The Indonesian Presidency

RENEWALS 458-4574

**WITHDRAWN
UTSA Libraries**

Asia/Pacific/Perspectives
Series Editor: Mark Selden

Identity and Resistance in Okinawa
 by Matthew Allen

Woman, Man, Bangkok: Love, Sex, and Popular Culture in Thailand
 by Scot Barmé

Making the Foreign Serve China: Managing Foreigners in the People's Republic
 by Anne-Marie Brady

The Mongols at China's Edge: History and the Politics of National Unity
 by Uradyn E. Bulag

Transforming Asian Socialism: China and Vietnam Compared
 edited by Anita Chan, Benedict J. Tria Kerkvliet, and Jonathan Unger

China's Great Proletarian Cultural Revolution: Master Narratives and Post-Mao Counternarratives
 edited by Woei Lien Chong

North China at War: The Social Ecology of Revolution, 1937–1945
 edited by Feng Chongyi and David S. G. Goodman

Social and Political Change in Revolutionary China: The Taihang Base Area in the War of Resistance to Japan, 1937–1945
 by David S. G. Goodman

Local Democracy and Development: The Kerala People's Campaign for Decentralized Planning
 by T. M. Thomas Isaac with Richard W. Franke

Islands of Discontent: Okinawan Responses to Japanese and American Power
 edited by Laura Hein and Mark Selden

Women in Early Imperial China
 by Bret Hinsch

Postwar Vietnam: Dynamics of a Transforming Society
 edited by Hy V. Luong

Wife or Worker? Asian Women and Migration
 edited by Nicola Piper and Mina Roces

Biology and Revolution in Twentieth-Century China
 by Laurence Schneider

Contentious Kwangju: The May 18th Uprising in Korea's Past and Present
 edited by Gi-Wook Shin and Kyong Moon Hwang

The Indonesian Presidency

The Shift from Personal toward Constitutional Rule

Angus McIntyre

ROWMAN & LITTLEFIELD PUBLISHERS, INC.
Lanham • Boulder • New York • Toronto • Oxford

ROWMAN & LITTLEFIELD PUBLISHERS, INC.

Published in the United States of America
by Rowman & Littlefield Publishers, Inc.
A wholly owned subsidiary of The Rowman & Littlefield Publishing Group, Inc.
4501 Forbes Boulevard, Suite 200, Lanham, MD 20706
www.rowmanlittlefield.com

P.O. Box 317, Oxford OX2 9RU, UK

Copyright © 2005 by Rowman & Littlefield Publishers, Inc.

All rights reserved. No part of this publication may be reproduced, stored in a
retrieval system, or transmitted in any form or by any means, electronic, mechanical,
photocopying, recording, or otherwise, without the prior permission of the publisher.

British Library Cataloguing in Publication Information Available

Library of Congress Cataloging-in-Publication Data
McIntyre, Angus.
   The Indonesian presidency : the shift from personal toward constitutional rule / Angus McIntyre.
     p. cm.—(Asia/Pacific/Perspectives)
Includes bibliographical references and index.
    ISBN 0-7425-3826-5 (cloth: alk. paper)—ISBN 0-7425-3827-3 (pbk.: alk. paper)
    1. Indonesia—Politics and government—20th century. 2. Indonesia—Politics and government—1998– 3. Presidents—Indonesia. 4. Soekarnoputri, Megawati, 1947– 5. Constitutional history—Indonesia. I. Title. II. Series.
   DS644.M28 2005
   959.803—dc22
                                                                           2004026496

Printed in the United States of America

∞™ The paper used in this publication meets the minimum requirements of American National Standard for Information Sciences—Permanence of Paper for Printed Library Materials, ANSI/NISO Z39.48-1992.

Contents

Acknowledgments	vii
Introduction	1
1 The Return to the 1945 Constitution	6

Part I

2 The Personal Rule of Sukarno	25
3 Suffering from the Quiet: Sukarno's Desolation and His Politics of Being Central	36
4 Aging and Fear of Death: Sukarno's Politics of Rejuvenation and His Quest for Immortality	61
5 Sukarno: Abandoned by History?	81

Part II

6 The Personal Rule of Soeharto	93
7 Soeharto's Composure	103

Part III

8 Megawati and the Emergence of Constitutional Rule	127
9 Childhood and Youth of Megawati Sukarnoputri	139
10 Megawati Sukarnoputri's Political Apprenticeship	151

11	Challenging Soeharto	161
12	The Fall of Soeharto	180
13	Democracy Returns	192
14	A Female President?	201
15	Megawati Sukarnoputri as Vice President	223
16	President Megawati Sukarnoputri	240

Conclusion	251
Postscript: The Indonesian Parliamentary Elections of 2004	261
Bibliography	267
Index	289
About the Author	303

Acknowledgments

Ibu Rachmulyadi, press secretary to President Sukarno, gave me access to the transcripts of his speeches stored in the State Secretariat. With the passing of Sukarno, this archive found its way onto the shelves of the Yayasan Idayu Library; and, in later years, its staff helped me expand my collection. Further assistance of a similar nature was provided by: Helen Sumardjo, formerly in charge of the Southeast Asian collection at Monash University; John Badgely, former curator, and Mary Crawford, administrative supervisor of the Echols Collection in the Kroch Library at Cornell University; as well as Ian Dawes, who spent a semester working as an intern in this collection.

I obtained a substantial proportion of the newspaper and magazine reports that inform this book from the clipping service provided by the same Yayasan Idayu Library. I was also a grateful client of another such service provided by Yayasan Geni in Salatiga. The thought of moving beyond clipping services to, with the arrival of the digital revolution, cutting and pasting in cyber space was a frightening prospect, and I would have struggled to cope at all but for the wonderful example and kindly guidance of John MacDougall at *Apakabar*.

To classify one's Indonesian friends and informants who were participants in many of the events described below as primary sources is to fail to do justice to their powers of reflection and analysis. In fact, they were both primary and secondary sources who invariably framed their eye-witness accounts in shrewd commentary. I am very pleased to be able to list some of them here: Mochtar Buchori, Karim, D. P., the late Karna Radjasa, Ali Sadikin, Aberson Marle Sihaloho, the late Manai Sophiaan, and Laksamana Sukardi.

It is often difficult to distinguish detached participants from passionately involved observers. Nevertheless, I have ventured to group the following people in the second of these two categories, and I would like to express my gratitude to them, both for their published works and for sharing their insights and knowledge with me. They are Ed Aspinall, David Bourchier, Arief Budiman, Lance Castles, Richard Chauvel, Bob Elson, Greg Fealy, the late Herb Feith, David Hill, John Ingleson, John Legge, Tim Lindsey, Hamish McDonald, Jamie Mackie, Chusnul Mar'iyah, Marcus Mietzner, Marthin Nanere, Douglas Ramage, David Reeve, Nazaruddin Sjamsuddin, Richard Tanter, Michael van Langenberg, and Ken Ward.

Colleagues at La Trobe University, the staff of Rowman & Littlefield, and my family and friends were also generous with their assistance. At La Trobe, Tony Pagliaro clarified Sukarno's confusing references to Mazzini; Novi Djenar and Harry Aveling prompted me through some difficult lines of translation; Sanjay Seth shared his insights on Marxism and modernity; Maxine Loynd put in hard work on the bibliography; and the staff of the Borchardt Library provided much valuable assistance. Helping to create a congenial working environment in the school of social sciences were John Miller, Robin Jeffrey, David de Vaus, Dennis Altman, Talis Polis, and, especially, Liz Byrne and Nella Dolceamore, who were unfailingly kind and helpful despite enormous demands being placed on their time and patience.

At Rowman & Littlefield, I would like to thank Mark Selden, the editor of the series of which this book is a part, for his many kindnesses, thoughtfulness, and remarkable editorial skill. I am also much indebted to Susan McEachern, Jessica Gribble, and Jenn Nemec for guiding me gently and thoughtfully through the publication process.

At home and nearby, I would like to thank: Jo Peck, for her kind support of my interest in Indonesian politics; my step-son, Alex, whose many activities and involvements have greatly enlarged my world, and who kindly contributed to the cover of this book; Willow Berzin, who also worked on the cover; and Robyn Williams, who taught me computer skills. Then there are my other families: the Sudjimans, with whom I lived in Jakarta during 1966–1967 (and for shorter periods on subsequent occasions), and where I was the eldest son with three remarkable, younger sisters: Ami, Isti, and Yanti. I had not managed to arrange things quite so well in my family of origin as there I was the youngest. Nevertheless, this position was not without many benefits, for I have over the years enjoyed the kindness and support of my elder brother and sister, Tony and Joanna; and, of course, our late parents.

Introduction

The Indonesian executive presidency has been in continuous existence since July 5, 1959, when Sukarno adopted by decree the so-called 1945 constitution. In the forty-three years since then (1959–2002) leadership at the apex of the political system has revealed itself in two forms. In the first thirty-nine years, there were only two presidents: Sukarno (1959–1967) and Soeharto (1968–1998). They were then followed by three more in as many years: B. J. Habibie (1998–1999), Abdurrahman Wahid (1999–2001), and Megawati Sukarnoputri (2001–2004). The lengthy tenures of Sukarno and Soeharto, far from indicating the construction of durable political settlements, were characterized by the personal rule of the incumbents, which undermined the autonomy of state institutions. The brief tenures of Habibie and Wahid, far from indicating profound instability, pointed to the emergence of a form of rule that is difficult to characterize but clearly shares some, if not all, of the attributes of constitutional rule. It took the form of presidential democracy with a legislature that was not only determined to limit the power of the executive but had been invigorated by free elections and the additional powers bestowed on it by two constitutional amendments.

Consequently, when Megawati assumed office on July 23, 2001, she found herself in a position quite different to that of her father when he was president. He had acknowledged few constitutional restraints; she, however, was obliged to abide by many. But even as she attempted to practice this partial form of constitutional rule, it became redefined by two further amendments to the 1945 constitution, one in November 2001 and one in August 2002, which by providing for, among other things, direct election of the head of government, enhanced its democratic attributes and promised to restore recently lost authority to the presidency.

Personal rule, which receives further clarification in the pages that follow, is a form of rule in which the leader governs in a highly personal and arbitrary fashion, quite free of any restraints imposed by binding laws, regulations, and a democratic constitution. The direct impact of a personal leader on the course of events renders his or her personality central to an understanding of the nature of the regime. To view Sukarno and Soeharto as personal rulers (especially in their later years of power) or to view "Guided Democracy" and the "New Order" as systems of personal rule alters some of the emphases of existing scholarship. First, it elevates the leaders' personalities into key explanatory factors for the nature of their respective regimes. To assert that the personalities of Presidents Sukarno and Soeharto were central in this way is to claim that their actions had distinctive consequences for their systems of rule. This work demonstrates that these were not actions we would have expected from other leaders in their place.[1] Of course, counterfactual propositions cannot be proved. The best one can do in this case is to show the highly personal and therefore individual nature of these actions and their decisive influence on the course of events and on the nature of their regimes, which I attempt to do in chapters 3, 4, and 5 (on Sukarno) and in chapter 7 (on Soeharto).

Second, this perspective emphasizes the significance of the personal form of rule that Guided Democracy and the New Order had in common for an understanding of the course of Indonesian history. From this point of view it becomes necessary to reassess the factor that had previously been given greater emphasis—namely, the ideological differences that distinguish the two. The massacre of Communist Party members in 1965 by anticommunists at the instigation of the army, for all its importance in shaping Indonesian history, was less a turning point than an event that marked the transition from personal rule of one ideological stripe to that of another. The real turning point occurred between 1957 and 1959 when Sukarno began fashioning his system of personal rule at the expense of constitutional democracy.[2] It goes without saying that the army must bear primary responsibility for the killings of 1965, but too little attention has been paid to Sukarno's inadvertent contribution to this event. In his hubris, he believed he was destined to lead the Indonesian revolution to socialism, but in fact—and this is the central argument of chapters 3, 4, and 5—he set the stage for the mass murder and middle-class counterrevolution that followed.[3]

The beginnings of personal rule in the 1957–1959 period was one turning point in the history of independent Indonesia, and the emergence of a rudimentary form of constitutional rule from its ruins from 1998 may prove to be another. Unlike personal rule, which is arbitrary and unrestrained, constitutional rule is "carried on in accordance with rules so clearly defined and so generally accepted as effectively to control the actions of public officers."[4] The nearest thing Indonesia had to such rules in 1998 was the 1945 constitution, which gave expression to some liberal democratic sentiments but did not provide the constitutional machinery to realize them.[5] Nevertheless, by providing "a set of familiar rules in a time of great turmoil,"[6] it was able to facilitate a shift in the direction of a constitutional order even before it underwent a process of detailed and elaborate amendment between 1999 and 2002. Once it was amended in this way, it did appear equal to the task of holding officers of the government—and, indeed, presidents—to exacting standards of public behavior in keeping with its expanded provisions. A history of the 1945 constitution, which culminates in this remarkable development, is one of the threads that runs through chapters 1, 2, 6, and 8.

The following study begins with the personal rule of Sukarno and Soeharto and, as such, enjoins us to consider the impact of their personalities on their manner of leadership and the nature of their respective regimes. We must resort to personality, but not at the expense of culture, for they were both Javanese (although of different regions), nor of history, for each was a member of a particular class and generation and, on more than one occasion, acted on as well as acting. History—at least contemporary history, in the sense of the history of the present—constitutes a large part of the subsequent narrative: the only thing we know for certain is the beginning of personal rule and a recent move away from it. I have been so bold to discern a trend from personal rule toward constitutional rule, but note the hedged nature of my claim. Conventionally, "history is lived forwards but it is written in retrospect."[7] This particular history is lived and written forward with myself and the political figures I am writing about hostage to tomorrow's events. Such an approach is not ideal, for it lacks the perspective that the passage of time bestows, although it does not suffer from the shortcoming of orthodox history whose author "know[s] the end before . . . consider[ing] the beginning and . . . can never wholly recapture what it was to know the beginning only."[8]

This contemporary history is mainly written in the form of a political biography of Megawati (chapters 9–16), for the perceived trend from personal toward constitutional rule has its individual counterpoint in the relationship between Megawati and her father and, indeed, the three other presidents who preceded her. Unlike the sharply focused thematic approach adopted in the chapters on Sukarno and Soeharto, this study of Indonesia's fifth president is created within the spacious, "life and times" tradition of political biography, written to encompass not only the details of Megawati's rise to political power but also the pertinent information about her predecessors. It is true that there is more to the history of this trend than Megawati's struggling to interpret her father's legacy, her resisting and yet being influenced by Soeharto, her opposing Habibie but also being a beneficiary of the democratic reforms that he instigated, and her contending with Abdurrahman Wahid; however, it is also true that these relationships lie at the heart of this trend. Personal circumstances inhabit the center of the broadest historical tendency. The prospects for constitutional rule in Indonesia do depend to some extent on what Megawati made of her father's words and deeds as she remembers them—and therein lies the justification for attempting this blend of history and biography, of historical time and interior time,[9] for reporting the emergence of Indonesia's new constitutional order from her perspective.

Indonesians still live in difficult economic times and are frustrated with the many shortcomings of their new democracy, not to mention the human frailty of their leaders; consequently, many display a nostalgia for the strong leadership of the past and place their hopes in the emergence of a new leader or savior. Nevertheless, if there is one thing to be learned from the history of presidential leadership in Indonesia since 1959, it is surely that such hopes are misplaced and that leadership, no matter how farsighted and well intentioned, can only be as good as the constitutional order that contains it. Between 1999 and 2001, this order took the form of a weak presidential system in which, in striking contrast to the period of personal rule under Sukarno and Soeharto, the latitude for independent action by the chief executive was substantially limited. Since 2001, however, additional amendments to the constitution have transformed it into one approaching a conventional presidential democracy. The amended document spells out a detailed democratic framework for Indonesia's new constitutional order, but it remains for all that a presidential constitution with the problematic qualities inherent in such a form of government. One of these qualities is the personal nature of the presidency, derived from executive power being concentrated in the hands of one person. The presidents in such a democracy will not enjoy the licence of a personal ruler such as Sukarno or Soeharto but will have considerably more scope for individual action than did the chief executives of the 1999–2001 period. In such an arrangement, good government may ultimately depend on its leaders' wisdom, yet one finds this attribute only rarely in top-drawer politics. I return to this and cognate issues in the conclusion, where I consider the prospects of Indonesia's constitutional order.

NOTES

1. See Greenstein, "Impact of Personality," 2.
2. Colin Brown adopts a similar periodization in his *A Short History of Indonesia*, 185.

3. Dick, "Rise of a Middle Class," 87.

4. Goodnow, *Principles of Constitutional Government*, quoted in Jackson and Rosberg, *Personal Rule in Black Africa,* 10n15.

5. Bourchier, "Lineages of Organicist Political Thought," 94–97; Lindsey, "Indonesia's *Negara Hukum,*" 367.

6. Liddle, "Indonesia's Democratic Transition," 375.

7. Wedgwood, *William the Silent,* 35, quoted in Mackie, *Konfrontasi*, 6.

8. Mackie, *Konfrontasi*, 35.

9. Richard Holmes, the biographer of Coleridge and Shelley, writes of "biographers using two *kinds* of time. One is historical time, which produces chronology, 'the plot,' the daily events of a life, set against their unfolding historical background. The other may be called interior time, the inner life of the subject, which makes patterns of impulse and imagery, repetitions and recollections, constellations of self-myth and self-understanding, links between childhood and adult experience, which obey the quite different, unhistorical, or 'dream laws' of memory and imagination" ("Biographer's Footsteps," 2; emphasis in the original).

1

The Return to the 1945 Constitution

The form of government envisaged by the 1945 constitution consisted of a president, a "super-parliamentary body" called the People's Consultative Assembly (Majelis Permusyawaratan Rakyat; MPR) in which the sovereignty of the people resides, and a legislature called the People's Representative Council (Dewan Perwakilan Rakyat; DPR). It is a form or government that is difficult to classify, even along the most fundamental dimensions.[1] The fact that the head of government is elected for a fixed term, cannot be forced to resign by the legislature, and enjoys an effective veto over draft laws suggests a presidential system—even a strong presidential system. However, members of the legislature serve as members of the People's Consultative Assembly, where they are joined by regional and group delegates; in this capacity, they exercise a level of supervision over the head of state that is seemingly inconsistent with presidential government. Not only do they elect the head of government, but they may also call that officeholder to account if he or she violates state policy as determined by the constitution or by the People's Consultative Assembly. This arrangement bears some resemblance to parliamentary government in which the tenures of the head of government and his or her cabinet members are dependent on the confidence of the legislature.[2] Presumably, it is for this reason that the 1945 constitution has been described as "presidential with parliamentary characteristics."[3]

The further question of whether this constitution is democratic cannot be easily decided, certainly not by a simple scrutiny of its contents. Rather, it requires some examination of the process by which this document came into being within the Committee for the Study of Preparation for Independence (Badan Penyelidik Usaha Persiapan Kemerdekaan Indonesia; BPKI),[4] established by the Japanese military administration on Java in May 1945.

Members of this body consisted of senior civil servants and nationalist politicians who had worked for the Japanese military administration.[5] Their deliberations on the constitution began in late May and soon revealed a division between the advocates of an Islamic state and those supporting a secular government. In the latter group, a further difference emerged between proponents of authoritarian forms of government and those favoring a constitutional democracy. Prominent in the first category was Supomo, the principal author of the constitution, who claimed that his theory of "integralism" had its roots in Indonesian political tradition. This body of thought esteems a governmental arrangement in which a ruler of unrestrained power presides over a state whose task is "not to guarantee the interests of either individuals or groups, but rather to protect the interests of the whole society."[6]

Sukarno assumed a similarly authoritarian disposition, but his stemmed not from integralist ideas (although he would embrace them briefly in the late 1950s) but rather from a form of radical collectivism. This disposition, however, was not apparent from his speech to the BPKI on June 1, in which he proposed five principles (*Pancasila*) to serve as the philosophical basis of the Indonesian state: nationalism, internationalism, "joint deliberation and representation," social welfare, and belief in God (with the last serving as an attempt to find common ground between Moslems and Christians). This proposal quickly gained favor, and "after being slightly reworded and rearranged to give 'Belief in the One God' . . . the top position," the principles were written into the preamble to the constitution, known as the Jakarta Charter.[7] This document strove to accommodate the theocratic aspirations of devout Moslems by an elaboration of the first principle, which enunciated "the obligation for adherents of Islam to carry out *Shariah* (the Islamic law)." This preamble was adopted on June 22, 1945, but on August 18, the Preparatory Committee for Indonesian Independence deleted these few words from it, as well as from article 29 (where they also appeared), fearful that they might threaten the unity of the newly proclaimed and religiously diverse Republic of Indonesia.[8]

Sukarno's radical collectivism and the authoritarian views to which it gave rise were evident in his tendency to speak of the people as a unified whole, from which it followed that each individual counted for little.[9] For example, he insisted to the members of the BPKI in another address on July 15 that the idea of the sovereignty of the people did not imply the sovereignty of individuals. Accordingly, he urged them "to accept that citizen's rights had no place in Indonesia."[10]

Foremost among the constitutionalists was Mohammad Hatta, the future vice president, who immediately took issue with Sukarno on this point. He argued that the constitution must guarantee freedom of opinion and association; otherwise, there was a danger that the Indonesian state would degenerate into a *negara kekuasaan* (power state) characterized by "cadaver discipline." He added presciently that "the principle of popular sovereignty" alone would not prevent this from happening, because this principle could be misused by the state, "especially in constitutions like this one, in which popular sovereignty resides in the People's Consultative Assembly which in turn entrusts its power to the president." Hatta stressed that the president must not have the constitutional freedom to establish a "power state."[11] Like-minded members of the BPKI—such people as Muhammad Yamin, Maria Ulfah Santoso, and Sukiman—supported Hatta's attempts to insert a guarantee of individual rights into the constitution. Sharing his concerns about the dangers of a power state emerging in Indonesia, they sought to give substance to the doctrine of popular sovereignty by calling for the direct election of the People's Consultative Assembly.[12]

The outcome of these differences of opinion in the BPKI was a compromise, but one that favored the authoritarians. The official elucidation of the 1945 constitution declares that "the Indonesian state is based on law (a Law State), and is not based on power (a Power State)."[13] Furthermore, article 1 of the constitution proclaims that "sovereignty is vested in the people and exercised fully by the People's Consultative Assembly," and article 28 refers to the right of individuals to associate and express opinions. However, the document not only ignores the democrats' call for elections for the MPR, but it has nothing to say at all about the method of selection of that body or, indeed, of the DPR; and the defense of individual rights to be found in article 28 amounted to very little after Supomo watered down Hatta's draft. Thus, as David Bourchier and Timothy Lindsey have argued, the provisions of the constitution did not provide the means to realize its proclaimed commitment to the sovereignty of the people and to a state based on law.[14] This, it seems, was precisely Supomo's intention.[15]

It is interesting to note that Sukarno and Hatta also found themselves at loggerheads in the debate on the territorial extent of the envisaged independent Indonesia. The terms of this debate were laid down by Muhammad Yamin, who in a speech to the BPKI on May 31 (the substance of which he repeated in another address before the same body on July 10) laid claim not only to Sumatra, Java, Madura, the Lesser Sundas, Dutch Borneo, Sulawesi, Dutch Timor, and Maluku (all of which fell within the territory of the Netherlands Indies) but also to Peninsular Malaya, North Borneo, Portuguese Timor, and Papua on the grounds that these territories belonged to the Indonesian fatherland (*Tumpah-Darah Indonesia*), whose territorial extent had been most recently determined by the fourteenth-century state of Majapahit.[16]

The following day, June 1, Sukarno alluded to these matters in his Pancasila speech. He "declared that a nationality consisted of the inhabitants of a

God-ordained geographical unity such as the Indonesian archipelago!" He then made reference to Borneo and Irian as part of this God-given unity without mentioning the colonial boundaries that divide both islands, and to that extent he revealed the similarity of his position to Yamin's. However, unlike Yamin, he did not refer to Malaya or Portuguese Timor, although the inclusion of the latter was implied by his observation that Indonesia extended from the northern tip of Sumatra to Irian.[17]

In a forceful speech on July 11, Mohammad Hatta strongly opposed Yamin's claim:

> By saying that we want this and we want that it is as if we who are not yet free are already recommending an imperialist policy. . . . But I propose here that we do not put out reasons which have about them something of the imperialistic spirit. . . . All our lives we have opposed imperialism, so let us not impart to our youth the content or spirit of imperialism, the spirit of expansion.

Finally, he spoke in favor of an Indonesian nation and state that did not extend beyond the boundaries of the former Netherlands Indies.[18]

Sukarno apparently considered himself to be the target of Hatta's criticism, for he followed him to the podium to say, "I am not an imperialist, definitely not. My life from the age of eighteen to my present age of forty-three, twenty-five years in all, I have devoted to struggling against imperialism." But he then added Malaya to Borneo and Irian on his list of territories outside the Netherlands Indies that properly belonged to Indonesia. Indeed, he even went so far as to cast an acquisitive glance at the Philippines but then added that it was already independent and that "we must respect the sovereignty of the Philippine nation."[19]

At the conclusion of the debate, the matter was put to a vote. A mere nineteen of the sixty-six members present, or 29 percent, voted for Hatta's proposal that the boundaries of Indonesia be coterminous with those of the Netherlands Indies, whereas thirty-nine members (59 percent) voted for Yamin's fatherland of the Netherlands Indies plus Malaya, North Borneo, Papua, and Portuguese Timor.[20] It was left to an officer in the Imperial Japanese Army to save the honor of Indonesian anticolonial nationalism, for it was only at the insistence of Marshal Terauchi, the Japanese commander in chief for Southeast Asia, that Sukarno subsequently declared that he would be satisfied with the territory of the former Netherlands Indies.[21]

To return to the consideration of the character of the 1945 constitution, we shall now examine the transitional provisions of the constitution to see what light they throw on the matter. Apart from providing for the election of a president and vice president by the Committee for the Preparation of Indonesian Independence (Panitia Persiapan Kemerdekaan Indonesia; PPKI), the successor body to the BPKI (which was duly done on August 18, 1945, the day after the proclamation of independence), the provisions declare in article 4 that "prior to the formation of the People's Consultative Assembly, the People's Representative Council and the Supreme Advisory Council, in accordance with the terms of this Constitution, their several powers shall be exercised by the President with the assistance of the National Committee."[22] According to A. K. Pringgodigdo, "by virtue of this stipulation the President was legally empowered to act with dictatorial authority since there was absolutely no basis for interpreting what was described as the assistance of a National Committee as a factor of restraint." He elaborated that the president, in the absence of the DPR, could issue all legislation and, in the absence of the MPR, could exercise the sovereignty of the people by, among other things, determining the broad outlines of state policy.[23] The National Committee itself was established by the PPKI on August 27 under the name of the Central Indonesian National Committee (Komite Nasional Indonesia Pusat; KNIP). The majority of its 137 members had worked for the Japanese, with the exceptions being the veteran nationalists Sutan Sjahrir and Amir Sjarifuddin.[24]

Although the additional provisions of the constitution limited the period in which the president could act in this way to six months, by which time he must "give effect to all requirements specified in this Constitution,"[25] the fact remains that the transitional provisions reversed the order of events implied in the body of the document as well as the relative standing of the key institutions involved. According to the constitution, it is the People's Consultative Assembly that elects the president, who is subordinate to the assembly, whereas the transitional provisions have the president performing the functions of the MPR and DPR until these institutions are established. It is understandable that drafters of the constitution would resort to such a measure in the difficult circumstances that attended the end of the Pacific War, but in reflecting on its consequences, perhaps it may be said that events conspired with the authoritarians on the BPKI to produce Pringgodigdo's presidential dictatorship. Among its early steps was the creation of a Staatspartij (State Party) on August 21, which "would take over [from the Jawa Hokokai] the function of mobilizing the population on a continuing basis behind the national leadership,"[26] and a presidential cabinet on September 4, which was disparagingly referred to by its opponents as the "Bucho Cabinet" (the Cabinet of Chiefs) because of the large number of its members who had served in senior positions in the Japanese administration.[27]

However, this presidential government—by dint of its authoritarian, Japanese flavor and its conservative composition—proved equally unsuited to negotiating with the Allies (whose troops landed on Java at the end of September), to gaining international recognition for the newly proclaimed Republic of Indonesia, and to responding effectively to the surge of revolutionary ferment among its own citizens. Stepping into this breach was Sutan Sjahrir, who had refused to work for the Japanese and for that reason enjoyed a strong following among the youth of Jakarta. He abhorred Sukarno's presidential government, subsequently declaring in a pamphlet released on November 10 that "those who have sold their souls and their honor to the Japanese fascists must be eliminated from the leadership of our revolution." Also, he took issue with the weak defense of individual rights in the 1945 constitution:

> The present constitution, which is still far from fully democratic, must be replaced by a wholly democratic constitution which will imprint on every organ of state administration the fundamental rights of the people: freedom of thought, speech and religion, freedom to write, to earn a living, to have an education, and to share in determining the organization and the business of the state through the right to elect and be elected to all bodies which participate in governing the country.[28]

On October 7, Sjahrir and his supporters on the KNIP proposed to Sukarno and Hatta a new interpretation of article 4 of the transitional provisions that would confer the powers of the DPR and MPR on the KNIP. Sukarno, mindful of the precariousness of his own position, readily agreed, and on October 16 Hatta read a proclamation to that effect (Proclamation X) before a plenary session of the aforementioned body. It stated that "the President . . . has decided: that prior to the formation of the MPR and the DPR, legislative power will be transferred to the Central National Committee, which will share in establishing the broad outlines of the aims of the state."[29] This proclamation also provided for a working body of the Central National Committee to carry out the main committee's expanded day-to-day responsibilities. Sjahrir and Amir Sjarifuddin became, respectively, the chairman and vice chairman of this body and enjoyed the assistance of thirteen other KNIP members, whom they appointed.[30]

Proclamation X substantially diluted the dictatorial nature of Sukarno's presidential government, but Sjahrir's goal was more radical than that.[31] He aimed to replace the presidential government with a parliamentary one, thereby relegating Sukarno to the position of head of state alone and enabling him to assume the office of prime minister and head of government. Also, it seems likely that Sjahrir regarded parliamentary government, as he had experienced it in the Netherlands between the wars, as a superior form of government to presidential democracy, let alone the form of presidential government envisaged by the 1945 constitution. Doubtless, it would be more acceptable to the Dutch themselves, with whom Republican representatives would sooner or later be obliged to negotiate.[32]

Accordingly, Sjahrir and his working committee pressed for the creation of a multiparty system, and they were successful in doing so: on November 3, Vice President Hatta signed an official decree permitting the formation of political parties and promising elections by January 1946. At this time, they urged on Sukarno a cabinet responsible to the Central National Committee serving as a legislature. On November 11, the working committee declared that the president had agreed to this proposal and had consented to appoint Sjahrir as cabinet formateur. Three days later, Sjahrir announced his new cabinet, thereby bringing to an end Indonesia's short-lived presidential form of government—at least for the time being.[33]

The consequent "pattern of government similar to that applying in the western European democracies," as Pringgodigdo described it, aided by the mutual cooperation of its principal members, worked flexibly and effectively during the years of armed conflict with the colonial power. Indeed, full power was again vested in the president on three occasions of emergency. In fact, for one comparatively lengthy period—January 29, 1948, to December 20, 1949—Vice President Hatta headed two successive presidential cabinets that were formed without close regard to party numbers in the KNIP and that, it was generally considered, "could not be forced to resign by the Working Committee."[34] This essentially parliamentary form of government continued to operate after the Republic of Indonesia became a member state of the Republic of the United States of Indonesia (RUSI) on the achievement of independence on December 27, 1949.

THE 1949 AND 1950 CONSTITUTIONS

The form of government for RUSI itself was spelled out in the 1949 constitution. It provided for a federal state, a bicameral parliament, a president as head of state "to be elected by delegates of the component states of the Republic of the United States of Indonesia"—there was no provision for a vice president—and a constituent assembly to draw up a new constitution. Pursuant to this constitution, sixteen delegates of the component states elected Sukarno president on December 16, 1949. He was sworn in the following day.[35] Hatta assumed the office of premier, and as the cabinet was not responsible to the lower house or House of Representatives,[36] his position may be compared to the one he occupied as premier in the presidential cabinets of 1948–1949.

Nationalist sentiment was hostile to the subordination of the Republic of Indonesia within a federal structure where it enjoyed only equal standing with the other, Dutch-created federal states. Accordingly, RUSI negotiated with its federal states for a return to the unitary "Republic of Indonesia." These parties reached an agreement on May 19 that set out some of the basic features of the new government—namely, a unicameral legislature and a parliamentary cabinet. "Further," writes Herbert Feith, "it established that President Soekarno would be President of the new state" and that "the constitution would be temporary; thus there would be no change from the provisions in the 1949 constitution whereby a Constituent Assembly was to be elected to make a permanent constitution."[37]

The details of the constitution were worked out by a joint RUSI–Republic of Indonesia (RI) Committee chaired by the deputy prime minister of the republic and the justice minister of RUSI. The latter was the very same Soepomo who had helped impart an authoritarian caste to the 1945 constitution.[38] Constitutional chameleon that he was, he now helped frame a very different document that not only "took over all provisions on human rights from the 1949 Constitution," which themselves were "drawn up largely on the basis of the United Nations Universal Declaration of Human Rights of 1948," but also added to them "a provision on the right to demonstrate and to strike" (article 21), which is not contained in either of the two said documents.[39]

Perhaps the most difficult issue for the RUSI–RI Committee to resolve was the relationship between the cabinet and the parliament. The RUSI cabinet was not responsible to parliament. However, cabinet responsibility to the legislature was introduced by the government of the Republic of Indonesia in November 1945. Nevertheless, a presidential cabinet that was not beholden to the political parties represented in the KNIP was installed on two occasions. The drafters of the new constitution were committed by the agreement of May 19 to a parliamentary cabinet. The question was whether they would draw up an escape clause to sanction such a step as this in the government of the unitary state. But the real issue, as Feith noted, was the role of Hatta. It was he "who had been appointed in 1948 to form a presidential cabinet when it seemed impossible to form . . . [one] on the basis of party strengths in parliament," and it was he "who was expected to step in if such a situation arose again and an escape clause were in existence."[40]

The RUSI position on the joint committee favored an escape clause and opposed the creation of the office of vice president, seeing it as an attempt to kick Hatta upstairs. Although it was supported by many leaders of the modernist Islamic Masjumi Party, in the end it was defeated by the RI side. Its position was also the position of the Indonesian National Party (PNI), and, notably, the Indonesian Socialist Party, which apparently hoped that, with Hatta removed from contention, Sjahrir would find his way back to the prime ministership. Thus, the final decision of the committee was "to reintroduce the vice-presidency and include no escape clause which would make a non-parliamentary cabinet possible." As Feith adds, "it was a decision which was to have important consequences in later years."[41]

On August 17, 1950, the new, unitary Republic of Indonesia came into being: Sukarno was head of state and Mohammad Natsir became the first prime minister. On October 14, the parliament voted in favor of recommending Hatta for appointment as vice president, and Sukarno duly appointed him in keeping with the provisions of the new constitution.[42] As recorded, they had worked well together. Their *dwitunggal* (two-in-one) leadership, as it was known at the time, may be understood as an informal consociational practice that contributed significantly to the effectiveness of the various governments between 1945 and 1950 and would continue to do so for a few more years, although Hatta's many talents were not fully utilized in the vice presidential office.[43]

Finally, elections for the parliament were held on September 29, 1955. The most successful party was the Indonesian National Party, which obtained 22.3 percent of the vote and appealed to the syncretist and nominally Islamic sections of the population, whose more meaningful religious adherence ranged from animism among the peasantry to forms of Hinduism and Buddhism among the remaining elements of the Javanese aristocracy. The Indonesian National Party was followed first by Masjumi, with 20.9 percent, which largely monopolized the support of modernist Moslems, who take their religion directly from the Koran; and second by Nahdlatul Ulama, with 18.4 percent, whose traditionalist followers adhere to the Syafi'i Law School within Sunni Islam. The Indonesian Communist Party, which had sunk roots among the animist peasantry, was next, garnering 16.4 percent. It was followed by a host of smaller parties (including Sjahrir's Indonesian Socialist Party), none of which polled above 2.9 percent of the vote.[44] And the same top four parties in the same order prevailed in the Constituent Assembly elections that fell on December 15.[45]

The holding of free elections not once but twice in the same year was a significant achievement of Indonesia's democracy. Nevertheless, it should not divert us from the fact that the persons who occupied the upper reaches of these political parties (not to mention the bureaucracy) or who were more broadly members of "the political public" adhered to an essentially populist understanding of this democracy.[46] This is not to say that they simply idealized the people (*rakyat*). At best, their attitude was ambivalent: on the one hand, they claimed to hold the people's interests at heart; on the other, they patronized them and even feared them. More particularly, they looked on the people as "an undifferentiated mass, whose interests were overwhelmingly common rather than mutually antagonistic."[47] Accordingly, political parties were viewed not as agents of public opinion but as instruments for shaping it. Even Hatta was to say that "political parties . . . are a means of organizing public opinion in order that the people may learn to feel responsibility as citizens of the state and members of society."[48] And Sjahrir, who suggested that Sukarno had sold his soul to the Japanese fascists and who criticized the 1945 constitution for its weak defense of individual rights, displayed a similarly authoritarian disposition himself in calling for the formation of a single, revolutionary party.[49]

RETURN TO THE 1945 CONSTITUTION

The new cabinet of Ali Sastroamidjojo, the first to be drawn from an elected parliament, came into being in March 1956, and the Constituent Assembly held its inaugural meeting on November 10, 1956.[50] One of the achievements of this cabinet was its success in ushering through the parliament law 1/1957, "which greatly increased the power of elected legislative councils in the provinces, regencies [or districts], and municipalities and provided for the gradual elimination of the *pamong pradja* [regional administrative corps] from territorial jurisdiction."[51] But it came too late to have any impact on its fortunes, facing (as it had since the previous year) an immense challenge posed by regional disaffection and unrest within the army and the civilian population. Military commanders in the exporting areas of North Sumatra and North Sulawesi, aggrieved by the government's unrealistic exchange rate, organized large-scale smuggling in mid-1956; and at the end of the year, military commanders in North, Central, and South Sumatra seized power from their civilian counterparts. They criticized Jakarta for "overcentralisation, corruption, and neglect of outer areas, for placing too many Javanese officials in these areas, and for leniency to communism" and demanded the resignation of Ali and his replacement by Mohammad Hatta as the head of a non-party business cabinet.[52] Hatta resigned the vice presidency on December 1, 1956, but clearly hoped to return to power as prime minister and attempted to use this demand to advance his claim.[53]

The principal alternative to the regional position was offered by President Sukarno. In a speech on October 28 (Youth Pledge Day), 1956, he declared that a very big mistake had been made in November 1945 when "we proposed the establishment of parties, parties, parties."[54] Sukarno genuinely believed that the behavior of the parties was having an injurious effect on the unity and well-being of the nation, but in phrasing it in this way he clearly meant to take a swipe at Hatta, who had signed the relevant decree.[55] Sukarno then declared himself to be in favor of the burial of the political parties: "Let us now together bury all parties."[56] But in the face of strong opposition from the parties themselves, he dropped this idea. Then, in February 1957, he advanced his *konsepsi,* which provided for the formation of a *gotong rojong* (mutual cooperation) cabinet, in which representatives of the major parties, including the Communist Party, would sit, suggesting by way of justification that it was not practical to exclude a group from the processes of government who received six million votes in the recent elections (those of 1955). He also proposed the establishment of a national council to serve as an advisory body to the cabinet. Revealing the recent influence on him of integralist or corporatist ideas, he suggested that the membership of this latter body should consist of representatives of functional groups in society and, as he saw it, thereby reflect the composition of society just as the cabinet would reflect the composition of parliament.[57]

Sukarno's *konsepsi* received a negative response from the regionalists. On March 2, the East Indonesia military commander placed his territory under martial law and added his voice to those of his Sumatran colleagues in a Piagam Perdjuangan Semesta (Charter of Total Struggle). Also, several major political parties rejected Sukarno's proposed *gotong rojong* cabinet and national council. At this point a compromise was brokered by the army chief of staff, General Nasution. Accordingly, Ali Sastroamidjojo returned his cabinet's mandate to President Sukarno on March 14. A half hour later, he proclaimed a state of war and siege for the whole country.[58]

It seemed possible that Sukarno would then call on Hatta to form a new government, but instead he appointed Suwirjo, the chairperson of the PNI, to be cabinet *formateur.* When Suwirjo failed to form a government, Sukarno "appointed himself, as 'Citizen Soekarno,' to form an 'emergency, extraparliamentary business cabinet.'" On April 8, he announced its composition: the leader was the nonparty, former cabinet minister Ir Djuanda.[59] He presided over a working cabinet in which the Communist Party was not represented.[60] Two months later the cabinet established by emergency law the functional group-based National Council.[61] Daniel Lev has described this development clearly: "After the proclamation of martial law and the formation of the Kabinet Karya [working cabinet] and the National Council, there were two overlapping political systems in force: . . . one system was based on the Constitution of 1950, the other on martial law—and the latter was in the ascendancy."[62]

It is a matter of history that Sukarno and the central government eventually won out in the regional conflict, but at the time, as Jamie Mackie has pointed out, such an outcome appeared unlikely. Indeed, contemporary observers believed that the regional forces would prevail because the outer islands produced almost all of Indonesia's export produce and foreign exchange earnings. Deprived of these, they reasoned, the Jakarta government would soon collapse. It seems that this assessment was largely shared by the protagonists, as it was the central government under Djuanda "that was the more conciliatory party and the regional authorities who remained intransigent and unwilling to compromise, being confident in their superior economic strength."[63]

But two factors then gave rise to a sudden upsurge of anti-Dutch sentiment: a vote in the UN on West Irian, one unfavorable to Indonesia, on November 29, 1957, followed the very next day by an assassination attempt on President Sukarno in which eleven persons died. In this angry climate it was possible for labor unions to take over all major Dutch enterprises and for the justice minister to require the departure of most Dutch citizens from Indonesia.

This sudden lurch to the Left in Jakarta politics had an exacerbating effect on the regional conflict, leading the Central Sumatra military commander and his supporters to issue an ultimatum to the central government on February 10 declaring that, unless a new cabinet under the leadership of Hatta and/or the Sultan of Yogyakarta was formed in five days, a separate govenment would be established in Sumatra. Jakarta failed to respond, and on February 15, 1958, the Revolutionary Government of the Republic of Indonesia (Pemerintah Revolusioner Republik Indonesia; PRRI) was proclaimed in Padang. Its prime minister was Sjafruddin Prawiranegara of the Masjumi Party, and his cabinet largely comprised people from Sumatra and Sulawesi.[64]

This decision by the regionalists to force a showdown with the central government proved an appalling miscalculation. Rather than wait for Jakarta's economic vulnerability to further weaken its political standing, their extreme action made it possible for Nasution to achieve something that would have been impossible even a few weeks earlier. By taking advantage of the sense of crisis that had been brought to a head by the proclamation, he was able to muster sufficient forces to launch an effective military operation against the regionalists. Indeed, the success of this operation by mid-1958 ensured a political victory for Sukarno and Nasution. But, as the above description of events makes clear, it was a near-run thing, hinging on an unsuccessful UN vote on one day and a failed assassination attempt on the next. Had this sequence of events not occurred, matters may well have turned out differently for Hatta and his regionalist supporters—certainly not with their discrediting and loss of all power, which no one had anticipated, and very possibly with their political success, which many had predicted earlier in the year.[65]

Mackie views the defeat of the Hatta forces in the PRRI rebellion as "a key factor in the demise of parliamentary democracy at the hands of Sukarno, Nasution and other advocates of a strong executive power under the 1945 Constitution."[66] But he does not argue that democracy would necessarily have survived had Hatta and company been victorious. Indeed, Hatta may not have been able to persuade his supporters in the regional military commands of the virtues of civilian control, especially against the backdrop of the Communist

Party's success in the regional elections held on Java in June, July, and August 1957. From these elections, it emerged "as the island's strongest party, with 27.4 per cent of the total vote as compared with 20.6 per cent in September 1955, a rise of over two million votes, and with an increased vote in every single one of the 100 *kabupatens* [districts] and municipalities."[67] However, there was no one in the Indonesian elite with a stronger commitment to democracy than Hatta, and given all that we know about him, it is most unlikely that, had he prevailed in this conflict, he would have gone so far down the authoritarian road as to abrogate the existing, parliamentary constitution and build a system of personal rule after the manner of his victorious opponent. Rather, Mackie's point, although hardly less momentous, is as follows:

> If the forces supporting Hatta had won out over President Sukarno in the power struggle that was being fought out through 1957–58 . . . as I believe they very nearly did in 1957, the latter course of Indonesian history might have been very different indeed. It could have meant no shift to Guided Democracy in 1959 (or a very different type of regime, not Sukarno's creation but Hatta's), no *Konfrontasi* against Malaysia in 1963–65, no hyper-inflation in the 1960s and the opportunities it provided for the PKI [Indonesian Communist Party] to surge towards the gates of power in 1963–65, no Gestapu [September 30 movement] and hence no New Order.[68]

Thus, there was nothing inevitable about the ascendancy gained by Sukarno and Nasution in mid-1958, but events thereafter assumed a more patterned quality.[69] Indeed, the turning point of 1957–1958, was followed by milestones on the road to the authoritarian government jointly managed by Sukarno and Nasution. However, the element of cooperation that existed between the army commander and the president at that time prevented people from seeing that this road would eventually lead to the personal rule of Sukarno, presiding arbitrarily over Guided Democracy.

One such milestone was reached on February 19, 1959, when the cabinet proposed that the Constituent Assembly—the same Constituent Assembly that had been elected in December 1955—adopt without amendment the 1945 constitution as the constitution of the Republic of Indonesia. In an attempt to placate devout Moslems in the assembly who were dissatisfied with the non-Islamic nature of this constitution, the cabinet proposal also declared that the government recognize the Jakarta Charter as a "historic document."

The cabinet's stance enjoyed the full support of a largely reunited military under Nasution; indeed, it was he who first suggested that the country return to its original constitution. On April 22, Sukarno sought to convince the Constitutional Assembly of the wisdom of this position.[70] Also, Djuanda acknowledged to the assembly that the 1945 constitution was not without its weakness: "The Government does not close its eyes to the shortcomings of the Constitution of Proclamation, among other things it does not contain sufficient provisions on human rights ... freedom of opinion and association."[71] Because a plenary session of the Constituent Assembly had already agreed to, but had not had an opportunity to finally endorse, twenty-two human rights to be included in a future constitution, the prime minister declared, on May 21, 1959, that such rights would be recognized as having constitutional force on the return to the 1945 constitution.[72] The government also promised elections for parliament and, eventually, for president and vice president by the People's Consultative Assembly.

But the real stumbling block was the Jakarta Charter, which was, it will be recalled, the original preamble to the constitution adopted on June 22, 1945, that elaborated on the principle of "Belief in the One God" by asserting "the obligation for adherents of Islam to carry out *Shariah* (the Islamic law)." The members of Moslem parties would not support a return to the 1945 constitution without the charter's incorporation. As the government would not agree to this stipulation, the assembly vote in favor of the government's proposal fell short of the necessary two-thirds majority.[73] Sukarno's response came on July 5, 1959. With the support of the cabinet and of Nasution—the latter had actually been pressuring Sukarno to take this action—he issued a presidential decree that dissolved the Constituent Assembly, enacted the 1945 constitution, abrogated the constitution of 1950, and contained a commitment to establish the institutions prescribed by the 1945 constitution in the shortest possible time. He made no mention of Djuanda's promise to attribute constitutional status to the decisions of the Constituent Assembly in the area of human rights.[74] Thus Guided Democracy came into being.

NOTES

1. Bourchier, "Lineages of Organicist Political Thought," 88–89.
2. Lijphart, "Introduction," 2–3.
3. National Democratic Institute, *Indonesia's Road to Constitutional Reform*, iii.
4. This committee is variously labeled depending on the writer's translation of its Indonesian title. In this matter, I have followed Bourchier's translation. See his "Lineages of Organicist Political Thought," 74–75.
5. Bourchier, "Lineages of Organicist Political Thought," 75–76.
6. Bourchier, "Lineages of Organicist Political Thought," 80.
7. Bourchier, "Lineages of Organicist Political Thought," 83–84.
8. Also, the requirement that the president be a Moslem was deleted from article 6 at this time (Nasution, *Aspiration for Constitutional Government*, 10–11, 104–6).
9. Sartori, *Democratic Theory*, 18–19.

10. Bourchier, "Lineages of Organicist Political Thought," 92; Reeve, *Golkar of Indonesia,* 70–71; Saafroedin Bahar, Ananda B. Kusuma, and Nannie Hudawati, *Risalah,* 259–260.

11. Bourchier, "Lineages of Organicist Political Thought," 92–93; Saafroedin Bahar, Ananda B. Kusuma, and Nannie Hudawati, *Risalah,* 262–63.

12. Bourchier, "Lineages of Organicist Political Thought," 91, 93–94; Reeve, *Golkar of Indonesia,* 71–75. Also, see Yamin's speech on this matter to the BPKI, quoted in Saafroedin Bahar, Ananda B. Kusuma, and Nannie Hudawati, *Risalah,* 181.

13. Saafroedin Bahar, Ananda B. Kusuma, and Nannie Hudawati, *Risalah,* 646.

14. Bourchier, "Lineages of Organicist Political Thought," 94–97; Lindsey, "Indonesia's *Negara Hukum,*" 367.

15. Personal communication, Timothy Lindsey, December 10, 2001.

16. McIntyre, "'Greater Indonesia' Idea of Nationalism," 81; Saafroedin Bahar, Ananda B. Kusuma, and Nannie Hudawati, *Risalah,* 46–61, 133–41. In his *Naskah-Persiapan Undang-Undang Dasar 1945,* 191–92, Yamin gives the date of his second speech as July 6.

17. McIntyre, "'Greater Indonesia' Idea of Nationalism," 81; Saadroedin Bahar, Ananda B. Kusuma, and Nannie Hudawati, *Risalah,* 73–4.

18. Saafroedin Bahar, Ananda B. Kusuma, and Nannie Hudawati, *Risalah,* 149. An English translation of an edited version of this speech may be found in Feith and Castles, *Indonesian Political Thinking,* 441–43.

19. Saafroedin Bahar, Ananda B. Kusuma, and Nannie Hudawati, *Risalah,* 150–51.

20. Also, six votes were cast in favor of the Netherlands Indies plus Malacca. Of the remaining two, one was blank, and the other specified a territorial arrangement not provided for in the ballot. Saafroedin Bahar, Ananda B. Kusuma, and Nannie Hudawati, *Risalah,* 159–60.

21. Terauchi met Sukarno and Hatta at his headquarters in Vietnam on August 12, 1945. At this meeting he refused to recognize the extensive territorial claims of the BPKI. It is possible he adopted this stance to avoid creating any additional obstacles to peace with the allied powers for which Japan was by that time desperately suing (McIntyre, "'Greater Indonesia' Idea of Nationalism," 81–83).

22. I have used Benedict R. O'G. Anderson's translation of this clause, as found in his *Java in a Time of Revolution,* 171.

23. Pringgodigdo, *Office of President,* 5–6.

24. Anderson, *Java in a Time of Revolution,* 91.

25. Pringgodigdo, *Office of President,* 6.

26. Anderson, *Java in a Time of Revolution,* 95.

27. Anderson, *Java in a Time of Revolution,* 110–12.

28. Sjahrir, *Our Struggle,* 28–29.

29. Anderson, *Java in a Time of Revolution,* 173.

30. Anderson, *Java in a Time of Revolution,* 173.

31. Pringgodigdo, *Office of the President,* 7.

32. Compare Anderson, *Java in a Time of Revolution,* 172.

33. Anderson, *Java in a Time of Revolution,* 175–78; Reid, *Indonesian National Revolution,* 71.

34. Pringgodigdo, *Office of the President*, 17.
35. Pringgodigdo, *Office of the President*, 19, 21.
36. See article 122 of the 1949 constitution in Nasution, *Aspiration for Constitutional Government*, 471.
37. Feith, *Decline of Constitutional Democracy*, 93.
38. Feith, *Decline of Constitutional Democracy*, 93.
39. Nasution, *Aspiration for Constitutional Government*, 28.
40. Feith, *Decline of Constitutional Democracy*, 95.
41. Feith, *Decline of Constitutional Democracy*, 96.
42. Feith, *Decline of Constitutional Democracy*, 96n84, 99; Pringgodigdo, *Office of President*, 30.
43. Lijphart, *Democracy in Plural Societies*, 199.
44. Feith, *Indonesian Elections*, 58–59; Liddle, "Coercion, Co-optation," 275–76.
45. Feith, *Decline of Constitutional Democracy*, 448–49; Feith, *Indonesian Elections*, 65.
46. "The political public . . . [consisted] of persons outside the political elite who nevertheless saw themselves as capable of taking action which could affect national government or politics" (Feith, *Decline of Constitutional Democracy*, 109).
47. Feith, *Decline of Constitutional Democracy*, 40.
48. Quoted in Feith, *Decline of Constitutional Democracy*, 41.
49. Sjahrir, *Our Struggle*, 29–30.
50. Feith, *Decline of Constitutional Democracy*, 462; Nasution, *Aspiration for Constitutional Government*, 41.
51. Feith, *Decline of Constitutional Democracy*, 552.
52. Feith, "Dynamics of Guided Democracy," 318–19.
53. See Kahin and Kahin, *Subversion as Foreign Policy*, 144.
54. Sukarno, *Pidato President Sukarno pada Hari Sumpah Pemuda tgl. 28 Oktober 1956 di Djakarta*, 11.
55. Compare this similar but more pointed remark from a speech of June 9, 1957: "I wash my hands of all wrong, because it wasn't I who ordered the existence of parties. Not I. In November 1945, a decree was issued to establish parties. Thank God, it wasn't Soekarno who signed that decree" (quoted in Lev, *Transition to Guided Democracy*, 55).
56. Sukarno, *Pidato President Sukarno pada Hari Sumpah Pemuda tgl. 28 Oktober 1956 di Djakarta,* 11.
57. Sukarno, *Menjelamatkan Republik Proklamasi,* 12, 13; Bourchier, "Lineages of Organicist Political Thought," 130–33.
58. Feith, *Decline of Constitutional Democracy*, 544–48; Feith, "Dynamics of Guided Democracy," 320.
59. Feith, *Decline of Constitutional Democracy*, 578–79; Kahin and Kahin, *Subversion as Foreign Policy*, 144.
60. Lev, *Transition to Guided Democracy*, 20–22; Feith, "Dynamics of Guided Democracy," 320.
61. Lev, *Transition to Guided Democracy*, 23.
62. Lev, *Transition to Guided Democracy*, 170.

63. Mackie, "Inevitable or Avoidable?" 29–30.
64. Mackie, "Inevitable or Avoidable?" 30–31; Feith, *Decline of Constitutional Democracy*, 583–86; Feith, "Dynamics of Guided Democracy," 321.
65. Mackie, "Inevitable or Avoidable?" 30–31; Harvey, *Permesta*, 153.
66. Jamie Mackie, "Inevitable or Avoidable?" 32.
67. Feith, *Decline of Constitutional Democracy*, 582. Despite the nationwide state of war and siege, regional elections, as provided for in law 1/1957, were held in Java, South Sumatra, and Riauw in 1957 and in Kalimantan in 1958 (Lev, *Transition to Guided Democracy*, 84).
68. Mackie, "Inevitable or Avoidable?" 27.
69. Compare Feith, *Decline of Constitutional Democracy*, 592: "The extreme unpredictability of the two years since mid-1956 had given way to more clearly patterned interaction, to what may be called a system."
70. Lev, *Transition to Guided Democracy*, 241–58; Feith, "Dynamics of Guided Democracy," 360.
71. Quoted in Nasution, *Aspiration for Constitutional Government*, 385.
72. Nasution, *Aspiration for Constitutional Government*, 387; Nasution, "Human Rights," 47–48.
73. Nasution, *Aspiration for Constitutional Government*, 397–98.
74. Nasution, *Aspiration for Constitutional Government*, 401, 408.

Part I

2

The Personal Rule of Sukarno

GUIDED DEMOCRACY

A broad account and history of Guided Democracy will be helpful before considering it as a system of personal rule by Sukarno. The first thing to be said in this regard is that Guided Democracy as a form of government severely tests the descriptive and analytical powers of those who attempt to describe and explain it. Indeed, Mackie argues that "it is unsafe even to talk about 'the government' after 1962, as if Sukarno, his ministers and the administration constituted a coherent, unified group exercising a collective responsibility for policy making." Mackie believes that "the notion of a 'court' in which every minister was striving to gain influence at the palace was more apposite in the later years."[1] Conceptual difficulties notwithstanding, it is possible to describe Guided Democracy as an authoritarian and centralized system and to add that power was divided between and struggled over by the president, the army, and the Communist Party. The initial configuration of these political actors was shaped by a competitive and cooperative relationship between President Sukarno and the army leadership under General Nasution, in which the former protected the PKI (Indonesian Communist Party) and resorted to its numbers and influence to counterbalance the power of the latter. Sukarno carried out this activity under the banner of NASAKOM, or unity between the nationalist, religious, and communist streams. Initially, he used this formula to rally the political parties as a counterbalance to military influence; subsequently, it became a formula to justify his attempts to include PKI members in the cabinet, and throughout this period he advanced it to promote unity between the increasingly antagonistic army and Communist Party (although some Indonesians came to fear that it was really a smokescreen under cover of which he hoped to bring the PKI to power).[2]

The "stable conflict," as Feith termed it, between the president and the army, whereby the "more or less equally matched partners" worked together and against each other, with the Communist Party being obliged to play a subordinate role did not last.[3] From 1963, the Communist Party became more assertive, challenging the army and even placing pressure on Sukarno. This new trend emerged from the fluid political circumstances that obtained in Indonesia between August 1962, when the Irian issue was resolved in Indonesia's favor by the New York Agreement, and September 1963, "when Sukarno's government was carried by events over which it had imperfect control to a more extreme position [on Malaysia] than it initially intended to assume."[4]

In the aftermath of the Irian campaign, First Minister Djuanda attempted to focus the president's attention on one of its casualties: the economy. Spending on the campaign had contributed to a huge budget deficit, which in turn exacerbated inflation that, in the latter part of 1962, showed signs of spiraling out of control. Djuanda enjoyed the support of the U.S. government and the International Monetary Fund (IMF) in this task, and together they negotiated a stabilization program to bring Indonesia's inflation under control. The program was sharply deflationary, insisting on a balanced budget, increased taxes, and a realistic exchange rate as a condition of loans. Mackie wrote, "Indonesia could hardly have hoped to check the inflation she was suffering from much less painfully"; he also noted that its implementation was going to impose immense political problems for its backers.[5] Nevertheless, Sukarno incorporated aspects of the program in his *Dekon* (Economic Declaration) of March 1963 and had this endorsed by the Interim People's Consultative Assembly in May. He then promulgated the "May 26 decrees," which contained the core of the stabilization package. Two further developments lent weight to the conclusion that Sukarno had embarked on a major shift to the Right in policy and direction: he settled a dispute between his government and three foreign oil companies, and he invited the Malayan prime minister, Tunku Abdul Rahman, to meet him for talks on the vexed issue of the proposed Federation of Malaysia.[6]

The Brunei revolt of December 8, 1962, provided Indonesia's leaders with an opportunity to condemn the formation of Malaysia as a British neocolonial device being imposed against the will of the people concerned.[7] On January 20, 1963, the Indonesian foreign minister Dr Subandrio declared, "We cannot but adopt a policy of confrontation against Malaya because at present they represent themselves as accomplices of the neo-colonialists and neo-imperialists pursuing a hostile policy towards Indonesia."[8] Sukarno endorsed this view in February 1963 at the very time Djuanda's negotiations with the IMF on the stabilization program had reached a critical stage.⁹ Nevertheless, Sukarno adopted a conciliatory stance toward Malaysia in May, and in Manila the following month the foreign ministers of Indonesia, Malaya, and the Philippines resolved that Indonesia and the Philippines "would welcome the formation of Malaysia provided the support of the people of the Borneo Territories is ascertained by an independent and impartial authority, the Secretary-General of the United Nations or his representative."¹⁰ This statement proved capable of more than one interpretation. Indeed, the ensuing summit meeting, also in Manila, between the heads of government of the three countries got off to a rocky start because Sukarno believed that the London Agreement—signed by Malaya and Britain on July 9, which determined that Malaysia would come into being on August 31—disregarded the clause in the accord signed in Manila relating to the ascertaining of opinion in Sabah and Sawarak.¹¹ However, a compromise was reached whereby Malaya would "permit some delay in the formation of Malaysia in return for Indonesia's abandonment of her previous demand for a full plebiscite."¹² But the announcement from Kuala Lumpur on August 29 that Malaysia would be formally proclaimed on September 16 stirred up the same cycle of distrust and recrimination; an enraged Sukarno claimed to "have been duped and humiliated by the British."¹³ This frame of mind may have inclined him not to accept the results of U Thant's investigation—namely, that "there is no doubt about the wishes of a sizeable majority of the peoples of these territories to join in the Federation of Malaysia"—which was released on September 12 and announced on September 14.¹⁴

The president was under pressure from various quarters. The Communist Party urged on him a stand of militant hostility toward Malaysia to destroy the stabilization program and to sever Indonesia's ties with the West. Others adversely affected by the program—including even business people suffering from its tight money policy—certainly realized that continued opposition to Malaysia would probably lead its Western sponsors to abandon it. However, food and clothing for the people formed one of the aims of Sukarno's government, and Sukarno was by no means insensible to its benefits, especially as it had already markedly slowed the rate at which prices were increasing. Also, Djuanda showed no sign of abandoning it. But he was unwell, and a number of ministers were already maneuvering to replace him.¹⁵

In this complex and volatile situation, Sukarno decided, on September 15, not to accept the UN report and to "withhold recognition of Malaysia" when it was proclaimed the following day.¹⁶ Mackie believes that the president, not wanting to jeopardize the foreign loans on which the success of the stabilization program depended, intended only a gesture of protest at the formation of Malaysia, but his "hand was forced by the burning of the British Embassy [on

September 18] and the PKI-sponsored take-over of British firms . . . on the same pattern as the take-over of Dutch firms in December 1957."[17] But one should not conclude from this account that Sukarno was simply the unwitting victim of an arbitrary sequence of events. If his apparent attempt to have it both ways—offer a gesture of opposition to Malaysia while maintaining the stabilization program—was nullified by the burning of the British Embassy, then it should not be forgotten that the rioters responsible for this action were themselves a product, in part at least, of Sukarno's inspired demagoguery and agitation against Malaysia in the preceding months of 1963.

On September 21, the government decided not to nationalize the British firms taken over by the Communist Party in the previous week, despite the party's demand that it do so. Rather, the decision was taken to sever all commercial and financial relations with Malaysia, of which Singapore was then a part. The following week, IMF standby credits and U.S. aid, without which the stabilization program could not survive, were stopped.[18] Moreover, no further attempt was made to contain inflation. First Minister Djuanda died on November 6, and with his death Sukarno lost, according to his personal physician, "an assistant who could contain his emotions."[19] He was replaced by the ambitious Dr Subandrio, who assumed the new title of first deputy prime minister.[20] Indonesian politics had lost the fluid quality that had characterized events from mid-1962 to mid-1963. From September 1963 a trend in favor of the Left was evident, but very few observers shared Sukarno's view that Indonesia was marching toward socialism. Rather, they noted the increasing polarization of Indonesian society and politics, especially between communists and anticommunists and the desperate rearguard action of the latter, not to mention signs that the president was in failing health. Accordingly, they anxiously sensed that they were witnessing the final scenes in a rapidly unfolding tragedy. Of course, no one foresaw the precise form that the disaster for Sukarno and his people eventually did take in the latter part of 1965 (detailed in the following chapter), but many were certainly expecting a disaster in one form or another.

PERSONAL RULE

Guenther Roth's influential interpretation of Max Weber's work on the forms of legitimate domination shapes our understanding of the concept of personal rule. Indeed, according to Roth, there are two types—not only the familiar case of charismatic leadership, which is based on a fascination with the person of the ruler, but also a derivative or attenuated form of patrimonialism, which stands "on the basis of loyalties that . . . are inextricably linked to material incentives and rewards." Roth calls this version "personal rulership" or "detraditionalized, personalized patrimonialism."[21]

The importance of this distinction cannot be gainsaid. Indeed, it is most helpful in bringing out the differences between the personal rule of the charismatic Sukarno[22] and the personal rule of the patrimonialist Soeharto.[23] Nevertheless, in this study, with its focus on the opposition between personal and constitutional rule, it is their similarity that is crucial. Thus, we will talk first of personal rule, to emphasize its arbitrariness as exercised by a leader free of restraints imposed by a legal order, and second of one of its two subtypes, to specify whether this arbitrary rule is based on a belief in the unique qualities of the ruler or one based on fear and favors (to put it at its broadest).

GUIDED DEMOCRACY AS A SYSTEM OF PERSONAL RULE BY SUKARNO

Sukarno was first and foremost a charismatic leader, although he also secured patrimonial loyalty by "the distribution of opportunities for personal profit."[24] As the account of Guided Democracy shows, he was not all-powerful, finding it necessary to take into account the influence and goals of the army and, after mid-1963, the Communist Party. Nevertheless, it also shows that at a certain point he was able to concentrate decision making in his own hands and to exercise it personally and arbitrarily—if not free of the restraint provided by countervailing political force, then certainly free of the restraint imposed by a legal order.

Many of the steps by which he reached this position were taken with the support or at least the acquiescence of the army, for both parties favored authoritarian government; indeed, the army led the way in this regard by championing the 1945 constitution and by urging it on Sukarno. If the first of such steps was his proclamation of this constitution in July 1959, then the second was his issuing of an edict two months later that severely limited the degree of regional autonomy provided for in law 1/1957. Indeed, it replaced regional heads elected by their respective legislatures with ones chosen solely by the president, in the case of first-level regions (or provinces), and with ones chosen by the Minister of Home Affairs "with the agreement of the President," in the case of second-level regions (or *kabupaten* and municipalities).[25] Then, in March 1960, he dissolved the elected parliament after it threatened to reject the government's budget. He endorsed the same budget by decree and, in the remaining months of a busy year, banned Masjumi, the modernist Islamic political party that had garnered almost eight million votes from its largely outer-islands constituency in the 1955 elections on the grounds of its involvement in the regional rebellion of 1958.[26] He also appointed a new legislature—whose members came from political parties, functional groups, and the armed forces—and an Interim People's Consultative Assembly (interim, that is, until elections were finally called).[27] But, as mentioned, they never were, and thus the sequence of events envisaged in the body of the constitution was again reversed. In 1945, the transitional provisions enabled the president to perform the functions of the MPR and DPR in their absence. In 1959, the members of the MPR did not elect the president; rather, the president selected them. Then, in 1963, they in their wisdom appointed him president for life. If we put to one side the egregious manner in which this constitution was reintroduced (Lindsey refers to it as a "coup"[28]), we must say that there was nothing unconstitutional in his selecting the members of the MPR and the DPR, for the 1945 constitution is silent on this topic. Nevertheless, it was a silence that opened the way to the derogation of both institutions and, with them, of the Indonesian people, whose sovereignty the MPR was supposed to exercise.

If regional autonomy and democracy were the first casualties of Sukarno's emerging personal rule, the law state (*negara hukum*), or rule of law, was the second. In February 1960, Sukarno made the chairman of the Supreme Court a cabinet member, and six months later he denounced the principle of the separation of powers.[29] In 1963, he introduced presidential decrees 5 and 11: the former required police permits for political gatherings, and the latter was directed against subversion, where the interpretation of what constituted subversive behavior was left entirely in the hands of the government.[30] These were followed by law 19 of 1964 and law 13 of 1965, which gave the president the right to intervene directly in court decisions.[31] According to Timothy Lindsey,

> the legislative process was effectively replaced by executive instruction and legal legitimacy lay in ideology as defined by the President rather than in written statute or a formal jurisprudence. This, combined with executive intervention in the judicial process and a culture of contempt for the rule of law, led to widespread legal uncertainty and the collapse of the legal process. The result was a system in which the citizen was vulnerable to, and defenceless against, the instrumentalities of state, where policy was the supreme source of legitimacy.[32]

Personal rule is often built on the subverting or abandonment of a constitution, and this was certainly the fate of the 1950 constitution, abrogated by Sukarno in 1959. But it is a telling measure of the flexible nature of the 1945 constitution that the president had no need to discard it to rule in a personal fashion. Although it gave the appearance of legality, it in fact opened the door wide to personal rulership.

Other steps taken by the president to draw the threads of power into his hands threatened the army's position of influence in Guided Democracy and were therefore met with varying degrees of opposition. The army's involvement in civilian matters in the Guided Democracy period was principally based on the proclamation of martial law in March 1957, under which General Nasution, as chief of staff, became central war administrator and his territorial commanders became regional war administrators. However, in December 1959, by which time the regional rebellion had been reduced to insignificance, the president "succeeded in reorganising the martial law system, establishing himself as head of a new Supreme War Authority . . . and thus creating an institutional framework in which the regional military commanders were his direct subordinates."[33] Then, in mid-1962, Sukarno managed to kick General Nasution upstairs, from chief of staff of the army to the weaker position of chief of staff of the armed forces, and replace him with the more tractable General Achmad Yani. In the following year he was able to lift martial law and thereby further limit the military's willingness and capacity to act against his wishes.[34]

It is impossible to date precisely Sukarno's advent as a personal ruler. His first steps in this direction go back to 1956–1957, when he spelled out his alternative to constitutional democracy and gave voice to his claim to be uniquely qualified to speak for the Indonesian people. He advanced his qualifications in this regard in his *konsepsi* speech of February 1957 in which he asserted that he was "the mouthpiece of the Indonesian people."[35] However, after the sidelining of Nasution in 1962, few would argue with the proposition that his style of leading broadly fitted this designation. It was later evident in the various positions he adopted and in the actions he took in relation to Malaysia—spectacularly so in his impetuous decision to withdraw from the United Nations on New Year's Eve 1964. However, this date may not be early enough, for he was displaying some of the characteristics of a personal ruler before that time—for example, in January 1962, he allowed his suspicions to get the better of him and ordered the arrest of political opponents.

PERSONALITY

The decisive influence of the personal ruler makes the personality of that figure central to an understanding of the nature of the regime. Accordingly, I attempt in chapter 7 to advance our understanding of Soeharto's inner self to better comprehend the character of his New Order regime; and in chapters 3–5, I show how various facets of Sukarno's personality influenced not only the course of events in the Guided Democracy years but also the nature of Guided Democracy itself. Much has been written on Sukarno's involvement in the politics of that period, but if the authors do not succumb to the culturalist view of him as the passive recipient of cultural imprinting, then they commit the "'intellectualist fallacy' [of assuming] that political activity is all calculation."[36] That is to say, "they posit rationality, defining away personal characteristics and presuming that the behavior of actors can be deduced from the logic of their situations."[37] What is missing from both these perspectives is "the presence of the determining personality,"[38] which is formed early and which shapes subsequent behavior, even political calculation, according to its lights. History is, of course, lived forward, but it is done so by participants whose personalities were largely formed in a preceding period.

Issues of separation appear to lie at the core of Sukarno's personality. As I argue in the following chapter, the feeling of desolation (*kesepian*) was Sukarno's constant companion and seemed to be based on a dread equivalence in his mind between separation and death. It almost overwhelmed him when he was placed in solitary confinement by the colonial authorities, but it still weighed heavily on him even when he was very much in the midst of others, whether as head of state alone or as both head of state and head of government. I assert that his efforts to fend off this feeling of desolation gave rise to a "politics of being central," which may be understood as the particular form his personal rule assumed whereby he placed himself at the center of fervent attention among government members and a large circle of followers and admirers beyond, to all of whom he looked for affirmation. The effect of this arrangement was to give scope for his other feelings (including suspicion) and for his state of health to impinge directly on the political process.

This part of the argument requires no elaborate analysis. Indeed, it is largely based on noting and taking seriously Sukarno's own frequent references to *kesepian* or cognate feelings in his speeches and autobiography.[39] However, if it is possible by these means to establish the salience of this disposition in Sukarno's mind and its consequences for his politics in the form of a distinctive manner of personal rule, then it is much more difficult, perhaps even impossible, to offer convincing evidence concerning the origins of this state of mind, although there is certainly reason to suspect an early and lengthy period of separation from his parents.

We also know from his many comments on the matter in his speeches that Sukarno had a pronounced fear of death. This fear was the other side of the coin to his fear of separation. If the latter gave rise to the "politics of being central," then the former fostered a contradictory approach to leadership that I have labeled the "politics of rejuvenation." Sukarno claimed to be on the side of youth and the future, and in politics he gave prominence to the role of contemporary youth and youthful qualities, such as reckless courage; yet, he reached into his own long-departed youth for inspiration and guidance. Its contribution to his manner of personal rule was to supplement its intense focus on his own self with a mobilization *politique* characterized by a quality of frantic risk taking on the one hand and an anachronistic frame of reference on the other. Like Mao Zedong, for whom the great proletarian cultural revolution was "a deliberate and nostalgic attempt on . . . [his] part to relive the cultural revolution of 4 May period [1915–1921]," Sukarno fell back on the notions of his youth to deal with the intractable political problems that confronted him in his old age.[40]

The theme of separation also appears in Sukarno's view of history and his place within it. He reveled in the belief that he was marching in step with an ascendant, anti-imperialist trend in world history of which Indonesian socialism was a culmination. However, he occasionally entertained doubts on this score, fearing that the imperialists had not yet exhausted their historic potential. Giving substance to these doubts were the events of 1965–1966—in particular, the massacre of the Communist Party and his removal from power by General Soeharto (the latter surrounded the palace with unmarked troops on March 11, 1966, at the very moment Sukarno proclaimed to his cabinet ministers inside that it was "Marxism that taught me historical thinking"). But the president would have none of it. He insisted on history's progressive character and of his inseparable relation to it. It was not he who had misread events but Soeharto, who would certainly be thrust aside when this progressive history reasserted itself. The alternative view, that he was an isolated figure who had been abandoned by history, was clearly too dreadful to contemplate.

Sukarno's embrace of the orthodox school of Marxism, with its view of history as a process governed by laws that are an extension of the laws of nature, appeared to reflect and perhaps served to restrain his narcissistic sense of himself as the coming man. It might be said that he substituted for himself as man of destiny the doctrine of historical necessity. The only lesson that such a man, with this view of how events happened, might derive from the catastrophe of 1965 would be one about not underestimating the last lunge of the waning imperialists and their local proxies. Furthest from his mind was the idea that hubris may visit disaster on a leader and his people—of course, this is a difficult lesson for any proud leader to learn. But of what did his hubris consist? He assumed that he could achieve results consistent with his intentions. There is debate about what precisely Sukarno's intentions were in the late Guided Democracy years: some argue that he was attempting to integrate the Communist Party within the existing order whereas others believe he was trying to smooth its path to power.[41] But we may be sure that he did not intend what he in fact contributed to: the mass killings of Communist Party members in the final months of 1965. He had not read those lines from *Hamlet* that state,

> Our wills and fates do so contrary run
> That our devices still are overthrown;
> Our thoughts are ours, their ends none of our own.[42]

NOTES

1. Mackie, *Konfrontasi*, 80.
2. Feith, "Dynamics of Guided Democracy," 325, 337–39; Crouch, *Army and Politics*, 43, 51.
3. Feith, "Dynamics of Guided Democracy," 325.
4. Mackie, *Konfrontasi*, 6.
5. Mackie, *Konfrontasi*, 135.
6. Mackie, *Konfrontasi*, 136–38.
7. Mackie, *Konfrontasi*, 111.
8. Mackie, *Konfrontasi*, 125.
9. Mackie, *Konfrontasi*, 127, 136.
10. Quoted in Mackie, *Konfrontasi*, 150.
11. Mackie, *Konfrontasi*, 154.
12. Mackie, *Konfrontasi*, 159.
13. Jones, *Indonesia: The Possible Dream*, 289.
14. Mackie, *Konfrontasi*, 175–76.
15. Mackie, *Konfrontasi*, 138–39, 178–79, 181.
16. Mackie, *Konfrontasi*, 181.
17. Mackie, *Konfrontasi*, 181.
18. Mackie, *Konfrontasi*, 181.
19. Soeharto, *Saksi Sejarah*, 136.
20. Mackie, *Konfrontasi*, 240.
21. Roth, "Personal Rulership," 196. Compare the similar approach of Jackson and Rosberg, *Personal Rule in Black Africa*, 73–74.
22. Ann Ruth Willner explains Sukarno's charismatic political leadership largely in terms of his identification with "sacred and legendary" figures and his oratorical ability (*Spellbinders*, 65, 151).
23. For a consideration of Soeharto's patrimonial rule, see Crouch, "Patrimonialism and Military Rule."
24. Crouch, "Patrimonialism and Military Rule," 573.
25. Legge, *Central Authority*, 60–61, 209–11.
26. Feith, "Dynamics of Guided Democracy," 363–64.
27. Feith, "Dynamics of Guided Democracy," 363–64.
28. Lindsey, "Overview of Indonesian Law," 7.
29. Feith, "Dynamics of Guided Democracy," 373.
30. Zifcak, "'But a Shadow of Justice,'" 356–57; Nasution, *Aspiration for Constitutional Government*, 426–27.
31. Lindsey, "From Rule of Law," 14.

32. Lindsey, "From Rule of Law," 13.
33. Feith, "Dynamics of Guided Democracy," 332.
34. Crouch, *Army and Politics*, 52–54.
35. Sukarno, *Menjelamatkan Republik Proklamasi,* 15. In subsequent years he returned to this theme, reformulating the nature of his link to the people in evermore intimate terms: "The language which comes out of my mouth," he said in the following year, "is already inscribed in the hearts of the Indonesian people themselves" (Sukarno, "Pidato P. J. M. Presiden [Sukarno] pada Rapat Umum di Saparua pada Tanggal 8 Nopember 1958," 1).
36. Graham Wallas, quoted in Davies, *Skills, Outlooks and Passions*, 293.
37. Greenstein, "Can Personality and Politics," 106.
38. Wallace Stevens, quoted in Edel, "Biography: A Manifesto," 2.
39. The analyses of Sukarno's personality and politics in chapters 3 through 5 are based on a careful and systematic reading of his preindependence writings as contained in *Dibawah Bendera Revolusi*, vol. 1, ed. H. Mualliff Nasution (Jakarta: Panitya Penerbit, 1965), and his postindependence speeches. My basic resource here has been the transcripts and published versions of the speeches, which I collected from the Indonesian state secretariat from 1966 to 1967 and from archives and libraries in the Netherlands, Indonesia, Australia, and the United States thereafter. An exchange of materials with Cornell University's John M. Echols Collection on Southeast Asia in 1993 plugged some gaps in our respective holdings, and I now have 269 in my collection, possibly making it, with Cornell's, the largest in existence.
40. Schram, *Mao Tse-tung*, 343.
41. See Hauswedell, "Sukarno: Radical or Conservative?"
42. Shakespeare, *Hamlet*, 3.2.203–5. The last line of this quote may be found, with commentary, in Bradley, *Shakespearean Tragedy*, 19.

3

Suffering from the Quiet: Sukarno's Desolation and His Politics of Being Central

But disappointment in Bung Karno—the shattering of belief in a symbol, in the flame—this could bring utter disillusionment. But what could be done? Perhaps one stage in becoming adult is becoming disillusioned in a leader.

—Goenawan Mohamad[1]

A person may be in solitary confinement, and yet not be able to be alone. How greatly he must suffer is beyond imagination.

—D. W. Winnicott[2]

Biographers and historians may cause pain to relatives by writing about the human vulnerability of their subjects, and if one of the subjects was a founding father of his country, it is likely that portrayal of this vulnerability will cause distress not only to his family but also to his country people. It is not simply that they feel offense; their very identity as citizens of this country may be shaken. This is what happened when John Ingleson's critical claims concerning Sukarno, contained in his book *Road to Exile: The Indonesian Nationalist Movement, 1927–1934* (1979), were summarized in the Indonesian newspaper *Kompas* in September 1980 by a critic of the former president, Rosihan Anwar.

Ingleson asserted in *Road to Exile* that Sukarno had not only abandoned his policy of noncooperation with the Dutch upon his second arrest, in August 1933, but had also written four letters to the attorney general of the Netherlands Indies in August and September 1933 "in which he pleaded for his release from jail, and in return promised to take no part in politics for the rest of his life."[3] The author's quotes from these letters reveal them to be abject in content and tone, giving the impression that Sukarno was shaken to the core at the prospect of having to endure a long period of isolation in jail or exile.

To read this account in the historical context provided by the author would be disconcerting enough for the Indonesian reader, as it is very much at odds with the received view of Sukarno in his country as a steadfast and heroic nationalist leader. However, to read it in the hostile framework offered by Rosihan Anwar would have been particularly troubling. Indeed, he used the information he obtained from Ingleson's book to paint a most unflattering picture of Sukarno, whom he also compared unfavorably to his former rival in the nationalist movement (and future vice president), Mohammad Hatta:

> Another difference lay in their political attitude to the Netherlands Indies colonial government. Hatta was firm and consistent. Sukarno was just the opposite, a ranting orator who quickly gave up if he faced a difficult situation which was not congenial to him personally.[4]

It is therefore not surprising to discover that some newspaper readers were shocked by Rosihan Anwar's account. H. Mahbub Djunaedi, for one, writing in the same newspaper in October 1980, gives a vivid report of its effect on him:

> My jaw dropped when I read the article by my good friend Ustad H. Rosihan Anwar. . . . I was so surprised that if a tiger had entered my room I would have extended to it the same hospitality as I would a kitten. That wasn't the end of the matter! The writing of my good friend . . . [threw my] digestive system . . . into chaos.[5]

Mohamad Roem, although once jailed at Sukarno's instigation, proved more detached than Rosihan Anwar. Indeed, he raised serious doubts about the authenticity of the letters on which Ingleson based his account and which he himself had read. He joined the discussion in the columns of *Kompas* in January 1981:

> The Soekarno letters in the Dutch archives which only constitute authentic copies do not convince me that it was Soekarno himself who wrote them. . . . When I read those letters I found a few mistakes in their Dutch. The knowledge of Dutch of Bung Karno (who attended the Hoogere Burger School) was at the very least on a par with mine (Algemene Middelbare School). In that time, we were very careful indeed not to make mistakes if we wrote letters in Dutch to Dutch officials.[6]

He also shared some of Mahbub Djunaedi's distress and suggested that the opinions of Indonesians concerning their first president affect the way they view themselves:

> I was also open-mouthed from surprise, like H. Mahbub Djunaidi, after reading the piece by Rosihan Anwar. . . .
> If we view Sukarno as a person who gave up, how must we view ourselves? When travelling along Proclamation Street we need not turn our gaze [to the monument that marks the place where Sukarno proclaimed independence on August 17, 1945].[7]

On February 19, another daily newspaper, *Merdeka,* entered the discussion by accusing Rosihan Anwar "and his group" of seeking to "blacken the name of Bung Karno." Furthermore, in a subsequent issue, the poet Sitor Situmorang accused John Ingleson of "character assassination of Sukarno and, simultaneously, of Indonesia as a nation."[8]

Rosihan Anwar's claims concerning Sukarno and their troubled and disputed reception in the pages of Indonesia's newspapers were noted with some concern at the highest level of the Indonesian government. On the same day as the aforementioned issue of *Merdeka* appeared, vice president Adam Malik informed reporters that he had just come from a discussion with President Soeharto about the argument in the press over Sukarno. *Kompas* reported his subsequent remarks as follows:

> "My assessment, like President Soeharto's, is that all Bung Karno's deeds have already been recorded in history," the Vice President said. According to Adam Malik, the airing of those problems again now will only damage the Indonesian nation itself by giving rise to conflict. Apart from that, it will, he added, also disparage the leader whom we have held in high esteem up until now. "For what reason would we find fault in a person whom we have already acknowledged as our leader. It is another problem whether one agreed with him or not. What is clear is that he was a leader who cannot be put in doubt again."[9]

A week later the government gave direct expression to its concern: censors blacked out two pages in the weekly magazine *Tempo* that referred to the Sukarno letters. However, they let through a thoughtful and scholarly treatment of the same issue by the historian Taufik Abdullah.[10] He argued that private matters in the life of a person have no necessary bearing on their historical role; therefore, "a historical figure is not really measured by the things he did in his private capacity."[11] He elaborated on this point in a subsequent interview by pointing out that even if Sukarno did write the letters, no consequences flowed from this event. The colonial authorities did not publish them or use them in some other way to discredit Sukarno. That being the case, they lie outside the historical process.[12]

Nevertheless, Taufik Abdullah did allow himself some speculation concerning Sukarno's state of mind. He invited his interviewer to recall the circumstances in which Sukarno found himself in August 1933 and to consider their likely effect on him:

> Imagine . . . Bung Karno jailed on the basis of the special powers vested in the Governor-General. In that situation Bung Karno loses the right to defend himself. He has come to be regarded as a hero and feels how great Ibu Inggit's sacrifice for him has been. Then they are forcibly separated and Sukarno does not enjoy the right to a trial. How would Bung Karno feel in that situation?

By way of answer to his own question, he offered three suggestions. First, "the letters which possibly were sent by him from Sukamiskin jail are a problem for Sukarno as an ordinary human being. Possibly he sent them because he felt lonely, isolated and the like." Second, "Bung Karno was possibly in a stressed state and very emotional when he was in jail because he had to leave his wife. The psychological factor becomes an issue here." These two suggestions clearly refer to the same state of mind, which can be briefly defined by reference to his third suggestion—namely, that Sukarno "felt kesepian."[13] *Kesepian* is derived from the adjective *sepi*, meaning "quiet," and the circumfix *ke-an,* which is borrowed from Javanese and means either "too" or, as in this case, "suffering from."[14] Thus, we may say that Sukarno was suffering from the quiet.

Taufik Abdullah conceded that a psychological consideration of the private individual may in the end throw light on his historical role: "Let those who are attracted by a psychological approach to history . . . search for the link between human beings in their private capacity and human beings as historical actors."[15] In this study, an attempt is made to do just that: to link personal aspects of Sukarno's life to his historical role or, more precisely, to link his emotions or affects to his style of political leadership. Mindful of Taufik Abdullah's speculations, a strong candidate in this regard would appear to be *kesepian*. However, a problem immediately presents itself with this particular affect. These speculations are based on the working assumption that the letters, which give powerful expression to this sentiment, are authentic; furthermore, as we know from his other remarks, Taufik, like Mohamad Roem, entertained serious doubts in this respect. But there is other, substantial evidence to suggest that Sukarno did indeed suffer this feeling on his arrest in 1933. And, to judge by his own remarks, he also suffered it following his initial incarceration in 1929, during his exile from 1934, and even when he was president of the Republic of Indonesia.

The question remains regarding how Indonesian readers will react to this exercise. Sukarno was their first president, and, as Mohamad Roem suggested, their opinion of him will influence their view of themselves as citizens of Indonesia. Those who found some comfort in the questionable authenticity of the letters may feel disconcerted by my claim that Sukarno's feeling of *kesepian* can be established without reference to these letters. Or they may suspect that this claim amounts to an indirect way of demonstrating the authenticity of the letters, for if Sukarno did experience the sentiment to which the letters give such strong expression, does this not increase the likelihood that the letters themselves are authentic?

And how will Indonesians react to the argument that central aspects of Sukarno's way of practicing politics were influenced by his attempts to keep this feeling of *kesepian* at bay? My answer is that this argument is advanced not to denigrate Sukarno; rather, it is put forward to trace the impact of his personality (or aspects thereof) on the manner of his personal rule and the nature of his regime. The picture that emerges of Sukarno and his leadership is certainly critical and bound to cause distress but is more human than the standard, idealized view of him in his country as a heroic leader and peerless founding father.

SUFFERING FROM THE QUIET

Sepi is an uncomfortable feeling for most Indonesians. They try to avoid it by embracing the opposite state, *ramai*, "which suggests conviviality, noises and crowds of people."[16] Even the mystically inclined are wary of it, tending to meditate in groups.[17] Thus, for Sukarno to be *kesepian* upon his arrest and incarceration in August 1933, as Taufik Abdullah suggested, is certainly consistent with our knowledge of the emotional world of the people of Indonesia. However, the pronounced severity of his reaction to this state of enforced isolation does seem extraordinary, even by the standards of his gregarious compatriots.

We first observe Sukarno's suffering from the quiet or from desolation upon his initial arrest, on December 29, 1929. This occurred after a hectic period of campaigning for independence as leader of the Indonesian Nationalist Party. The event proved shocking to him: "when that heavy door [of Bantjeuj Prison in Bandung] locked me in that first time, I died."[18] Sukarno was sentenced to four years in jail by the Bandung District Court in December 1930 and was then moved to the even less-hospitable Sukamiskin Prison. Reflecting on his experiences in Sukamiskin in 1931, Sukarno commented, "The worst cruelty that can be inflicted on a human being is isolation."[19] After a remission of part of his sentence, he was released from jail on December 31, 1931. Tjipto Mangunkusumo later wrote that Sukarno came out of Sukamiskin a "psychic patient."[20]

Just eighteen months later, on August 1, 1933, he was arrested again and sent back to Sukamiskin. He recalled being locked in "a special cell set up in the midst of a large hall that had been stripped." He added, "There I sat penned in a small cage within a large room. And all alone. For eight months I lived like a dumb hermit."[21] The consequences of this manner of imprisonment are described by J. E. Stokvis, a member of the Indies Social Democratic Party and "a tireless defender of Indonesian interests in the Volksraad":[22]

> The treatment he experienced and still experiences, now that he again is detained, is like torture to him. In contrast to the 1929–30 period of detention, he then had some freedom of movement, and even after his sentence in 1930 when imprisoned in Soekamiskin, although set to work, he was allowed communication with his fellow-prisoners. But now in an isolation cell he is prohibited to talk to anyone, even his warders. This situation has shocked Soekarno deeply in a psychological sense. . . . In the opinion of every visitor he is completely at the end of his tether.[23]

Thus, when the colonial authorities plucked Sukarno for a second time from the center of the nationalist movement and replaced the orator's podium with solitary confinement, he all but collapsed. As he later recalled, his exile on the island of Flores, beginning in February 1934, only served to prolong his suffering:[24] "Besides idleness, loneliness, and friendlessness, I was also suffering acute depression. Flores was utter torture in the early days. I needed something stimulating, or I should kill myself."[25]

It was only with the coming of the Japanese in March 1942 that Sukarno once again had an opportunity to return to the political stage. As a nationalist leader (1942–1945), but especially as president of the Republic of Indonesia after the proclamation of independence on August 17, 1945, he practiced politics in an open fashion, mixing freely with his political colleagues, addressing large rallies and the like. Although he was officially relegated to the position of head of state in December 1949, he nevertheless had almost unlimited opportunities for contact with his people. It therefore comes as a surprise to discover that this contact did not seem to be quite sufficient to keep away the feeling of desolation that he had experienced in states of enforced isolation. For example, having told an audience on September 24, 1955, that they were too far away from him, he urged the organizers of the occasion to allow the audience members to approach him more closely to relieve the feeling of torture that he felt when he was separated from his people.[26] Even during the Guided Democracy years (1959–1966), when Sukarno was very much at the center of things as head of government and head of state, this feeling of desolation was his constant companion. In a speech of March 25, 1963, Sukarno praises the shining look of the young members of his audience for their capacity to disperse this feeling:

> The feeling in my heart, if I am face to face with young men and women, if I see the gleam . . . see the gleam in the eyes of the young men and women, then I feel like Kokrosono when he had just returned from the retreat of Argodunjo. . . . That is the feeling in my heart, no longer discouraged, no longer without hope, no longer lacking courage in facing my great and heavy responsibilities imposed on me by the Revolution, but proud, like Kokrosono, crushing all these difficulties.[27]

Sukarno expresses similar sentiments in a speech of March 11, 1965:

> I myself, personally speaking, once I have seen the glow in the eyes of the young men and women, although I am tired, I feel strong, although I am, let us say, almost despairing, I feel enthusiastic again, it is as if I have obtained an electrical charge, a charge of strength from you, from you, from you, from you, from you, from you, from you, from you, from all the young men and women of Indonesia.[28]

In light of the said account, there can be no doubting Sukarno's desolate state when the colonial authorities forcibly separated him from his friends and supporters and plunged him into a state of isolation. However, the fact that cognate feelings of being "discouraged," "without hope," and "almost despairing" (his words) threatened his sense of well-being, even when he was very much in the midst of others during his presidency in the late Guided Democracy period, suggests that his *kesepian* was not only a reaction to extreme situations of emotional deprivation but also a more pervasive and severe condition that weighed on him even when circumstances were very *ramai* indeed. In the next section, I note how his efforts to keep this desolation at a distance gave shape to a distinctive style of political behavior that I call "the politics of being central."[29]

THE POLITICS OF BEING CENTRAL

We may assume that Sukarno's *kesepian* predates the first direct manifestation of it to reach our notice—the consequences of his arrest on December 29, 1929; therefore, we are committing no anachronism in regarding the politics of being central as having its origins before this date. Certainly, it was discernible since 1927 during Sukarno's inclination as the leader of the Indonesian National Party (Partai Nasional Indonesia; PNI) to make his own powerful anticolonial oratory the principal focus of the party's activities. The consequence of this approach, as his colleagues quickly realized, was to link its fate too closely to his own. His mentor, Tjipto Mangunkusumo, wrote from exile in Banda: "You have not yet prepared a replacement: if you fall the PNI will be without a leader. Should you not moderate? I think there have been enough speeches."[30] These remarks proved only too prescient: dissatisfaction with the policy of the leaders who replaced Sukarno after his arrest contributed to a split within the party.

As noted, Sukarno was released from jail on December 31, 1931, after the remission of part of his sentence. He immediately plunged back into the thick of nationalist politics. The day after his release, he set out to attend a congress of nationalist organizations in Surabaya, and the crowd of approximately five thousand at the railway station shouting *Long live Sukarno!* presumably helped dispel for a period the loneliness and distress he had endured in prison.[31] Sukarno's leadership style did not change with his release from jail, but he no longer enjoyed the authority that had been his before December 1929. After failing to heal the differences between the Indonesian Party (Partai Indonesia; Partindo) and the New PNI (Pendidikan Nasional Indonesia; PNI Baru)—the two organizations that grew out of the split in the original PNI—he joined the former and gave further expression to his now familiar talent for stirring oratory.[32]

Sukarno's enduring state of *kesepian* fostered the politics of being central as its antidote. In its most benign form, this style of politics gave substance to his nation-building aspirations by reaching out to an expanding circle of supporters, and it achieved its apotheosis a few months before the Declaration of Independence with Sukarno's formulation and delivery of the engaging and inclusive *Pancasila* speech on June 1, 1945. But it is likely that Sukarno's feeling of *kesepian* was exacerbated by the approach of old age and the growing proximity of the final separation and isolation of death. This may be the reason that merely being at the center of various groups, as well as mediating and seeking to foster cooperation between them, did not continue to satisfy him. As can be seen from the preceding account, he had to be at the very center of fervent attention; indeed, his 1963 and 1965 speeches quoted earlier certainly suggest that all eyes had to be on him. Nothing less, it seems, would keep his desolation at bay. Certainly, this helps to explain the fact that the president spoke frequently—sometimes two or three times per day—to ever-larger gatherings. For instance, he delivered his *Dwikora* speech on May 3, 1964, in tones of undiminished militancy "to a mass rally of (allegedly) one million volunteers [to crush Malaysia] outside the . . . [presidential] palace."[33]

The president's major campaigns of the Guided Democracy period—the incorporation of West Irian and the "confrontation" of Malaysia—have usually been explained in terms of the nationalist and anti-imperialist ideology of the president on the one hand and his desire to contain the centrifugal forces of Guided Democracy on the other. But underpinning both was Sukarno's basic emotional need for a style of politics that fostered activity, movement, and above all a high pitch of enthusiasm among Indonesians that had him as their principal focus, for it was this factor that predisposed him to embark on these campaigns in the first place.

Sukarno's politics of being central was an agitational and oratorical style of politics that placed a "high value . . . on the emotional response of the public" with whom it sought to deal directly.[34] It was essentially populist in nature and inimical to institutionalization. It may be likened to Feith's account of Sukarno as the most prominent of the "solidarity makers," or members of the Indonesian political elite possessing "integrative skills, skills in cultural mediation, symbol manipulation, and mass organization"[35] whose aspirations were "incompatible with the emphasis . . . on law, rules, and the efficient operation of agencies concerned to solve particular problems," which was the preoccupation of the opposite and opposed skill group, "the administrators."[36] Although his conceptualization is in terms of a "skill role" and mine has its roots in personality, there is reason to believe that we have hold of the same stick, though at opposite ends. When the president's inclination to conduct such politics was combined with his willingness to exercise the power he had acquired from 1957 in an authoritarian fashion, the stage was set for his own person to impinge directly on the political process. In Guided Democracy a "president for life" ruled by decree, and "revolutionary law" undermined the independence of the judiciary.[37] In this arrangement his state of mind and state of health had direct consequences, not only for the working of Guided Democracy, but for its very survival. As we shall see, his suspicions led directly to arrests; his callousness, to elite indifference; and his illness, to the collapse of the system.

STATE OF MIND

Suspicion

Sukarno's state of mind consisted of emotions other than desolation, and just as desolation contributed to the politics of being central, this style of politics gave his other feelings the scope necessary to leave their mark on the political system. One of these feelings was suspicion. Sukarno had not always been a suspicious person; indeed, he had reached out to people in a gregarious and charming manner, confident of their love. Although these attributes never deserted him, they proved difficult to maintain in the face of no fewer than five assassination attempts. But if these attempts provided solid grounds for suspicion, then his ability to come through unscathed on each occasion offered equally strong evidence in favor of his sense of destiny. "Allah must approve of what I am doing, otherwise I would long ago have been killed," he declared to the American ambassador after surviving the fifth such attempt, on May 14, 1962, in which a person fired on him as he attended prayers at the mosque in the palace grounds in Jakarta.[38]

The first assassination attempt occurred on the evening of November 30, 1957, when hand grenades were thrown at him while he was visiting a fete at his children's school in the Cikini area of Jakarta. Sukarno was unhurt, but eleven others died and at least thirty were seriously injured. The chief suspect was the former army intelligence chief Colonel Zulkifli Lubis. Because some of his supporters were members of the youth organization of the Masjumi political party, the president's first reaction was to believe that some Masjumi leaders were behind the attempt. Fearing arrest, Lubis fled to West Sumatra, where the regionalist leader Colonel Hussein offered him protection. This fact, combined with subsequent overwhelming evidence that the Central Intelligence Agency (CIA) was backing the dissident colonels, led Sukarno to eventually conclude that the Cikini assassination attempt had been masterminded by the CIA.[39] Thereafter, he was quick to accuse the CIA of involvement in Indonesia's political life. For example, in 1964 Sukarno came to believe that the Body of Support for Sukarnoism (Badan Pendukung Sukarnoisme; BPS), which sought to advance Sukarnoism as an alternative to communism and which received strong backing from the Murba Party, was being manipulated by the CIA. Apparently this is what foreign minister Dr Subandrio had alleged, and the president believed him: "I obtained information," he declared, "info, information, secret information, that the CIA, the Central Intelligence Agency, made use of the BPS." Accordingly, Sukarno banned the BPS on December 17 and suspended the operations of the Murba Party on January 6, 1965. In doing so he abandoned the members of these organizations, many of whom had rallied to him in 1956 when he began "staking an ideological claim to the heirship of the party and parliamentary regime" to a dangerous political isolation while he enabled the Communist Party to consolidate its position.[40]

There were two further assassination attempts: on November 1, 1958, a mortar was fired near his car between Mandai airport and the city of Makassar; and on March 9, 1960, an airforce lieutenant flying a MIG 17 strafed the presidential palace with machine-gun fire.[41] Presumably, they did nothing for the president's equanimity as he contemplated a report from Subandrio's

Central Intelligence Body (Badan Pusat Intelidjen; BPI) that subversive actions against the state had been discussed among guests of Mr Anak Agung Gde Agung on the occasion of the cremation of his father—the former raja of Gianyar, Bali—in mid-August 1961.[42] Sukarno had known that the gathering was going to take place: General Nasution recalled him discussing with Subandrio the invitations Anak Agung had issued to such figures as former vice president Hatta and former prime minister Sjahrir, and he recalled his subsequent order that government ministers who had received an invitation were not to attend.[43] By the time Sukarno issued his ban, Anak Agung realized that he had made a mistake in only inviting his personal friends and political allies—most of whom had connections to the Masjumi Party or the Socialist Party, both recently banned by Sukarno for their alleged involvement in the regional rebellion of 1958. Afraid that he may have offended the president, he then sent Sukarno an invitation. But Sukarno declined to attend, thereby confirming Anak Agung's fears. In reflecting on these events at a later date, Anak Agung came to believe that the president's feeling of hurt at being overlooked had quickly been replaced by a feeling of suspicion regarding the motives of the host and those who had been invited.[44]

Sukarno ordered an investigation into the allegation contained in the BPI report, but no arrests were made. Four months later, on January 7, 1962, three hand grenades were thrown at his car as it made its way along Cenderawasih Street in Makassar (subsequently, Ujung Pandang).[45] Three onlookers were killed by the grenade and another twenty-eight were injured. On January 15, two Dutchmen were arrested on suspicion of involvement in this event, and "it was rumoured that something pointed towards the 'Bali connection.'"[46] The following day, Anak Agung and his former guests—Sjahrir, Subadio Sastrosatomo, Sultan Hamid of Pontianak, and Mohamad Roem—were arrested with some Masjumi leaders who had not attended the funeral. However, Hatta, who had been at the cremation, was not arrested, and on January 19, 1962, he wrote to Sukarno in protest:

Soekarno,
   Now society is in commotion . . . because of the arrest of several well known people, amongst others Sjahrir, Prawato, Roem, Soebadio, Anak Agung Gde Agung, and I don't know who else. It is said about a dozen people. People do not know the reason. According to some accounts they have been accused of involvement in the Tjenderawasih Affair in Makassar. I think that human beings of sound mind condemn terrorist deeds such as occurred in Makassar. And I am convinced from the history of our struggle that Sjahrir and the others would as a matter of principle oppose all forms of terror in politics because it is in conflict with socialism, and with humanity. And Mr Roem is well known as a person happy to ply the trade of politician [*politicien satisfait*]. They are

not averse to practising robust opposition in politics, as was apparent in their movement formerly, but it is inconceivable that they would participate in a terrorist deed. . . .

We always boast that our state is based on Panca Sila but where is the justice, humanity and democracy in fact. Is it democracy if the people on the average feel afraid, have to keep their mouths shut, and criticism is not allowed, with the consequence that various matters which cannot be justified occur freely? What we condemned and opposed formerly in the Dutch colonial period now occurs again carried out in your name. You should reflect on these matters as deeply as possible.[47]

Two months later, a young associate of Sjahrir's, Rosihan Anwar, wrote in his diary that Hatta's letter had had "no effect whatsoever."[48]

In the aforementioned account, the progression from presidential suspicion to arbitrary arrest is explained as a consequence of a highly personalized form of rule—the politics of being central—combined with the authoritarian exercise of power. However, it is also plausible to view this suspicion as the defining element of a soured version of the politics of being central itself; to see matters in this way, it will be helpful if we return to the funeral for Anak Agung Gde Agung's father. Anak Agung, it will be recalled, believed that Sukarno had felt hurt at not being invited and that this sentiment had quickly changed into suspicion regarding the motives of the host and the persons he did invite. This seems a shrewd insight and can be readily appreciated in light of the observation made here that each assassination attempt not only aggravated Sukarno's suspicion but also offered proof of his higher calling. In this exalted frame of mind, it was perhaps more palatable for Sukarno to suspect the funeral guests of plotting against him than to accept that he had simply been ignored. It can be seen that this is still the politics of being central; only here it is being conducted under a negative sign.

Callousness

In addition to Sukarno's feelings of desolation and suspicion, his callousness (if, indeed, this may be called a feeling) also left an impression on Indonesian politics. The point here concerns the president's evident refusal at a particular point to acknowledge the deteriorating social and economic conditions within his country and his lack of concern over the growing signs of distress in his midst. Even before this point, a question mark hung over the extent of his commitment to the material welfare of the people of Indonesia. Certainly, he was capable of giving the impression that his ambition was focused on more lofty goals than the well-being of ordinary peasants. For example, in 1956 he said,

Yes, definitely we want to see A or B or C and so forth live safely and soundly. But as mortal creatures they will disappear in the end. No, we are not struggling above all else for mortal individuals, but rather for the idea of the glorious and powerful nation which sustains the eighty million Indonesians.[49]

Nevertheless, Sukarno made food and clothing for the people one of the three goals of his new, presidential government, formed in July 1959. The other two were the restoration of security and the "return" of West Irian to Indonesia. "Soekarno assumed responsibility for this program," Lev wrote, "though he hedged somewhat in saying that if it were not fulfilled within two or three years he would consider himself one-half a failure."[50] Nevertheless, Sukarno continued for a few years to hold himself to these goals and was quite frank about his difficulties in realizing the first one—food and clothing for the people. For example, on December 14, 1961, he told his audience,

> The Government . . . will make every effort so that the problem of rice and sugar and food and clothing can be resolved and I myself, brothers and sisters, God willing, will do my upmost so that what I said two and a half years ago, that after three years I would bring the three-fold program of the Government before the Indonesian people, and ask: has the three-fold program of the Government been implemented or not? It goes without saying that I myself—there is still half a year to go, brothers and sisters—I will do all in my power to try to solve these matters.[51]

A week later, sounding thoroughly exasperated, he returned to this issue:

> Brothers and Sisters, it has been the case for some time that I have made myself dizzy thinking about the fact that the implementation of the Three-fold Program of the Government, above all in the area of food and clothing, has been experiencing difficulties. The price of rice has risen. . . . And I as the leader of this Government, which included the Three-fold Program in its lists of tasks—food and clothing, the restoration of security, West Irian—I often become a target of criticism: "It is said that you wish to establish Socialism in Indonesia. So how come the price of rice increases to fifty, sixty rupiahs." "It is said that you wish to establish Socialism in Indonesia, so how come sugar sometimes cannot be purchased."[52]

On Independence Day 1962, the president admitted giving priority to the restoration of security and to the "return" of West Irian over solving the food and clothing problem, although he also argued that the recent achievement of the former goals would enable greater resources to be devoted to the latter: "Brothers and Sisters! With the settling of the security problem, with the settling of the problem of Irian Barat, our resources for solving the economic problems will greatly increase." He continued,

We have used almost three-quarters of our national product to solve the problem of security and to implement Trikora. . . . Do you understand, Brothers and Sisters, this is one of the main causes of the difficulty in our economic life? Do you understand, Brothers and Sisters, that with the pouring out of more than 70% of that national product, the "Food and Clothing" program was not able to be fully implemented in a satisfactory manner? I can appreciate the suffering here and there and I bow my head before that suffering. . . . Only I wish to explain here that it is of course true that I have given priority to the settling of the problem of security and the problem of Irian Barat, although I knew, that in order to do these things almost three-quarters of our national product had to be spent.[53]

Frank as this statement was in some respects, it failed to fully acknowledge the damage the West Irian campaign had done to the national economy and therefore to the government's goal of providing adequate food and clothing for the people. As Mackie has pointed out, inflation caused by budget deficits was a constant feature of the Guided Democracy period. First minister Djuanda had tried hard to hold the budget in balance in 1961, but his efforts were destroyed by Sukarno's West Irian campaign. As a result, prices and the volume of money doubled between September 1961 and September 1962, making the achievement of the government's final goal an even more elusive prospect. In the face of this disturbing development, the government tried again to balance the budget in 1963, but this time it was the "crush Malaysia" campaign that wiped out its efforts. Consequently, the annual doubling of prices and the volume of money continued until 1965 when inflation reached an annual rate of 600 percent. Observers, alarmed at this trend, wondered how much longer events could go on as they did; but Sukarno was no longer remorseful, and he boasted that Indonesians could continue living with inflation until Malaysia had been crushed.[54]

Indeed, by 1965 he seemed quite indifferent to the suffering of his people, judging by the remarks he made in a speech on May 23 at the forty-fifth-anniversary celebrations of the Indonesian Communist Party:

But Bung Aidit [the first secretary and chairman of the Communist Party] said — as a rebuttal to the imperialists who say that Indonesia is suffering a shortage of sustenance, that Indonesia is suffering a shortage of food — that the people of Indonesia, on account of the abundance of food, actually use cassava to stop up holes in the sidewalk. Which other people in this world stop up holes in their sidewalks with cassava, brothers and sisters? Only Indonesia itself, on account of the abundance of its food.

At this point, Sukarno improvised a song in the form of a pantun:[55]

> Who says I am from Blitar,
> I am from Prambanan,
> Who says the Indonesian People are hungry [*lapar*],
> Our people have enough food [*makanan*].[56]

Sukarno's politics of being central ensured that his callousness did not pass unnoticed. It reinforced the already widespread indifference to public suffering present in the political elite of Guided Democracy.

STATE OF HEALTH

President Sukarno's centrality to the working of Guided Democracy, which lacked even a vice president after the resignation of Mohammad Hatta in 1956, ensured that his state of health and mortality would have a direct bearing on its very survival. No one saw this earlier or more clearly than Hatta himself. In his 1960 article entitled "Our Democracy," he wrote,

> World history . . . shows that a dictatorship which depends on a single man's authority does not last long. And so the system to which Sukarno has given birth will last no longer than Sukarno himself. No man can live for ever. When Sukarno is alive no longer, his system will collapse of its own accord like a house of cards.[57]

Subsequent academic studies point to Sukarno's mortality as the Achilles' heel of Guided Democracy or, more precisely, the *modus vivendi* between the army and the president that underpinned it. Feith commented in 1962 that

> the Sukarno–army balance is not expected to outlive the President; indeed, few men doubt that Sukarno's disappearance would set tremendous changes in motion, and thus assassination attempts, like rumours of illness and impending coups, focus attention on the instability which underlies the balance.[58]

Sukarno did indeed suffer from a serious illness, and it is therefore not surprising that various rumors about it circulated among persons in political circles well aware of its implications for the durability of the regime. The illness was *urolithiasis*, or kidney stone disorder, which was diagnosed by Dr Soeharto at the beginning of the Japanese occupation after Sukarno turned up at his clinic in Jakarta complaining of nausea and pain in the lower part of the body. Soeharto devised a program for its management, but Sukarno rarely abided by its requirements, especially after he became president. Consequently, his condition showed signs of worsening by the 1950s, driving the doctor to suggest to the president that he enter hospital for a thorough examination. After repeated attempts to convince Sukarno of the wisdom of this course of action, Sukarno eventually agreed and entered a hospital in Jakarta on January 7, 1959. The result, however, was inconclusive: although it was confirmed that the president was still suffering from the same disorder, the eight examining doctors lacked the facilities to clarify certain aspects of it. Accordingly, they recommended that he visit an overseas clinic for further tests and treatment. Sukarno reluctantly agreed but said that it would be impossible to do so in the near future.[59]

After a lapse of two years, in which time Sukarno passed nine stones in his urine and was frequently in pain, Dr Soeharto tried again. This time the president responded immediately, and in October 1961 he placed himself in the hands of Dr Fellinger of the medical faculty at the University of Vienna.[60] Fellinger discovered that the president's left kidney had ceased to function, and he recommended that it be removed by operation. Dr Soeharto urged the president's compliance, explaining that if the left kidney was not removed, it might become infected or have a deleterious effect on his heart and blood circulation. But he was most reluctant, eventually saying, "No, later. If we have already liberated Irian Barat."[61]

As was to be expected, Sukarno's sudden departure for medical treatment in Vienna triggered speculation concerning his condition and consequent leadership changes, as General Nasution reported:

> In October 1961 he was forced to seek medical treatment in Vienna. Various rumours arose, and again my name was dragged into the calculations of people who were discussing the leadership of the state. After he returned, news continued to circulate that his left kidney was no longer functioning and that he could only be helped by an operation, but that was what he was unwilling to contemplate. The state of his health was kept a closely guarded secret so that even officials like me were not allowed to know.[62]

Upon his return to Indonesia, Sukarno summoned a medical team from the People's Republic of China to treat his kidney disorder (in addition to commenting himself on the speculation concerning his health: "Each time it is announced that I am sick or have gone overseas for medical treatment . . . all kinds of speculation is offered, not only by enemies outside the country but also by the bedbugs at home").[63] It was led by Dr Wu Jieping, a urologist, and consisted of specialists in Western and traditional Chinese medicine. Indonesian government officials claimed that under the care of the Chinese doctors the president was restored to "perfect health" and that he "would not have to undergo an operation that doctors in Vienna had thought would be necessary."[64]

Two years later, in May 1963, Sukarno was proclaimed "President for Life of the Republic of Indonesia" by the appointed Interim People's Consultative

Assembly in recognition of his various services to the nation—in particular, his securing of the transfer of West Irian to Indonesian control. Sukarno clearly cherished the title, perhaps because its appropriateness could not be gainsaid in terms of his needs. If Hatta informed us that Guided Democracy could not survive without Sukarno, Sukarno himself seemed to be saying, by the adoption of this title, that he could not live except as president. It is not difficult to see the psychological truth in this claim: the need to be at the center of things to keep his desolation at bay guaranteed that life without the presidency would be grim indeed.

The president suffered an attack of influenza in mid-August 1963, which was followed a week later by a recurrence of his kidney stone disorder. Seven doctors were called to the presidential palace on August 20 to attend to it.[65] He also appears to have been sick again in the last months of 1964. In September of that year he returned to Vienna, where two doctors were reportedly successful in removing an offending kidney stone.[66] In December, it was announced in Jakarta amidst intense speculation about his prospects that the president was "walking with a limp, from a swollen leg, and looked tired from overwork."[67] But in January at a ceremony at which he decorated his five Chinese doctors, Sukarno "dismissed charges that he said were being circulated by the imperialist, colonialist and neo-colonialist forces that he was 'seriously ill and even dying.'" He claimed, on the contrary, to be in "top condition," adding, "I am now as fit as ever. This is, among other things, due to the treatment given me by the Chinese physicians."[68]

Presumably, no one was convinced by these words: seven months later, mere fears concerning his impending death, rather than the thing itself, were sufficient to set in motion a chain of events that brought his presidency and Guided Democracy to an end. These fears were aroused when Sukarno suddenly fell ill on August 4, 1965. D. N. Aidit, who was in China at the time, was convinced that the death of the Communist Party's protector would lead to the party's being attacked by the army. Perhaps worried that the precise nature of the president's condition would be withheld from him by Sukarno's Indonesian doctors, he arranged for the same team of Chinese doctors whom Sukarno had decorated in January to accompany him back to Jakarta, where they arrived on August 7. After meeting the president and consulting Dr Wu Jieping and his colleagues, it seemed that Aidit formed the impression that the president's condition was indeed precarious. He subsequently informed a meeting of the politburo that "the doctors informed him that it was likely that the president would either die or be paralysed unless he changed his style of life."[69]

In light of this and subsequent gloomy prognoses, the communist leaders decided to anticipate the expected attack on the party by the army. They contacted some dissident officers and together laid their essentially defensive plans.[70] These were, according to one account, to arrest the army's leading generals and hand them over to a revolutionary council, which would investigate their plans to carry out a coup.[71] But matters did not go according to plan. Instead of arresting these generals, the September 30 movement killed them, provoking a countermove from the generals it had failed to apprehend. In a short period, the latter group, under the leadership of Major General Soeharto, destroyed its military opponents and then encouraged and directed anticommunist civilian groups to wipe out the Communist Party. This they did with appalling thoroughness, killing approximately one-third of a million people.

Sukarno was appalled to witness his life's work as a nation builder being undone before his very eyes, crying out, "Stop, stop, stop, stop, Brothers and Sisters! Stop, don't go on like this!"[72]

> I recently said that I had never experienced such sadness as I do now, especially a few weeks ago, sadness that the Indonesian nation tears at its own chest, sadness that there are people who wish to turn this revolution from the left to the right, sadness that revolutionary enthusiasm has for all intents and purposes disappeared altogether.[73]

Thus deprived of this power base, but unwilling to abandon long-held policies, Sukarno clung to power until a fateful cabinet meeting of March 11, 1966. At this gathering one of his aides handed him a note informing him of the presence of unidentified troops in front of the presidential palace. Sukarno left the meeting hurriedly and retreated by helicopter to his Bogor palace. Later that day, in the presence of three emissaries from General Soeharto, he signed the "Letter of March 11," in which Sukarno "ordered" Soeharto "to take all measures considered necessary to guarantee security, calm, and stability of the government and the revolution, and to guarantee the personal safety and authority of the President . . . in the interests of the unity of the Republic of Indonesia."[74]

This event constituted a grievous political setback for Sukarno, and just how grievous it was became apparent to him in the following months as he helplessly watched cherished policies, such as the confrontation of Malaysia, become abandoned by the army-dominated government. In March 1967, Soeharto had himself declared acting president by the Interim People's Consultative Assembly. Exactly one year later the same body elected him president. The house of cards that was Guided Democracy in Hatta's metaphor had indeed collapsed but not because Sukarno had died as the former predicted. Rather, his anticipated death triggered a sequence of events that resulted in the destruction of the Communist Party, his presidency, and Guided Democracy itself.

ALIVE BUT NO LONGER PRESIDENT

According to Hartini, Sukarno's third wife, "Bung Karno was completely shattered" by Soeharto's accession to the presidency and "lost all interest in politics."[75] To be alive but no longer president was a terrible outcome and was made worse by the imposition upon him of house arrest—or "political quarantine," as it was officially called. Sukarno was confined to the Bogor palace in 1967 and, beginning July 1, 1968, to his private house in Batu Tulis Street, Bogor. Finally, on October 30, 1968, the former president was moved to the vacant house of his Japanese wife, Ratna Sari Dewi, in Jakarta. Hartini visited him there, but her departure at the end of a visit caused him considerable anxiety, even though she was seeing him every day. She recalled,

> Often, when I was about to leave, he would ask: "Are you coming back tomorrow, Tien?" I would say: "Yes." He would ask again: "Will you? At what time?" like a small child who was afraid he would never see his mother again.[76]

In 1969, the military authorities banned the family from visiting Sukarno for a four-month period while they interrogated him as part of their investigation concerning his alleged part in, as they saw it, the communist-led coup attempt of October 1, 1965.[77] The effect of this prolonged period of isolation, not to mention the interrogation itself, was devastating. According to Hartini,

> After about four months we were allowed to see him again. He wept like a child as soon as he saw us. His health and spirit were irreparably broken. The loneliness of those four months had been more than he could stand. It tipped the balance in the battle against his illness.[78]

Sukarno died the following year, on Sunday, June 21,[79] and, in light of the said account, it seems no exaggeration to say that the principal cause of death was his *kesepian*.[80] Furthermore, there is even the suggestion that one of Soeharto's motives in imposing this isolation on Sukarno was to hasten his end. This seems to have been Sukarno's own opinion, to judge by a remark of his quoted by Hartini: "The Government is smart, by making me like a fish in an aquarium without water, sooner or later I will die."[81]

Given the unusual strength of Sukarno's feeling of desolation and its considerable consequences for his politics, it is frustrating not being able to offer a detailed account of its origins. To be sure, there are clues, such as Hartini's likening Sukarno's behavior to that of a child being afraid of never seeing his mother again, and there are one or two pertinent facts, such as his early and prolonged absence from his parents (more on this in chapter 4), but not much else. Indeed, it is striking how little information we have on Sukarno's early years. But if it is not possible to provide a close account of the particular circumstances that gave rise to this state of mind, it is still possible to explore something of the meaning that it acquired for him in later years. In this regard, his fondness for the *wayang* story of Prabu Bomanarakasura, with which he occasionally regaled his audiences, is suggestive.[82]

> In the story of the Mahabaratha it is said that Kresna, Sri Bathara Kresna, has a number of wives, Rukmini, Setiaboma, Pratiwi, Djembawati. Thus amongst Kresna's wives there is one wife whose name is Pratiwi. And Pratiwi, according to the legend, emerged from the earth, and was not a normal woman, she was a daughter of the soil, her name was Pratiwi. Then Kresna took her as his wife. As a result of her marriage to Kresna, Pratiwi gave birth to a son, his name was Boma. In the Javanese language he is called Boma.
>
> In this legend it is said that as long as Boma was united with his Mother, was united with the earth, was united with Pratiwi, he could not die; he has magical powers, magical powers of the highest order, as long as he is united with his Mother, as long as he is united with the earth, as long as he is still at one with the earth, as long as he still stands on the ground, as long as he still sprawls on the ground, he will not die. But whenever he is separate from the earth, he can be easily killed. That is the story of Boma.
>
> In one battle, Brothers and Sisters, Boma was killed several times by his enemies. But each time Boma made contact with the earth, with the ground, he came back to life. Killed by his enemy, he fell down becoming one with the ground, with the earth, with his Mother, with Pratiwi, and he got up again.
>
> Then his enemy adopted a strategy. His strategy was as follows: the instant Boma died, that is to say was lying on the ground, he was lifted up, and was placed on a trellis, was placed on a stretcher, he was separated from the earth, he was separated from the ground, he was separated from the land, he was separated from Pratiwi; and he remained dead.[83]

The personal meaning of this story to Sukarno seems clear: separation equals death.

Although we can only surmise as to the precise circumstances that forged this dire equivalence in his mind, the fact that he did equate one with the other conveys something of the bleakness and severity of his feeling of desolation. Is it any wonder then that his characteristic way of going about politics was to place himself at the very center of attention and admiration?

NOTES

This chapter is a revised version of a paper entitled "Sukarno Kesepian: His Desolation and the Politics of Being Central," which was presented to the Asian Studies

Association of Australia Conference, convened at the University of Melbourne between July 3–5, 2000. A psychologist at the University of Indonesia, Bagus Takwin (see his "Bung Besar, Ideolog yang Kesepian," *Kompas Cyber Media*, June 1, 2001, www.kompas.com), came to the same conclusion as I did—namely, that Sukarno's feeling of desolation was central to his psychology and, indeed, his politics. However, as the text makes clear, the first person to draw attention to this aspect of the president's makeup was Taufik Abdullah.

1. Goenawan Mohamad, "Bung Karno," 186.
2. Winnicott, "Capacity to Be Alone," 416.
3. Ingleson, *Road to Exile*, 218.
4. H. Rosihan Anwar, "Perbedaan Analisa Politik Antara Sukarno dengan Hatta," *Kompas*, September 15, 1980, iv–v.
5. H. Mahbub Djunaidi, "Itu Mah Pamali, Itu Mah Mustahil: Kata Ibu Inggit," *Kompas*, October 7, 1980, iv.
6. Mohamad Roem, "'Surat-surat' dari Penjara Sukamiskin," *Kompas*, January 25, 1981, vi, x.
7. Mohamad Roem, "'Surat-surat,'" vi, x.
8. Edi Sudarjat, "Sejarah Riuhnya Perdebatan Surat Mohom Ampun Sukarno," *Republika*, April 10, 1995; Sitor Situmorang, "Tanggapan Atas Persoalan 'Surat-surat Soekarno' dari Penjara Sukamiskin (1933)," *Merdeka*, February 19, 1981, viii.
9. "Adam Malik tidak Yakin Soekarno Minta Ampun," *Kompas*, February 20, 1981, i, ix.
10. Edi Sudarjat, "Sejarah Riuhnya."
11. Taufik Abdullah, "Biografi dari 'Surat-surat' Itu," *Tempo*, February 28, 1981, 14–15.
12. "Surat-surat yang mengandung polemik," *Zaman*, March 1–7, 1981.
13. "Surat-surat yang mengandung polemik," *Zaman*, March 1–7, 1981.
14. Echols and Shadily, *Indonesian–English Dictionary*, 504; Sneddon, *Indonesian Reference Grammar*, 49–50; Robson, *Javanese Grammar for Students*, 44–45.
15. Taufik Abdullah, "Biografi dari 'Surat-surat' Itu."
16. Aveling, *Thematic History of Indonesian Poetry*, 29.
17. According to Geertz, *Religion of Java*, 309: "In theory, one can meditate and study one's inner life as well by oneself as with others, but to do so in a group is considered preferable because individual meditation smacks too much of a hermit-like isolation from daily life of which most people disapprove."
18. Adams, *Sukarno: An Autobiography*, 97. In a speech of August 31, 1964, Sukarno also referred to his experience in a Bantjeuj prison: "I was once imprisoned by the Dutch, this wasn't Sukamiskin yet, but Bantjuej prison in Bandung. I was placed in a cell on my own. Now, in that cell I often, in the quiet of the night, sat or lay alone and I thought, what am I sitting here, sprawling here, for? Who says that being in jail is comfortable and nice, there is no one. Being in jail, well, it is extraordinarily unpleasant, Brothers and Sisters" (*Madju Terus Pantang Mundur Sampai "Malaysia" Hantjur Lebur!* 13).
19. Adams, *Sukarno: An Autobiography*, 110. In his autobiography, Soeharto recorded the following remarks, which Sukarno made to him in 1942: "Wherever I

am in Indonesia I feel happy . . . provided I can enjoy the company of friends and books, and am always in a position to carry out a task, whether small or large. What I don't like is a lengthy period of solitude. In Sukamiskin I did not feel the solitude so long as I had an opportunity to associate with the jailers even though they were not friendly in the beginning" (*Saksi Sejarah*, 115).

20. Hering, *Mohammad Hoesni Thamrin*, 177.
21. Adams, *Sukarno: An Autobiography*, 125.
22. Dahm, *Sukarno and the Struggle*, 47.
23. Hering, "Once More the Four Letters," viii–ix.
24. Ingleson, *Road to Exile*, 222.
25. Adams, *Sukarno: An Autobiography*, 130.
26. Sukarno, *Apa Sebab Negara Republik Indonesia Berdasarkan Pantja-Sila?* 6.
27. Sukarno, *Amanat Presiden Sukarno pada Konperensi Besar IPPI*, 3. Raden Kakrasana is a well-known mythological character from the Javanese *wayang*, or shadow theatre, who becomes king of Madura and, in that position, becomes known as Prabu Baladewa. He is a first cousin to the Pendawa who, unlike his brother Kresna, sides with the Kurawa in the fratricidal war known as the Bharata Yudha. In one of the *lakon*, or dramas, "Kokrosono is the legitimate heir to the land of Mandura, ruled by the demon Kongso. The father of Kokrosono cannot defend himself against the usurper. Kokrosono withdraws to live as a hermit, and after his purification receives from a god the magic weapon Nanggala, with which after various adventures he succeeds in overcoming the demon Kongso" (Dahm, *Sukarno and the Struggle*, 134n25; Hardjowirogo, *Sedjarah Wayang Purwa*, 99–102; Anderson, *Mythology and the Tolerance of the Javanese*, 14–15).

28. Sukarno, *Indonesia Tetap Tegak Berdiri sampai Achir Zaman*, 6.
29. I borrowed the expression from A. F. Davies but developed my argument separately. See *Human Element*, 89–90.
30. Quoted in Ingleson, *Road to Exile*, 87.
31. For the details of Sukarno's reception in Surabaya, see Ingleson, *Road to Exile*, 159.
32. Ingleson, *Road to Exile*, 185.
33. Mackie, *Konfrontasi*, 244, 278–79.
34. This is how Harold D. Lasswell defines the political agitator (*Psychopathology and Politics*, 78).
35. Feith, *Decline of Constitutional Democracy*, 24.
36. Feith, *Decline of Constitutional Democracy*, 118.
37. Lindsey, "Overview of Indonesian Law," 7.
38. Jones, *Indonesia: The Possible Dream*, 49. For Nasution's account of this assassination attempt, see Nasution, *Memenuhi Panggilan Tugas*, 5:238–39.
39. Kahin and Kahin, *Subversion as Foreign Policy*, 112–15.
40. Feith, *Decline of Constitutional Democracy*, 515; Crouch, *Army and Politics*, 66; Mortimer, *Indonesian Communism under Sukarno*, 377; Sukarno, *PWI Benar-Benar Mendjadi Alat Revolusi*, 9.
41. Sukarno refers to the five assassination attempts in a speech of May 19, 1963 (see Sukarno, *Hantjurkan Kontra Revolusi*, 8). See also *Bintang Timur*, March 10,

1960, 1; H. Mangil Martowidjojo, *Kesaksian tentang Bung Karno,* 315–16; and Jones, *Indonesia: The Possible Dream,* 49, 216–17. However, the newspaper *Merdeka* (November 3, 1958, 1) did not report the Mandai-Makassar affair as an assassination attempt. According to its account, those responsible for the president's security directed machine gun and mortar fire at two people who were moving near the road and whose behavior had given rise to suspicion. Whatever the facts of the matter, Sukarno certainly came to believe that it was an attempt on his life, as the May 19 speech bears witness.

42. Mrazek, *Sjahrir,* 461–62.
43. Nasution, *Memenuhi Panggilan Tugas,* 5:395.
44. Mrazek, *Sjahrir,* 462.
45. H. Mangil Martowidjojo, *Kesaksian,* 325; *Bintang Timur,* January 9, 1962, 1–2.
46. Mrazek, *Sjahrir,* 463.
47. Mochtar Lubis, *Hati Nurani Melawan Kezaliman,* 70–71.
48. Quoted in Mrazek, *Sjahrir,* 465.
49. Sukarno, *Susunlah Konstitusi jang Benar-Benar Konstitusi Res Publica,* 6. Sukarno spoke in a similar vein six weeks after being obliged to hand over substantial power to General Soeharto: "Later when I am dead I do not want the Indonesian people simply to recollect or remember that in the time of Bung Karno, well, we had enough to eat. Do human beings only eat! I want when I am dead and gone from this land of Indonesia, that there are also matters which the Indonesian Nation can be. . . . Yes, we are a great nation; yes, we have things of which we are rightly proud" (Sukarno, "Amanat PJM Presiden Sukarno pada Pelantikan/Penjumpahan Major Djendral KKO Ali Sadikin," 5). Is it possible that Sukarno was ambivalent with respect to the well-being of the people at large because he saw them as inadequate vehicles for his immortality? Peasants, even well-fed ones, do not live very long; certainly not long enough to preserve for the duration the memory of their erstwhile leader. Compare Kapuscinski, *Emperor,* 131: "Were he to give ear to the whispers and murmurs that it would be better to feed the hungry than to build dams. . . . Well, the hungry, even if they are satiated at last, will eventually die, leaving behind not a trace—neither of themselves, nor of the Emperor."

50. Lev, *Transition to Guided Democracy,* 282.
51. Sukarno, *Persatuan Total dengan Poros Nasakom,* 17.
52. Sukarno, *Tidak ada Bangsa jang Besar tanpa Perbuatan,* 5.
53. Sukarno, "Tahun Kemenangan," 2:511–12.
54. Mackie, *Konfrontasi,* 88–90.
55. The pantun stems from classical Malay literature and has been defined by A. Teeuw as "an epigrammatic quatrain with the rhyme scheme abab, in which the first pair of lines in some way alludes to the second pair which contains the explicit intention of the poet" (*Modern Indonesian Literature,* 1:12).
56. Sukarno, *Tenaga Gadungan lebih Berbahaja daripada Imperialis!* 7.
57. Mohammad Hatta, "Dictatorship Supported by Certain Groups," 140.
58. Feith, "Dynamics of Guided Democracy," 358.
59. Soeharto, *Saksi Sejarah,* 115–18.
60. Soeharto, *Saksi Sejarah,* 118–21.

61. Soeharto, *Saksi Sejarah*, 122.
62. Nasution, *Memenuhi Panggilan Tugas*, 5:230.
63. Sukarno, "Pidato PJM Presiden Sukarno pada Rapat Raksasa berkenaan dengan Peringatan Hari Pahlawan di Semarang," 10 November 1961, 1.
64. *New York Times*, May 6, 1962, 64. Leaving aside the official version, the various accounts by the doctors involved concerning Sukarno's health are incomplete and occasionally contradictory. Dr Soeharto states that although the president's left kidney had ceased to function altogether, the president did respond well to the traditional Chinese medicines and acupuncture administered to him by members of the Chinese medical team (*Saksi Sejarah*, 123–24). However, in an interview with Rahmat Edi Irawan of the Indonesian magazine *Medika* (February 1995), the head of the Chinese team, Dr. Wu Jieping, a urologist, gave a slightly different account of Sukarno's left kidney: "Bung Karno suffered from quite a large stone in one of his kidneys which often caused severe abdominal pain that could affect his appearance in public. The kidney affected by the stone functioned very badly but the other kidney still worked well." Also, he added that the specialists in traditional Chinese medicine did not succeed in dislodging the offending kidney stone. Sukarno, however, believed that they did (or was he referring to another kidney stone?): "By drinking Chinese medicine, by having acupuncture, the stone came out" (Sukarno, *Kumpulkan Ilmu Pengetahuan untuk Pembangunan*, 17).
65. *New York Times*, August 14, 1963, 2; August 21, 1963, 4.
66. *New York Times*, September 26, 1964, 2.
67. *New York Times*, December 14, 1964, 12.
68. *New York Times*, January 4, 1965, 3.
69. This was a reference to the president's sexual activity. At the trial of Dr. Subandrio in 1966, Peris Pardede, a candidate member of the politburo, quoted Aidit as saying at that meeting of the politburo that "what most disturbed . . . [Sukarno's] health was a private matter, that is meeting the desires of his wives" (Crouch, *Army and Politics*, 110n23).
70. Crouch, *Army and Politics*, 133–34.
71. Crouch, *Army and Politics*, 125–26.
72. Sukarno, *Suatu Bangsa jang Besar tidak akan Tenggelam, ketjuali djikalau Robek-robek Petjah dirinja sendiri dari dalam*, 30.
73. Sukarno, "Amanat PJM Presiden Sukarno pada Pembukaan Sidang Pimpinan MPRS ke-X di Istana Negara, Djakarta, 6 Desember 1965," 13.
74. Crouch, *Army and Politics*, 187–89.
75. Hartini, "Oriental Love Story," *Australian Women's Weekly*, December 16, 1970, 43.
76. Hartini, "Oriental Love Story," 43.
77. Labrousse, "Second Life of Bung Karno," 175.
78. Hartini, "Oriental Love Story," 43. Compare the comments in a similar vein by Ibu Supeni, formerly a roving ambassador of the Republic of Indonesia and close associate of Sukarno, in response to the question "Were there bitter experiences from the time of Sukarno's political quarantine?" "There were many such experiences; for example, in 1968 [read: 1969] Bung Karno was interrogated by the prosecutor. While he

was being interrogated he was not permitted to receive visits from his wife and children. That was for about eight or nine [read: four] months. That was the most bitter experience of all. And the interrogation was conducted in a very impolite way. And Sukarno, because he got no visits from his family, and because he was treated in a cruel fashion, suffered greatly. Also, apparently there was a tape of Subandrio besmirching Bung Karno's name, which was played by the interrogators. He was very hurt that the interrogators seemed to believe Subandrio more than him. When the interrogation was over Hartini was able to visit him, bring bananas, which Sukarno used to enjoy, but he was no longer clear in his thinking. He could only see that he was being visited by a woman. 'Who is that?' 'Hartini.' 'Oh, it has been torture, how I have suffered. Why didn't you visit me?' 'I wasn't allowed.' The children were very distressed to see their father treated like that" (personal interview, Jakarta, July 15, 1997).

79. Legge, *Sukarno*, 408.

80. This is also the opinion of Riza Sofyat. See his "Kala Senja Putra Sang Fajar," *Forum Keadilan* 9, no. 12 (June 25, 2000).

81. Quoted in Sofyat, "Kala Senja Putra Sang Fajar."

82. Hardjowirogo, *Sedjarah Wajang Purwa*, 108–9.

83. Sukarno, *Rapatkan Barisanmu dengan Pemerintah dan Sukseskan Triprogram Gaja Baru*, 4.

4

Aging and Fear of Death: Sukarno's Politics of Rejuvenation and His Quest for Immortality

> Man is a history-making creature who can neither repeat his past nor leave it behind.
>
> —W. H. Auden[1]

FEAR OF DEATH

Death, despite being such an overwhelming and unambiguous event, can constitute a "projective ecology," if not for the full range of our feelings and experiences, then at least for each individual's own private list of fears and dreads.[2] What then did it mean to Sukarno? In the previous chapter we noted that his powerful feeling of desolation, or *kesepian,* seemed to derive from his equating separation or isolation with death. In light of the general propositions that children know absence before death and that if the experience of the former is severe, then it is likely to color their sense of the latter,[3] it seems likely that he also equated death with separation.[4] However, there is more to be said concerning Sukarno's fears in this regard, especially as it seems appropriate to extend the object of this fear from death alone to the aging process that preceded it. As we shall see, if death for Sukarno meant separation and if he feared it as such, then death for him also meant decay and he feared that as well; therefore, the aging that preceded his death not only portended these future horrors but also reflected his present torments, such as physical decline as well as loss of virility and beauty.

What modern fears these are. It is plausible to search for their origins in terms of his membership of the small, Westernized Indonesian elite. Indeed, an examination of his early years shows just how far removed Sukarno was in some respects from the confines and comforts of the traditional Javanese world. His father, Raden Sukemi Sosrodihardjo, was an adherent of Theosophy and a teacher whose pursuit of his career in the Second Class Native School System took him from his native East Java to Singaradja in Bali, where he married a Balinese woman, Ni Njoman Rai Siremben, who came from an old *pasek* (elevated commoner) family in Boeleleng. Her family was outraged by this violation of tradition and subsequently disowned her. Nevertheless, she remained in Singaradja until the birth of her first child and daughter, Soekarmini.[5]

Husband, wife, and child then moved to Surabaya, where Sukemi had secured a new posting and where Sukarno was born in 1901. Perhaps the financial burden of two children was too heavy for the couple to bear on his salary, as the infant was sent to stay with his paternal grandparents in Tulung Agung. According to the account Sukarno gave a Japanese journalist during the war, his removal to his grandparents' house took place just after he had been weaned, and it was not until he turned six that he was reunited with his parents in Surabaya.[6] There, he studied at a primary school until he accompanied his family to Modjokerto, where he continued his education at the primary school to which his father had just been appointed *mantri guru* (chief teacher).

Subsequently, Sukemi was able to place him in the local Dutch-language elementary school (Europeesche Lagere School). After some years of study, he was again obliged to leave home, for in 1916 his father enrolled him in the Dutch High School (Hogere Burger School) in Surabaya, where he stayed with many other guests at the house of—and, one might say, under the influence of—Umar Sayed Tjokroaminoto, who was a friend of his father and the leader of the modern, protonationalist organization Sarekat Islam. The Surabaya Dutch High School was one of only three on the island of Java, and success there guaranteed him entry into a tertiary institution: he chose the recently opened technical college in Bandung, which he entered in 1921. He graduated from the college in 1926 with the title of *Ingenieur* (Ir) and in the following year played a leading role in establishing the Indonesian Nationalist Party.[7]

Sukarno emerged from this modern world as a Marxist, but it is important to note in this regard that Marxism in the colonial world quite lacked the ambivalence of the original theory toward modernity; indeed, far from expressing misgivings about modernity, it actively underpinned the modernizing impulse in Asian nationalisms.[8] The Marxism of Ir Sukarno was no different in this respect, encouraging rather than cautioning the future president in his enthusiastic embrace of the modern world. However, it seems that certain emotional costs offset Sukarno's attraction to living in this mobile and secular world, not to mention the optimistic theorizing to which it gave rise. The mobility of this world—or, rather, the consequences of such mobility—helped foster his fear of separation, whereas its secularism deprived him of the traditional and religious means of coming to terms with aging and death, all of which imparted a modern intensity to his evolving fears.[9]

Unlike his elder nationalist colleague Sutomo (b. 1888), who was able to fulfill the traditional Javanese ideal of living in rhythm with the movement of life toward death despite being a medical doctor familiar with Western notions of life as decay and death as the end,[10] Sukarno expressed his distress about aging and death on numerous occasions. For example, in 1948, on the eve of his forty-seventh birthday, he declared,

> If I look at the face of an old person who is eighty or ninety or seventy years old, what I see in fact is a grave hovering before my eyes. But if I look at your faces, hey, young men and women and my children, I see an image of the future. The look in your eyes is, for me, like the eternal glow of a star.[11]

Old age seemed to Sukarno quite lacking in redeeming qualities; indeed, he viewed it simply as a harbinger of dreadful death, from which he fled into the sustaining gaze of young men and women.

THE POLITICS OF REJUVENATION

In the previous chapter we observed Sukarno's finding a temporary cure for his feelings of *kesepian* in the gleam in the eyes of the young men and women in his audience. This same quality of youth also served as a healing remedy for, even a denial of, his own aging and related feelings of infirmity—that is, to judge by the following excerpt, from a speech that he delivered in May 1964, when he was sixty-two.

> For me, personally, it is a great pleasure to meet with you all. To be frank, I feel weary, tired, but you must understand that I am already old, and my eyes are watery so I carry Kleenex with me. If my eyes are watery, I wipe them with Kleenex. But although I am tired and although my eyes are watery, yet I feel fit again because I am face to face with you. Yes, if I see the gleam in the eyes of young men and women, and especially the gleam in the eyes of the . . . young women from Irian Barat, well, I feel that I have become young again! In the words of the puppeteer, if I see the glow in the eyes of young men and women, *rasanja kojo dadi Kokrosono* [I feel like I have become Kakrasana].[12]

In light of such a preoccupation, it is not surprising that Sukarno addressed many rallies of young people, gave attention to their role in politics, and expected them to make a significant contribution to their country. "I always say that young men and women are the most important pillar of the state,"[13] he said in 1948. Likewise, as one claiming that he was a "student from the Historical School of Marx"[14] and who therefore studied the past not as an academic pursuit but as a quest to divine the future, he tended to view youth not only as "an image of the future" but also as a natural constituency for his prophetic leadership. "I reverse the Dutch saying," he wrote in 1940. "Not 'whoever has the youth has the future' but, as I say, 'whoever has the future has the youth.'"[15]

Sukarno's admiration toward youth also manifested itself in the considerable lengths to which he went to promote what he saw as youthful qualities in politics—in particular, activism, dynamism, and reckless courage. In the final analysis, however, it is safe to say that it was his own youth that interested him most; such was his intense focus on it, perhaps even his idealization of it. Cognate with these responses to advancing years and approaching death was a desire that his political achievements and teachings would be remembered and indeed revered long after his own passing. I have labeled these related dispositions as the promotion of youth and youthful attributes, the idealization of his own youth, and the quest for immortality; and I regard these dispositions and their political manifestations as "the politics of rejuvenation."

Youth

As noted, Sukarno saw youth as the natural constituency for his prophetic leadership. It therefore became a matter of irony that in the immediate aftermath of the Japanese surrender (news of which was received in Jakarta at noon on August 15, 1945), the youth (*pemuda*) of that era, who were enraged by Sukarno's caution on the matter of declaring independence, kidnapped him and Hatta as a way of forcing a declaration on them. The two elder leaders, however, refused to accede to the demands of their kidnappers and on August 17 made the fateful declaration only after they had received a measure of Japanese support for this deed.[16]

Eleven years after the declaration of independence, in 1956, Sukarno sought to close the generational gap between his former kidnappers and himself by drawing on their support and on that of other young radicals of the revolution in establishing his new regime. In making the case for what eventually would be called Guided Democracy—or, rather, in making the case against the parliamentary regime that preceded Guided Democracy—the president spoke of the divisiveness of the political parties and expressed the wish that their leaders agree to a dissolution. To reinforce his point, he drew on an article by Chairul Saleh, chief among his erstwhile kidnappers and an exponent of the vaguely articulated "Generation of 1945."[17] "Chairul Saleh ... wrote about 'the sovereignty of youth.' That's right, that's right Brothers and Sisters, that's right! Hey, young men and women, assert your sovereignty, and don't parrot the political parties!"[18]

In the face of strong opposition from the parties themselves, Sukarno abandoned his wish that they be dissolved. As noted in chapter 1, he called for the formation of, first, a *gotong rojong* (mutual help) cabinet—in which representatives of the major parties, including the Communist Party, would sit—and, second, a national council, which would offer advice on policy to the cabinet. The membership of this latter body would consist of representatives of functional groups, such as peasants, workers, and youth, to reflect the composition of society just as the membership of cabinet reflected the composition of parliament.[19]

Vehement opposition from the army and anticommunist political parties obliged Sukarno to retreat again, this time concerning his desire to include the Communist Party in the *gotong rojong* cabinet. Accordingly, he had to settle for less in the form of a working cabinet without Communist Party representation. However, he was able to appoint to this cabinet some of the young radicals of the revolution, such as A. M. Hanafi and Chairul Saleh.[20]

The working cabinet established the functional group-based National Council by emergency law in May 1957.[21] The concept of functional group representation had its origin in European corporatism and was new to Sukarno's political thinking; but the partiality he subsequently displayed for the idea of a youth-based functional group was consistent with his recent attempt at generational realignment.[22] The functional group of youth, he said in a speech of 1960, would be

> the most important functional group, more important than other functional groups. Forgive me if I say, for example, that it is more important than the functional group of workers, more important than the functional group of peasants, because in making their contribution to the completion of the revolution, these other functional groups definitely bring hopes, demands and claims of their own, and they are appropriate demands, I say. But for young men and women, such demands practically don't exist. So far as young men and women are concerned, you simply give.[23]

In actual fact, the idea did not receive clear organizational expression in the Guided Democracy period owing to the unwillingness of the political parties to surrender their mass organizations to army-sponsored regrouping along functional lines. Sukarno himself lost interest in functionalist ideas once he drew the conclusion that the army stood to benefit from their antiparty impulse more than he did.[24]

Thus, the functional group of youth eventually came to be nothing, but Sukarno did manage to include some youngish figures in the working cabinet of April 1957. Also, he found additional ways to impose youthful attributes on his government and people, one of which was to urge a policy of rejuvenation on his fellow Indonesians.

The Attributes of Youth

Rejuvenation

Sukarno's emphasis on youth can be understood within the context of a flight from old age and death, and that link is especially clear in his advocacy of national rejuvenation. Indeed, it seems to have been a direct extension of Sukarno's personal preoccupation with physical rejuvenation. Not only did the president expatiate frequently on the invigorating and rejuvenating qualities of youth, but he was also, as was Mao Zedong at one stage, a client of Dr Ana Aslan, the general director of the National Institute of Gerontology and Geriatrics of Romania who, in the words of an official publication of the institute, discovered the use of procaine as a basic substance in "the prevention and treatment of ageing."[25] In addition to procaine (Novocain), Sukarno also used vitamin tablets for the same purpose, as Louis Fischer has testified. Describing a lunch with Sukarno in the grounds of the Bogor palace, he wrote, "A battery of vitamin bottles stood before Sukarno. As he opened them he invited me to partake. 'They'll keep you young,' he suggested."[26]

In October 1959, President Sukarno drew on a sentence of Mazzini's to lend authority to his call for national rejuvenation. In an essay entitled "Europe: Its Condition" Mazzini wrote,

> Man is not changed by whitewashing or gilding his habitation; a people cannot be regenerated by teaching them the worship of enjoyment; they cannot be taught a spirit of sacrifice by speaking to them of material rewards.[27]

Sukarno elaborated as follows (and in the process wrongly attributed Mazzini's remarks to his book *The Duty of Man*):

> Brothers and Sisters, my younger brothers and sisters, I remind you of the statement of a great Italian leader, Giuseppe Mazzini . . . who in his book "The Duty of Man" said: "A nation does not become youthful because its young men and women are always enjoying themselves." There is another statement of Giuseppe Mazzini, which is also in his book "The Duty of Man," . . . which declares "A nation does not become youthful because it white washes the outside wall of its house." . . . What Mazzini meant was that a nation can only become youthful if it changes its way of thinking, not towards frivolity and enjoyment,

but in daring to live, in daring to become a nation which is united, in daring to become a nation which carries out great deeds, in daring to bring about a society which can provide happiness to all its people. . . . Don't we all, including you young men and women, wish that our nation can become young again, in the sense that Mazzini intended. Can become a nation which is vital, a nation which can truly, like a young hero, be game to face all the big problems; and not a nation which is old and senile; not a nation which is decrepit; not a nation which is fearful; not a nation which suffers from an inferiority complex; but a young nation which is game to solve problems and overcome difficulties within the country and moreover is game to face up to problems of a global nature.[28]

Living Dangerously

In October 1962, Sukarno returned to the theme of national rejuvenation, but on this occasion he formulated it in more radical terms by giving prominence to the youthful attribute of reckless courage. He also cast it in the imperative mood and again cited Mazzini as his source:

What did Giuseppe Mazzini say to young men? Giuseppe Mazzini said to young men in his book "The Duties of Men" [sic] . . . he said to them: "Giovinezza"—"giovinezza" means "hey, young men"—"live dangerously!"[29]

Actually, Mazzini had not said this; rather, it was Nietzsche who coined the expression *Live dangerously!*

The secret of the greatest fruitfulness and the greatest enjoyment of existence is: to *live dangerously!* Build your cities under Vesuvius![30]

But the phrase was later adopted by Mussolini, who offered it as advice to the delegates at the national council of the Italian Fascist Party in August 1924.[31] It seems likely that Sukarno realized the expression was popularized by the fascist leader and wished to disguise this fact by attributing it to Mazzini, although one wonders why he did not simply attribute it to Nietzsche. Also, the expression *Giovinezza* may come from Salvatore Gotta's song of youth of the same title, which was initially sung by the Arditi and subsequently became one of the most popular songs of Fascist Italy.[32]

Living dangerously was a task for youth and for those intent on rejuvenation, such as Sukarno himself: "We all, and not only young men and women, I myself have asked God Almighty so that I, even though an old person, can be game to live dangerously."[33] The aging president's attempt to live according to this maxim, not to mention his exhortations to the nation to follow his example, contributed to a mood in the country that was conducive to perilous action, such as the expansion of the armed conflict with Malaysia to the

Malay peninsula on August 17, 1964; Indonesian Independence Day; and the very day the president delivered his anniversary speech entitled "A Year of Living Dangerously."

On that day a force of Indonesians landed near Pontian about thirty miles north of the Straits of Johore, and it seems likely that the object of this incursion "was either to arouse pro-Indonesian elements among the Malay communities there or to provoke further communal conflict in an area where serious anti-Chinese riots had broken out in 1946."[34] Then, on the night of September 1, the Indonesian air force dropped a large group of commandos at Labis in Johore, which had been a communist stronghold during the Malayan emergency. Apparently, their purpose was to recruit dissidents from the large Chinese community in the area "to stir up the embers of the earlier Communist insurrection."[35] It seems that common to both these landings was an intention to incite communal uprisings in the wake of the Singapore race riots of July. Furthermore, it is pertinent to note that the second round of race riots in Singapore—on September 2, in which Indonesian provocateurs probably had a hand—coincided exactly with the Labis landing.[36]

Rex Mortimer has argued that these two raids were the brainchild of the Indonesian military high command, and he gives the impression that Sukarno was not directly involved; his only evidence, however, is the assertion of Communist Party leaders themselves. In fact, as we know from Harold Crouch's subsequent work, the raids "did not have the approval of the army leadership," and, as Mackie has made clear, Sukarno was directly involved. If political decisions are often based on a complex mix of rational calculation and personal inclination on the part of the leader concerned, then it is difficult to see any element of calculation behind the carrying out of these two raids. Opposed to these actions were both the Communist Party, which feared that an escalation of the conflict with Malaysia would lead to a military takeover in Indonesia, and the army leadership, which feared being "drawn into a much wider conflict than it was prepared for." Thus, there can be no question in this case of Sukarno's seeking to accommodate the aspirations of one or the other or of his trying to find some common thread between them for the sake of wider unity.[37] We are therefore left with a president acting solely on his personal inclinations. In retreat from aging and death, he was trying to live up to his own injunction to live dangerously. As Mackie concluded,

> If the two operations had succeeded both Singapore and the peninsula might have burst aflame with communal conflict. Malaysia promptly reported the Labis landings to the UN Security Council, while British naval and air forces were alerted to strike at Indonesian bases if any further major attacks were launched. All this made September 1964 the period of most dangerous tension

during the entire period of confrontation. "Vivere pericoloso," the President had told his people on 17 August—and the following month he was certainly putting that advice into effect.[38]

The Young Sukarno

The president's attitude toward contemporary youth was not wholly positive. In his Independence Day speech of 1953, for example, he expresses some misgivings concerning the commitment of the young men and women in the audience:

> Especially you, hey, young men and women of Indonesia, you from the present generation who, it is possible, have never consciously experienced taking part in the journey of History, are you already aware that the moment will quickly come when you will have to take part? And you young men and women who are already taking part, do you already think and act in such a way that you feel yourself to be living in an obsession, feel yourself to be instruments of History, living instruments, with whose help History can destroy backwardness and greed, destroy slavery and colonization, forge a New World for your own nation and a New World for all nations? Have you, all the young men and women of Indonesia, already stopped treating pleasure as the most important thing, as I asked of you two years ago?[39]

There were also times when he expressed anger and exasperation with youth. How could he create a situation conducive to the leap into socialism, he wondered in 1964, when young Indonesians could only imitate the fashions and bad habits of the West in violation of their own national identity?

> This matter of creating a favourable situation, it is that which is very difficult, Brothers and Sisters, because the majority of us just want to copy, copy, imitate, imitate, imitate, imitate. Oh, especially the young women . . . what a pity it is if they imitate. I repeat, we must become a nation with its own identity, Indonesian identity. Why do you, there are many who imitate the bouffant hair style? . . . A few days ago there came to these parts some confused young men from England called "The Beatles"; their hair reaches down to their eyebrows. . . . Young men, if there are any among you who imitate them, beware! I will issue an order to the police throughout Indonesia, if there is an Indonesian youth who imitates, has his hair "Beatled," hold him, shave him completely bald. Hey Pak Tjipto [Sutjipto Danukusumo, the police commander], is he here or not? Are the police here or not? Make a note, make a note of my order.[40]

But more telling than this critical stance was the fact that Sukarno could be envious and competitive with respect to the very qualities he admired. For example, in his address on Youth Pledge Day in 1960, he said, "Perhaps among the young men and women there are those who ask: 'Pak Karno is already old, how come he joins in The Oath of Youth'? Hey, I am not old, I still feel young."[41] In April 1964, he said, "Brothers and Sisters, and my children, I was once young like you, but now I am 62. Although I am now 62, I do not wish to be defeated, I do not wish to be defeated in youthfulness of spirit by any young person at all."[42]

The following year he gave expression to the same sentiments, and his accompanying remarks on the politics of the day show how this envious and competitive attitude toward contemporary youth, no less than his emphasis on the need for dynamism and reckless courage, contributed to Guided Democracy's radical mobilization *politique*:

> The tumult of the people is extraordinary. People who do not understand think this is a competition [*djor-djoran*]. Do you understand the meaning of *djor-djoran*? A contest, between the Communist Party and the National Party! . . . But Brothers and Sisters, even if it is a competition, even if it is a contest, I do not object. . . . Yes, indeed, Brothers and Sisters, in a struggle, each group, even each individual in that struggle contributes enthusiasm, contributes energy, contributes everything they have for the achievement of the goal of the revolution. Take me for example, Bung Karno. I am already 64 years old. But I do not want to be defeated by anyone, so let us compete. Compete to struggle, compete to struggle.[43]

Ultimately, though, Sukarno appears to have sought refuge from his fear of aging and envy of contemporary youth in an intense focus on, even an idealization of, his own youth. Something of this process may be gleaned from the remarks he made to a congress of young people in 1964 in which he displayed no more than a fleeting interest in them before fixing on the topic of his own youth:

> I do not know whether I look more handsome wearing this cap or more ugly. Please answer, more handsome or more ugly? [The audience replies, "Younger, Bapak."] You say, "younger, Bapak." In fact, I wished to try this cap on because I wanted to know what it feels like to be a young person at the present time. If we are asking what it felt like to be a young person in the previous period—you realize that I was once young—I certainly know. I am now 63 but I once experienced a time when I was 18, 20; indeed, I experienced a time when I was 15. Now, I wish to compare my feelings at the time I was 15, 16, 17, 18, 19, in my twenties, with my feelings now.[44]

In keeping with this degree of self-absorption, Sukarno believed that it was only his youth and that of his generation that were of any historical consequence. Far from admiring contemporary youth when in this frame of mind, he held their youthfulness against them. They did not suffer; they did not sacrifice themselves; indeed, they had not even been born when Sukarno and other patriots of his acquaintance and generation were enduring great hardship in their heroic struggle to achieve Indonesian independence.

> I, brothers and sisters, was active for forty years in the people's struggle, I truly know what the message of the people's suffering is. For forty years I accompanied the people, accompanied them in their suffering, consequently I know why they were suffering, know what they were crying over, know what were their appeals to Almighty God, know why they courageously went to jail . . . know why they smiled as they climbed the gallows as happened formerly in Tiamis. I know more than you because I am older than you and because I participated in the people's movements for forty years.[45]

Also, in a later speech:

> I whom you have elevated to become Great Leader of the Revolution, to become President for life, I was forty-five years in the struggle, forty-five years. Before many of you were born, I was already in the struggle.[46]

Sukarno seemed unable to draw on the resources of his culture—respect for age, cultivation of wisdom, and the like—to arrive at a degree of acceptance of advancing years and approaching death. Accordingly, he sought an untraditional and modern comfort in an absorption in and idealization of his own youth. Thus neither here, nor in his other speeches, nor in his autobiography does Sukarno find anything to criticize in his own youth. On the contrary, he invariably represents it as exemplary. The idea, even within a modern perspective that adult life might be constructed differently—say, on a skeptical attitude toward one's past from which one might conceivably learn or simply on the acknowledgement of youthful difficulties and troubles—never seems to have occurred to him although in his early period as a leader of Indonesian nationalism something went wrong, as we have seen.[47]

The consequence of this attitude for his politics was apparent from the late 1950s onward. At first, Sukarno searched for a more satisfactory means than he believed parliamentary democracy provided for addressing Indonesia's problems; then, after briefly flirting with corporatist ideas, he reverted in wholly uncritical fashion to the political programs and ideology that he had espoused as a young nationalist leader between 1926 and 1933.

We may observe something of this process in his bringing forward the doctrine of NASAKOM from 1960. Nowhere was this process of reverently returning to the programs and policies of his youth clearer or more significant than in the case of Sukarno's idea, which he first advanced in 1926, that close cooperation between nationalist (*nasionalis*), religious (*agama*), and socialist forces was essential to the unity of Indonesia. At first, however, his motivation for reviving this notion seemed to be based on largely pragmatic political considerations. As noted, he lost interest in functionalist ideas when he realized that the army stood to benefit from their anti–political party orientation more than he did. In this frame of mind, the president called for a broad alliance in 1960 between the various political parties that represented nationalists, devout Moslems, and communists (*komunis*)—under the banner of what he called NASAKOM unity (*NASionalis, Agama, KOMunis*)—and he sought their support in his contest for influence with the military. However, it almost immediately became apparent that his attachment to it had an emotional dimension not explained by reference to political utility alone. Indeed, as tensions grew between the Communist Party and its NASAKOM partners (the traditionalist Islamic Nahdlatul Ulama and the Indonesian National Party) and between the Communist Party and the army in the following years, the appropriateness of the doctrine to the circumstances of the day became increasingly problematic. But this is to anticipate the argument below.

In 1926, when Sukarno turned twenty-five, he published three articles in the nationalist journal *Indonesia Muda* (Young Indonesia) entitled "Nationalism, Islam, and Marxism." In them, he argued for close cooperation between the people and the organizations representing these three outlooks in the struggle for Indonesian independence:

> There is nothing to prevent Nationalists from working together with Moslems and Marxists. Look at the abiding relationship between the nationalist Gandhi and the Pan-Islamicists, Maulana Mohamed Ali and Shaukat Ali! When the non-cooperation movement in India was at its height, they were virtually inseparable. Look at the Chinese Nationalist (Kuomintang) Party's readiness to accept the Marxist ideas of opposition to militarism, opposition to imperialism and opposition to capitalism![48]

However, the "abiding relationship" between Gandhi and the two brothers who led the Pan-Islamic movement in India came to an end in 1928 as a result of the growing antagonism between their respective communities. The cooperation between the Kuomintang and the Chinese Communist Party ended in bloodshed, with Chiang Kai-shek's massacre of the Shanghai workers in April 1927.[49] To make this observation may seem unfair, for Sukarno could not be expected to anticipate the future, prophetic pretensions notwithstanding. However, the future president was certainly aware of these events and commented at least twice on the fate of the communists in Shanghai but did not see fit to revise his formulation.[50] When he reintroduced it into Indonesian politics in 1960 under the rubric of NASAKOM unity, it was as if the events had never taken place.

Moreover, Sukarno appeared not to take into account the deteriorating relationships between the components of this proposed coalition. Arguably, his 1926 appeal for unity between nationalist, religious, and socialist forces was not altogether unrealistic despite the questionable arguments he advanced in its favor. At that time these groupings were not as sharply divided as they were later to become, and the colonial government was their common enemy. However, by 1960, the Dutch had long departed. Furthermore, deep divisions had opened up in society in the intervening years, the management of which seemed to require some form of institutional separation, not an imposed unity.

In 1958 and 1959, Sukarno sought to protect the Communist Party (Partai Komunis Indonesia, PKI) from the army's efforts to circumscribe its activities. Matters came to a head in July 1960 when the party issued a statement highly critical of various government ministers and the army. The latter responded vigorously by summoning all members of the politburo to an interrogation, and in August the military commanders of South Sumatra, South Kalimantan, and South Sulawesi banned communist activity in their respective regions.[51] The account by the army's chief of staff at the time, General Nasution, of Sukarno's subsequent attempt to have these bans lifted shows the strong emotional investment that Sukarno was once again making in his early thinking on the need for cooperation between nationalist, religious, and socialist forces:

> After the "Three Souths" incident occurred the President shifted to the political front in opposing the anti-PKI attitude in the Army. . . . The President called a national level meeting at the Palace. Ministers, the Armed Forces leadership, and commanders, governors and police chiefs in the regions attended. . . . The Army General Staff prepared a plan of action: The commanders would report on the PKI and its mass organizations in the regions, and would draw the conclusion that they endangered political and social stability and so forth. . . . The President listened patiently while preparing his response. He then delved again into the origin of the national movement and the precision of Marxism as an analytical tool. . . . He challenged those present, asking who amongst them had read and studied more Marxist books than him. In the final analysis, he could not envisage the Indonesian national struggle separately from the former line whereby Nationalists, Religious People and Communists all played a part. He said that Nasakom has been a tendency in our national struggle since former times. Saying this affected him and tears flowed down his cheeks.[52]

Once the president had reinvested in his "Nationalism, Islam, and Marxism" of 1926, he proceeded to explicate and advocate it at every opportunity. Indeed, by 1964–1965, he seemed determined to place NASAKOM as a doctrine that acknowledged the existence of a communist stream within Indonesian society and the PKI as its representative on an equal footing with the state ideology of *Pancasila*.[53] Neither the fate of the Pan-Islamic movement in India nor the massacre of the Chinese communists in Shanghai—not to mention any number of other cautionary tales—impinged on the confidence and conviction he displayed in advancing NASAKOM unity as a precondition for the successful completion of the Indonesian revolution. In 1962 he even claimed to a Communist Party audience that he had been successful in substantially reducing the amount of "communist phobia" in Indonesian society:

> And one matter which gives me satisfaction is that I have already succeeded in ridding the inner feelings of the Indonesian people—or a large proportion of them—of Communist phobia (lengthy clapping). You know that the Communists decades ago and even in recent times were considered by some of the Indonesian people to be like devils (the audience laughs) on this earth (further laughter). And it troubled me that the Communists were considered to be like devils by a section of the Indonesian people. Whereas I know that the intentions of the Communists are good, and especially in the struggle to smash imperialism in Indonesia the contribution of the Communists has not been small (lengthy clapping)....
> So brothers and sisters, one source of satisfaction to me in recent times is that Communist phobia has already greatly declined, to such a degree that, yes, I see it as extraordinary. Aidit [chairman of the PKI] is on the same level as groups from A [*agama*, religion], Aidit is on the same level and works together with groups from Nas [*nasionalisme*, nationalism], and likewise leaders from Nas work with the leaders of Kom [*komunisme*, communism]. Moreover, the green shirts [military] at the present time often work together with Kom (lengthy clapping).[54]

But 1962 was also the year in which the traditionalist Moslem political party Nahdlatul Ulama established within its youth group Ansor a paramilitary corps called Banser, or Barisan Serba Guna Ansor (Ansor Multipurpose Brigade). According to a historian of the Nahdlatul Ulama, Greg Fealy, "its official purpose was to give physical protection for party activities and supporters, but its unstated aim was to prepare for confrontation with the PKI."[55] This was not the only sign that the president's faith in the efficacy of his NASAKOM concept was not well founded. Most obvious was the fierce cultural and religious opposition to the Communist Party's class-oriented attempts in 1964–1965 to unilaterally implement the Land Reform and Crop Sharing Laws of 1959–1960. Amid growing violence between communists and anticommunists—in the villages of Central and East Java in particular—the president intervened to save NASAKOM unity. On December 12, 1964, he met with the leaders of ten political parties, and after a tense meeting lasting thirteen hours, they felt obliged to sign a unanimous declaration "that reaffirmed the common adherence of the parties to revolutionary national unity based on Nasakom and committed them to doing their utmost to act in accordance with the spirit of Nasakom."[56]

Surely the evidence was in, if not by 1960 or 1962, then certainly by the 1964–1965 period: it was courting disaster to bring together groups of such diverse and, indeed, antagonistic interests within an environment shaped by soaring inflation and serious food shortages and to persist in such efforts despite an increasing incidence of violence between them. But still the president remained optimistic about the fit between his concept and the contemporary circumstances in Indonesia. In addressing a meeting of the Communist Party's student front on September 29, 1965—the very unruly nature of which might also have given him pause, as the students kept up a chant demanding that the government ban the modernist Islamic student organization Himpunan Mahasiswa Indonesia—he reiterated his confidence in NASAKOM and claimed that it had taken root in Indonesian society:

> And as a practice, an application of the principle of bringing together all the revolutionary forces, a fusion of all the revolutionary forces, already in '26 when I was perhaps younger than, which one of you . . . at that time I was twenty-five years old, younger, perhaps, than you, hey, who is sitting over there, you are, perhaps, already 28 or thereabouts. Possibly I was younger at that time than you, how old are you? Oh, 23 now. In '26, I, as an adaptation, as an application of the principle of the struggle of bringing together all the revolutionary forces, of fusing all the revolutionary forces, in '26 I formulated the idea of Nasakom. I expressed this idea of mine in a rather lengthy article called "Nationalism, Islam and Marxism." This is before Panca Sila brothers and Sisters. . . . The idea of Nasakom was in '26. The word Nasakom appeared only later once Indonesia had gained its independence, but the idea of Nasakom, the gathering together of all revolutionary forces, not only Islam but also Nationalists, and also Marxists, was born in Indonesia in '26, brothers and sisters. Now, brothers and sisters, this Nasakom, for which I say Thank God, has already become national property. By this I mean that it is already owned by all the Indonesian people. Except the false ones brothers and sisters. Except the people who are in fact traitors of the nation. Except the people who are in fact counter revolutionaries. Now Nasakom has become a national asset, the property of all the Indonesian people. Ninety-nine per cent of the Indonesian people hold Nasakom in high esteem.[57]

President Sukarno offered no argument here or, indeed, in any of his other remarks concerning Nasakom regarding its appropriateness for the conditions of Guided Democracy. However, he frequently mentioned that the idea for which the term NASAKOM was later coined occurred to him in 1926 when he was twenty-five. In this particular speech he even expressed the view—the envious thrust of which cannot be mistaken—that he was younger then than some of the students in his audience on this occasion in September 1965. Could it be that this was the principal justification of the idea in his eyes, that it had occurred to him when he was a young man? If such an idealization of his youthful self did indeed underpin the president's faith in NASAKOM, then it becomes clear why he failed to discard or adapt it in the face of evidence that it was not a realistic strategy for the circumstances of Guided Democracy. For what relevance can such processes of adaptation or adjustment have to a president who held himself as a young man and his creations at that time in such elevated esteem. After those glorious years (glorious in retrospect at least), which probably came to an end in his mind with his arrest in 1933 when he was thirty-two years old, it must have seemed to him that there was nothing more that he could learn, not even from experience.[58]

Between October 1965 and February 1966, the army encouraged, supported, and directed the killing of communists by the nationalists and the Moslems. Nahdlatul Ulama's paramilitary youth corps, Banser, was very active in this regard. However, this massacre, which shockingly falsified President Sukarno's claim that 99 percent of the Indonesian people held NASAKOM in high esteem, did not bring about a change in his thinking. In his Independence Day speech of 1966, four months after General Soeharto had seized substantial power, he further jeopardized his political standing by insisting that NASAKOM was essential not only for Indonesia but for humankind in general, as he warned his fellow country people against further slaughter:

> I say that Nasakom or Nasasos or Nasa plus whatever else one calls it if not Communism or Socialism is an essential element in the development of the Indonesian Nation! Nationalism, a belief in the one God, Socialism (or call it what you will) constitute a striving in each human soul, in each nation, a striving of all mankind! . . . The soul of Pancasila and the soul of Nasasos or Nasa whatever has to become the lodestar of the modern revolution now, that is the revolution of all mankind! For that reason, I always warn the nation and my people, "Don't engage in conflict!!" "Don't slaughter each other!" Because such behaviour will shatter the integrity and unity of the nation, destroy the true essence of our revolution. And besides that, hundreds of thousands of killings, hundreds of thousands of arrests, will in fact become a burning social and political problem which will exacerbate the conflicts between us.[59]

The Quest for Immortality

A fear of and retreat from old age and death were behind Sukarno's preoccupation with youth, youthful values, and in particular his own youth. This preoccupation gave shape to a manner of politics that stressed dynamism and reckless courage on the one hand and privileged the doctrines that he had formulated at that stage of his life on the other. Cognate with this response to advancing years and approaching death was a desire that his political ideas and teachings would be remembered and indeed revered long after his own passing. In his Independence Day speech of 1965, he said:

> One of our poets declared that he "wanted to live for a thousand years." And I want to live for a thousand years. But that is clearly not possible. There is not one human being who has reached the age of a thousand years. But I pray, O God, O Lord, may my ideas, my teachings, which are now included in the *Five Talismans*, may those teachings and those ideas of mine live for a thousand years![60]

This is a wish of breathtaking proportions and as such is perhaps some measure of the desperation Sukarno felt in the face of death. For, as a Marxist, the president would have been well aware of the implications of such a desire: if his ideas and teachings were to last a thousand years, then history would have to end with him.

CONCLUSION

We are accustomed to interpreting Sukarno's behavior in terms of the Javanese tradition, yet nothing could be more remote from that tradition than his response to his advancing years and impending death. Accordingly, it is possible to view the "politics of rejuvenation" not as a culturally shaped response to aging and death but as a modern substitute for it. The president's focus on youth and youthful qualities such as reckless courage, his attempt to repeat his youthful past and fix history in its final form, and his frantic style of politics to which these various behaviors gave rise all form less an exclusively Javanese story than the modern one of a leader imagining himself still young with a young man's power in the face of old age and death.

NOTES

1. Auden, *Dyer's Hand*, 278.
2. The expression is David Gutmann's.
3. See, for example, J. Robertson: "He [the child aged from eighteen to twenty-four months] does not know death, but only absence; and if the only person who can satisfy his imperative need is absent, she might as well be dead, so overwhelming is his sense of loss" (quoted in Bowlby, *Attachment and Loss*, 3:10).

4. Compare Zygmunt Bauman, who asserts that fear of separation is always implicated in our fear of death (*Mortality, Immortality, and Other Life Strategies,* 128).

5. Hering, *Soekarno,* 14–15; Izarman, *Bung Karno,* 8; Vickers, *Bali: A Paradise Created,* 166.

6. Kanzoo Tsoetsoemi, quoted in Hering, *Soekarno,* 21–22.

7. There are some discrepancies among Sukarno's three biographers, Legge, Dahm, and Hering, regarding the details of his primary and secondary schooling. In particular, they do not agree on the period of his attendance at the Europeesche Lagere School in Modjokerto. Consequently, I have only included those dates on which all three authors agree—namely, those related to his attendance at the Hogere Burger School in Surabaya. See Legge, *Sukarno,* 16–30, 62–63, 77; Dahm, *Sukarno,* 23, 28, 30, 43–44; Hering, *Soekarno,* 21–5.

8. For a discussion of Marxism as an expression of and a protest against the process of modernization, see Berman, *All That Is Solid,* 87–129; and for a consideration of the process by which Marxism's stance with respect to modernity shifted from ambivalence to endorsement, thereby facilitating "its appropriation [in the colonies] by a nationalism of the Nehruvian type," see Seth, "Nehruvian Socialism," 466–71.

9. Compare Bauman's discussion of the "resigned equanimity with which death was treated in pre-modern times" (*Mortality,* 96–97).

10. Anderson, "Time of Darkness," 231–32.

11. Sukarno, "[Pidato] disampaikan dalam rapat samudera di Bukittinggi, bertetapan dengan peringatan Israk dan Mikraj," 14–15.

12. Sukarno, *Bertjita-tjitalah Setinggi Bintang Dilangit!* 5.

13. Sukarno, "[Pidato] disampaikan dalam rapat samudera di Bukittinggi, bertetapan dengan peringatan Israk dan Mikraj," 14.

14. Sukarno, "Tabir adalah Lambang Perbudakan [1939]," 1:351.

15. Sukarno, "Me-'Muda'-Kan Pengertian Islam [1940]," 1:372.

16. Anderson, *Java in a Time of Revolution,* 66–84.

17. Lev, *Transition to Guided Democracy,* 21–22; Feith, *Decline of Constitutional Democracy,* 515–20.

18. Sukarno, *Pidato President Sukarno pada Hari Sumpah Pemuda tgl. 28 Oktober 1956 di Djakarta,* 12.

19. Sukarno, *Menjelamatkan Republik Proklamasi,* 12.

20. Lev, *Transition to Guided Democracy,* 20–22.

21. Lev, *Transition to Guided Democracy,* 23.

22. Bourchier, "Lineages of Organicist Political Thought," 130–33.

23. Sukarno, *Pidato Presiden Soekarno pada Pembukaan Kongres Pemuda Seluruh Indonesia tanggal 15 Pebruari 1960 di Bandung,* 14.

24. See Lev, *Transition to Guided Democracy,* 65–67, 204–5, 223–24; Feith, "Dynamics of Guided Democracy," 335–36.

25. Soeharto, *Saksi Sejarah,* 123; *Gerovital H3,* 10; Li Zhisui, *Private Life of Chairman Mao,* 104.

26. Fischer, *Story of Indonesia,* 308.

27. Clarke, *Essays,* 289.

28. I am indebted to Dr. Tony Pagliaro of La Trobe University for tracing Sukarno's Mazzini references to their correct source. Sukarno, *Kuliah Umum Presiden Soekarno pada Pembukaan "Studium Generale" bagi Gabungan Mahasiswa2 Bandung,* 4–5.

29. Sukarno, *Persembahkan Hidupmu kepada Tanah Air dan Bangsa,* 28.

30. Kaufmann, "Gay Science," in *Portable Nietzsche,* 97.

31. Smith, *Mussolini,* 12, 82.

32. Smith, *Mussolini,* 36, 47. I am grateful to Dr. Tony Pagliaro for this point and for his guidance with this part of the argument.

33. Sukarno, "Amanat PJM Presiden Sukarno pada Peringatan 'Hari Sumpah Pemuda' Tanggal 28 Oktober 1962 jang diutjapkan di Istana Olah Raga Senajan Gelora Bung Karno, Djakarta, 30 Oktober 1962," 9.

34. Mackie, *Konfrontasi,* 259.

35. Mackie, *Konfrontasi* 260.

36. Mackie, *Konfrontasi,* 259–60.

37. Mortimer, *Indonesian Communism,* 232, 242–43; Crouch, *Army and Politics,* 62.

38. Mackie, *Konfrontasi,* 259.

39. Sukarno, "Djadilah Alat Sedjarah!" 2:189–90.

40. Sukarno, *Membangun Sosialisme Indonesia dengan Konsepsi Sendiri!* 16–17. The reference to the police commander comes from Crouch, *Army and Politics,* 85.

41. "Amanat PJM Presiden pada Peringatan 4 Windu Hari Sumpah Pemuda di Istana Negara Djakarta pada Tanggal 28 Oktober 1960," 1.

42. Sukarno, *Laksanakan Pantja-Logi: Irigasi-Edukasi-Emigrasi-Industrialisasi-Indoktrinasi,* 6.

43. Sukarno, "Amanat PJM Presiden Sukarno pada Peringatan Hari Ulang Tahun PNI ke-38 di Stadion Utama Gelora Bung Karno, Senajan, Djakarta, 25 Djuli 1965," 1.

44. Sukarno, *Djadilah Kader Bangsa dan Kader Revolusi!* 5.

45. Sukarno, *Komando Presiden Soekarno Pemimpin Besar Revolusi kepada Angkatan 45,* 7.

46. Sukarno, *Komando Presiden: Adakan Gerakan Sukarelawan Indonesia untuk Mempertinggi Ketahanan Revolusi Kita!* 24.

47. Compare Kerrigan, "Life's Iamb," 186.

48. Soekarno, *Nationalism, Islam, and Marxism,* 40–41.

49. Soekarno, *Nationalism, Islam and Marxism,* 40–41nn10–11.

50. In 1928 Sukarno wrote, "The chaos in the ranks of the Chinese nationalists last year did not fail to arouse the concern of us all" ("Indonesianisme dan Pan-Asiatisme," 1:74). And in an article he wrote in 1941, in which he summarizes Trotsky's criticism of Stalin, he had the following to say about China: "In fact it was this country in which Stalin's policy recently devoured thousands of victims from the ranks of the communists when in December 1927 in Canton they were annihilated by the national government" ("Batu Udjian Sedjarah," 1:528).

51. Feith, "Dynamics of Guided Democracy," 338–39.

52. Nasution, *Memenuhi Panggilan Tugas,* 5:35–36.

53. Hauswedell, "Sukarno: Radical or Conservative?" 133–34.

54. Sukarno, *Go Ahead!* 6, 8–9.

55. Fealy, "Ulama and Politics in Indonesia," 237.
56. Mortimer, *Indonesian Communism*, 322.
57. Sukarno, "Amanat PJM Presiden Sukarno pada Rapat CGMI di Istora, Senajan, Djakarta, 29 September 1965," 4–5.
58. Compare Stuart Schram's interpretation of the great proletarian cultural revolution, quoted in part in chapter 2, "as a deliberate and nostalgic attempt on Mao's part to relive the cultural revolution of the 4 May period and to recapture his own youth by projecting another generation of adolescents on to the political stage as his own generation suddenly came to the fore fifty years ago, as the promoters of a new attempt to renovate China" (*Mao Tse-tung*, 343).
59. Sukarno, "Jangan sekali-kali Meninggalkan Sejarah!" 4:209–10.
60. Sukarno, "Capailah Bintang-Bintang di Langit (Tahun Berdikari), 4:194.

5

Sukarno: Abandoned by History?

"ONE CANNOT ESCAPE HISTORY"

Sukarno was introduced to Marxism by C. Hartogh, one of his teachers in the Hogere Burger School (Dutch High School) in Surabaya.[1] With the passage of time this "intrinsically European current of thought" permeated his thinking and influenced the outlook of his mature years, including his view of history.[2] He proudly acknowledged this debt, saying on more than one occasion, "I am a student of the Historical School of Marx."[3] Such historical thinking led him to see history as a process that possessed logic and direction: he studied the past not as an academic pursuit but as a pursuit to divine the future direction of events, which he then sought to facilitate.[4]

Within Marxism, Sukarno's particular view of history owed a good deal to the orthodox school, with its emphasis on the laws of history as an extension of the laws of nature and the cognate notion of historical necessity, of which Engels was the progenitor and the *Anti-Duhring* an important text.[5] One can imagine the appeal of this form of Marxism to a Javanese who was familiar with the traditional "cosmo-magic principle" concerning parallelism between macrocosmos and microcosmos; further, it is not surprising that Sukarno occasionally spoke as if the ancient task of organizing the empire as an image of the universe could be accomplished by acting in concert with the Marxist or Marxist-derived laws of history.[6] In his Independence Day speech of 1954, entitled "Attuned to the Cosmos," he says, "Humankind must have the courage to embrace the consequence that flows from the necessity of being attuned to the cosmos. And what is that consequence? That consequence is the wiping out of all colonial domination of one nation by another."[7]

The centrality of the notion of historical necessity in orthodox Marxism has often led to the disparagement of the latter as a form of historical fatalism. But this is an unjust criticism in the case of one of its most influential figures, Karl Kausky, who distinguished sharply between necessity and inevitability, defining the former as "the only possibility of further development."[8] As Walicki explains, "In other words, socialism would not come about as an inevitable, though unintended, result of human history. . . . The necessity of socialism derived from its role as a prerequisite to further development, since the alternative would be the demise of civilization."[9] Or, as Kautsky put it, "in his commentary on the Erfurt Program: 'As things stay today capitalist civilization cannot continue; we must either move forward into socialism or fall back into barbarism.'"[10]

Sukarno made a similar distinction in a course of lectures he gave in 1947, and although he cited Marx as his authority—as Marx was, of course, in the ultimate sense—Sukarno may have been drawing more directly from Kautsky, with whom he was by no means unfamiliar:[11]

> Karl Marx himself made it clear in one of his writings that the collapse of capitalism does not automatically mean the emergence of socialism. Socialism will only come into being if steps are taken to ensure that. If there are no forces at work building socialism then the inevitable collapse of capitalism (an historical necessity) certainly will be followed for years by chaos without limit or equal! Of course there are many people who think that the phrase "social historical necessity" means that at a particular stage of evolution capitalism definitely will of its own accord be replaced by socialism. But as Marx said above, it is not like that! Capitalism at a particular stage of evolution will definitely be replaced by socialism only when the common people take steps to replace it with socialism.[12]

Another important influence on Sukarno was Lenin, especially in his endorsement of anticolonial nationalism as a kind of second front in the struggle for liberation of the European proletariat. Sukarno's call in *To Achieve an Independent Indonesia* (1933) for the formation of a vanguard party organized according to the principle of democratic centralism that would guide a mass movement of common people in the struggle for independence clearly revealed its Leninist provenance. But perhaps a more important influence than these specific ideas was the impatient, voluntarist stance that underpinned them. Sukarno never quite seized the day with the same audacity as Lenin did in 1917, but then circumstances never quite presented themselves to him in the same auspicious terms. Such voluntarism in both men existed in an uneasy relationship with their adherence to orthodox Marxism. Lenin strained against the laws of history as he saw them, terrified that he might miss the revolutionary moment; Sukarno spoke and wrote as if he had lapsed into a belief in historical inevitability, though his activism indicated otherwise.

Finding clear expression in President Sukarno's Independence Day speech of 1950 are each of the aforementioned themes and influences: first, a Marxist view of history as a process governed by laws that are themselves an extension of the laws of nature; second, a notion of historical necessity that, under the influence of Lenin, attaches itself not to the class struggle in the metropolitan countries but rather to the multiclass, nationalist struggle in the colonies.

> Do not see in the transfer of sovereignty on 27 December last year a manifestation of the good character of the Dutch—see in that event the reality of a historical law proclaiming the definite demise of colonialism and the sure realization of the aspirations of a certain nation! Just as we recognize the reality of the law of gravity in the falling of a mango—which cannot be denied, which cannot be lessened, which cannot be defied, and which cannot be reversed—then the transfer of sovereignty on 27 December signalled the existence of a historical law asserting that the aspirations of a certain nation cannot be damned up and defied; rather, they will triumph and prosper and will be totally fulfilled! Likewise, the rolling back of the federal states is no more nor less than a sign of national aspirations at work, as is the coming into being of the unitary state. For that reason, the rolling back of the federal states cannot be defied and opposed, and the coming into being of the unitary state cannot be defied and opposed! For that reason also I state clearly and with conviction: a day will definitely come when West Irian will return to the Motherland! The reason for the return of West Irian lies in our national aspirations which, as I said before, cannot be defied and cannot be opposed, cannot be suppressed and cannot be extinguished. On the contrary, they will triumph, they will definitely triumph! Come, let us all, all of humankind, understand this matter! Come, let us all not try to "escape history." Come, let us all respect and facilitate the working of history![13]

The transfer of sovereignty over the Indonesian archipelago from Dutch to Indonesian hands on December 27, 1949; the subsequent discarding of the federal state system imposed on Indonesia by the Dutch (the Republic of the United States of Indonesia); the establishment of the unitary Republic of Indonesia on the date of this speech as well as the transfer of—or, as Sukarno put it, the "return" of—West Irian to the mother country at some time in the future were all manifestations of a historical law at work, one that worked with the same silent certainty as the law of gravity and one that proclaimed the death of colonialism and the achievement of nationalist aspirations. This was the "history" that one should not try to "escape" and should indeed honor and facilitate.

Sukarno is quoting the words of Lincoln here, but he has altered their meaning. The expression comes from Lincoln's State of the Union address of December 1862, and it is clear from its context that Lincoln is asserting that he and his fellow citizens cannot escape the judgment of history, not the direction of history, as Sukarno would have it—specficially, the anticolonial direction of history.[14] Sukarno repeated this expression in his 1953 Independence Day speech, this time acknowledging Lincoln as his source and thereby enlisting the authority of the American president for his own distinctive viewpoint.[15]

In subsequent speeches, Sukarno reiterated his view concerning the inescapable anticolonial and pronationalist direction of history. "Don't toy with 'fate'!" he warned the Western powers hostile to Nasser's nationalization of the Suez Canal. "Because what Egypt is doing is nothing other than 'The course of history.' Once again, for the second time in this speech, I will imitate the words of Abraham Lincoln: 'One cannot escape history.'"[16] In his speech to the General Assembly of the United Nations in September 1960, he said, "This is the era of emerging nations and the turbulence of nationalism. To close the eyes to this fact is to become blind to history, to ignore destiny and to reject reality."[17] A year later, at the Conference of Nonaligned Nations in Belgrade, he spoke of "the emergence of nations" as "a process which meets with the resistance of the old forces of domination at every turn." "But," he continued, "this resistance is blind, it is a resistance that refuses to recognise reality, refuses to recognise the march of history."[18]

President Sukarno exploited international trends with great energy and skill to achieve the "liberation" of West Irian. The details need not concern us here: suffice to say that Sukarno, by exploiting international rivalries, was able to persuade the Kennedy administration that a transfer of sovereignty in the disputed territory from Dutch to Indonesian hands was in its Cold War interests. This was an extraordinary achievement for Sukarno, yet in his Independence Day address of 1962, he was content to give the credit to history and, in an un-Marxist addition, to God:

> This victory is History's victory. Each struggle to oppose colonialism finally will be won by the side striving for independence, for the course of History desires the victory of the independence side. Each struggle to maintain colonialism will be defeated, for the course of History desires the defeat of colonialism. We have acted in keeping with the course of History, and for that reason we have triumphed. The Dutch acted against the course of History, and for that reason they have been defeated. Therefore, don't let this victory of ours make us arrogant! Besides, we should all look up to God. This victory is God's gift. God's present! God's compassion! It was he who did this. It was he who bestowed this gift. For that reason you should not be arrogant.[19]

Sukarno achieved success in securing the "return" of West Irian to Indonesia as well as in predicting it by many years. Doing so must have enhanced an already powerful conviction that he understood not only the workings of history but also the functioning of the universe, given the overlap between the laws of history and the laws of nature in orthodox Marxism. In terms of his own culture, which is perhaps how he preferred to see things, he had attuned his political leadership to the cosmos.

Perhaps even more gratifying for Sukarno than the verification that West Irian offered to his profound insight into the workings of history was the proof that it offered that history was working in his favor as a nationalist leader. Of course, it had not always been thus: history had not always proceeded in an anticolonial or anti-imperialist direction, as he himself made quite clear. Speaking in English in Manila on August 5, 1963, at the closing ceremony of the Manila conference, Sukarno said,

> When I was making a speech at the University of the Philippines, I told for example about the history of the 17th and 18th century, the century of the commercial revolution of the West. By that commercial revolution . . . we lost our political independence. And then came the 19th century and the 20th century with the industrial revolution of the West. And again we could not escape history, the history of the industrial revolution of the West. By that industrial revolution of the West, we lost our economic independence. So that in the beginning of the 20th century most of us . . . have become . . . a nation of coolies and a coolie among nations.[20]

But, then, at the beginning of the twentieth century, Sukarno explained, "History awakened. We Asians awakened"; and so it was the turn of Sukarno and other nationalists to relish the fact that they were marching in step with history.[21] The fact that this awakening of history coincided with Sukarno's birth—he was born in 1901—may have appeared to him as, to use an expression common among Marxists, "no accident"; at the very least, it would have been tempting for him to view this coming together of his youth and nationalist history in portentous terms.

Sukarno's great confidence in the anticolonial direction of history, enhanced by the success of the West Irian campaign, may explain in part his embarking on a policy of confrontation of Malaysia in 1963. Certainly, he justified this policy in familiar terms, referring to Malaysia as a neocolonial project of the British "to oppose the Indonesian people, to 'contain the Indonesian revolution,'" which was destined to fail "as each and every attempt which is in conflict with nature's wish and history's wish must fail."[22] One of his most telling criticisms of the British was that they were anomalous figures whom history had passed by—they were not merely yesterday's men but last century's men:

> I say we live in the year 1963. Times have changed since the middle of the eighteenth century or the beginning of the nineteenth when a British poet wrote "Britannia rules the waves, Britains never shall be slaves." ... That was a voice at the beginning of the nineteenth century or the middle of the eighteenth. Now it is one thousand nine hundred and sixty three. The Indonesian people have already risen up. The people from the new emerging forces have already risen up, all progressive human beings in this world have already risen up and are firmly united to smash imperialism-colonialism and all exploitation of man by man.[23]

Or, as Sukarno also put it in his Independence Day speech for 1963,

> In the 20th Century Indonesia arose, Asia arose, Africa arose, Latin America arose, the socialist countries arose. ... And—especially for us, yes for us—this century is our century. The century in which we arose. The century in which we obtained our freedom. The century in which we waged revolution. The century in which we again became a very powerful nation.[24]

This confidence on the part of the Indonesian president would seem impervious to self-questioning, yet it is possible that Sukarno occasionally doubted his reading of history. He noted in his 1964 Independence Day speech that the imperialists remained influential:

> Of course there are various ruses from the imperialists: they toppled the Goulart government in Brazilia; they continue to launch attacks against Cuba; they installed Tsombe in the Congo; and they want to pour a quarter of a million foreign soldiers into Southeast Asia.[25]

Observing these developments, perhaps he feared that the imperialists had not yet played out their historical role after all and that he was living not in Asia's or Indonesia's or his time but in their time—still. If a doubt of this nature did cross his mind, it was quickly banished. "But all this is not the main current of History!" he explained to his audience.

> All this is the back wash of History, which is therefore only of a temporary nature, and will not be able to withstand the pull of the main current. It will certainly wash away, it will certainly disappear! It is certain, as certain as the sun will rise tomorrow![26]

Sukarno returned to this theme in 1965, but on this occasion he added a new element. Not only would imperialism definitely come to an end in the twentieth century and not only would it be replaced by what he called the *Pax Humanica*, but this *Pax Humanica* would last for ever.

> Again and again I have said that the 20th Century is the century in which world imperialism will come to an end. The *Pax Imperialistica* has oppressed, extorted and enslaved us for too long, and the bell of history has rung out with the message that the moment for the formation of the *Pax Humanica* has arrived! Yes, the *Pax Humanica*! Peace for all humankind! Welcome *Pax Humanica*, welcome forever.[27]

Thus, Sukarno adopted the standpoint of Marx and indeed of Hegel in anticipating an end to history. What he envisaged, however, was much closer to the classless society than it was to the Prussian state—namely, a world free of imperialism, based on national independence and, by implication, socialism.[28] Indeed, history's final form and Sukarno's crowning achievement were essentially the same. Not for him, therefore, was the fate of the world's imperialists: dominant and renowned in one century and failing and despised in the next, ignorant individuals who did not even realize that history had abandoned them.

Socialism had in fact been an official objective of the Indonesian nation since 1959. According to a schematization of Sukarno's Independence Day speech of that year, undertaken by the country's Supreme Advisory Council, the goal of Indonesian socialism was to be realized via two revolutionary stages: the national democratic stage, in which imperialist and feudal influences would be eliminated, and, subsequently, the socialist stage.[29] But in July 1964, the president, seemingly impatient with the slow progress of history and keen for it finally to coalesce in the shape of an ultimate achievement on his part, fancifully declared that Indonesia was capable of making the leap into socialism.[30] Then, in April 1965, Sukarno stated that Indonesia was entering the stage of *sosialisme Indonesia,* but he was forced to back down by the Communist Party, which was alarmed to have the appalling social distress and hardship then existing in Indonesia so described. He recanted the claim in his Independence Day speech of August 1965; however, the world of his fantasy reasserted itself, and the president twice repeated his grand claim in the following month.[31]

"NEVER ABANDON HISTORY"

Needless to say, this socialism of Sukarno's was not forged in the crucible of social forces but in the smithy of his mind, a testimony more to the power of his imagination than to the perspicacity of his historical judgement. Nevertheless, the president believed it and presumably derived considerable satisfaction from it—until he was disabused most rudely by what followed: first, the killing of almost the entire general staff of the army by the September 30 movement and, second, the mass murder of Communist Party members and sympathizers at the hands of the remaining generals and their civilian accomplices. Rivers clogged with dead bodies; orphaned children huddled in market places, terrified. Whatever else this was, it clearly was not socialism, and Sukarno was aghast.

Sukarno's thoughts returned to Marx at the fateful cabinet meeting of March 11, 1966, telling his ministers that it was "Marxism that taught me historical thinking."[32] Moments later, an aide handed him a note informing him of the presence of unidentified troops in front of the palace. Sukarno withdrew to his Bogor palace, where later in the day he signed over substantial authority to General Soeharto in the form of the "Letter of March 11." He never recovered from this political setback and was unable to resist the fundamental shift in ideology and policy that Soeharto now pursued.

As he sat down to write his Independence Day speech for 1966, it was, of course, the calamitous events of the last ten months that impinged on his consciousness and of which he sought to make sense in terms of his Marxist understanding of history. On August 17, he offered his view to an unreceptive audience:

> There was a leader, namely Abraham Lincoln, who said "one cannot escape history." . . . I too say that! But I add: "Never leave history." . . . Never abandon the history of your past, O, my people, for if you abandon the history of your past, you will find yourself standing in a vacuum . . . and then you will become confused, and your struggle will, at the most, be just mere running amok! Running amok, like monkeys in the dark!

He then elaborated as follows:

> In my speech on 17 August 1953 I declared that all of us, without exception, cannot escape history—History, which in this 20th Century shows its character and direction with increasing clarity and increasing conspicuousness. In the past, we, the Indonesian nation, truly acted in keeping with that character and direction of history, until eventually we came to where we are now. But history does not stop, history has never stopped, history keeps moving onwards—and do we want to stop, do we want to deny the history of our past, do we want to change direction? Come, let us continue to move onwards with that history, and not stop, for whoever stops will nevertheless be dragged along by history itself.[33]

As the president wandered through the ruins of his aspirations, noticing a new building slowly taking shape that was much closer to Hegel's Prussian state than it was to Marxian socialism, his old formulation that "one cannot escape history" would have offered him no comfort. It implied that he had misread history, that he had mistaken the backwash of history for its main current, that he was still living in colonial and imperial time, and that his destiny was not to be remembered as an instrument of history but to be forgotten as an anomalous figure abandoned by history—a Martov, not a Lenin. It is therefore understandable that he changed this formulation and replaced "one cannot escape history" with "never abandon history." From this viewpoint, the progressive character of history is restored, as is Sukarno's unity with it. From this viewpoint also, we can see that it is not Sukarno but Soeharto who had mistaken the backwash for the main current. As such, his regime, like Tsombe's, would be temporary, only lasting until progressive history reasserted itself. At this point Indonesia's glorious future would be secured and Sukarno's historical greatness guaranteed.

NOTES

1. Sukarno, "Mendjadi Pembantu 'Pemandangan,'" 1:510–11. For more information concerning Hartogh's Marxist beliefs, see Dahm, *Sukarno*, 30–31; and for a full discussion of the early influences on Sukarno, including Marxist ideas, see Legge, *Sukarno*, chap. 3.
2. Carrere d'Encausse and Schram, *Marxism and Asia*, 4.
3. Sukarno, "Tabir adalah Lambang Perbudakan," 1:349–51.
4. Compare Lichtheim, *Marxism*, 40, and Walicki, *Marxism and the Leap*, 20.
5. For an account of orthodox Marxism, see Lichtheim, *Marxism*, 236–38, 245–47; and Walicki, *Marxism and the Leap*, 116, 120, 122, 171–72, 179, 212. That Sukarno was partial to *Anti-Duhring* may be seen from some advice he offered in one of his speeches to students. "If you wish to understand Marxism, read first of all those thin volumes which provide a commentary on Marxism. . . . When we have read those thin books, then we read the thicker ones, and only then do we come to the centre of Marxism, where we read '*Das Kapital*,' where we read other books of Marx. For example, the '*Anti-Duhring*' which was written by Friedrich Engels is very good" (Sukarno, *Tjeramah Presiden Soekarno kepada Peladjar-Peladjar di Surakarta Tanggal 26 Djuli 1960*, 12).
6. Heine-Geldern, *Conceptions of State*, 1–2.
7. Sukarno, "Berirama Dengan Kodrat," 2:211. For remarks in a similar vein, see Sukarno, "Djerit-Kegemparan," 1:55.
8. Walicki, *Marxism and the Leap*, 210, 212.
9. Walicki, *Marxism and the Leap*, 210, 212
10. Walicki, *Marxism and the Leap*, 210, 212.
11. Sukarno drew on Kautsky's *Sozialismus und Kolonialpolitik* (1907) and *Der Weg zur Macht* (1909) in his defense speech "Indonesia Meggugat!" before a colonial court in 1930. For further details, see Paget, "Introduction," xxxi, lviii.

12. Sukarno, *Sarinah: Kewajiban Wanita dalam Perjuangan Republik Indonesia*, 222.
13. Sukarno, "Dari Sabang Sampai Merauke!" 2:117–18.
14. See Donald, *Lincoln*, 398.
15. Sukarno, "Djadilah Alat Sedjarah!" 2:189.
16. Sukarno, "Berilah Isi kepada Hidupmu!" 2:271–72.
17. Sukarno, *To Build the World Anew*, 6.
18. *From Non-alignment to Coordinated Accumulation of Moral Force toward Friendship, Peace and Social Justice among Nations*, 13.
19. Sukarno, "Tahun Kemenangan," 2:509.
20. Quoted in Modelski, *New Emerging Forces*, 78.
21. Modelski, *New Emerging Forces*, 78.
22. Sukarno, *Indonesia Tetap Tegak Berdiri sampai Achir Zaman*, 12.
23. Sukarno, *Amanat Presiden Sukarno pada Rapat Raksasa Front Nasional "Mengganjang Malaysia,"* 13.
24. Sukarno, "Genta Suara Republik Indonesia," 2:552.
25. Sukarno, "Tahun Vivere Pericoloso," 2:590.
26. Sukarno, "Tahun Vivere Pericoloso," 2:590.
27. Sukarno, "Capailah Bintang-Bintang di Langit," 4:172.
28. See Carr, *What Is History?* 114–15.
29. Mortimer, *Indonesian Communism*, 95–96.
30. Sukarno, *Membangun Sosialisme Indonesia dengan Konsepsi Sendiri!* 16.
31. Mortimer, *Indonesian Communism*, 170–71; Hauswedell, "Sukarno: Radical or Conservative?" 127–28, 128n73. For Sukarno's first mention of Indonesia entering the socialist phase, see his speech *Berdiri diata Kaki Sendiri (Berdikari)*, 8–9. For his subsequent recanting, see "Capailah Bintang-Bintang di Langit," 4:182.
32. "Amanat PJM Presiden Sukarno pada Sidang Kabinet Paripurna di Istana Negara, Djakarta, 11 March 1966," 5.
33. Sukarno, "Jangan Sekali-kali Meninggalkan Sejarah!" 4:210–11. I was greatly assisted in translating the two excerpts from this speech by Molly Bondan's provisional translation in "Never Leave History! Address by the President of the Republic of Indonesia on the Twenty-first Anniversary of Independence 17 August 1966," 18–19.

Part II

6

The Personal Rule of Soeharto

The beginning of the so-called New Order regime may be dated to March 11, 1966, when, under duress, President Sukarno signed a "letter of command" transferring substantial powers to General Soeharto. Fearful that he might subsequently withdraw this letter, the army leaders called the Interim People's Consultative Assembly into session in late June. Those members who had been murdered or incarcerated in the persecutions of the previous months were replaced by persons loyal to the military line, and the ones who had been appointed by Sukarno were placed under enormous pressure to support the new dispensation. It came as no surprise, therefore, that they made the letter irrevocable. Also, they canceled the "president for life" title that the assembly had bestowed on Sukarno in 1963, and they expressed dissatisfaction with the speech that he addressed to the assembly entitled "Nawaksara."[1] In a final decision, they called on him to follow up this speech with an account of his responsibility for the coup attempt. He did so six months later, submitting a report on January 10 in which he said that the September 30 movement "was a complete surprise for me." Unsatisfied, the Interim People's Consultative Assembly, meeting in March, dismissed Sukarno from office and declared Soeharto acting president. Exactly a year later the same body reconvened and named Soeharto president.[2]

PERSONAL RULE

Soeharto presided over his New Order regime from its beginnings in 1966 in broadly patrimonial fashion. In an influential article, Crouch wrote, "The New Order . . . bore a strong resemblance to the patrimonial model. Political competition among the elite did not involve policy, but power and the distribution of spoils."[3] President Soeharto worked cautiously and skillfully in the following years to accumulate more and more power in his own hands. By the early 1990s his success was sufficient to warrant a refined classification of his regime in terms of that highly personal form of patrimonialism known as sultanism.

From 1965 to 1974, as Mackie and MacIntyre have argued, General Soeharto was at best *primus inter pares* in a military-dominated government in which the bureaucracy was weak and ineffectual. He owed his power to the support of the armed forces, but his control over them was limited. Anticommunist civilians, including devout Moslems, offered the New Order strong support, beginning at its inception. But during this period, the government progressively limited the terms on which they could participate in the political process.[4] Elections were held in 1971, but they were not free: the newly created government party, Golkar, was able to profit from its privileged position, gaining 62.8 percent of the vote.

Part of the explanation for Golkar's success—as, indeed, for the abject failure of the Indonesian National Party, whose vote fell from 22.3 percent in 1955 to 6.9 percent in 1971—is to be found in the fact that the regional bureaucracy felt obliged to abandon its allegiance to the Indonesian National Party and to vote for the government party. The Partai Muslimin Indonesia (Parmusi) also fared poorly, garnering only 5.4 percent of the vote, in stark contrast to the political party from which it derived, Masjumi, which obtained 20.9 percent in 1955. Only the Nahdlatul Ulama—which enjoyed strong support among the *kiyayi*, or traditional Moslem leaders of the villages of East and Central Java—was able to withstand "the Golkar onslaught," even improving on its 1955 result. It obtained 18.4 percent then and 18.7 percent in 1971.[5] In the following two years, the government gave further expression to its antiparty animus by forcing the nine parties that had competed in 1971 to reconstitute themselves into two groupings: the Moslem Unity Development Party (Partai Persatuan Pembangunan) and the secular and Christian Indonesian Democracy Party (Partai Demokrasi Indonesia). The government's expectation, it seems, was that the bundling of diverse parties into two new organizations would leave the groups plagued by disunity—and they were certainly not disappointed in this regard. In their divided and weak states, neither group was fit to challenge Golkar in the subsequent New Order elections of 1977, 1982, 1987, and 1992.[6] Nevertheless, Soeharto left nothing to chance: he exercised close, personal control over the selection of the parties' candidates and over the election process itself, with the result that only persons willing to accept his leadership uncritically entered the DPR and MPR, and even then only on sufferance.

Hence, Soeharto, like Sukarno, was able to evade the oversight and control of his presidency that the constitution assigned to the members of the DPR and MPR. Sukarno did so by taking advantage of the constitution's silence on the selection method of DPR and MPR members and simply appointed them himself. Such members became mere extensions of his executive power, and, as we may see from the aforementioned account, Soeharto's approach did not differ in substance from that of his predecessor. Ultimately, the 1945 constitution proved a false friend to constitutional rule and a true friend to its opposite.

From 1974 to 1983, the military remained decisive, whereas the bureaucracy and the state enterprises were transformed into effective instruments of government. An exception was the state oil enterprise Pertamina, which incurred a $10 billion dollar debt in the 1974–1976 period. This event—with the president's progressive alienation of students, Moslems, professionals, and recently retired military contemporaries of the revolutionary generation of 1945—ensured that his position remained vulnerable throughout the 1970s.[7]

The same cannot be said for the next period, 1983 to the early 1990s. The president's policy successes (especially in the field of agriculture) as well as his longevity—the joke about the military opposition's moving to the outpatients' department of the Gatot Subroto military hospital contained a good deal of truth—enabled him to build his authority independently of his close association with the armed forces, which were coming to be led by a younger, postrevolutionary generation of officers who looked up to Soeharto.[8] The bureaucracy, characterized by a growing technical expertise, also assumed a certain independence with respect to the military at this time. It remained, however, very much subject to the will and whim of Soeharto, whose behavior assumed a dynastic quality in these years, as he promoted the business, political, and military careers of family members and retainers. Mackie and MacIntyre have commented that this dynastic tendency "thwarted earlier hopes that the New Order would become sufficiently institutionalised that the succession issue would pose no great problems."[9] Having traced the steps by which President Soeharto was able to accumulate a direct and personal form of power beginning in 1983, Mackie and MacIntyre observe that "the concentration of political, military and economic power in what . . . looks increasingly like an embryonic family dynasty has become very worrying to many Indonesians." They concluded that "Soeharto has . . . imposed the stamp of his personality and political style upon the New Order so strongly (as did his predecessor, Sukarno, upon the 'Guided Democracy' years, 1959–65) that we simply cannot disregard the personal factor in any analysis of the political, social or structural dynamics of the regime."[10]

These details of Soeharto's personal style of leadership as it developed in the 1980s and early 1990s seem to point beyond Crouch's patrimonialism or Roth's "detraditionalized personalized patrimonialism" toward that extreme version of patrimonialism known as *sultanism*. In this form of rule, the leader exercises "maximum discretion," wielding his power "without restraint" and without regard for "the binding norms and relations of bureaucratic administration." And he is aided in this regard by "members of his family, friends, business associates, or individuals directly involved in using violence to sustain the regime."[11]

In this account of sultanism we find perhaps a closer match with the details of Soeharto's rule as Mackie and MacIntyre described it for the period from 1983 to the early 1990s. If it is objected that the concept of sultanism refers to a form of leadership behavior more extreme than that found in their account, then it is appropriate to point out that they were writing in the early 1990s and that, by the end of the New Order regime in 1998, there could no longer be any doubt on this score. Certainly, Aspinall sees 1997 as a turning point by which time "the New Order regime was deep into the transition to a more sultanistic form of rule," and he points by way of evidence to, among other things, Soeharto's attack on Megawati ("The attack on Megawati bore the typical sultanistic hallmarks of pursuit of the ruler's personal power at the expense of the longer-term interests of the government, regime or state"); the activities of the president's children in accumulating, with Soeharto's help, wealth and power (although this did not stop them from feuding among themselves); and the rapid promotion of the president's son-in-law, Prabowo Subianto, through the ranks of the army, well ahead of his classmates.[12]

The claim by Mackie and MacIntyre that "we simply cannot disregard the personal factor in any analysis of the political, social or structural dynamics of the regime" accords well with the statement of Chehabi and Linz that it is "almost tautological to point out that the personality of the ruler is a key element in understanding a sultanistic regime."[13] Accordingly, I attempt in chapter 7 to advance our understanding of Soeharto's inner self to comprehend the character of his New Order regime, at least in its later years. My central argument is that Soeharto organized his personality around thinking where thinking principally means thinking ahead in the service of his composure and is associated with a kind of emotional autarchy. Furthermore, my position goes some way toward explaining his cautious, realistic, and ultimately successful approach to politics and the complex and demanding task of maintaining himself in power for over three decades. If we take into account my further argument that this personal disposition manifested itself in solipsism (other people did not loom large on Soeharto's mental screen) and coldness (he likened his mind to a computer), then we have at least the beginnings of an explanation for what the president's biographer R. E. Elson calls "a characteristic soullessness and pragmatism at the centre of the New Order."[14]

FAVORS

However, if Soeharto's rule resembled Sukarno's, in that Soeharto came to preside over the country's affairs via a personal and arbitrary rulership unhindered by legal restraint, then it differed in other respects. Whereas Sukarno gained support for his leadership largely on the basis of his charisma, Soeharto achieved the same end by engendering fear and distributing favors. In particular, he employed the latter method to secure the loyalty of the armed forces. As Crouch writes, Soeharto used his political influence

> to reward loyal supporters and win over dissident and potentially dissident officers with appointments to civilian posts that offered prospects of material gain. Other officers were encouraged to go into business, with a promise of help from the administration whenever they needed licences, credit or contracts. Control over the machinery of patronage was thus the key factor that enabled Soeharto to win and maintain the support of the armed forces for his leadership.[15]

But the president's patrimonial embrace was by no means confined to the military. With the passage of time, it appeared that Soeharto sat at the apex not only of the political structure but also of "a system akin to business franchising" in which he bestowed privileges and "awarded franchises to other government officials at lower levels to act in similar manner. This included many of his ministers and senior bureaucrats, government administrators at all levels—from provinces down to rural villages—and top executives in the state enterprises . . . such as the food logistics agency, Bulog."[16] Soeharto ran this system with his characteristic shrewdness, displaying, according to Elson, "remarkable skill in establishing and maintaining an elaborate patronage machine which ensured that virtually all the actors in the New Order were so thoroughly compromised and in his debt that they had no room for effective political manoeuvre."[17]

The president also proved adept for many years at balancing the opposing logic of a capitalist economy and patrimonialism.[18] He was aware that the viability of the latter depended on the continuing growth of the former, and when a substantial decline in the price of oil between 1982 and 1987 threatened Indonesia's export earnings—three-quarters of which derived from oil—and revenue—two-thirds of which derived from oil—he undertook substantial deregulation and reform, especially in the area of government-granted import monopolies, for these were undermining the international competitiveness of downstream enterprises. Soeharto acted in this way to foster industrial exports in the private sector, although he knew that this step would reduce opportunities in this area of the economy for rent taking, especially for his children and for a tight circle of largely Sino-Indonesian cronies.[19]

But they were quick to find and accept other opportunities, and one can only conclude that Soeharto's political judgment and customary restraint had departed him altogether in permitting such behavior to continue. Not only did it lack a rationale derived from traditional patrimonialism — the loyalty of this tiny, favored group had already been secured many times over — but also it drained away the political support he had so far enjoyed; and because of his presumed desire to remain in office to protect the business empires of his children, it complicated the already vexed issue of the succession.[20] Consequently, by the time the next economic crisis struck Indonesia, during the 1997–1998 period, President Soeharto was quite unable to take the larger view of things as he had done ten years before. Far from ordering the children and the cronies to retreat to secure the interests of the economy and the country as a whole, he sought to sidestep pressure from the International Monetary Fund to rid the economy of its sultanistic features as a precondition for the provision of credits. In Liddle's assessment, "Suharto at age 76 . . . was no longer willing or able to distinguish between the interests of his family and his cronies and those of the nation."[21]

The influence of Soeharto's essentially patrimonial style of rule, before it developed into a parody of itself in the form of sultanism, extended beyond securing support for his rule. It also helped shape business–state relations in general and by so doing influenced the class structure of New Order Indonesia. As Howard Dick has argued, the middle class, broadly understood, "was to be counted among the winners" of the political upheaval of 1965–1966. After the depredations of the Guided Democracy period, when "its members had for the most part suffered a marked decline in living standards, and their privileges had been further threatened by the power of the PKI," their fortunes improved markedly under Soeharto. Inflation came down from 600 percent in the 1965–1966 period to 10 percent in 1969. Large increases in the price of oil in 1974 and 1979 contributed massively to export earnings and government revenue and underpinned an average growth rate in the economy of 8 percent between 1970 and 1980. "Even allowing for a population growth rate of about 2 percent, this has meant an impressive rise in real income per capita" of which the middle class has been a substantial beneficiary.[22] As noted, Soeharto successfully averted the threat that the subsequent drops in the price of oil posed to this remarkable growth by shifting the orientation of the economy from the state sector and oil to nonoil exports by the private sector. Consequently, economic growth continued apace, but this should not blind us to the fact that Indonesian prosperity in the 1990s could only be described as modest. In 1994, Indonesia's gross national product per capita was US$790, somewhat less than the Philippines (US$960) but well beneath Thailand (US$2,210), let alone South Korea (US$8,220).[23]

This moderate level of economic prosperity provided some impetus toward the appearance of a robust and politically independent middle class in Indonesia. For example, the private sector growth from the late 1980s fostered self-confidence and self-assertion among the business people involved.[24] Nevertheless, it was quite insufficient to overcome the debilitating effect on class formation of the mutually reinforcing phenomena of persisting patrimonialism on the one hand and a Sino-Indonesian minority on the other whereby "pariah entrepreneurs," far from being able to convert their economic strength into a corresponding political influence, felt obliged to seek the protection of *pribumi,* or native patrons. And "big *pribumi* business" also, as Crouch explained in the early 1990s, "is still very closely tied to the regime and has no interest in challenging its patrons while middle-level *pribumi* business, which might have an interest in a more open political system, is not strong enough to take the lead."[25] Before being tempted to place constitutional and democratic expectations on this last category, it is sobering to recall Liddle's general conclusion offered in the late 1980s: "I suspect that the great majority of professionals and entrepreneurs are not in fact liberals but rather are quite willing to trade some dependence for a larger share of the benefits of state largesse."[26] So long as patrimonialism, in the particular form of patron–client relations, joined what an expanding capitalist economy might otherwise have separated (state officials and entrepreneurs; the bureaucracy and the business class; the state and civil society) and separated what it might otherwise have joined (Sino-Indonesian and pribumi entrepreneurs), then a strong middle class with an energetic business strata at its core—that is to say, a bourgeoisie—would be unlikely to emerge in Indonesia.

FEAR

Soeharto's granting favors in return for political support was not his only means of securing acceptance for his regime. He also had recourse to fear and, indeed, those measures that gave rise to fear, such as in the case of those whose politics and beliefs were judged to fall on one side or the other of the New Order mean or of those who proved resistant to Soeharto's patrimonial blandishments. Communist scaremongering was one of his principal tactics in this regard, and with the massacre of communists in 1965 serving as a ghastly warning of what he and the army were capable of, it proved most effective in bringing people into line. If it failed or if a person's transgressions were considered unforgivable, then the security apparatus of the state was brought to bear. At the center of this was the Operations Command to Restore Security and Order (Komando Operasi Keamanan dan Ketertiban; Kopkamtib), which was established under Soeharto's direction in October 1965 with the objective of hunting down communists. However, its charter was later extended to cover not only a wider range of opponents of the regime—including, at times, university students and devout Moslems—but also a broader range of activities. It supervised newspapers, granting and sometimes withdrawing publication permits; it was entrusted with maintaining order during election campaigns; and it interfered closely in the affairs of labor, putting down strikes and arresting recalcitrant employees.[27] According to Crouch, "with virtually unlimited power, the Kopkamtib was a key instrument in maintaining the government's authority."[28] Furthermore, Soeharto did not fail to bend Sukarno's instruments of oppression to his own purposes. In 1969, he gave statutory force to presidential decrees 5/1963 and 11/1963—the former requiring police permits for political gatherings and the latter designed to combat subversion.[29] He finally dismantled Kopkamtib in 1988, but he did not disown the intimidation and arbitrary arrest that it had practiced, although such instances were carried out with less frequency during a period of "openness" in the early 1990s.[30] Indeed, these coercive instruments and the fear that they engendered remained part and parcel of the regime's so-called security approach to government until the very end.[31]

In addition to giving citizens solid reason to fear the New Order regime, it endeavored to make them fearful on other accounts. For example, they were encouraged to fear divisiveness in society and disunity in the nation, as well as what was purportedly responsible for both: the parliamentary democracy of the 1950s and the alien, liberal philosophy that allegedly informed it. According to Bourchier, "in the language of the New Order, the fifties stand for Westernism, national disintegration, economic backwardness and chronic political instability, the mirror image of the New Order's accent on indigenism, national unity, development and political stability."[32] Schwarz's testimony suggests that such fears, if they did not actually take hold for the first time in the period of the New Order, were exacerbated by the regime's pronouncements. Schwarz observed that "the philosophical underpinnings of the New Order are infused with fears of national disunity—fears which emanated from the 1950s and were further strengthened by the societal breakdown in 1965-66—and these fears have been bought by the public."[33]

Finally, the regime fostered a fearful attitude toward the people at large. This was not a new fear in the Republic of Indonesia. As noted, the more prosperous and educated inhabitants of the cities and towns had, at best, an ambivalent attitude toward those who were less so—in particular, the urban poor and the small farmers and peasants of the countryside. The better-off claimed to have the latter's interests at heart but feared them for their large numbers, presumed ignorance, violent inclinations, and willful tendency to assert their own views of matters. Sukarno's stance toward them was somewhat less patronizing and certainly did not seem to be based on fear: he addressed them in his speeches as "Brothers and Sisters." But the people—other than as a unity distinguished by their collective uniqueness, other than as a source of affirmation to his own self, and other than "as a chorus for what was increasingly a palace-centered politics" [34]—in all their clamorous individuality were missing from his vision for Indonesia. Soeharto, however, did not participate in even these patrician forms of populism. When Sukarno was displaced by Soeharto, populist politics, if not fear, was put aside.[35]

If Soeharto's security chiefs continued to warn, as they did right up to 1998, of the continuing threat of communists undermining the New Order, then one assumes that the fear in question was not simply a fear of the people but rather a more specific fear, if not of their consciences, then of retaliation for the massacre of 1965.[36]

Fear was ubiquitous in the New Order regime, attacking the people's sense of well-being and impeding their preparedness not only to speak openly but to think freely about their personal, social, and political circumstances. If it was difficult to resist these debilitating consequences of fear, then the dispensing of favors in return for support only served to open another front in the assault on the individual's autonomy. Much has been written about the damaging legacies of such regimes as the New Order. For example, Chehabi and Linz noted that "under sultanistic rule the distinction between regime and state is . . . blurred . . . [whereby] the ruler and his associates directly intervene in the structures of governance, disregarding their internal norms, professional standards, and ethos . . . This renders the 'state structures' less serviceable after a regime change."[37] However, comparatively little has been documented about the severely diminished possibilities for good behavior by the bribed and battered citizenry obliged to live under such structures.

NOTES

1. This was the title Sukarno gave to the speech. As he explained it, it is short for the Sanscrit words *nawa aksara* ("nine basic points"). See Sukarno, *Nawa Aksara (Nawa Aksara)*, 11–12.
2. Crouch, *Army and Politics*, 201–2, 212–13, 216–20.
3. Crouch, "Patrimonialism and Military Rule," 578.
4. Mackie and MacIntyre, "Politics," 7, 9–10.

5. Crouch, *Army and Politics*, 270; Ward, *1971 Election in Indonesia,* 90–113.
6. Mackie and MacIntyre, "Politics," 13.
7. Mackie and MacIntyre, "Politics," 8, 14–15.
8. This remark is recorded by Michael R. J. Vatikiotis in his *Indonesian Politics under Suharto,* 161.
9. Mackie and MacIntyre, "Politics," 46.
10. Mackie and MacIntyre, "Politics," 4, 46.
11. Roth, "Personal Rulership," 203; also, Chehabi and Linz, "Theory of Sultanism: 1," 4-7.
12. Aspinall, "Political Opposition," 273–74.
13. Chenabi and Linz, "Theory of Sultanism: 2," 37.
14. Elson, *Suharto,* 200.
15. Crouch, "Patrimonialism and Military Rule," 577.
16. McLeod, "Government–Business Relations," 149.
17. Elson, *Suharto,* 305.
18. Crouch, "Patrimonialism and Military Rule," 579, 585, 587.
19. MacIntyre, *Business and Politics in Indonesia,* 56–58.
20. Schwarz, *Nation in Waiting,* 160.
21. Liddle, "Indonesia's Unexpected Failure of Leadership," 25.
22. Dick, "Rise of a Middle Class," 88.
23. Eccleston, Dawson, and McNamara, *Asia-Pacific Profile,* 221.
24. Schwarz, *Nation in Waiting,* 270.
25. Crouch, "Democratic Prospects in Indonesia," 117.
26. Liddle, "Middle Class," 51.
27. Tanter, "Totalitarian Ambition," 253–61; Schwarz, *Nation in Waiting,* 257–63; Elson, *Suharto,* 242.
28. Crouch, *Army and Politics,* 223.
29. Zifcak, "'But a Shadow of Justice,'" 356–57.
30. Elson, *Suharto,* 261–62.
31. For a full account of the security apparatus of the New Order regime, see Tanter, "Totalitarian Ambition," 213–88.
32. Bourchier, "1950s in New Order Ideology," 50.
33. Schwarz, *Nation in Waiting,* 295.
34. McVey, "Beamtenstaat in Indonesia," 86.
35. Siegel, *New Criminal Type in Jakarta,* 4.
36. Siegel, *New Criminal Type in Jakarta,* 6.
37. Chehabi and Linz, "Theory of Sultanism: 1," 10.

7

Soeharto's Composure

In the previous chapter, I draw principally on the work of Mackie and MacIntyre to note the steps by which President Soeharto was able to accumulate a direct and personal form of power in his hands. It is now appropriate to return to the authors' conclusion concerning the consequent impact of his personality on the character of the New Order regime. "In both its achievements and its shortcomings," they write, "the New Order has been shaped by Soeharto's personal qualities as much as the Old Order was by Sukarno's." Yet, as they also point out, a full appreciation of these qualities is difficult to acquire because

> the inner man remains curiously unknown, almost cryptic and elusive, even to his closest associates. He generally presents himself as calm, dignified, restrained, soft-spoken, almost avuncular—"the Smiling General." Unlike Sukarno, whose entire life, even down to his love affairs, seemed to be conducted on a public stage, Soeharto has remained an intensely private man, devoted to his family, and his cattle farm. Indonesians refer to him as *tertutup* (reserved, shut off)—a quality respected by Javanese and utterly unlike the extrovert Sukarno. "No one knows what that man thinks . . . That is the secret of his power," commented one senior politician who had watched him closely for years. Only occasionally does Soeharto lose his cool, or reveal much of his inner feelings and thinking.[1]

In this chapter, I attempt to advance our understanding of the inner man by drawing on certain biographical and autobiographical materials. These consist of two editions of a semiofficial biography by O. G. Roeder, published in 1969 and 1976; some remarks Soeharto made at a press conference in 1974 in response to the publication of his alleged genealogy by a Jakarta magazine;

and his collaborative autobiography, published in 1989. These sources are examined in chronological order, as the timing and circumstances of the president's remarks can themselves be informative.

Inevitably, the use of such traditionally self-serving material raises questions about its reliability, and the reader is certainly obliged to view the subject's various claims with skepticism. However, it is not only Soeharto's truthful comments that have a just claim on our attention. His words in his order (autobiographical collaborators notwithstanding) are, by dint of that fact, meaningful although the particular meaning one attaches to them will depend to some degree, of course, on an assessment of their truthfulness. For example, Soeharto's autobiography contains numerous assertions about his high intelligence and his ability to outsmart political and military opponents. It is not always possible to have confidence in the veracity of these claims—did he really disarm untrained revolutionary youth in the clever and skillful way described in the autobiography?—but the mere fact that he makes them in this area (of his mind) as opposed to some other is already telling.

Furthermore, Soeharto's *Autobiography (Otobiografi) as Related to G. Dwipayana and Ramadhan K. H.* was written in the shadow of *Sukarno: An Autobiography As Told to Cindy Adams.*[2] Thus, a full appreciation of the *Otobiografi* requires a knowledge of his predecessor's similarly structured chronicle, and in this regard we are aided by Adams's account of her experience as the first president's "autobiographer," in her book *My Friend the Dictator*.[3]

The fundamental impression that I gained of President Soeharto from the aforementioned texts was of a man taxing his mind to maintain his composure. By thinking ahead, trying to anticipate events (especially disruptive ones), and thereby avoiding shocks, he tried to create the inner calm that more predictable parental behavior than he enjoyed bestows naturally on its beneficiaries.

SUKARNO'S AUTOBIOGRAPHY

Cindy Adams—a "good-looking wise-guy babe," in the estimation of one of her journalist friends—first met Sukarno in August 1961 when she interviewed him for the North American Newspaper Alliance. She appears to have made a deep impression, for shortly after her return to the United States, she received a letter from him. A correspondence ensued, and Adams realized that she had become, as she put it, "a pen pal of the President-for-life of the Republic of Indonesia."[4] They continued to correspond for two years. Then, in August 1963, Adams received a letter from Howard Jones, the U.S. ambassador to Indonesia, that said, "In talking with the President today I commented that somebody ought to do a biography of him soon. He said, 'I'll wait until I'm gone for that.' He hesitated a moment, then grinned boyishly, 'Cindy could do a good biography of me. If ever I do my life story only one person will do it—Cindy Adams.'"[5] When Sukarno repeated this sentiment a few days later and Jones duly conveyed it to her, Adams decided to take him at his word.[6]

She arrived in Jakarta in December 1963 to begin work on a collaborative autobiography (Adams does not explain how the task came to be redefined in this way). Sukarno, however, seemed more intent on seduction, and it was only after Cindy had managed to fend him off that they were able to begin work.[7] The president would not allow a tape recorder, so she was obliged to take notes. Referring to himself in the third person, he expressed his hope that the autobiography would contribute to "a better understanding of Sukarno and with that a better understanding of my beloved Indonesia."[8] He then turned to his origins, laying claim to the last king of Singaradja (on his mother's side) and the sultan of Kediri (on his father's side) as ancestors, and he related his mother's prophecy of his future greatness based on the fact that he had been born at sunrise.[9]

Adams completed her interviewing in June 1964 and went home to New York to write up the fruits of her labor. She had an understanding with Sukarno that she would return to Indonesia by the end of the year with a manuscript for his inspection. True to her word, she arrived in Jakarta in time to attend a speech by the president on New Year's Eve. This was the address in which he announced Indonesia's withdrawal from the United Nations.[10] While she was waiting for Sukarno to find time in the midst of such events to check her work, she showed Ambassador Jones the part relating to Allen Pope, the American pilot shot down and captured by the central government after siding with the rebels in Indonesia's civil war. Sukarno had told Adams that he had had a long talk with Pope to discover his motives and find out who was behind him. She found him, as she put it, "phenomenally retentive in this instance. He remembered huge chunks of his conversation with . . . Pope. It was a most moving sequence." It therefore came as a considerable surprise when Jones summoned her and said, "I think there's something you ought to know. Sukarno never met Allen Pope."[11] When the president acknowledged that this was indeed the case (but in an irritated way, as if objecting to having such a fine distinction forced upon him), Adams found herself recalling something he had once said to her: "I'm always pursuing ideals instead of cold facts. I'm constantly trying to remake circumstances so they can be vehicles to reach what I'm pursuing."[12] She also took fright at the possibility that he had concocted other stories, and she believed that she had no choice but to check the accuracy of his account from beginning to end.

After the manuscript had been in his hands for several months, Sukarno declared that he wanted it rewritten as a biography. "I have asked my ministers and my friends," he stated, "and they agree it is too egotistical for me to say good things about myself. They said you should say them instead."[13] Adams fought back, claiming that she had already signed publishers' contracts for a "first-person story by Sukarno." She also pointed out that the research as well as the writing had been carried out from his point of view and that a biography would therefore require not only rewriting but also fresh research. After further fierce argument, Sukarno backed down and gave her permission to publish the manuscript in its present form. (Adams believed that the president's obstructionist stance was a response to pressure from the Communist Party, keen to sever Sukarno's few remaining ties with the West. She gambled on her belief that he really wanted to have his say.)[14]

Adams left Indonesia in March amid signs of impending political catastrophe. The failed coup attempt of October 1, 1965, threatened Sukarno's presidency, and he evidently saw in the publication of Adams's book one month later an opportunity to retrieve something of his lost standing in the world. When she returned to Jakarta in January 1966, this time as a television reporter for the American Broadcasting Company, she found him, despite his rapidly deteriorating political position, welcoming and grateful to her for the book she had written. "All agree," he said as they drank coffee together in a palace surrounded by hostile student demonstrators, "that this book is Sukarno. Every page sounds like him."[15]

No doubt these words came as a relief to Cindy Adams. She had allowed herself to be possessed by him to represent his character clearly, but in the process she too had possessed him in narrative form.[16] This, it seems, is exactly what Sukarno wanted. Consider in this regard some comments he made in a speech to the Indonesian Publishers' Association in the presence of Adams a few days after the aforementioned meeting:

> Here is Cindy Adams . . . who has already, as you know, published a thick book "Sukarno, An Autobiography as Told to Cindy Adams." . . . And in that book of Cindy Adams I say, "I take leave of this material world . . . . I went into the world of the mind . . . ." And in the world of the mind, this is what is written by Cindy Adams, I met great people . . . . I met—Cindy Adams writes—Sidney and Beatrice Webb, leaders of the workers in England.[17]

Toward the end of this speech the president asserts that American publishers do sometimes publish good books, and he offers the following as examples: "Edgar Snow, 'Red Star over China,' Edgar Snow, 'The Other Side of the River,' Cindy Adams, 'Sukarno.'"[18] If King Lear "mad'st . . . [his] daughters . . . [his] mothers,"[19] then Sukarno, at a similar age and in a comparable condition, has promoted Adams into the author of his life.

ROEDER'S *THE SMILING GENERAL*

The first account of Soeharto's childhood is found in O. G. Roeder's biography entitled *The Smiling General,* which first appeared in 1969. Roeder, a German who came to Indonesia in 1959, chose to write his book in English and explained his biographical impulse in the following unidiomatic terms: "The reason for writing this book was to present the portrait of a newly born national leader, widely unknown to the world."[20] He denied that it was hagiography and explained its status by stating that "despite some official Indonesian assistance, this book is not an authorized biography."[21] However, he did secure Soeharto's approval of his biographical task, and on the back cover of the second edition (1970) there is a photograph of Roeder, his publisher, Masagung, and President Soeharto himself, admiring a copy of the first edition.

Roeder's account of President Soeharto's childhood, for which Soeharto was presumably the main source of information, emphasized its ordinariness and revealed its disrupted nature. Unaccompanied by holy signs or by son of the dawn–type prophecies, such as those that accompanied the birth of his predecessor, Soeharto was born in the hamlet of Kemusuk in the village of Godean in 1921. He was the son of Kartoredjo, a village irrigation official, and his wife, Fatimah.

Two years later, Kartoredjo separated from his wife, and Soeharto was left in the care of his paternal grandmother, who had also been the midwife at his birth. Kept busy by her occupation and working without servants to assist her, she was obliged to take the infant with her on her rounds. After remarrying a few years later, Fatimah reclaimed her son, who was then four years old, and shortly thereafter presented him with a half brother, Sutjipto. When Soeharto was nine, his father, who was "disappointed with the poor way his son was being brought up," resolved to place him in the care of his younger sister, Ibu Prawirowiardjo, who lived in Surakarta. Presumably fearful of not gaining his ex-wife's permission to take this step, Kartoredjo managed to avoid her upon his arrival, only allowing his son to say good-bye to two people: his grandmother and the teacher at his school in Tiwir. Shortly after Soeharto joined the Prawirowiardjos, they moved to Wuryantoro, where he finished his primary school education. Subsequently, Soeharto, with his cousin and good friend Sulardi, moved to Selogiri so that they could attend the lower middle school in nearby Wonogiri. They stayed at the house of one of Sulardi's elder brothers, who worked as an agricultural official in the district.

Soeharto was circumcised at the relatively late age of fourteen and shortly thereafter was obliged to move once again—this time to the house of Pak Hardjowijono, a friend of his father who lived in Wonogiri. This man was an enthusiastic follower of the magic specialist, traditional healer and Islamic religious teacher Daryatmo,[22] who was also, like Kartoredjo, a village irrigation official. Hardjowijono allowed his new boarder to accompany him on his frequent visits to Daryatmo. Before long, Soeharto found himself living at the Daryatmo's house and enthusiastically learning his various skills.

This high point in Soeharto's young life came to an end when he was obliged to return to Kemusuk to complete his middle school classes. He attended a Muhammadiyah school in nearby Yogyakarta. Upon completion of his studies, he returned to Wuryantoro, where he obtained a job as apprentice to a clerk in the Volksbank. However, one day he tore his *sarong* while riding a bicycle in the course of his duties and was rebuked by the clerk and by Ibu Prawirowiardjo, who had provided him with the cloth in the first place. Without a *sarong* to wear, Soeharto was unable to continue in his work. While still employed by the Volksbank, Soeharto applied to join the Royal Netherlands Indies Army, and, as Roeder says, "the young man, well built and intelligent, was accepted without any difficulty at . . . [its] military school . . . at Gombong, Central Java, on June 1, 1940."[23]

THE *POP* AFFAIR

Soeharto did not tell Roeder the full story of his childhood. This became apparent in October 1974 when the president provided a more detailed picture of his background to discredit a royal genealogy attributed to his family by the Jakarta fortnightly magazine *POP*, which was actually owned by a person in the employ of presidential adviser and intelligence chief Lieutenant General Ali Murtopo.[24] According to the magazine, the president was the son of R. Rio Padmodipuro (subsequently, R. L. Prawirowiyono). This man was descended from Sultan Hamengku Buwono II. He was forced to entrust his wife and seven-year-old child, R. Soeharto, to a villager named Kertorejo to fulfill an obligation to marry the daughter of an influential district chief. Thereafter, neither side attempted to make contact with the other, and the father died in 1962 without setting eyes on his son again.[25]

The publication of this most recent "version of Soeharto's alleged aristocratic links" greatly angered the president and his family.[26] This outcome must have dismayed Ali Murtopo, whose intention, one assumes, was ingratiation during a year of unstable relations among the inner circles of the regime.[27] Be that as it may, the following day Soeharto's half brother, Probosutejo, held a press conference in the company of four inhabitants of the *desa* of Kemusuk who had been flown to Jakarta that morning, including the younger brother of Soeharto's mother, Prawirosudarmadi. He described *POP*'s genealogy as a slander of their parents and ancestors.[28] On October 28, the president himself elaborated on the charges of his half brother in the presence of approximately one hundred journalists from the local and foreign press, the attorney general, the head of the State Intelligence Service, the minister of information, the minister responsible for the state secretariat, and a chastened Lieutenant General Ali Murtopo, to all of whom he distributed copies of his family tree as corrected by Probosutejo and Prawirosudarmadi a few days before.[29]

Soeharto stated that the article in *POP* gave the impression that he was "'a person who didn't respect his parents,' an 'insubordinate child.'"[30] In saying this he probably had in mind its claims that, at the end of his life, Prawirowiyono "'suffered anxiety which could not be resolved because he very much yearned for his child, Raden Soeharto'" and that "Prawirowijono's grave seems neglected now, 'a fact which cannot be reconciled with his son's position as President of the Republic of Indonesia.'"[31] Perhaps allowing his suspicions of Ali Murtopo to get the better of him, Soeharto also claimed that the article cast doubt on his legitimacy and may have been intended to undermine his presidency.[32] Many had believed that the wily intelligence operator—who had outwitted and defeated his principal rival, General Sumitro, the previous January—was hoping to oust and replace the president himself.

> It can give the impression, if one asks why a wife and six-year-old son were handed over with such ease, that possibly the marriage was not valid. And, if invalid, that means a child born out of wedlock or an illegitimate child. Won't this have a bearing on the good name of the nation and the state? Looking at it in the long term we can see that it not only concerns me personally, and my ancestors, but it also concerns me as one who, as it happens, has now obtained the trust of the people. Therefore, it is possible that this material is being used subversively and in politically destabilizing activities.[33]

To avoid this possibility, President Soeharto declared his intention of setting his family record straight, even though doing so would involve the revealing of private matters. True to his word, he then spoke about an ordinary village background, relieved only slightly by a faint aristocratic link on his mother's side,[34] which he said in an emotional voice was "'full of suffering which possibly was not experienced by others.'"[35] Unlike Sukarno, who told a fabulous story of being a child of the dawn who had kings and sultans for ancestors, Soeharto angrily rejected an aristocratic lineage. Central to him, it seems, were his sense of himself as a dutiful son and a plain man of realistic bent.

ROEDER'S *ANAK DESA*

In speaking openly about his childhood, Soeharto provided enough new detail to warrant a revised version of Roeder's semiofficial biography, a work to which I now turn. It was published in Indonesian in 1976 under the title *Anak Desa: Biografi Presiden Soeharto* (Child of the Village: A Biography of President Soeharto).[36] This edition differed from its predecessor on a number of minor points. For example, according to this edition, Soeharto joined the Prawirowiharjos (as their name is spelled in *Anak Desa*) in Wuryantoro, not Surakarta. Two other points of difference should be noted for the sake of clarity in the ensuing narrative; they concern the name of Soeharto's mother and the nature of his relationship to the woman who served as the midwife at his birth. Fatimah of *The Smiling General* becomes Sukirah in *Anak Desa* (and the *Otobiografi*), whereas his midwife is transformed from his father's mother to the wife of his father's uncle (and is given his name Kromodiryo). In the *Otobiografi* she undergoes a further change, simply becoming his father's aunt.[37]

Other details are consistent with this picture of the disrupted nature of the Soeharto childhood; indeed, they reinforce it. We learn, for example, that the marriage of Kertosudiro (the Kartoredjo of *The Smiling General*) to Soeharto's mother was his second of a total of three and that he changed his name with each marriage, from Panjang to Kertoredjo to Kertosudiro to Notokariyo. This name changing suggests, according to McDonald, that he was a restless man, dissatisfied with his lot in life, for "a Javanese custom is to change a name, particularly a child's, after a run of bad luck or illness."[38] We also learn that the midwife, Mbah Kromodiryo, rather than always carrying the infant Soeharto with her on her rounds, frequently entrusted him to the care of her adult daughter, Mbok Amat Idris.[39] In the *Otobiografi*, Soeharto adds Mbah Kromodiryo's husband to the list of his carers and gives the impression that it was he who dominated his affections in that household.[40] We are also told that Sukirah's second marriage (to Atmopawiro) yielded not only Sutjipto (Sucipto) but a total of seven children, of whom Sucipto was the second. The first, a girl called Sukiyem, lived for only a year or two.[41]

Finally, we are informed that after just one year with the Prawirowihardjo family in Wuryantoro, by which time he had begun to feel at home, Soeharto was visited by his stepfather, Atmopawiro; his half brother, Sumowiyatmo; and his half sister's husband, Sastroharyono. Roeder explains that Sumowiyatmo and Mrs Sastroharyono were Kertoredjo's children by his first marriage.[42] It was the fasting month at the time, and Atmopawiro, who said that Sukirah longed to see her son again, promised the Prawirowihardjos that he would return Soeharto to them at the end of Lebaran so that the boy could continue his schooling in Wuryantoro. But the promise was not kept, and Soeharto ended up back in the school at Tiwir, near Kemusuk, where his mother lived. A year later his father and aunt returned him to the aunt's home in Wuryantoro.[43]

Unquestionably, the most important new information to be found in *Anak Desa* concerns the circumstances of Soeharto's separation from his mother. We discover that Soeharto was not entrusted to the care of his midwife at about the time of his second birthday, as stated in *The Smiling General*. Rather, this event occurred less than forty days after his birth, and the cause was not the separation of his parents (which occurred later) but his mother's inability to continue feeding him after undertaking a fast in the wake of a family quarrel.

> When Soeharto was not yet 40 days old, his mother wandered off on her own because of a family quarrel. This behaviour is called *"ngebleng"* in Javanese. Some time elapsed before she was found. She was alone in the central room of a *"rumah joglo"* [Javanese house] and initially there was not one person who suspected that she was there. She was found in an exhausted condition, her lack of strength being due to the fact that she had gone without food and drink for quite some time. She was not able to suckle her child in this state, and Soeharto was taken to the house of his great-aunt who had helped with his delivery.[44]

Although *ngebleng* is a normal Javanese ascetic practice that "consists of entering some enclosed space, usually the rice-storage area in the innermost part of the house, and remaining there for three days and nights without eating and as far as possible without sleeping,"[45] the fact that Ibu Sukirah undertook it while still feeding her infant raises questions regarding her mental stability and serves to underline still further the disrupted nature of Soeharto's early days.

SOEHARTO'S AUTOBIOGRAPHY

The eldest child of President Soeharto, Siti Hardijanti Rukmana, was at the center of Soeharto's autobiographical enterprise: her holding company, Citra Lamtoro Gung Persada—well known for its involvement in wood, pulp and paper, toll roads, trading, and telecommunications—printed and published the autobiography.[46] The funding, however, was provided by one of Soeharto's Sino-Indonesian cronies, Prajogo Pangestu, who by 1991 had "accumulated some 5.5 million hectares of forest concession areas, a tract of land slightly larger than Denmark."[47]

In the publisher's preface, she (or her ghostwriter) began by making an invidious allusion to Cindy Adams's foreign citizenship in the course of explaining the collaborative process as it prevailed in the case of her father's work: "The book which discusses the life story of President Soeharto was related by him to two *Indonesian* writers, G. Dwipayana and Ramadhan K. H."[48] Elsewhere we learn that this process began in February 1985 when Soeharto was sixty-three (a year older than Sukarno when he began his collaboration with Cindy Adams in 1963) and that it concluded in March 1988.[49] And we quickly gather from her subsequent remarks that these two writers—the former, an assistant minister in the state secretariat with responsibility for documentation and the mass media; the latter, a journalist and author—experienced a less intimate and less equal relationship with their subject than Cindy Adams enjoyed with hers: "Both writers were able to translate clearly the thoughts and expressions of President Soeharto into plain language thereby making the book accessible to the most lay of readers."[50] Dwipayana and Ramadhan had been assigned minor roles of translating Soeharto's words into plain Indonesian. Such relegation is less surprising where Dwipayana is concerned, for he was a longtime assistant of the president's; but the role is certainly noteworthy in the case of Ramadhan K. H., who has led a distinguished literary career as poet, novelist, and Indonesian translator of works by Garcia Lorca. Unlike Sukarno, who found comfort in his advanced years by imagining himself possessed by his beautiful young collaborator, Soeharto entertained no such reaching out, let alone fusion, in his autobiographical enterprise: old age has not disturbed his self-containment;[51] possibly, it has accentuated it, making him, as Vatikiotis suggests, "more imperious—as well as impervious."[52]

Rukmana was keen to portray her father as a man of humble birth whose early life was not marked by signs or portents of future greatness. Once again, we encounter a comparison with Sukarno calculated to sharply distinguish him from Soeharto:

> The young Soeharto was not the son of an aristocrat who had been prepared by his parents to become a national leader. He was also not a child whose birth was accompanied by signs of his future greatness. He was merely a village child who was born into the family of a poor peasant.[53]

Although the president's daughter wanted her father to reach a large Indonesian readership, her preoccupation was not to win understanding as it was Sukarno's, which he sought for himself and his people—the two seemed indivisible in his mind—from Cindy Adams and her American readers. Her preoccupation, rather, was to portray her father's life of struggle as an example to be held up for the educational benefit of the young generation of her country people:

What can be studied from this autobiography is how the child of a poor peasant was able to achieve the highest level of leadership in this country. And, all that was carried out with honesty, diligence and determination in facing life's challenges. May his attitude and actions, and his manner of leadership, become an example and model for Indonesians of the young generation, who will steer the ship of state in the future.

As a last word, I say enjoy your reading and may you draw appropriate lessons from this book.[54]

In Rukmana's and her father's expectation that readers should approach the autobiography in a mood of self-improvement, we see a self-satisfaction not confined to Soeharto alone but present in some other surviving members of the 1945 generation. Alien to them, especially to Soeharto, is the capacity for self-criticism, reflected in the remark of an exceptional member of this generation, Ali Sadikin, a retired marine general and former governor of Jakarta. He said, "Never mind the generation of 1945, they are all *brengsek* [rotten], I know because I'm one of them."[55]

SOEHARTO'S COMPOSURE

Mackie and MacIntyre said that President Soeharto "presents himself as calm, dignified, restrained, soft-spoken, almost avuncular." The implication of this remark is that calm, dignity, and the like are not traits that Soeharto assumed as a matter of course; rather, they are states of mind that, with some effort, he could plausibly imitate. This is a case not of calm but of its appearance or simulacrum, and as Adam Phillips points out in an insightful and apposite essay, a person who only appears calm can be better understood in terms of the attribute of composure.[56]

Phillips described composure as a "self-cure for the experience of traumatic excitement . . . a belated refusal [to feel that excitement]; it becomes, in fact, a superstition of confidence in the integrity of the self." Drawing in particular on the work of D. W. Winnicott, he added that composure is a form of self-holding undertaken when the mother's care becomes tantalizing and unpredictable. More specifically, this self-holding may take the form of using the mind "to make up for failures of mothering." "One mothers oneself, or rather, foster-mothers one's self, with one's mind," and putting the mind to such use, he argues, stimulates its precocious development. This foster-mothering of the self enables the person concerned to lay claim to an early independence, but it is only simulated and brittle and "by communicating a relative absence of neediness, renders the other dispensable." "Hell is not other people but one's need for other people."[57]

There is a consonance between President Soeharto's composure and the "emotional equanimity . . . [the] certain flatness of affect" that, Clifford Geertz claimed, is "the mark of the truly *alus* [refined Javanese] character."[58] Therefore, it is possible to view Soeharto's composure as a product of his culture and, in particular, the mystical strand within it, with its emphasis on the control of unruly emotions.[59] In this respect, he may be viewed as more Javanese than the Javanese. However, it may have also been the circumstances of his childhood, profoundly unstable even by the standards of the Javanese nuclear family with its high rate of divorce and widespread fostering of children, which, with the guidance of Prawirowihardjo and Daryatmo, led him fervently to embrace Javanese mysticism in the first place with its offer of culturally approved methods for gaining composure.[60]

At the press conference President Soeharto called on October 28, 1974, to respond to *POP* magazine's attribution to him of a royal genealogy, he stated that his childhood had been "full of suffering which possibly was not experienced by others." A review of its various circumstances suggests that he was not exaggerating. For example, when he was less than forty days old, the infant Soeharto was entrusted to the care of the midwife at his birth, Mbah Kromodiryo, who shared this responsibility with her daughter and her husband. The reason was attributed to the inability of his mother, Ibu Sukirah, to continue feeding him after undertaking a fast in the wake of a family quarrel. About four years later, Ibu Sukirah reclaimed him from Mbah Kromodiryo. Soeharto went to live with her and her second husband, Atmopawiro, but his life became immensely complicated by the arrival of seven offspring from this marriage (the eldest of whom, Sukiyem, died in her infancy) and the presence of numerous cousins (for his mother was one of nine siblings). Soeharto told how one of these cousins was favored by their great-grandmother in the matter of a new shirt; however, one suspects that the resentment he expressed toward her on this account was also directed at his mother for failing to defend his interests adequately in the context of the extended family.[61] Subsequently, Soeharto's father, Kertosudiro, who was apparently concerned about his son's education, took him from his mother's house and placed him with his sister's family, the Prawirowihardjos, about sixty kilometers away in Wuryantoro. According to Roeder, Soeharto, who was about nine years old at the time, was only allowed to say good-bye to the midwife and his teacher. A year later, during the fasting month, Atmopawiro arrived in Wuryantoro to take Soeharto back to his mother. His promise to return him by the end of Lebaran was not kept, and another year passed before his father and his aunt brought Soeharto back to Wuryantoro.

In view of this background—one that included a mother of questionable mental stability, to judge by her decision to fast while still feeding her infant; a largely absent father, whose intermittent interest in Soeharto's education led to an occasional, momentous intervention in his childhood affairs; an incomplete acceptance within the extended family; the death of his half sister, with the survival of another six half siblings perhaps being almost as disconcerting—it is not surprising that we should discover Soeharto at the age of twelve (and still living with the Prawirowihardjos) working on his composure:

> It was at that time that I became acquainted with the lesson of the three "*ajas*", "*aja kagetan, aja gumunan, aja dumeh*" (don't be startled, don't be overwhelmed by anything, don't feel superior), which later became a personal philosophy and a source of support in facing problems which were capable of shaking me up.[62]

Thereafter, the three don'ts became a mantra that Soeharto would invariably utter when his composure was threatened by a sudden change of events or a shocking development. For example, in recalling his part in putting down the coup attempt of September 30, 1965, he described his reaction to an early report that unidentified troops had taken up positions near the presidential palace. "I remembered what I had to do in situations like that. First of all I had to be calm. I remembered in an instant, as if it was a reflex action, the Javanese saying "*Aja kagetan, aja gumunan, aja dumeh*" [Don't be startled, don't be overwhelmed by anything, don't feel superior].[63]

This summoning of the appropriate instrument of thought at a difficult time can be seen as the president's second line of defense against a loss of composure. His first line was to think ahead, anticipate the disruptive event, and thereby avoid being startled by it, with his composure remaining intact and secure. He frequently informs us how such thinking ahead, anticipation, and advanced planning enabled him to remain composed in difficult circumstances, such as facing British military forces at Ambarawa at the outbreak of the Indonesian National Revolution or in dealing with the death of former president Sukarno in 1970.[64]

There is much to contemplate in this picture of Soeharto's thinking hard and thinking ahead to maintain his composure. Phillips's remarks prompt the question, Does this thinking amount to—or at least have its origins in—that form of self-holding that he regards as a reaction to unpredictable mothering and that he characterizes as foster-mothering oneself with one's mind? Certainly it is a drastic form of adaptation to substitute mind for mother, but the circumstances here were themselves drastic, causing Soeharto, one imagines, much confusion, bitterness, and despair; it is a form of adaptation that is consistent with all that we know of his childhood.

It also makes sense of his adult preoccupation with thinking, as reflected in the *Otobiografi*. For example, Soeharto takes considerable pride in his intelligence as, indeed, does his eldest child and publisher.[65] Rukmana informs the reader in her introduction that her father "always got the best marks in his class." In the body of the text, the president himself tells us of how the official in the village bank formed a high opinion of Soeharto's intelligence. The president was also happy to record that he was top of his training group in the Royal Netherlands Indies Army and the Keibuho (Japanese Police), even though these achievements may be seen as casting some doubt on his nationalist credentials.[66] He further mentioned that he entered the Indonesian army's Staff and Command College in Bandung in November 1959 and subsequently graduated at the top of his class.[67] Also, to judge from the following quote, the president greatly valued and actually cultivated, from the standpoint of Javanese mysticism, a particular way of working through a problem in the mind (finding the computer to be an appropriate metaphor for the mind).

> There are people who say that I wait on the whispers of the *dukun* (magic specialist) before I take a decision concerning the problems which I face. . . . In fact, my philosophy here is "*cipta, rasa, karsa*" ("thought, feeling, wish").[68] That is my philosophy of life . . . Of course, our individual responses to a particular matter vary . . . Because of that, if we view it from the point of view of the tactics and strategy of war, a military explanation on its own is something quite raw, and needs to be worked up into an intelligence report. And it is this report which amounts to something ripe, which can be relied on, and which can be used as a standard.
>
> And it is like that also with whatever we hear, see or feel. We must gather together all this material so that it can be processed, entered into our "*komputer*", into our "*cipta*". Then we allow it to settle in order to be felt. If we feel it to be right, if our "feeling" says it's right, then an intention will emerge as of its own accord. After that I put forward choices, and make a decision.
>
> That's how it works in theory, and everyone can do it. But, actually, practice is the most important thing.[69]

Having provided evidence of his intelligence and having explained his method of making decisions, Soeharto then portrayed himself as putting these attributes to good use. If Sukarno was pleased to think of himself as dominating opponents by the force of his personality, Soeharto immodestly recalls many episodes in which he outsmarted his.[70] Invariably taciturn, analyzing, thinking hard, as if playing a game of chess ("I wracked my brains searching for a way"), he solved the problem—whether it is how to disarm untrained revolutionary youth or by what means to restore civilian faith in the military after Dutch forces entered Yogyakarta without substantial opposition in December 1948.[71]

How much credence should we give to the president's claims concerning a superior intelligence and an ability to outsmart others? Without accepting them at face value—we will later see that one of them is exaggerated—it is still possible to accept in general terms his high estimation of himself as a thinker. In all probability, the vital maternal role that thinking played in maintaining Soeharto's composure had given rise to a precocious development in this area—as Phillips has led us to expect. Of course, successful politics requires more than hard thinking. But if we think of thinking as "an experimental, small-scale kind of acting—an essential element in 'reality-testing,'"[72] then it is possible to envisage how Soeharto's early efforts and precocious development in this area proved a great asset to him as a political leader.

Soeharto's childhood belief that he could not rely on his mother had a corollary: the only person he could rely on was himself. This conclusion did not underpin independence of mind, which accommodates a degree of mutual dependence. It established an emotional autarchy that denied dependence and neediness in himself and demanded deference of his friends and associates—recall Phillips's remark that hell is one's need for other people![73] It is this frame of mind that explains Soeharto's reluctance in the *Otobiografi* to give others their due for the achievements of the New Order.[74] It also explains why he is so quick to contradict the view that he was in any way dependent on his former supporter and crony Sudjono Humardani for guidance in the matter of Javanese mysticism.

> One hears people talk about Sudjono Humardani as if he knew more about Javanese mysticism than me. In point of fact, Djono himself usually deferred to me. He considered me more senior and more knowledgeable about mysticism. . . . Of course, it is true that Djono liked to bring me books of his writings. He had faith. And he liked to offer suggestions. I accepted his suggestions to please him. But I did not swallow them just like that. I considered whether they were rational or not. If they were rational, if they were reasonable, then I accepted them. If not, then I definitely did not make use of them.
>
> Therefore, those who think that Djono was my mysticism teacher will be disappointed. Such suppositions are not true. And Sudjono asked more questions of me about mysticism than the reverse. He himself once said, "I am a student of Pak Harto."[75]

Even someone as prominent, as highly esteemed, and indeed as entitled to deference by the Yogyanese Soeharto, as the sultan of Yogyakarta did not escape this process of relegation. However, it was not always like this. In charting the vicissitudes of this relationship, we find it possible to advance our understanding of Soeharto's way of dealing with other people. I have in mind here the president's changing view over the years concerning his own and the sultan's respective roles in the so-called General Attack of March 1, 1949.

According to *The Smiling General*, published in 1969 and 1970, Soeharto and the sultan enjoyed a close relationship across social barriers and shared responsibility and credit for this military success.

> There were long conferences between the scion of a noble family and the son of a peasant . . . Sri Sultan was the heart of the national resistance. Lieutenant Colonel Soeharto was his trusted field commander. . . .
>
> During one of the secret meetings between Sri Sultan Hamengku Buwono, who held the rank of a colonel in the Indonesian Army, and Lieutenant Colonel Soeharto, a bold decision was taken to launch a general attack on Jogjakarta and to hold the town "even if it was only for a few hours." The aim was to demonstrate to the world that the persistent Indonesian resistance had not vanished, as was being alleged by the Dutch representatives at the United Nations.[76]

Exactly the same account appears in *Anak Desa,* which appeared in 1976. At this time, from 1973 until 1978, the sultan was serving as Soeharto's vice president. However, in the wake of antigovernment protests by students in anticipation of the quinquennial meeting of the People's Consultative Assembly in March 1978, the sultan announced that, for reasons of health, he would not stand for reelection as vice president.[77] The president's few terse remarks on this topic in the *Otobiografi* suggest that he was deeply offended by the sultan's action.[78] When we turn to his latest account of the General Attack in the same volume, we discover that the sultan's agency in this event has been obliterated and that his own contribution has become all encompassing.[79]

As David Jenkins showed in his book *Suharto and his Generals*, a similar fate befell three prime ministers from Indonesia's period of quasi-democratic and democratic government, between 1945 and 1957, all of whom had the temerity in 1980 to sign a petition that criticized President Soeharto for unconstitutional behavior. Violating the custom of providing such office holders with a place of honor at the country's Independence Day celebrations, the president ordered them to be removed from the invitation list. This action provoked one of them, Mohammad Natsir, to comment: "After the Petisi 50 [Petition of 50] no one is invited to August 17 at the palace. . . . We don't exist any more."[80] The abiding impression one is left with after reviewing such material is just how dimly lit other people are on Soeharto's mental screen and how readily he extinguishes the light on those who violate his simulated independence.

Adding to the above observations is the view that Soeharto is a cold and secretive man, which should come as no surprise for such characteristics are consistent with the ones already enumerated. Nevertheless, there is considerable independent evidence that this is an accurate description of him. For example, according to Adam Schwarz, "those who meet him regularly find him hard to read and, more so since the mid-1980s, aloof. 'I find him kind of scary,' one cabinet minister told me, 'cold, hard eyes that look right through you.' "[81] Schwarz also stated that even the president's top aides were mystified regarding how policies were formulated.[82] We may also recall the observation of the senior politician quoted in the introduction who said, "No one knows what that man [Soeharto] thinks. . . . That is the secret of his power." Soeharto's coldness is also apparent in his choice of metaphors: a computer for the mind; and, one which is especially telling in view of his lifelong effort to anticipate and avoid shocks and surprises, "shock therapy" for the intended effect on Indonesia's gangland of the state-sponsored murder of suspected criminals and the display of their corpses in public places.[83] These murders took place between 1983 and 1985 and claimed over five thousand lives.[84] Of course, his coldness is also apparent in his very ability to formulate and implement such a drastic policy response to rising criminal activity.

CONCLUSION

I have been trying to build a case for viewing Soeharto as someone who has organized his personality around thinking, where thinking principally means thinking ahead in the service of his composure and is associated with a kind of emotional autarchy. In these respects I have sought to contrast him to the gregarious Sukarno. My evidence for these differences between the two presidents begins with the nature of the relationships that they established with their autobiographical collaborators. We see Sukarno possessing, and being possessed by, Cindy Adams, and we see Soeharto controlling Dwipayana and Ramadhan K. H. from a distance and keeping them in their place. I believe this argument contains a significant truth; nevertheless, it must be incomplete, for it does not adequately prepare us for the fact that it is the outgoing Sukarno who retreats into the autistic world of omnipotent fantasy ("I'm constantly trying to remake circumstances so they can be vehicles to reach what I'm pursuing," he told Adams) and that it is the aloof Soeharto who in striving to anticipate the emergence of threats to his composure reveals a vested interest, as it were, in engaging with the world realistically.

NOTES

1. Mackie and MacIntyre, "Politics," 45.
2. Adams, *Sukarno: An Autobiography.*

3. *My Friend the Dictator* is the title of the American edition. It was subsequently republished as *Sukarno My Friend*.

4. Adams, *Sukarno My Friend*, 11, 14, 33. In fact, as noted in chapters 2 and 3, the title of "President for Life" was bestowed on Sukarno in 1963 by the Interim People's Consultative Assembly.

5. Adams, *Sukarno My Friend*, 15.

6. Adams, *Sukarno My Friend*, 16.

7. Adams, *Sukarno My Friend*, 79–82, 87–89.

8. Adams, *Sukarno: An Autobiography*, 16. See also, Adams, *Sukarno My Friend*, 184.

9. Adams, *Sukarno: An Autobiography*, 17, 19.

10. Adams, *Sukarno My Friend*, 206–7, 224–25.

11. Adams, *Sukarno My Friend*, 254.

12. Adams, *Sukarno My Friend*, 255. Having appreciated the significance of this statement, the author gives it a certain prominence by placing it near the beginning of the autobiography (Adams, *Sukarno: An Autobiography*, 2).

13. Adams, *Sukarno My Friend*, 265.

14. Adams, *Sukarno My Friend*, 265.

15. Adams, *Sukarno My Friend*, 277–78, 273–74.

16. See Lejeune, *On Autobiography*, 190–91.

17. Sukarno, "Amanat PJM Presiden Sukarno Kepada Ikatan Penerbit Indonesia (IKAPI) di Istana Bogor, 26 Pebruari 1966," 3.

18. Sukarno, "Amanat PJM Presiden Sukarno Kepada Ikatan Penerbit Indonesia (IKAPI)," 6.

19. Shakespeare, *King Lear*, 1.4.163–64.

20. Roeder, *Smiling General*, 279. An Indonesian translation of this book appears under the title *Soeharto: Dari Prajurit sampai Presiden*.

21. Roeder, *Smiling General*, 280.

22. My description of Daryatmo is based on the fact that he was both a *kiyayi*, or Islamic religious teacher, and a *dukun*, or, in Ward Keeler's words, "a magic specialist to whom people turn for cures, advice, and other mystical assistance" (*Javanese Shadow Plays*, 269).

23. Roeder, *Smiling General*, 79–93. The quotes may be found on 83 and 93.

24. This was Colonel Aloysius Sugianto, the chief of staff of Special Operations (*Operasi Chusus,* or, as it is usually known, *Opsus*). It was originally created by Ali Murtopo as a combat intelligence unit attached to the army's Strategic Reserve but subsequently evolved "into a body notorious for political manipulation under the Suharto Government" (McDonald, *Suharto's Indonesia,* 35–36). Sugianto himself was "an elegant moustachioed former Special Forces (RPKAD Regiment) officer who held side-interests in publishing and film-making" (198).

25. Quoted in "Disekitar 'Silsilah POP' itu," *Tempo*, November 9, 1974, 45–46. See also McDonald, *Suharto's Indonesia*, 9, 141, 198.

26. McDonald, *Suharto's Indonesia*, 9.

27. See McDonald, *Suharto's Indonesia*, 141.

28. "Disekitar 'Silsilah POP' itu," 46.

29. "Disekitar 'Silsilah POP' itu," 45.
30. "Disekitar 'Silsilah POP' itu," 46.
31. "Disekitar 'Silsilah POP' itu," 46.
32. I am indebted to the late Herb Feith for these points.
33. Quoted in Roeder, *Anak Desa,* 142.
34. Notosudiro, Soeharto's great-grandfather on his mother's side, was a descendent, five generations removed, of a prince who was a son of Hamengku Buwono V by his first concubine. See "Disekitar 'Silsilah POP' itu," 47.
35. Roeder, *Anak Desa,* 140, 142–43.
36. See McDonald, *Suharto's Indonesia,* 23n10.
37. Roeder, *Anak Desa,* 130–31; Soeharto, *Otobiografi,* 6.
38. Roeder, *Anak Desa,* 129–30, 162, 374; McDonald, *Suharto's Indonesia,* 10.
39. Roeder, *Anak Desa,* 133–34.
40. Soeharto, *Otobiografi,* 8.
41. Roeder, *Anak Desa,* 134–35.
42. Roeder, *Anak Desa,* 162. Soeharto's *Otobiografi* talks of "Atmopawiro, together with his elder brother, Sumowijatmo and his brother-in-law, Sastroharjono" (12). I assume that there is a mistake here in the choice of personal pronoun and that it should read, "Atmopawiro, together with my [i.e., Soeharto's] elder brother, Sumowijatmo and my brother-in-law, Sastroharjono."
43. Roeder, *Anak Desa,* 162–63.
44. Roeder, *Anak Desa,* 133.
45. Keeler, *Javanese Shadow Plays,* 42.
46. Adam Schwarz, "All Is Relative," *Far Eastern Economic Review,* April 30, 1992, 57.
47. Schwarz, *Nation in Waiting,* 141.
48. Soeharto, *Otobiografi,* ix; emphasis added.
49. Soeharto, *Otobiografi,* xiv.
50. Soeharto, *Otobiografi,* ix; see also, 586–87.
51. See Lejeune, *Autobiography,* 185. The biographical details about K. H. Ramadhan come from the cover of his historical novel about Sukarno, entitled *Kuantar Ke Gerbang: Kisah Cinta Ibu Inggit Dengan Bung Karno.*
52. Vatikiotis, *Indonesian Politics under Soharto,* 150–51.
53. Soeharto, *Otobiografi,* ix–x.
54. Soeharto, *Otobiografi,* xii.
55. Quoted in Jenkins, *Suharto and His Generals,* 170.
56. Phillips, "On Composure," in his *On Kissing, Tickling, and Being Bored,* 40–45.
57. Phillips, "On Composure," 40–45.
58. Geertz, *Religion of Java,* 240.
59. Geertz, *Religion of Java,* 241.
60. See Mulder, *Mysticism and Everyday Life,* 62–63. Compare McDonald, *Suharto's Indonesia,* 9–10: "Even by Javanese standards, which accommodate a high rate of divorce and remarriage and the frequent fosterage of children by relatives, Suharto's early life was a remarkably disturbed one, full of family disruption, and to-ing and fro-ing across the boundary of peasant and official classes."

61. Soeharto recalls this event as follows (*Otobiografi*, 9–10): "One day I was playing with Mas Darsono in front of the house of mBah Buyut Notosudiro, my mother's grandfather. At that time great-grandmother was sewing a shirt. Then I heard her calling me. I half leapt up, happy to be called by her. She kept on calling me. 'Come here,' she said. Then I was ordered to try on the shirt she had made. I put it on cheerfully. But then my great-grandmother said: 'Oh, it's you Harto.' Call over your cousin, Darsono. I ran to carry out her instruction. And when Mas Darsono stood in front of her, he was ordered to try on the shirt which I was wearing. I took it off. Apparently that shirt was big enough for him. Moreover, Mas Darsono was ordered to keep wearing that shirt. That proved that it was indeed for him. At that time I did not wear a shirt. Only trousers. My heart whispered, 'Oh, great-grandmother likes my Aunt's son, Mas Darsono, more than me.' Mas Darsono was, in fact, the son of a rich person, the son of my mother's older sister. Mas Darsono's parents were better off than my parents. But how come the one who was given that shirt was the great-grandchild who already had one. I felt humiliated. I felt sorry for myself, and very sad. At that time I felt 'Oh, why is life like this?' I thought, we are both her great-grandchildren but we are treated differently. Mas Darsono already has a shirt whereas I don't. Why was I not made one and Mas Darsono was?"

62. Soeharto, *Otobiografi*, 13. For the difficulty that *aja dumeh* poses for the translator, see the comments of Anderson, "Cartoons and Monuments," 315n36.

63. Soeharto, *Otobiografi*, 119.

64. Soeharto, *Otobiografi*, 33, 245.

65. B. J. Habibie, who served in Soeharto's cabinets between 1978 and 1998, has supported Rukmana's view on this matter with his own comment that "Soeharto is a wise leader." "'Low profile,' very modest. He clearly has a high IQ, and his memory is strong. As long as I have been connected to him, I have enriched myself by obtaining lessons from him about the philosophy and culture of the Javanese, his attitude to leadership, nationalism, integralism, and the like. Pak Harto also teaches me about Islam. Not many know that Pak Harto can read and write in Arabic script. For more than 19 years I have received an intensive course of study from 'Professor' Soeharto. If I had made use of it at university, I would have got a doctorate three times over" ("Saya tak Sebodoh yang Dikira Orang," *Tempo*, October 10, 1992, 25–26).

66. See Anderson, "Old State, New Society," 487.

67. Soeharto, *Otobiografi*, x, 17, 20, 22, 94. The army's Staff and Command College provided a broad education for its students to prepare them for military and social responsibilities. Military subjects formed only half the curriculum. The other half consisted of courses in economics, law, political science, sociology, and philosophy, which were taught by visiting professors from various Indonesian universities. These people provided Soeharto with his first systematic knowledge in these areas, and when he became president, he appointed his former economics teachers as advisers and ministers (Sadli, "Recollections of My Career," 39).

68. Paul Stange defines *rasa* as follows: "In Indonesian the word 'rasa' means 'feeling', both in the physical and emotional sense; in the more spiritually resonant

Javanese it also means 'intuitive feeling'. Rasa is at once the substance, vibration, or quality of what is apprehended and the tool or organ which apprehends it" ("Logic of Rasa in Java," 119).

69. Soeharto, *Otobiografi*, 234–35. President Soeharto's reference to an intelligence report in the midst of this account of his thinking processes is suggestive. The prominence of intelligence agencies under Suharto's New Order regime has been explained by Richard Tanter as follows: "Just as the dominance of the military within the state yields the familiar Third World militarized state, so the particular character of the militarized state in Indonesia derives from that stream of the military which is dominant—in this case, the intelligence stream" ("Totalitarian Ambition," 214). Can this dominance of the intelligence stream within the Indonesian military be explained in terms of a predilection on Soeharto's part? One may readily suppose that his concern with thinking ahead to anticipate and, if possible, avoid shocks would incline him to give surveillance a prominent role in his government. I am indebted to Richard Tanter, who has discussed these matters with me.

70. Adams, *Sukarno: An Autobiography*, 27–28.

71. Soeharto, *Otobiografi*, 28–30, 50, 58, 106.

72. Editor's footnote to Sigmund Freud, lecture 32 of the "New Introductory Lectures on Psycho-Analysis," entitled "Anxiety and Instinctual Life," in *The Standard Edition of the Complete Psychological Works of Sigmund Freud*, ed. James Strachey, 24 vols. (London: Hogarth Press / Institute of Psycho-Analysis, 1973), 22:89n1.

73. General Benny Moerdani's close relationship with the president appears to have been based on his stance of filial deference, to judge by one of David Jenkins's informants, who states, "Even Benny says his relationship with the president is like that of father and son" (Jenkins, *Suharto and his Generals*, 20n16). The relationship came to an end, it seems, when Moerdani presumed to criticize the business dealings of Soeharto's children. A similar filial responsiveness on the part of B. J. Habibie produces a delighted response from the president in the *Otobiografi*: "He considers me as his own parent. It is very apparent that he does not want to do wrong. He always asks for my guidance. And he jots down the points of philosophy I offer him" (457). Habibie looked on Soeharto as a kind of stepfather since the death of his own father in 1950, when he was thirteen. For Habibie's own account of this event, see "Mister Crack dari Pare-Pare," *Tempo*, October 10, 1992, 28.

74. Soeharto's emotional autarchy lies behind the depleted feeling engendered in me by simply reading the *Otobiografi*. This feeling of depletion seems not inconsistent with the responses of Indonesian readers, as reported by various commentators. For example, Barry Wain stated, "Some of the intellectuals who have worked with Mr. Suharto during his term in office are upset and angry over the exaggerated role he ascribes to himself" ("Suharto: Slowly Losing Touch with Indonesia," *Asian Wall Street Journal*, April 5, 1989). And Peter Hastings reported, "At dinner parties and social gatherings, Jakarta's elite, including formerly close Cabinet colleagues and some senior serving generals, now criticise . . . [Soeharto] openly, if politely, as being too old, too arrogant, too out of touch as evidenced by his narcissistic autobiography" ("Soldiers Hold the Key to Soeharto's Future," *Sydney Morning Herald*, July 5, 1989).

75. Soeharto, *Otobiografi*, 441–42. Compare Graham Little's remarks concerning Sir Francis Bacon's essay "On Followers and Friends," in *Friendship: Being Ourselves with Others,* 20, 23.

76. Roeder, *Smiling General*, 120.

77. Bresnan, *Managing Indonesia,* 201; Jenkins, *Suharto and His Generals*, 84n63. Bresnan explained the Sultan's misgivings about Soeharto as follows: "An aide said later that a chief source of the Sultan's disenchantment was his constantly encountering a lineup of Chinese businessmen outside the president's office when he went there to pay a call. As the 1978 election to the presidency and vice presidency neared, the Sultan also found himself increasingly hemmed in. One morning, when he was expecting to receive a delegation of students, he woke to find that his personal security guard had been changed without notice. The new officer of the guard informed him that the student visit had been cancelled. That was the moment, the aide said, when the Sultan realized the time had come to bow out" (201).

78. Soeharto, *Otobiografi*, 332, 372.

79. Soeharto, *Otobiografi*, 58–64. Soeharto first put forward his revised view of the General Attack on November 1, 1985. The Sultan gave his version of events (which does not differ substantially from Roeder's) in an interview with the BBC on November 23, 1985. See A. H. Nasution, *Memenuhi Panggilan Tugas*, 2A:323–27.

80. Jenkins, *Suharto and his Generals*, 184–85.

81. Schwarz, *Nation in Waiting*, 44.

82. Schwarz, *Nation in Waiting*, 85.

83. Soeharto, *Otobiografi*, 390; Bourchier, "Crime, Law and State Authority," 177.

84. Bourchier, "Crime, Law and State Authority," 177.

Part III

8

Megawati and the Emergence of Constitutional Rule

The modest levels of prosperity among the Indonesian population in the late New Order period and the absence of a robust middle class deriving its energy from an independent business strata did not augur well for the emergence of a durable democracy in Indonesia.[1] Furthermore, the antidemocratic and antiliberal propaganda that the New Order directed against the citizenry—which was already fearful of the regime—did not favor the appearance of popular government. Finally, the merging of regime and state under Soeharto undermined the integrity of the state, reducing the prospects in the post-Soeharto era for effective government, let alone effective democratic government.[2]

Nevertheless, a measure of constitutional rule did emerge in the post-Soeharto period from these broadly inauspicious conditions. An explanation of this phenomenon lies partly in the severe economic downturn of 1997 and in the student and middle-class mobilization of 1998 to which it gave rise.[3] However, if the sudden emergence of an economic crisis contributed to the advent of a rudimentary democracy at that time, then the failure of Indonesia to return to strong economic growth placed a heavy burden on its democracy and cast doubt on its long-term prospects. (Its economy has been growing at 3.5–4.5 percent per annum since 2000, whereas 6 percent is needed to absorb the 2.0–2.5 million persons who enter the labor market each year.)[4] Another part of the explanation lies in the readiness to hand of that chameleon-like document, the 1945 constitution, and the preparedness of President Habibie to breathe democratic life into it by specifying that the method of selection of the DPR and MPR would be by free elections.

There is one as yet unremarked aspect of this constitution that contributed to the emergence of constitutional rule after Soeharto's forced resignation.

This is article 8, which provides for a vice president to succeed the president "in the event of the President's death, resignation, removal from office or inability to exercise his duties during the term of his office."[5] As detailed in chapter 1, Hatta resigned from the vice presidency in December 1956. In the following Guided Democracy years, Sukarno made no attempt to replace him, and (as noted in chapter 3) this failure aggravated the succession crisis of 1965–1966. Soeharto was more punctilious in this regard: from 1973 until 1998, the MPR chose a president and a vice president at its quinquennial sessions, and at its 1973 session it even provided for a succession mechanism "in the event of the incapacity of both president and vice-president to perform his duties."[6] However, after experiencing difficulties with his first two deputies—the independent minded sultan of Yogyakarta (1973–1978) and Adam Malik (1978–1983)—Soeharto ensured that their successors would be beholden to him. Indeed, when a besieged Soeharto came to select his last vice president, at the beginning of 1998, in anticipation of the MPR session scheduled for March, it seems that he chose B. J. Habibie on the calculation that the prospect of his becoming president would reconcile the opposition to Soeharto's continued rule.[7] Nevertheless, he did at least ensure that there was a vice president, and so Habibie was there to succeed him constitutionally when he stepped down on May 21.[8]

TOWARD CONSTITUTIONAL RULE

To become president was one thing; to remain so in an atmosphere hostile to the regime in which he had been a minister for twenty years was another altogether. Habibie immediately realized that he would have to discard the methods of his predecessor and mentor; indeed, he could not have failed to notice what Liddle has also pointed out: that Soeharto's manipulation of the electoral process, like his empty constitutionalism, served only to discredit him while creating a longing in the populace for the real thing.[9] Consequently, Habibie resolved to close the 1945 constitution's infamous loophole by immediately offering free and fair elections as the method of selecting members of the DPR and MPR. According to Liddle, Habibie "promised to implement a . . . process that was procedurally within the frame of the 1945 Constitution, and thus familiar to all elite players, but substantively new in that it would be genuinely instead of cosmetically democratic."[10] Accordingly, they and most of the advocates of reform accepted this offer and began preparing for elections.[11]

By early February 1999, Habibie had attached his signature to three laws: one on political parties; one on elections for national, provincial, *kabupaten,* and *kotamadya* parliaments; and one on the composition of these various legislatures. In the case of the national parliament, or People's Representative Council (Dewan Perwakilan Rakyat; DPR) and the People's Consultative Assembly (Majelis Permusyawaratan Rakyat; MPR), the law provided for the free election of 462 members of a 500-member DPR, in which the remaining 38 seats would be occupied by appointed military members. These 500 members of parliament would then join 135 regional delegates and 65 group members to constitute the MPR.

If free elections were the first priority of the government's legislative program, then local autonomy was the second. No sooner had Habibie signed off on the these laws than did the parliament pass legislation introduced by the government in the form of laws 22 and 25 of 1999, which provided for what has been described as the "one of the most radical decentralisation programs attempted anywhere in the world."[12] These laws embodied the aspirations of the long-abandoned law 1/1957 by providing for the further democratization of government in the province, *kabupaten*, and municipality, as well as for bestowing substantial autonomy and corresponding fiscal powers on *kabupatens* and municipalities. Law 22 also overruled the New Order regime's undemocratic village government law (law 5/1979)—it had attempted "the transformation of local government into an arm of the central bureaucracy"[13]—by providing for an elected Village Representative Board of between five and thirteen members to whom the village head would be accountable.[14]

The elections themselves were held on June 7, 1999, and the first MPR to consist of freely and directly elected members (albeit only 462 from a total membership of 700) convened in October 1999 to consider Habibie's accounting for his period in office and to elect a president. On October 14, Habibie read his so-called accountability speech before the assembly, which, after several days of deliberation, rejected it by a narrow margin. Habibie then believed he had no choice but to withdraw from the presidential race, which he did in the early hours of October 20. On the same day, the assembly elected Abdurrahman Wahid and Megawati Sukarnoputri president and vice president, respectively.

Failing to see how the ground had shifted since the fall of Soeharto and, in particular, since the holding of the elections, the new president treated the new DPR with contempt, slandering and even sacking cabinet ministers from political parties that were enjoying strong parliamentary support. The parliament reacted by asserting its long-dormant interpellation right, questioning the president over his behavior. Abdurrahman responded in words that did not fully encompass the complexity of the situation: "This is a presidential system of Government. . . . The President is not accountable to the House. The President will give his account at the end of his term to the People's Consultative Assembly."[15] The president may not be responsible to the DPR, but the body does have an oversight role and, under the 1945 constitution as it stood then, was able to call the MPR into a special session to seek an accounting from the president when under suspicion of having violated state policy. This was precisely what happened the following year (details in chapter 12) and was immediately followed by the MPR's dismissal of the president, an action that lay within its power.[16]

Thus, Abdurrahman was dismissed, with Megawati installed in his place on July 23, 2001, by actions in keeping with the 1945 constitution. What a difference free elections had made. By breathing life into the DPR and MPR, the two bodies had transformed a strong presidential system into a weak one; or, they changed a presidential system with parliamentary characteristics into one in which the parliamentary characteristics were more evident.

Finally, we may conclude that once the stipulation had been made that elections were to be the method of selecting DPR and MPR members, then the 1945 constitution—that former accomplice of personal, presidential rule—proved capable of ushering its opposite into being: constitutional, presidential rule. Liddle viewed this development as "an extraordinary irony of history, a striking instance of the way in which authoritarian institutions and ideologies can be turned against politicians who have spent decades fashioning them as instruments of autocratic power."[17]

AMENDMENTS TO THE 1945 CONSTITUTION

The ability of the 1945 constitution to underpin constitutional rule did not mean that it was satisfactory in all respects. Consequently, in 1999, reform-minded members of the MPR turned their minds to amending it that it might better serve Indonesia's emerging democratic order. That these reformers thought only of revising the 1945 constitution—and not, say, resuming the substantial work of the Konstituante or reintroducing the 1950 constitution—was perhaps a sign of the Sukarno and Soeharto regimes' effectiveness in maligning parliamentary government over a forty-year period.[18] It also appears to be a sign of how deeply the 1945 constitution had lodged itself in the minds of Indonesians—"more honour'd in the breach than the observance" but honored nevertheless. Whatever the precise explanation, these reformers undertook their task with energy and care. Indeed, if free elections enhanced the authority of the DPR and MPR at the expense of the presidency, then the first two amendments to the constitution, undertaken by MPR members in 1999 and 2000, reinforced this shift in the institutions' relative standing. On October 19, 1999, the general session of the MPR passed the first amendment to the 1945 constitution. It limited the previously unrestricted number of presidential terms to two; it obliged the chief executive to heed the opinions of the People's Representative Council (in such matters as the appointment of ambassadors) and the Supreme Court (in matters of clemency and the like); and, at the expense of the president, it gave the DPR a stronger role in the legislative process.[19]

The same general session instructed the working body of the MPR to continue the process of constitutional review, which it subsequently did by setting up Ad Hoc Committee 1 (Panitia Ad Hoc I) for this purpose. Furthermore, the MPR decided to institute annual sessions at which it could consider further constitutional amendments and pass decrees and to which the president would be required to present reports, in addition to the accountability speech at the end of the presidential term. Ad Hoc Committee 1 then reviewed the constitution in detail and made proposals for further amendments, to be considered by the first annual session of the MPR. This took place in August 2000, and approximately one-third of these proposed amendments were adopted by the annual session as the second amendment.[20]

Much has been made about the failure of the 1945 constitution to require the election of DPR and MPR members and of its adverse consequences for Indonesian politics. Attention has also been given to the 1999 laws on parties, elections, and the composition of the DPR and MPR and on the transforming effect that their enactment had on relations between the president and the DPR and MPR. It is therefore significant that the second amendment, which was approved by the MPR on August 18, 2000, gave constitutional force to the requirement that members of the national parliament and regional parliaments—whether at the provincial, regency, or municipal level—be chosen via general elections. In addition to making a reversion to past practices less likely, this change effectively ended the appointment of military and police representatives to these bodies. However, this particular democratic gain was substantially compromised by MPR decree 7/2000, which permitted the police and military forces to maintain their representation in the assembly until 2009.[21]

Furthermore, the second amendment wrote into the constitution the general principles and core details of laws 22/1999 and 25/1999. These two laws, as noted, had their antecedent in law 1/1957 and were designed "to democratise the local government, and to devolve certain powers" as well as "support that shift of power to the local government by providing more fiscal resources."[22] They had been passed by the parliament in April 1999 in response to the government's dawning realization that the Sukarno and Soeharto regimes' centralized approach to regional government was counterproductive.[23]

The second amendment strengthened still further the DPR's "legislative function" and enhanced its "oversight function" (to quote this amendment's wording) by giving "constitutional force" to the DPR's "powers of interpellation . . . and investigation . . . into government activities."[24] It likewise greatly expanded and strengthened article 28—which was originally drafted by Hatta, then revised and weakened by Supomo—by substantially drawing on the United Nations Universal Declaration of Human Rights of 1948.[25]

As Lindsey and Ellis have noted, Indonesian human rights activists hold the Universal Declaration of Human Rights in the highest esteem, but they were dismayed the incorporation of one of its articles into the Indonesian constitution. Article 11(2) of the declaration, which proclaims "the right not to be tried under a law with a retrospective effect," was incorporated into article 28I of the Indonesian constitution, which asserts "the right not to be prosecuted under retrospective laws" as a basic human right "that may not be interfered with under any circumstances at all." In essence, this right would provide members of the armed forces found guilty of human rights abuses under law 26/2000 on human rights courts with solid grounds for appeal, as well as make the process of bringing the military under civilian control that much more difficult. However, this amendment contributed to civilian control in other respects: it confirmed and provided a formal rationale for President Habibie's separation of the police from the military (Tentara Nasional Indonesia) in 1999 by making a "distinction between external defence, as the responsibility of Tentara Nasional Indonesia, and internal security, law enforcement and maintenance of public order, as the responsibility of . . . [the police]."[26] It also assigned the ordering and regulation of this new arrangement to the parliament.[27]

The fact that a number of proposals from Ad Hoc Committee 1 were not included in the second amendment was testimony to their fundamental and controversial nature. Indeed, these proposals suggested a basic change in the manner in which the sovereignty of the people would be expressed in the constitution. They were eventually considered by the MPR at its annual session, convened in November 2001, when, in an extraordinary act of self-denial, it produced the third amendment, which declared that the sovereignty of the people, rather than be exercised by itself, would be implemented by the constitution.[28] Accordingly, the MPR lost its previous authority to lay down the broad outlines of state policy (*garis besar haluan negara*). Furthermore, its indirectly elected regional representatives were rendered redundant by the creation of a new, directly elected Council of Regional Representation (Dewan Perwakilan Daerah). In the absence of the MPR in its previous role as the body that elects the president and the vice president, the amendment provided for the direct election of these two officeholders. They would be placed on joint tickets put forward by political parties or coalitions of political parties in which the winning pair would obtain over 50 percent of the total votes cast and would garner at least 20 percent of the vote in more than half the total number of provinces. Finally, it sought to underpin judicial authority and a degree of independence by requiring the establishment of an independent Judicial Commission and a Constitutional Court with the power to review legislation. In this new, constitutional environment, the functions of the MPR were confined to amending the constitution (in response to a proposal by one-third of its members), swearing in the elected president and vice president and dismissing one or the other or both on the basis of a proposal from the People's Representative Council. The council could propose the impeachment of the president for various misdeeds—but no longer on policy grounds—in those cases where the Constitutional Court decided a solid case existed for such action.[29]

The loose ends to this far-reaching amendment—in particular, the composition of the MPR and the nature of the second-round election for president and vice president—were tidied up with the passage of the fourth amendment at the third annual session of the MPR, in August 2002. It declared the MPR to consist of "members of the People's Representative Council and members of the Council of Regional Representation who have been chosen via a general election,"[30] thereby effectively excluding group and military representatives from this bicameral body from the 2004 general elections, despite the previous reprieve until 2009, which was granted to military members. On the matter of the second-round presidential election, it was decided that if no one pair of candidates for the position of president and vice president achieved the thresholds stipulated in the third amendment, then there would be a second-round, or runoff, election between the top two pairs of candidates.[31]

In light of its exclusion of military members from both houses of the MPR, it is not surprising that the fourth amendment was viewed with particular misgivings by military leaders. Two days before the opening of the MPR session at which it was to be considered, General Endriartono Sutarto, the commander of the armed forces, went so far as to assert to that the Indonesian military would support Megawati if she emulated her father by reintroducing the original 1945 constitution by decree. However, she ignored this request and did not oppose her party members' voting for this amendment, thereby ensuring its smooth passage through the MPR, despite military objections.[32]

But there remained one issue for the MPR to deal with at this session: the Jakarta Charter. It will be recalled that this document contained the stipulation that the state of Indonesia would be based on "Belief in the One Supreme God with the obligation for adherents of Islam to carry out *Shariah* (the Islamic law)." The charter was adopted as the draft preamble to the constitution on June 22, 1945, but then replaced on August 18 by another preamble, identical in all respects save that the words "with the obligation for adherents of Islam to carry out *Shariah* (the Islamic law)" were absent. Also, these very same words were removed from article 29, leaving it to declare simply that "the state is based on belief in the One Almighty God." Moslem political leaders in the Konstituante had tried to retrieve the situation in 1959 when they made their acceptance of the reintroduction of the 1945 constitution by President Sukarno conditional on the inclusion of the Jakarta Charter. As we know, Sukarno rejected this arrangement and enacted the constitution by decree. There the matter sat until Soeharto's resignation in May 1998 raised hopes among the devout that their religion would finally achieve constitutional recognition. Accordingly, in 2000, a fresh proposal to include the Jakarta Charter in the 1945 constitution was listed for consideration by the relevant committee of the MPR, Ad Hoc Committee 1. This did not take the form of returning the crucial words to the preamble—MPR members had already agreed that the preamble should not be touched—but rather to returning them to article 29, from which they had also been deleted in 1945.[33]

This suggested constitutional change did not enjoy unanimous support within the Islamic community. Its advocates came from Islamic political parties and individuals of an essentially modernist orientation, including Megawati's vice president, Hamzah Haz; but they were opposed by the equally modernist Islamic educational organization Muhammadiyah, as well as by the traditionalist Nahdlatul Ulama, both of whom saw the attempt to introduce the change as likely to exacerbate the already strained relations between the various religions in Indonesia.[34] Once it became evident to the supporters that the proposed amendment would not be accepted—they could only claim 100 votes from a total MPR membership of 695—they withdrew it.[35] And owing to a subsequent constitutional amendment, future attempts to have this proposal considered by the MPR will require the support of at least one-third of its members.[36]

The four amendments of 1999–2002 have substantially moved the 1945 constitution in a democratic direction. However, they have not stipulated a full presidential democracy in that the grant of independence to the judiciary is qualified, as provided in the third amendment. As Lindsey has argued in his interpretation of the relevant clauses of this amendment, "the judicial power is not actually vested in the highest court, but reserved to the legislature for allocation by statute." Yet, as he also points out, the amending body's provision of this qualified independence to the courts does not signify an adverseness to the doctrine of the separation of powers; rather, it points to well-founded misgivings on the part of legislators in the competence of the Supreme Court.[37]

Shortcomings notwithstanding, the passage of these amendments amounts to a considerable achievement; nevertheless, it is also possible that MPR members, still living in thrall to Sukarno's and Soeharto's attack on parliamentary democracy, made light of the more problematic characteristics peculiar to presidentialism.[38] In the conclusion, I consider these characteristics and speculate on their likely affect on Indonesia's emerging constitutional order.

MEGAWATI: RELUCTANT CONSTITUTIONALIST

The move in the direction of constitutionalism in Indonesia is remarkable when considered against the unpromising economic, social, and political circumstances that existed at the end of the New Order period. Part of the explanation for this disparity lies in the role of individuals—in particular, the readiness of Habibie on becoming president to offer free elections within the framework of the 1945 constitution. Of course, Habibie had no history of commitment to democracy, but was he not a Gorbachev-like figure who, realizing that the old way of doing things simply did not work, resolved to change it?[39] There is some truth in this observation, yet it is also true, in light of the sudden upsurge in middle class and student activism, that if he had not brought on some degree of democracy, he would in all probability have been driven from power. In this latter respect, the more appropriate comparison would be to Egon Krenz, reforming with his back to the wall. The final portrait is not altogether flattering, but the fact remains that Habibie, by bringing on democratic politics within the framework of the 1945 constitution, contributed more substantially to the emerging constitutional order than the other Indonesian leaders of that time and place. Another way of appreciating the significance of Habibie's contribution to Indonesia's rudimentary constitutional order is to try to imagine what things would have been like without him. Suppose Soeharto had overlooked Habibie and called on the incumbent vice president, retired general Try Sutrisno, to serve a second term. Would he, too, have embraced democratic reform as a way of staying in power or, more likely, attempted to resist it at every turn?

It is a further irony of Indonesian history that this task should fall to a loyal protégé of Soeharto and the longest standing minister in the cabinets of the Old Order, whereas Megawati, who contributed to the erosion of the president's legitimacy by making a brave and sometimes lonely stance against him and, for that matter, Habibie, had no direct hand in the most significant achievements of the post-Soeharto period: the substantial decentralization of government to the district and municipal level, in keeping with laws 22 and 25 of 1999; the parliamentary and presidential elections of the same year; and the fundamental revision of the 1945 constitution between 1999 and 2002. She was a beneficiary, rather than a creator, of the new system of constitutional rule: her political party won a plurality of votes in the 1999 parliamentary elections, and she was elected vice president in 1999 and president in 2001. Her own political style, although populist, reflected a certain distrust of and condescension toward the people at large. Also, her anxiety to preserve what she saw as her father's principal legacies—the unitary state and the 1945 constitution—made her willing to resort to military force to deal with separatist movements and to query the value of the constitutional amendment process, even though she did not in the end oppose it. Finally, she appeared uneasy with the degree of freedom and outspokenness that existed in the new governmental arrangements; nevertheless, she continued to act within the terms of the constitution, and it may be that her accommodating attitude to the army enabled it to adjust to constitutionalism rather than seek to defy it. In attempting to pull together the threads of this account, we might describe Megawati since the fall of Soeharto as a reluctant constitutionalist.

How Megawati became like this is, of course, a complex issue that will preoccupy us in the chapters to follow as we consider the influence that her father and President Soeharto had on her. As a prelude to the argument, we can say that her authoritarian populism and her anxiety to preserve the unitary state and safeguard the 1945 constitution appear to have roots in her past and in her personality, as shaped by her interaction with her father. However, her qualified commitment to the rule of law seems to have sprung from her experience as a victim of the arbitrary actions of the Soeharto regime, especially in 1996 and 1997. If this aspect of her political behavior was shaped by opposition to Soeharto, other aspects seemed to derive from a New Order way of looking at the world. Wariness toward the people has been a constant of Indonesian politics since 1945, but it was under Soeharto's rule that wariness calcified into suspicion and even fear; and it is even possible that Megawati was influenced by this climate of opinion, especially as she and her family were beneficiaries of the regime in a material sense, notwithstanding her father's fate and Soeharto's later hostility to her.

NOTES

1. Crouch, "Democratic Prospects in Indonesia," 94–99.
2. See Elson, *Suharto,* 308.
3. For a shrewd and balanced account of the social bases and character of the opposition to the Soeharto regime, see Aspinall, "Political Opposition," 341–46. For a full account of the economic downturn, see Hill, *Indonesian Economy,* 260–98.
4. Ray, "Survey of Recent Developments," 245, 248; Przeworski and colleagues claim that "per capita income is by far the best predictor of the survival of democracies" (*Democracy and Development,* 137).

5. I have employed Lev's translation of the 1945 constitution (*Transition to Guided Democracy*, 292).
6. Elson, *Suharto*, 201.
7. Schwarz, *Nation in Waiting*, 361–62.
8. Liddle, "Indonesia's Democratic Transition" 385–86.
9. Liddle, "Soeharto's Indonesia," 29.
10. Liddle, "Indonesia's Democratic Transition," 387.
11. Liddle, "Indonesia's Democratic Transition," 388.
12. Aspinall and Fealy, "Introduction," 3.
13. Warren, *Bureaucratisation of Local Government*, 4.
14. Antlov, "Not Enough Politics!" 79–80. For further detail, see his "Village Government," 193–214.
15. "President Strikes Back," *Jakarta Post Online*, July 21, 2000, http://thejakartapost.com.
16. Aspinall, "Downfall of President Abdurrahman Wahid," 35.
17. Liddle, "Indonesia's Democratic Transition," 397.
18. Bourchier, "1950s in New Order Ideology," 50–62.
19. National Democratic Institute for International Affairs, *1999 Presidential Election*, 18; "UUD 1945, Perubahan Pertama dan Perubahan Kedua," *Kompas*, August 21, 2000, 31.
20. *1999 Presidential Election*, 6, 20; Blair A. King, "Constitutional Tinkering: The Search for Consensus is Taking Time," *Inside Indonesia* (January–March, 2001), 25.
21. National Democratic Institute for International Affairs, *Indonesia's Road to Constitutional Reform*, 2, 6; "UUD 1945, Perubahan Pertama dan Perubahan Kedua," 31.
22. Wihana Kirana Jaya and Dick, "Latest Crisis of Regional Autonomy," 216.
23. See van Dijk, *Country in Despair*, 400.
24. Fealy, "Parties and Parliament," 105.
25. National Democratic Institute for International Affairs, *Indonesia's Road to Constitutional Reform*, iii; "UUD 1945, Perubahan Pertama dan Perubahan Kedua," 31.
26. National Democratic Institute for International Affairs, *Indonesia's Road to Constitutional Reform*, 6; van Dijk, *Country in Despair*, 339.
27. Lindsey, "Indonesian Constitutional Reform," 252, 254–55, 296; Ellis, "Indonesian Constitutional Transition," 132–33. Law 26/2000 on Human Rights Courts was actually established after the passage of the second amendment. For a full and fascinating account of the creation of this law in seeming breach of the second amendment passed only a few months beforehand, see Clarke, "Retrospectivity and the Constitutional Validity," 14–18.
28. Many supporters of the reform process in Indonesia had argued that a thoroughgoing amendment of the 1945 constitution could only be carried out by a special commission removed from the governmental process. Presumably, such critics did not anticipate—indeed, it may be unprecedented—that the amending body would be willing to surrender a substantial portion of its own powers to achieve a more democratic outcome. I am indebted to Tim Lindsey for drawing my attention to these points. See also, in this regard, the comment of Carl J. Friedrich that "certain amendments to a constitutional document are unlikely if the power of amending the document is vested

in an official or a group of officials whose own power might conceivably be curtailed by such an amendment" (*Constitutional Government and Democracy*, 142).

29. National Democratic Institute for International Affairs, *Fundamental Changes That Nobody Noticed*, 6.

30. "MPR Sahkan Amendemen Keempat UUD 1945," *Kompas Cyber Media*, August 11, 2002, www.kompas.com.

31. "MPR Sahkan Amendemen Keempat UUD 1945"; Ellis, "MPR Annual Session 2002," 1–3.

32. Crouch, "Political Update 2002," 22.

33. See Nasution, *Aspiration for Constitutional Government*, 106.

34. "Amendemen Pasal 29 PK Tawarkan Jalan Tengah," *Tempo Interaktif*, August 4, 2002, www.tempo.co.id; "Soal Tujuh Kata Piagam Jakarta," *Pikiran Rakyat Online*, August 8, 2002, www.pikiran-rakyat.com; "Sharia Last Point of Contention in Constitutional Amendments," *Jakarta Post Online*, August 10, 2002.

35. National Democratic Institute for International Affairs, *1999 Presidential Election*, appendix 9.

36. Ellis, "MPR Annual Session 2002," 3.

37. Lindsey states the Supreme Court "is widely regarded as being one of the most corrupt institutions in Indonesia and its competence is also subject to much criticism. Although the stewardship of Professor Bagir Manan, the Chief Justice . . . has recently produced signs of improvement in Supreme Court decisions, it remains a profoundly troubled jurisdiction. The result is that many in the legislature and the government think it would be dangerous to fully release it too quickly from the oversight by the Ministry of Justice. The dilemma is a real one: the democratic *trias politika* obviously demands an independent third branch but is it prudent to place the final level of appeal in the hands of an unchecked rogue court?" (Lindsey, "Indonesian Constitutional Reform," 264–65).

38. A similar view was expressed by Daniel Lev in August 2002 in a contribution to an electronic discussion group convened by Edward Aspinall.

39. Compare Miller, *Mikhail Gorbachev*, 53–74.

9

Childhood and Youth of Megawati Sukarnoputri

Female political leaders have occasionally emerged in postcolonial Asia who are the daughters of the "founding fathers" of their countries. As such, they have sought political power to protect or redeem what they see to be their fathers's reputations and achievements or to avenge their ill treatment at the hands of others. For example, when Aung San Suu Kyi was two years old, her father and almost the entire membership of his provisional government were gunned down on July 19, 1947; yet, she "reappeared like an avenging nemesis to haunt Ne Win with the memory of Aung San, the only truly unifying name in Burmese politics today."[1] Addressing a mass rally in Rangoon on August 26, 1988, she said, "I could not as my father's daughter remain indifferent to all that was going on. This national crisis could in fact be called the second struggle for national independence."[2] Then there is Sheikh Hasina Wajed, the daughter of the first prime minister of Bangladesh, Sheikh Mujibur Rahman, who led her father's Awami League back into office in the 1996 general election almost twenty-one years after army officers assassinated him and most of his family. She was twenty-eight at the time of his murder, and it was said by one commentator that "years of exile in India, followed by a decade of struggle to rebuild the Awami League under hostile military governments, left deep scars on Mrs Wazed [Wajed], who often seemed driven by a burning zeal for revenge against her family's killers."[3]

Although perhaps not as neatly as Suu Kyi and Sheikh Hasina, Indira Gandhi fits here, too: she served as a companion and housekeeper to her widower father, Jawaharlal Nehru, before becoming president of the Congress Party and subsequently, with the death of Lal Bahadur Shastri in 1966, prime minister. No doubt she saw herself as being loyal to her father in some deep sense; however, as the emergency of 1975–1977 bore witness, she was in fact impatient with the democratic institutions he had so carefully nurtured.[4]

By pushing the boundaries of the category out a little, we can also include former prime minister Benazir Bhutto, who was "born into one of the largest landowning families in Sind" and whose father was president and subsequently prime minister of Pakistan, but not its founding father.[5] He was executed by General Zia ul-Haq on April 4, 1979, and as Stanley Wolpert related, "At twenty-six, Benazir took up the mantle of her father's leadership, first of his party, and later of his nation . . . Benazir was her father's true political heir, and wherever she went or spoke, people cried aloud, 'Jiye Bhutto!' . . . Each time the chosen day drew near, it became clear to the . . . General-President . . . that he could never win a 'free and fair' election against Zulfi Bhutto, who 'lived' through his dauntless daughter Benazir."[6] Finally, there is Megawati, the second child and eldest daughter of Indonesia's first president, Sukarno. Before becoming president in 2001, she posed a challenge in 1995–1996 to the man who deposed her father and, by doing so, belongs in this category as well.

To classify these women is one thing; to understand their motivations fully and explain their success in all its aspects is a task that has hardly begun. It is one made especially difficult by the fact that they are viewed, initially at least, as mere symbols of their fathers or simply as leaseholders of patriarchal power. For example, Najma Chowdhury writes that "the emergence of Sheikh Hasina . . . in political leadership . . . represents a paradox in a patriarchal culture that is best explained by . . . kinship . . . to male authority. The political capital of Sheikh Hasina . . . is . . . [her] kinship to the powerful male political . . . [leader] Mujibur Rahman (leader of the Awami League)."[7] To be explained as such has certainly been the fate of Megawati: she is just a symbol, they say;[8] or, more harshly, "Suppose she was not the daughter of Bung Karno, she wouldn't be any one at all: only a housewife with simple thoughts."[9] Admittedly, however, there is some truth to this perspective. No one would deny that Megawati owes much of her political success to her ability to symbolize her much-loved father, the first president of the Republic of Indonesia. Her younger brother, Guruh, explained the matter this way:

> It's like this, according to my intuition, the Indonesian people still love Bung Karno. But because Bung Karno is already deceased, the people will instinctively support a leader who symbolizes the spirit of Bung Karno, and in this case that is Mbak Mega.[10]

But in reflecting on the "just a symbol" and "leaseholders of patriarchal power" perspectives, it is important to recall that Aung San Suu Kyi, Benazir Bhutto, and Megawati Sukarnoputri all have brothers: in Suu Kyi's case, Aung San Oo, who has shown little interest in politics and now lives in the United States; in Benazir's case, Murtaza and Shah Nawaz; and in Megawati's case, Guruh and the eldest child, Guntur—all of whom do not appear to have had the same success in symbolizing their fathers or in acquiring their power.[11] Why should this be so? Why did President Sukarno's legacy slip through Guntur's fingers only to end up in Megawati's hands? The answer is not easily given, but it certainly concerns Guntur's and Megawati's feelings for their father and the way that these two siblings were perceived by the Indonesian people.

As far as the issue of perception is concerned, there is reason to believe that Megawati's gender handed her an advantage. According to Benedict Anderson, a woman such as Megawati, Cory Aquino, Aung San Suu Kyi, or Benazir Bhutto can

> symbolize purity as she is not the family head, nor a gang leader, nor the head of a conglomerate, nor a general and so on. If for example it had been Guntur or whoever else that may have appeared as the representative of Bung Karno's spirit, they would not have been as successful as Megawati, that is the important thing.[12]

However, if family name and female gender are the only factors in Megawati's success, we are left wondering why her two sisters, Rachmawati and Sukmawati, do not enjoy a similar political importance. This is a difficult issue to resolve, but we can at least inquire into the talents she possesses that distinguish her from her sisters and go some way toward explaining her political success. These include a certain flexibility in interpreting some aspects of her father's legacy, thereby enabling her to adjust to changed circumstances. More significant, this relatively inarticulate woman—relative, that is, to her father, a charismatic orator—acquired a comparable eloquence by her ability to symbolize not just her father and purity but other, cognate qualities, such as decency. Contrary to her critics of the "just a symbol" school, this particular ability should not be taken for granted, as it clearly depended on more than family name and female gender. In her case, it seems to have a great deal to do with her silences, and silent suffering at the hands of the arbitrary and corrupt New Order government of President Soeharto.

CHILDHOOD

Sukarno came to parenthood late, when Fatmawati (his second wife) gave birth to Guntur in 1944. He was forty-three and elated by the arrival of his "precious son."[13] However, the birth of his first daughter on January 23, 1947, also seemed to be an occasion for delight, and in a speech eighteen months later he was already fantasizing about his infant daughter's future suitors. "I have frequently whispered into Megawati's ear: 'Don't look favourably on a marriage proposal from a young man without ideals.' Therefore the youths here who do not have ideals, you have no chance."[14]

Paternal enthusiasm notwithstanding, Megawati's early years were not easy. Her teeth chattered, as did Guntur's, when the Dutch military shelled the capital of the republic, Yogyakarta, in December 1948.[15] Her father's subsequent arrest and exile separated him from his children for six months. Then, shortly after the birth of Guruh in January 1954, Fatmawati left her husband in response to his decision to take another wife. She took Guntur with her but left the other children—Megawati, Rachmawati, Sukmawati, and Guruh—in Sukarno's care. In her autobiography, Rachmawati vividly described her distress at this event and how relations between the children's servants and, ultimately, the children themselves deteriorated in the vacuum created by the absence of their mother and by their father's preoccupation with his duties. Then Megawati and her siblings were obliged to watch as their father took a third, fourth, and even fifth wife over the following years.[16] None was more critical than Guntur, who took his mother's side in the marital dispute and refused to have anything to do with her successor, Hartini (let alone Hartini's successors).

An assassination attempt on President Sukarno compounded the family's distress. This took place on Saturday evening, November 30, 1957, at his children's school in Cikini. As he was leaving a ceremony to mark the school's fifth anniversary, a number of hand grenades were thrown at him. Guntur and Megawati accompanied their father to this event but then stayed on to watch a film.

> It so happened that because of their plan to watch a film, Guntur and Megawati did not come out into the yard. Rather, they remained in a room on the upper level of the school as a consequence of which the two children of the President were safe from the fatal catastrophe which otherwise would have threatened them. After the event occurred Guntur and Megawati were taken to the palace by their guards. One of the guards of the two children, Ngadino, who was on duty in front of the door of the school building at the time of the explosion, suffered a number of wounds and required hospital treatment.[17]

Apparently the children arrived back at the palace sometime before their father and were unsure of his fate.[18] As they eventually discovered, he was unhurt, but eleven had died and over thirty were wounded. Rachmawati was seven years old at this time and had just entered the first grade at the Cikini school. She had not attended the school fete but was badly shaken nevertheless. "Since the 'Tjikini [Cikini] Affair,'" she wrote, "I have been dogged by a fear of losing my father."[19] This fear could only have been reinforced by another four assassination attempts, one of which she actually witnessed.[20]

Rachmawati made no attempt to conceal the scars of her early years; indeed, her distress is palpable on almost every page of her autobiography. Megawati, however, emerged from childhood with a rather different personality. People noted a soft, maternal quality in her from a very early age. Dullah, the artist in residence at the palace, wrote, "Even as a child Mega's appearance and behaviour brimmed with motherly qualities."[21] The servant from her childhood years, Mbok Tjitro, said that "from when she was small until now [1993] she was indeed always like that, soft and motherly."[22]

One can imagine that this maternal quality was reinforced when the children's mother left the family and Megawati struggled to respond to her younger siblings, who looked to her as a substitute. Yet, her sister was disappointed with her efforts: "Since mother left, we who were still very young of course looked on Megawati as a substitute mother. But Mbak Ega herself had not reached maturity so that in the end our expectations of her were not realized."[23]

The breakup of the marriage affected Megawati in other ways as well. According to Rachmawati,

> I am indeed different from Megawati because I am more open. My older sister is a very sensitive person and she maintains her anger for a long period of time. But I easily forget my anger and can quickly forgive. It is not like that with Mbak Ega who tends to be more taciturn and sensitive. It is clear that her feelings which are so sensitive were hurt by the event which struck our parents' household.[24]

Through Dullah's, Mbok Tjitro's, and Rachmawati's eyes we catch a glimpse of a child with maternal qualities and a stoical disposition, who is sensitive and says little. However, a discussion of individual character traits can leave much unsaid, and it is therefore appropriate to try to understand something of her underlying disposition.

It is clear that Megawati enjoyed great privileges as a child—her own bodyguard, her own servants, a palace for her home—but the emotional climate in which she grew up, especially after the divorce of her parents, can only be described as bleak. It is possible that her personality was shaped in part by the interaction of these two factors. If her defensive pride was made to work overtime amid the hurts and rejections of the family circle, then the extraordinary circumstances of her childhood would only have served to reinforce it, giving rise to a feeling of entitlement and correspondingly imperious behavior.[25]

As Megawati entered adolescence, her father's interest in her prospective husband continued apace. In his speeches, Sukarno would occasionally point to his mixed background—Balinese mother, Javanese father—and say that, as he had then married a woman from Sumatra, it would be a good idea if Megawati chose a spouse from Sulawesi. But in Sukarno's mind, there was always one proviso concerning this nation building in the bedroom: Megawati's Sulawesian husband had to be a man of high ideals; and Sukarno was proud to tell his audience that, on that score, she had already had occasion to reject numerous suitors.

> I suggested to Megawati that she marry later with a youth from Sulawesi—if he is compatible and has ideals. If this young man is not a young man of high aspirations I will not give my permission for the marriage even though he may look like Robert Taylor. Mega, Megawati, Mega, I also call her Dis, Gadis [Girl], don't marry a young man who has no ideals, even though he looks like Robert Taylor. And I want you to know that Megawati has already answered, "yes, I also am not willing, father, to consider young men who lack ideals." The number of young men turned down by Megawati is already large, you know![26]

By 1963 the president's involvement in such matters moved beyond the realm of fantasy. According to retired general Benny Moerdani, Sukarno approached him and raised with him the prospect of marriage to his daughter in the following terms: "As a matter of fact, I want my child to marry a hero. Yes, like you."[27] Moerdani did not say which "child" Sukarno intended, but presumably it was Megawati, the eldest daughter. Major Moerdani (as he then was) was not from Sulawesi, but he clearly qualified in terms of ideals, as the president had recently decorated him for his role as a parachutist in the West Irian campaign. Nothing came of the suggestion, however, as the major was already betrothed.

As Moerdani was a Christian, it is clear that Sukarno's preoccupation with the qualities of Megawati's suitors did not extend to their Islamic religious adherence. This is not surprising in light of the diversity of faiths to be found in his own family. His father was a Theosophist, his mother Hindu-Balinese, and his own attachment to Islam was only a subordinate element in a complex of beliefs that included Hinduism and Buddhism in their local forms. In keeping with this background, Megawati developed a similar religious orientation. Like other syncretists, she became wary of devout Islam in its modernist form and displayed a marked preference, if not for the pre-Islamic world of Hindu Java, then certainly for that form of Islam that was closest to that world.

In this particular religious and, indeed, cultural tradition to which both father and daughter belonged, women enjoyed more standing and freedom. It was therefore in keeping with this attribute that Sukarno, when he was not preoccupied with Megawati's suitors, envisaged an active role for her in adult life. Indeed, he could be eloquent on the prominence of women in traditional society. In the election of a female village head or in the promotion of women to officer rank in the armed forces, he saw proof that Dutch colonial influence, in its patriarchal aspect, was waning.

> Yes, of course, in former times before the Dutch came here, we had a large number of female village heads, brothers and sisters. And leaving aside female village heads, we had queens and female heroes at that time. Up until the beginning of the twentieth century, before South Sulawesi was colonized by the Dutch, for example, in South Sulawesi there were still female monarchs. For example, the monarch from Tanete. Are there any Buginese here. No. The monarch of Tanete was a woman, brothers and sisters . . . . Until the beginning of the twentieth century in those places where there were no Dutch, we still had female monarchs. And especially female heroes. Tjut Nja' Din, a woman from Atjeh. Tjut Mutia, a woman from Aceh. Ratu Wandansari, a woman from East Java. Women, all of them women.
>
> Therefore when Saudari Rolifah [a recently elected female village head] stood here, I was moved, moved because we have entered the realm of our own identity. And, of course, we cannot arrange our society to become truly a just and prosperous one, cannot make our state firm and strong, if men are not together with women.[28]

He also referred with pride to the ambition of "my beautiful child, Megawati" to become an agricultural scientist.[29] In a speech he gave in December 1964, he recalls the following conversation:

> "Hey, Mega, what do you want to become?"
>
> "I want to become an agricultural engineer, father."
>
> "Do you wish to become an agricultural engineer who works in the field?"
>
> "No, father, I want to become an engineer who works in a laboratory. I want to put my brain to work on research, so that we can have enough food."
>
> "Hey, child, you really are my child."[30]

Indonesia had suffered a bad rice harvest in 1963, and the president was concerned by the country's dependence on rice imports.[31] Accordingly, he made a number of speeches in 1964 in which he urged the people to eat corn and called for more research into rice strains suited to dry cultivation. It was in this context that Megawati declared her intention of becoming an agricultural scientist, and a clearly delighted president held her up as an example to other students to encourage them to embark on research careers in areas relevant to Indonesia's problems. Thus it can be seen that while Sukarno had been brooding on his eldest daughter's future and importuning handsome young men of high ideals on her behalf, she had been thinking about the problems he was facing and had resolved to come to his aid. As a result, she was as good as her word: on graduating from the Cikini Senior High School, she enrolled in her father's alma mater, the Institute of Technology, Bandung, to prepare for her chosen career.

THE FALL OF SUKARNO

Sukarno's being overthrown by General Soeharto and his subsequent but also consequent decline in health and spirits weighed heavily on the shoulders of his children. They shared his humiliation at the hands of the new rulers—Megawati returned to the palace one day "to find the army throwing her belongings onto a truck"[32]—and they struggled to adapt to the drastic change in their social circumstances, with both she and Guntur discontinuing their university courses at the time. After the Interim People's Consultative Assembly installed Soeharto as president in March 1968, Sukarno was placed under a form of house arrest (or political quarantine, as it was officially called) in the Bogor palace and then at his private house in Batu Tulis Street, Bogor, while the government investigated his alleged part in the communist-led coup attempt of October 1, 1965.[33] Sukarno's morale quickly deteriorated as he witnessed the overturning of some of his most cherished policies and as his contact with people was confined to family members only.[34] In this latter regard, matters were made more difficult by Guntur's reluctance to visit his father in Bogor because of the presence of Hartini.[35] "His illness grew worse as his spirit continued to take a battering. The solitude gnawed dreadfully at his spirit," Rachmawati wrote.[36]

In October 1968, the former president was moved to the vacant house of his Japanese wife, Ratna Sari Dewi, in Jakarta. His condition continued to deteriorate to the point where this most articulate of leaders, who while in office gave speeches once, twice, or even three times a day, stopped talking. According to Rachmawati,

> I fully understand how father's spirit rebelled at his shackled existence in the Wisma Yaso. His connection with the outside world was completely broken. Eventually this state of affairs broke his spirit, and then I witnessed father lose the will to speak and become mute. This was a change which greatly disturbed me.[37]

The youngest daughter, Sukmawati, shared responsibility for her father's care and painted a similar picture of his plight at this time:

During those miserable times, I often nursed father. His spirit was well and truly broken. He could not be said to be alive but neither was he dead. A person who was alive but also dead. All his aspirations at that moment lay in ruins, thwarted and defeated. Father was truly sad at that time. So he often wept.[38]

She added that "we are not yet able to forget 100 per cent the wrong-doing inflicted on our leader and father, Bung Karno."[39]

During this most difficult time Sukarno lost Megawati to an air force lieutenant, Surindro Supjarso (Mas Pacul).[40] There seems to be no record of what he thought of the young man, but one can imagine that he would have experienced difficulty in forgiving even the most idealistic son of Sulawesi for taking Megawati from him, especially as they planned to live in distant Madiun, where Mas Pacul was stationed. Misfortunes piled up: Rachmawati informs us in her autobiography that Megawati suffered a miscarriage some time later and that their father felt the loss keenly.[41] (Megawati eventually had two children by Mas Pacul: Mohammad Rizki Pratama and Mohammad Prananda.)[42]

Rachmawati followed suit, seeking her father's permission to marry Tommy Marzuki. He reluctantly gave her his blessing, preoccupied not by her suitor's ethnic origin (he was not from Sulawesi either) or his ideals but with the simple fact that he was about to lose another one of his daughters. "What other friends do I have? Who else is there to be close to me?" he cried out, much to Rachma's distress.[43]

When Sukarno's health deteriorated further in June 1970, Megawati rushed back to Jakarta to join the other children at his hospital bedside.[44] He died on June 21. President Soeharto granted him a state funeral but for security reasons would not allow him to be buried at Bogor, despite his own request and the pleadings of Hartini and Ratna Sari Dewi. Instead, his body was laid to rest alongside his mother's in his home town of Blitar, East Java.[45] Thereafter, he passed, as Pierre Labrousse has phrased it, "into purgatorial silence by the official erasing of his historical role—particularly in relation to the birth of the [state ideology of] *Pancasila*—and by the embargo on the republishing of his political writings."[46]

DEATH OF HUSBAND

Worse was to follow for Megawati: her husband's plane crashed in difficult terrain near Biak in Irian Jaya on January 22, 1971.[47] The public record is silent on the ensuing period, and one can only assume that, as on previous occasions, Megawati suffered in silence. However, her subsequent behavior spoke loudly of her continuing distress and indeed added to it. Approximately a year later she became enamored of an Egyptian, Hassan Gamal Ahmad Hassan, who had served in his country's diplomatic service in Jakarta. The family had known him since the time he visited Fatmawati to extend his condolences on the death of Sukarno. With the passage of time family members had come to suspect him of dishonesty and were appalled by Megawati's fondness for him. She was urged to break off the relationship and, apparently resolved to do so, met him at the Sarinah Department Store in Jakarta on June 27, 1972. But rather than act on her resolve, she eloped with him to Sukabumi, where they were married in the Religious Affairs Office (Kantor Urusan Agama). Their married life seems to have lasted only one-and-a-half hours before Mega was somehow reclaimed by the family. Husband and wife met again two weeks later in the Special Islamic Court of Jakarta (Pengadilan Istimewa Agama Islam Djakarta), where Guntur, acting at his mother's behest, managed to have the marriage dissolved on the grounds that the death of Megawati's first husband had not yet been clearly established (although according to the well-known Indonesian Islamic scholar Hamka, a wife is only obliged to await the return of a missing husband for four months and ten days).[48] Megawati does not seem to have said much at this time, but she was in such a palpable state of distress and indecision that she obliged two journalists from *Tempo* to reach for their copies of Shakespeare in their attempt to describe her condition.

> To this point the commotion, it seems, was caused by Megawati who is soft, vacillating and meek, as Shakespeare said in *Hamlet*: "Frailty, thy name is woman!" But who wishes to blame the young woman who is afflicted by grief because of the death of her father and the loss of her husband? They say that when she was born twenty-five years ago, the day was full of rain clouds and showers, so that her father, the first President of the Republic, called her "Megawati" [daughter of the rain clouds]. Now it appears that a gloomy mist still hangs over her life.[49]

Megawati would come to stand for other qualities, but she appeared frail again in 1996 when she took her stand against Soeharto, which perhaps explains the solicitude with which she was often regarded by her supporters at that time.[50]

NOTES

1. Smith, *Burma*, 421; Aris, "Introduction," xvi.
2. Aung San Suu Kyi, *Freedom from Fear*, 199.
3. John F. Burns, "After 21 Years, Bangladeshi Party Is Returned to Power," *New York Times*, June 14, 1996, A3.

4. Nayantara Sahgal, *Indira Gandhi*, 1, 209, 240.
5. Ayesha Jalal, *Democracy and Authoritarianism*, 78.
6. Wolpert, *Zulfi Bhutto*, 329.
7. Najma Chowdhury, "Bangladesh," 100.
8. For example, Takashi Shiraishi interviewed by Ben Abel on *Apakabar@clark.net* (an Indonesian news service moderated by John MacDougall), July 6, 1996.
9. Quoted in Goenawan Mohamad, "Mega, Mega," *Suara Independen*, June 1996, 2.
10. "Guruh Soekarnoputra: 'Dari dulu Kami tak pernah Dendam,'" *Forum Keadilan*, July 15, 1966, 15.
11. Lintner, *Aung San Suu Kyi*, 16; Wolpert, *Zulfi Bhutto*, 53.
12. Ben Anderson interviewed by Ben Abel on *Apakabar* (see n. 8), July 12, 1996.
13. Adams, *Sukarno: An Autobiography*, 184.
14. Sukarno, "Pidato disampaikan dalam Pertemuan dengan para Pelajar dan Pemuda di 'Atjeh Bioskop,' June 16, 1948, 8:30pm," 70, 76.
15. "Ibu Fatmawati bercerita tentang Bung Karno," *Pos Kota*, July 26, 1977, 1, 12.
16. Rachmawati Soekarno, *Bapakku Ibuku,* 31, 34–35, 46, 179; "Ibu Hartini dan Anak-anak tentang Fatmawati," *Kompas*, November 9, 1994.
17. "Pertjobaan Pembunuhan terhadap Presiden Sukarno," *Mimbar Indonesia* 49, no. 11, December 7, 1957, 6.
18. Guntur Soekarno, "Granat Maut," 132–140.
19. Rachmawati Soekarno, *Bapakku Ibuku*, 41, 46.
20. Rachmawati Soekarno, *Bapakku Ibuku*, 171–72.
21. "Bung Karno: Pemimpin, Presiden, Seniman (dari kumpulan surat-surat pelukis Dullah kepada isterinya Biby Fatimah)," *Merdeka*, September 5, 1982.
22. "Megawati Soekarnoputri,"*Apa dan Siapa* (Pusat Data dan Analisa Tempo), www.pdat.co.id/ads/html/M/ads,20030701-01,S.html.
23. Rachmawati Soekarno, *Bapakku Ibuku*, 35.
24. Rachmawati Soekarno, *Bapakku Ibuku*, 37.
25. Compare Shore, "Henry VIII," 374.
26. Sukarno, *Bertjita-tjitalah Setinggi Bintang Dilangit!* 11.
27. Pour, *Benny Moerdani,* 241.
28. Sukarno, *Pamong Desa Salah Satu Sokoguru Revolusi Indonesia,* 9. See also, Brown, "Sukarno on the Role of Women," 68–92.
29. Sukarno, *Amalkan Ilmu daripada Kehidupan Sehari-hari (The School of Life),* 12.
30. Sukarno, "Amanat PJM Presiden Sukarno pada Upatjara Peringatan Tri Pantjawarsa Universitas Gadjah Mada di Siti Hinggil, Jogjakarta, 20 Desember 1964," 10.
31. Mackie, *Konfrontasi*, 217.
32. David Jenkins, "In the Name of the Father," *Sydney Morning Herald*, July 21, 2001, 21.
33. Labrousse, "Second Life of Bung Karno," 175.
34. Suripto, *Bung Karno,* 18–19; Rachmawati, *Bapakku Ibuku*, 204–5.
35. Rachmawati Soekarno, *Bapakku Ibuku*, 222.
36. Rachmawati Soekarno, *Bapakku Ibuku*, 205.

37. Rachmawati Soekarno, *Bapakku Ibuku*, 208, 233.
38. Sukmawati Soekarnoputri, "Karisma Bung Karno tidak bisa Dihapuskan 100 persen," *Forum Keadilan*, June 8, 1995, 73.
39. Sukmawati Soekarnoputri, "Karisma Bung Karno," 74.
40. *Tempo*, December 25, 1993, 17.
41. Rachmawati Soekarno, *Bapakku Ibuku*, 223.
42. "Megawati: Kisah Tjinta dan Tinta," *Tempo*, July 22, 1972, 47; Nababan, *Gerak dan Langkah Megawati Soekarnoputri*, 43.
43. Rachmawati Soekarno, *Bapakku Ibuku*, 208.
44. Rachmawati Soekarno, *Bapakku Ibuku*, 251, 254.
45. Brooks, "Rustle of Ghosts," 65.
46. Labrousse, "Second Life of Bung Karno," 175.
47. "Megawati: Kisah Tjinta," *Tempo*, July 22, 1972, 47; *Tempo,* December 25, 1993, 17.
48. "Megawati: Kisah Tjinta," *Tempo*, July 22, 1972, 8–9, 47–50; *Tempo*, December 25, 1993, 17–18.
49. "Megawati: Kisah Tjinta," *Tempo*, July 22, 1972, 50. The journalists were Toeti Kakiailatu and Goenawan Mohamad.
50. This claim is based on personal observations made in Jakarta in June and July 1996.

10

Megawati Sukarnoputri's Political Apprenticeship

STANDING FOR PARLIAMENT, 1987 AND 1992

About six months after the debacle with her second, though temporary, husband, the "gloomy mist" appeared to lift for Megawati. In March 1973, she married a man of modest means, Taufik Kiemas, who hailed from South Sumatra and had been an activist in the Indonesian National Party's university student front. Their marriage produced a daughter, Puan Maharani, and while Mega devoted most of her time in the ensuing years toward raising her three children, Taufik managed a chain of petrol stations provided to the family by the state oil enterprise, Pertamina, at the behest of President Soeharto himself.[1] She and her siblings must have also derived some satisfaction from Soeharto's partial rehabilitation of their late father, signified by the building of "a funerary complex in Blitar dedicated to the Father of the People, the Proclaimer of Independence, the first President of the Republic of Indonesia, Bung Karno," which Soeharto himself opened in June 1979.[2] No doubt, the Sukarno children were buoyed by the high regard with which the Indonesian people continued to regard their father, as evidenced by the fact that 1,458,057 people visited his grave the following year (from June 1, 1980 to June 1, 1981).[3] This peaceful period came to an end thirteen years later, in 1986, when the new general chairman of the Indonesian Democracy Party (Partai Demokrasi Indonesia; PDI) sought to involve members of the Sukarno family in its campaign for the elections scheduled for April 23, 1987.

The PDI was a lineal descendant of the pro-Sukarno and nonconfessional Indonesian National Party (PNI) formed in early 1946 and the remote descendent of another PNI, which Sukarno himself led before independence. This PDI was established in 1973 on the basis of a government-enforced merger with, among others, the Protestant and Catholic political parties. The 1946 PNI was by far the largest of these parties, and its experiences in the preceding years did much to shape the character of the PDI. Although the PNI was itself responsible for the murder of many communists in 1965, it had since endured considerable hardship. Members of its left wing were killed or arrested, and even its anticommunist members suffered because of their association with Sukarno. They were purged from the civil service, which then became a preserve of the Government Party (Golkar), and had no choice but to accept the latter muscling in on the PNI's nominally Islamic (non-*santri*) constituency not to mention the merger referred to earlier. These events—in particular, the arrest or murder of some of their members—ensured the fearful acquiescence of its successor organization in continuing government interference.[4] The most recent example of which occurred at the third party congress in April 1986 when the government imposed its choice of leaders on the party: as general chairperson, Soerjadi, a former member of the PNI's tertiary student front; and Nico Daryanto, a member of the former Catholic Party.[5]

This did not seem a promising beginning, but Soerjadi threw himself into the job with considerable enterprise and energy. One of his first moves was to embrace members of the Sukarno family. He hoped that such family involvement would affirm the PDI's pro-Sukarno orientation and thereby persuade the large (and growing) numbers of similarly inclined youth to vote for it. These young people perceived Sukarno as an idealized figure, even as an object of longing and nostalgia in "the image of the unknown Father"[6] and, increasingly, as a symbol of opposition to President Soeharto. "The virtues praised in Sukarno," one author commented, "are exactly those missing in Soeharto."[7] Chief among these was the claim that the former president did not use his office to advance the material welfare of his children. The fact that this comparison worked to the benefit of the Sukarno children is not without its irony when we recall that Soeharto had provided—quite handsomely, as it turned out—for the Sukarno children as well.

In response to Soerjadi's invitation, Megawati emerged from her suburban fastness to stand as a PDI candidate for parliament from Central Java. (Her husband did likewise, seeking to be one of the representatives from South Sumatra.)[8] Her decision seems to have been underpinned by a certain amount of postparental freedom. She said, "I had no thoughts of becoming a leader. At the time I felt that since my children were already independent, I might as well become active in politics."[9] Her brother Guruh also responded favorably to Soerjadi but did not run for parliament; yet, with his musical group Swara Mahardhika (The Voice of Freedom), he took part in a PDI parade in Jakarta during the course of the election campaign.[10]

Rachmawati, however, ignored Soerjadi's invitation and publicly criticized her sister for becoming involved in the PDI. She believed in perpetuating their father's teachings but felt that this could not be achieved by Megawati's associating herself with a particular political party that would only seek to exploit the family name.[11] She said that they must instead follow their father's example and remain above party loyalties; indeed, she reminded her sister, the Sukarno children had promised one another to do so four years previously. From this disagreement it is possible to see that Rachmawati was burdened by her responsibility as her father's daughter. As she herself put it, "I feel nervous if I haven't carried out the request of my late father to perpetuate his teachings."[12] Megawati wore the mantle of family loyalty more lightly than her sister, and was therefore able to give it more flexible expression. However, the difference between them on this matter was very much one of degree. As we shall see, Megawati could be anxious and inflexible, too, when key aspects of her father's legacy were called into question.

Guntur did not respond to Soerjadi either, although he enjoyed great affection in PDI circles as the eldest child and son who also bore a striking resemblance to his father and no doubt would have done well in an electoral contest.[13] However, he may not have felt much inclination to become involved in the business of symbolizing and vindicating his father; after all, he was a mother's boy, as his father once said.[14] Instead, he stayed resolutely out of the public eye, tending to his construction business, his staid monogamous lifestyle a silent reproach to his father's glamorous polygamous one.[15]

Sukmawati, like Rachmawati, is an articulate and outspoken defender of her father. Also like Rachmawati, she stood apart from the PDI campaign. Her reason for doing so, though, was not the same as her sister's. Although once connected by marriage to one of the royal houses of Java, Sukmawati became more militant and made no secret of her admiration for Che Guevara. From her point of view, the PDI was insufficiently radical, being unwilling to oppose the government and lacking the courage to discuss Sukarno's teachings; she preferred to involve herself instead in the Marhaen People's Movement, a small organization established in 1981 by former leaders of the old Indonesian National Party.[16]

Megawati attracted large crowds to her public meetings, although this phenomenon was due in part at least to the more neutral and less intimidating stance adopted by the armed forces under their commander, General Benny Murdani, during this election campaign. He apparently believed that a vigorous PDI under a sympathetic leadership—Soerjadi and Nico Daryanto were associated with a think tank in which his influence was strong—and enjoying a larger vote than it had managed to obtain in 1982 was in his political interests.[17] In Pekalongan, generally considered a stronghold of the Islamic Unity Development Party (Partai Persatuan Pembangunan), about five thousand people turned out to hear Megawati on March 26, 1987, which was twice the number that attended a rally of the Golkar Party in the same place on the previous day. She also drew one hundred thousand listeners in Banyumas on March 31 and seventy thousand in Medan on April 5.[18] Something of the atmosphere of the campaign can be gathered from this account of the PDI's last rally:

> At PDI's final rally in Jakarta on 17 April, local newspapers estimated that as many as one million people jammed the capital's main thoroughfares wearing red PDI T-shirts and flashing the party's three-finger sign. The display doubled as a mass act of worship for the late president, with many PDI supporters wearing Sukarno T-shirts and brandishing his portrait. "Oh Bung Karno . . . kamilah penerusmu [we are your followers]," read one slogan. [A better translation for *kamilah penerusmu* would be "We are carrying on your ideals."—AM] "Hidup Sukarno [Long Live Sukarno]," one of the late president's daughters, Megawati, shrieked to an ecstatic crowd.[19]

The party did well at the elections, significantly improving on its 1982 result. It increased its vote from 5,919,702 votes (8 percent of the total) to 9,324,708 (10.87 percent of the total) and its seats in the parliament jumped correspondingly from twenty-four to forty. Regional increases were marked in North Sumatra; South Sumatra, where Taufik Kiemas was on the party list; West Java; Jakarta; and Central Java, where Megawati was standing.[20] Approximately 10.7 million young people voted for the first time in 1987;[21] but, as Liddle pointed out in an article published in 1988, it is impossible to determine from the available data if the PDI's additional votes came disproportionately from this source. It is clear, however, that they were cast in cities. The large increase in the PDI's share of the vote in Jakarta has already been noted, and most of the rise in West Java came from cities such as Bandung and Bogor (with their large university student populations) and from districts bordering Jakarta. "It is thus certainly possible," Liddle concluded prophetically, "that the youthful crowds at PDI's Jakarta rallies could become the seeds of a future challenge to the government."[22]

Another 13.5 million were added to the electoral register for the June 9, 1992, elections. For many in this cohort, the rock star Iwan Fals was second only to God. As Margot Cohen explained, he "built a nation-wide following with straightforward lyrics that attack the insensitivity of the rich, the hypocrisy of the media, the blindness of parents, and a society that leaves no room for idealism." But if Fals was number two, Sukarno was number three, lionized by "youths who know very little about him." Cohen continued,

In opinion polls and press interviews, high school and college students talk of the former president's charisma, his bold revolutionary stance, his rivetting speeches and the "freedom" he afforded to various political parties. . . . In Blitar, the East Java site of Sukarno's tomb, the former president shares superhero status on T-shirts also printed with Batman. Students surreptitiously trade old recordings of his speeches and look for old textbooks describing his exploits.[23]

In this environment the PDI's electoral prospects looked promising, especially as Guruh underlined the association between the PDI and Sukarno by joining Megawati and Taufik Kiemas as a parliamentary candidate on this occasion. Well known not only as the youngest child of Sukarno but also as the leader of Swara Mahardhika, his appearances during the campaign attracted large numbers of people. At a rally in Banjarmasin, South Kalimantan, the film star Sophan Sophiaan, who was a recent recruit to the party, nominated him as a presidential candidiate. Guruh's response that he was "even at this moment . . . ready and willing" to replace President Soeharto was received with rapturous applause by the twenty thousand supporters present.[24] Also helping the party was the more-or-less neutral posture of the armed forces, although by this time Moerdani had been kicked upstairs by Soeharto to the less powerful position of minister of defense. The election results were indeed satisfying for the PDI: it increased its share of the vote from 10 to 15 percent, thereby gaining an additional fifteen seats in the parliament. Most of its gains were made in Central and East Java and seem to have been won largely at the expense of the Golkar Party, whose overall vote dropped by 5 percent (from 73 to 68 percent).[25] Emboldened by this success, nineteen of the PDI's parliament members, including Megawati, signed a letter calling on the party to nominate an alternative to Soeharto as its presidential candidate. But Soerjadi blocked this step, mindful that his leadership could not survive such effrontery.[26]

CANDIDATE FOR THE PARTY LEADERSHIP

This act of compliance, however, was insufficient to save him. The electoral gains made by the PDI in 1987 and 1992 had not endeared Soerjadi to the government. He is also said to have antagonized Soeharto in the 1992 campaign by advocating that presidential tenure be limited to two terms and by criticizing the high levels of official corruption.[27] Finally, his links to Moerdani were no longer an asset, as Moerdani's political influence was by this time in decline.[28] Consequently, the minister of home affairs, Yogie Memet, with the objective of preventing Soerjadi's reelection, encouraged some dissident members to disrupt the party congress convened in Medan in July 1993. They and their thuggish supporters did so by crashing a jeep into the conference building. Undeterred, the general chairperson's supporters managed to reendorse him by acclamation on the following day. On hearing this, the minister called in the thugs of the previous day and, in the ensuing chaos, was able to declare Soerjadi's election invalid. He then appointed the party dissidents to a caretaker executive and effectively charged them with getting the government's preferred candidate, Budi Hardjono, elected at an extraordinary congress later in the year.[29]

Other party members tried to thwart this interference: on September 11, approximately one hundred party officials from 70 of the party's 304 branches visited Megawati at her home in South Jakarta to ask her to stand for the chair at the extraordinary congress.[30] This was an audacious move, challenging the managers of the corporatist-style political system with a candidate who was enjoying popular support. Megawati's agreement to run proved to be a courageous and inspiring decision for many people, not only party members. Greeted with great enthusiasm, it immediately triggered declarations of support from a variety of people, including human rights lawyer Adnan Buyung Nasution, who had been an active opponent of her father.[31] Rachmawati, however, maintained her former objection, whereas Guruh offered the following commentary on their differences: "If Rachma is still being unbending, Mega is attuned to the changing situation."[32]

Megawati and her supporters sought to consolidate her position.[33] In the space of ten weeks they managed to compile and publish a booklet containing an outline of her thinking on various issues. Entitled *Bendera Sudah Saya Kibarkan* (I Have Unfurled the Flag), it gave a human rights cast to the state ideology of *Pancasila* and focused on those who failed to benefit or who were actually excluded from the *pembangunan* (development) of the last thirty years. Perhaps its most evocative image was of peasants dispossessed of their land to make way for the golf courses of the elite and the housing estates of the newly rich.[34] Her booklet was launched at the Hotel Indonesia on November 23 before a gathering of approximately two hundred people comprising family members, such as Hartini and Sukmawati; members of the 1946 PNI and close associates of Sukarno, such as Roeslan Abdulgani, Manai Sophiaan, and B. M. Diah; members of a younger generation, including Manai Sophiaan's son and PDI member Sophan Sophiaan and, standing out somewhat in a sea of syncretist (or nominally Islamic) faces, Sri Bintang Pamungkas, a parliamentary representative of the Islamic Unity Development Party and a member of the Association of Indonesian Islamic Intellectuals (Ikatan Cendiakawan Muslimin Indonesia); and well wishers, including Ria Moerdani, the daughter of retired general Moerdani, and her husband.

In her reply to the various addresses, Megawati said, "Silence does not mean not thinking." This remark, one newspaper explained, was aimed at those who viewed her silences with misgivings.[35] Certainly, there were a number of critics who claimed that Megawati's involvement in the affairs of parliament had been infrequent and characterized by her usual reticence. However, this slight record did not seem to have worked against her in the eyes of her growing band of enthusiastic supporters: if her critics viewed her as inactive or even lazy, her supporters saw a woman unsullied by political and factional involvement who might even be able to heal the divisions of not only the party but the nation.[36] (Megawati had actually identified herself with the reform-minded group within the PDI as demonstrated by her signing the letter that called on the party to nominate an alternative to Soeharto.)

The extraordinary congress was convened in Surabaya between December 2 and 6. Megawati stopped in Blitar to seek her father's blessing before facing the congress delegates. This was a well-trodden path for her and one on which she was occasionally accompanied by Abdurrahman Wahid (Gus Dur), the partly blind leader of the large Islamic social organization Nahdlatul Ulama. He had been there on the ninety-first anniversary of Sukarno's birth, on June 22, 1992, at the invitation of the children, and had spoken movingly about the cooperation and friendship that existed between his father, Kiai Haji Abdul Wahid Hasjim, and Sukarno at the time of the country's declaration of independence.[37] Doubtless, Gus Dur's Islam was more profound and learned than Megawati's more nominal variety, but in the final analysis they were both Javanese Moslems who seemed to mourn their dead fathers in ways more typically Javanese than obviously Islamic.[38]

When Yogie Memet opened the extraordinary congress on December 2, he must have realized that his plan to have Budi Hardjono elected general chairman of the PDI was facing tough opposition. Even if he had not witnessed the pro-Megawati crowds outside the conference building,[39] he could hardly have remained insensitive to the mood of defiance within. No wonder he suggested in his opening speech that taking a vote might not be the best way of determining who the next leader of the PDI would be. Confirmation of his fears was not long in coming: on December 4, 256 of the party's 305 branches, resisting enormous pressure from home affairs officials in the regions and on the conference floor, declared their support for Megawati as general chairperson of the PDI. On the last two days of the congress, desperate members of the caretaker board resorted to spoiling tactics, even absenting themselves from the floor to prevent a vote being taken for chairperson and other executive positions. Consequently, when the congress's licence expired on the last night, the party remained leaderless, though Megawati declared herself to be the de facto party chairperson.[40]

Amid appeals to the government from a former chief of Golkar and an ex-minister of home affairs to accept the fact that the PDI rank and file clearly wanted Megawati as party leader, Yogie Memet planned a "national consultation" of the leaders of the party's provincial councils to be held in Jakarta in late December. He had consulted President Soeharto about Megawati's candidature on December 4, 9, and 14 (the first during the extraordinary congress) and seemed to be in retreat. After discussions with Megawati on December 13, Yogie Memet said, "There was a large possibility that Megawati would become chairperson of the PDI." The woman herself remained calm, saying, "I have become accustomed to managing well all the psychological pressures which impinge on me."[41] Furthermore, she did not neglect to maintain the contact with the senior military figures that had been initiated by her supporters in September, at the time of her nomination for the leadership.

These officers were concerned by the growing political influence of the research and technology minister, B. J. Habibie, whose most recent offense had been to engineer the appointment of a civilian, information minister Harmoko, as chairperson of Golkar at the party's congress in October. They were fearful that Habibie would stand for president in 1998 with Golkar support. These sentiments were most clearly expressed by Major General Radja Kami Sembiring, the deputy leader of the armed forces faction in parliament, in his angry commentary on the recent Golkar congress and in his raising the possibility (however hypothetical) of the armed forces abandoning Golkar and lending support to the PDI in the next elections. Although these signs of a split in the inner circle of the regime on the question of the presidential succession may have provided Megawati and her supporters with hope that they would be the beneficiary, the reality of the situation proved less promising. It is true that Major General Hendropriyono, the commander of the Greater Jakarta military region, and Brigadier General Agum Gumelar, the special forces commander, took over the management of the one-day national consultation and presided over the election of Megawati as party chairperson. But it is also true that they did this in the absence, as they saw it, of a practical alternative and not because they had struck some deal with Megawati beforehand. Unwilling to indulge in yet another round of attempted manipulation of increasingly bold party delegates and believing (wrongly, it seems) that Soeharto was resigned to Megawati's elevation, they allowed her election to proceed but only on the condition that she accept dissident party members into her leadership council. The date of her election was December 22, 1993.[42] A day or two later she reflected on her experience over the last month with the comment, "It's not that easy to be elected a leader from below."[43]

NOTES

1. Panda Nababan, *Gerak dan Langkah Megawati*, 44; "Megawati: Saya belum Memikirkan," *Forum Keadilan*, February 12, 1996, 103; Patrick Walters, "Megawati:

The Enigmatic Democrat," *Australian*, August 2, 1996, 13; Tim Dodd, "The Man behind the Throne," *Australian Financial Review*, February 5, 2003, 43.

    2. Brooks, "Rustle of Ghosts," 66–67.

    3. Labrousse, "Second Life of Bung Karno," 177. The number of Indonesians visiting Sukarno's grave declined in subsequent years: in 1991, it totaled 279,626. See "Makam Bung Karno di Blitar makin dilirik Wisman," *Pelita*, August 20, 1992.

    4. Aspinall, "Political Opposition," 197–99.

    5. Aspinall, "Political Opposition," 199.

    6. Aspinall, "Political Opposition," 195.

    7. Brooks, "Rustle of Ghosts," 69, 75–76, 85.

    8. Adriana Elisabeth Sukatmo, Ganewati Wuryandari, and M. Riza Sihbudi, *PDI dan Prospek Pembangunan Politik*, 5n5.

    9. Walters, *Australian*, August 2, 1996, 13.

    10. Adriana Elisabeth Sukatmo, Ganewati Wuryandari, and M. Riza Sihbudi, *PDI dan Prospek Pembangunan Politik*, 5n5.

    11. *Far Eastern Economic Review*, April 30, 1987, 38.

    12. Quoted in "Mereka Ahli Waris Nama Besar," *Tempo*, December 18, 1993.

    13. "Mereka Ahli Waris Nama Besar," *Tempo*, December 18, 1993.

    14. "Guntur is not as close as could be. He is a mother's child. I cannot blame him. I was myself" (Adams, *Sukarno: An Autobiography*, 285).

    15. "Mereka Ahli Waris Nama Besar," *Tempo*, December 18, 1993.

    16. "Sukmawati Soekarnoputri: Karisma Bung Karno," *Forum Keadilan*, June 8, 1995, 70–71.

    17. Adriana Elisabeth Sukatmo, Ganewati Wuryandari, and M. Riza Sihbudi, *PDI dan Prospek Pembangunan Politik*, 15; Aspinall, "Political Opposition," 200–201.

    18. Adriana Elisabeth Sukatmo, Ganewati Wuryandari, and M. Riza Sihbudi, *PDI dan Prospek Pembangunan Politik*, 5n6.

    19. Rodney Tasker, "Bung Karno's Charisma: Former President Proves a Potent Symbol in Polls," *Far Eastern Economic Review*, April 30, 1987, 38.

    20. Adriana Elisabeth Sukatmo, Ganewati Wuryandari, and M. Riza Sihbudi, *PDI dan Prospek Pembangunan Politik*, 16–24; "Hollow Victory for Soeharto," *Inside Indonesia*, August 1987, 4.

    21. Adriana Elisabeth Sukatmo, Ganewati Wuryandari, and M. Riza Sihbudi, *PDI dan Prospek Pembangunan Politik*, 17.

    22. Liddle, "Indonesia in 1987," 187.

    23. Margot Cohen, "Born to Be Meek," *Far Eastern Economic Review*, October 24, 1991, www.library.ohiou.edu/indopubs/1992/01/13/0000.html.

    24. Menuk Suwondo, "Indonesia: Following in the Bung's Footsteps," *Sunday Age*, May 24, 1992, 3; Aspinall, "Political Opposition," 167.

    25. Suhaini Aznam, "No Surprises: Elections Confirm Golkar's Firm Grip on Power," *Far Eastern Economic Review*, June 25, 1992, 14–15.

    26. Aspinall, "Political Opposition," 205.

    27. John McBeth, "Orders Awaited: Party in Disarray over Sukarno's Daughter," *Far Eastern Economic Review*, December 16, 1993, 20.

    28. Aspinall, "Political Opposition," 206.

29. van Klinken, "Sukarno's Daughter," 2–3; Aspinall, "Political Opposition," 206–7.
30. van Klinken, "Sukarno's Daughter," 3; "Mega didukung dan disanjung," *Forum Keadilan*, October 14, 1993, 21.
31. Brooks, "Rustle of Ghosts," 86.
32. "Keluarga Bung Karno Dipecahbelah?" *Jakarta-Jakarta*, October 16–22, 1993.
33. Edward Aspinall notes that following Megawati's agreement to stand for the position of chairperson, "a tightly knit group of her core supporters formed what became known as . . . [her] *Tim Sukses*, 'Success Team.' This included outspoken PDI legislators and campaigners like Mangara Siahaan, Djathi Koesoemo and Sophan Sophiaan (all Soerjadi-era recruits) and . . . senior journalists like Eros Djarot of *DeTik*, and Panda Nababan of *Forum Keadilan*. Team members discussed tactics, organised 'lobbying,' distributed vast amounts of material to branches and coordinated a vigorous press campaign" ("Political Opposition," 208).
34. *Bendera Sudah Saya Kibarkan!* 18–19. For further commentary on this publication, see Aspinall, "Political Opposition," 209–10.
35. "Mega Disimbolkan Tanda-Tanda Zaman," *Jawa Pos*, November 24, 1993; Joko Supono, "Mengintip Strategi Mega," *Editor*, December 2, 1993, 28.
36. For the expectations of Megawati held by her supporters just before the extraordinary congress, see the polling data and interpretation in Idrus F. Shahab, "Suara Banteng Muda terhadap Mega," *Editor*, December 9, 1993, 25–26.
37. "Mega tak Merasa Dibayangi Nama Besar Bung Karno," *Suara Pembaruan*, November 30, 1993; *Merdeka*, June 22, 1992. For full details of Abdurrahman Wahid's life, see Barton, *Gus Dur*.
38. Personal communication, Greg Fealy, November 27, 1996.
39. For details, see Brooks, "Rustle of Ghosts," 86–87.
40. "Detik-detik Perjuangan Mega," *Forum Keadilan*, December 23, 1993; "Orders Awaited," *Far Eastern Economic Review*, December 16, 1993, 20.
41. *Forum Keadilan*, January 6, 1994.
42. I have altered my earlier interpretation of these events as contained in *In Search of Megawati Sukarnoputri* in the light of Edward Aspinall's detailed and persuasive interpretation. See his "Political Opposition," 216–19.
43. Patrick Walters, "Suharto in Campaign to Eliminate Poll Rival," *Australian*, January 23, 1995, 14.

11

Challenging Soeharto

PARTY LEADER

Minimal as their assistance to Megawati had been, Agum Gumelar and Hendropriyono were transferred to positions of lesser authority in 1994, a sure sign of the president's disfavor.[1] In the meantime, Soeharto's loyal delegates Yogie Memet and the armed forces commander Feisal Tanjung gave full and active support to dissident party elements, such as the chairman of the former caretaker board, in their attempts to undermine her leadership. They set up alternative leadership boards in East Java and at the national level and accused hundreds of party members, including Megawati's husband, Taufik Kiemas, of having had links in the past to the Indonesian Communist Party. Patrick Walters summarized the plight of Megawati and her party supporters at year's end: "After only 12 months as PDI leader Ms Megawati finds her party on the brink of disintegration after a concerted campaign of destabilisation conducted by party rebels backed by influential forces in the government."[2]

At that time, East Java provided sixty-two of the four hundred elected seats in the Indonesian parliament. This was more than any other province in Indonesia, and it was mainly here that Golkar lost votes to the PDI in 1992. For these reasons it became the principal battleground between the PDI and the government in anticipation of the 1997 elections. But the contest was a most uneven one, for having Megawati as PDI leader hardly outweighed the advantages Golkar enjoyed by being the government party in a closely managed political system. It is therefore hard to understand why the PDI leader and her supporters were hounded so relentlessly, as indeed they were.[3]

The answer could only be that Soeharto was planning—in fact, had been planning all along—to stand again for president in 1998 and that he intended to build his bid on an improved Golkar vote, which at the very least would retrieve the ground lost to the PDI in 1992. Doubtless, this is why he "dropped" Harmoko, an effective political campaigner, into the Golkar chair in 1993 and had his eldest daughter, Siti Hadijanti Rukmana, appointed a vice chairperson on its new executive board, with responsibility for coordinating the party's election campaign in East and Central Java.[4]

As noted, the possibility of Habibie running for president in 1998 with Golkar support had angered some military men and inclined them to look favorably on the PDI; but once it became clear that Soeharto was to be the candidate, this stance lost its raison d'être. Whatever scope remained within military circles for a sympathetic hearing for the PDI was further limited in February 1995 when President Soeharto appointed General Hartono to replace General Wismoyo Arismunandar as army chief of staff. Although related to the president's wife, Wismoyo was a soldier's soldier with a strong professional disposition. Hartono, by contrast, was a palace general, enjoying close ties with the president's eldest daughter.[5] Like Feisal Tanjung, he was sympathetic to Islam's playing a role in state affairs; but in other respects, the two men were rivals. Feisal Tanjung enjoyed a close relationship with Habibie whereas Hartono shared the Soeharto children's antipathy for him. Indeed, they competed with each other in their efforts to undermine Megawati as a way of proving their loyalty to the president. By contrast, the defense minister, General Edi Sudrajat, and the commander of the armed forces staff college, Major General Theo Syafei, were supporters of a secular state and were correspondingly sympathetic toward the like-minded PDI but lacked the influence to protect it.[6] Their main concern was not only the stance of the Islamically inclined "green" officers but also the activities of their mentors, Soeharto and Habibie, who had been seeking to court and co-opt modernist Islam since they approved the foundation of the Association of Indonesian Islamic Intellectuals (Ikatan Cendiakawan Muslimin Indonesia; ICMI) in 1990.

One month after his promotion, General Hartono offered army backing to the Gokar Party such as it had not received since the 1970s: he appeared with the president's daughter on the stage at a Golkar rally, clad in the yellow jacket that serves as a uniform for party members, and declared that "every ABRI [Indonesian armed forces] member is a Golkar cadre." He added that "as a Golkar cadre, it is legally binding for me to accept the advice and guidance of the Golkar board chair, Mbak Tutut [Siti Hadijanti Rukmana]."[7] Soeharto was going to extraordinary lengths to meet the electoral challenge posed by the PDI under Megawati's leadership. In addition to the campaigning talents of Harmoko were the inducements of the president's daughter—for example, five billion rupiahs were distributed to *pesantren* (Islamic boarding schools) in East Java in 1995–1996[8]—and the intimidation of the armed forces.

Megawati was left in a precarious position, but every time the government dealt her or her party a new blow, the people's esteem and affection for her rose considerably—especially when the government's tactics were of a personal nature, such as accusing her husband of being tainted by communism or preventing the Sukarno family from organizing the annual pilgrimage to their father's grave in Blitar on the anniversary of his birth. Her close friend, Abdurrahman Wahid, noted that "she expresses her protest in a silent way; she doesn't say things easily" and, perhaps sensing the power of this, advised her "to be silent." He added, "She's a leader and she leads by not doing anything. . . . That she is not being coopted by the government, that is enough."[9] But this silence and inactivity spoke volumes: Megawati became a mute symbol, or, rather, a symbol because she was mute, a sign for decency amid the abuse of power of the Soeharto regime. Her ability to harness her silence and her stillness in this way—to speak in sign language, as it were—was an interesting variation on her father's volubility, and perhaps no less eloquent.[10]

NOMINATION FOR PRESIDENT

We have seen the lengths to which Soeharto was prepared to go in order to secure his reelection as president in 1998 on the basis of an enlarged Golkar vote, so we can therefore imagine the nature of his reaction to the news, in October 1995, that Megawati had not repudiated a statement issued by seven PDI branches in Central Java calling on her to stand as a candidate for the presidency at the next opportunity.[11] In failing to repudiate this statement, she ignored the warnings of her advisers, who certainly had no trouble in imagining Soeharto's response (that it would render her already precarious position more precarious by focusing the president's wrath on her)[12] and of one newspaper (that "daring to nominate herself as presidential candidate would seem likely to speed her downfall").[13] By behaving in this way and by deciding, in effect, to challenge the man who had toppled her father, the observer is confronted with the possibility that this woman, famous for her soft, maternal qualities, was actually seeking to avenge his overthrow and humiliation. Of course, her maternal appearance greatly contributed to her appeal, but if we recall the reason she gave in 1987 for entering politics—"my children were already independent"—it is possible to surmise that what we are dealing with here is not the softness and nurturing of a motherly figure but the toughness and androgyny of the postparental woman.[14] A comment about Megawati by Aberson Marle Sihaloho, one of her main backers in the PDI and the chief facilitator of her presidential nomination, gives some plausibility to this claim: "She is a strong person. She would be one female with virile courage."[15]

By challenging Soeharto for the presidency, Megawati was living dangerously—recall her father's 1964 Independence Day speech, "The Year of Living Dangerously"—and this was perhaps one circumstance that caused her to reflect on the matter of fear. In a speech before five thousand of the party faithful in Maumere, Nusa Tenggara Timur, on September 28, 1995, she said,

> The feeling of fear is everywhere in the territory of the unitary state of the Republic of Indonesia, and its presence does not mature but rather stunts the autonomy of the people. We have been independent for fifty years, and have just now celebrated that anniversary with great joy. But, and I say this apologetically and with respectful feelings for this Republic, how come the feelings of its people and citizens are still blanketed in fear? Please ask yourselves, each of you, do you feel that fear?[16]

But her concern with this issue predated her challenge to Soeharto. She told Aspinall that "after joining the . . . [PDI], she had always viewed her main task as 'breaking down the old trauma' (the legacy of 1965) in the party's mass support base."[17] She may also have been influenced by Aung San Suu Kyi's thoughts on the same topic. The two women had not met, although as a young girl Suu Kyi was introduced to President Sukarno while he was visiting Rangoon.[18] But Megawati may well have read an Indonesian translation of the Burmese leader's 1991 essay "Freedom from Fear," in which Suu Kyi wrote vividly of "the people of Burma [who] had wearied of a precarious state of passive apprehension where they were 'as water in the cupped hands' of the powers that be."[19] Certainly, both leaders were concerned by the prevalence of fear under the authoritarian governments in their respective countries and its debilitating consequences for the citizenry at large.

GOVERNMENT COUP

In early 1996, Soeharto let it be known that he wanted Megawati removed from the leadership of the PDI. He then left its principal implementation to the minister for home affairs Yogie Memet; the armed forces commander Feisal Tanjung; and the chief of staff for social and political affairs Lieutenant General Syarwan Hamid. Like Feisal Tanjung, Syarwan Hamid was supportive of political Islam, close to Habibie, and through Habibie linked to the modernist Moslems of ICMI.[20] In May of that year this trio embarked on a clumsy charade: they cajoled dissident members of the PDI to petition for an extraordinary congress of the PDI as a way of removing Megawati from the leadership. They then portrayed the consequent call for a congress as the democratic expression of opinion within the party, to which they as a government were obliged to respond—provided, of course, that the petitioners had acted in keeping with the party's constitution. No one was fooled by this performance, certainly not Megawati's supporters. The PDI treasurer, Laksamana Sukardi, told Walters that "the government was trying to 'facilitate a coup' against Mrs Megawati and predicted an outburst of 'mass anger' if the PDI leader was deposed."[21] He added, "This is a critical situation not only for Mrs Megawati but for Mr Soeharto. This is happening because the Government thinks she is a threat. Mrs Megawati is the first popularly elected political leader in the history of the New Order and she won't compromise."[22]

In early June, in an atmosphere of deepening crisis, Megawati loyalists took up guard at the party's headquarters in Diponegoro Street, Central Jakarta, and displayed banners on bamboo poles declaring "Mega Yes, Congress No" and "I am willing to die for Mbak Megawati."[23] Other similarly motivated supporters in various parts of Indonesia took to pledging their loyalty to the PDI leader by signing their names in their own blood.[24] This evidence of self-sacrificing devotion on the part of some of her followers suggests that for them Megawati had indeed become a charismatic leader.[25] However, there is reason to believe that discovering the extent of her influence over young people left her in two minds: on the one hand, she was tempted to realize her widespread and often devoted public support in a people's power–type movement; on the other, she hesitated at the prospect of young people laying down their lives for her.

Events now moved quickly. On June 14, representatives from thirty non-governmental organizations (NGOs) gathered in front of the parliament building. The chairperson of the Indonesian Workers' Welfare Union, Muchtar Pakpahan, read out a prepared statement condemning the government's interference into the internal affairs of the PDI and declaring the support of the NGO community for Megawati's leadership of the party.[26] Similar demonstrations in Jakarta and other cities of Java took place in the ensuing days.[27] On June 19, the PDI leader dismissed sixteen members of her central executive board for convening the rival congress but offered no comment on the fact that it enjoyed the endorsement of President Soeharto. On the same day approximately five thousand people marched through Central Jakarta in support of her right to continue leading the PDI.[28] The following day, June 20, protesters again rallied in the streets of Jakarta as the rival congress convened in Medan. According to Walters, the "rally started peacefully with Mrs Megawati urging supporters to remain orderly 'and show that we can be as democratic as our father when he proclaimed independence.'" But when the security forces blocked its progress in front of the Gambir railway station, "red-shirted PDI supporters hurled rocks at police and tried to charge through . . . [their] lines. The security forces, backed by armoured vehicles, retreated, regrouped and then bore down on a group of about 1500 protesters who turned and fled." It is possible that one protester was killed in the clash. The number of injured, including members of the military, reached at least one hundred.[29]

In the meantime the government-managed congress in Medan removed Megawati from her position as general chairperson of the PDI and chose Soerjadi in her place. This was the very same Soerjadi whose election at the July 1993 party congress the government had refused to recognize, thereby precipitating the sequence of events that led to Megawati's election as party head at the end of that year. However, Megawati refused to be intimidated by the government. On the afternoon of June 23, she arrived at the PDI office dressed in the party's colors of black and red and addressed a crowd that overflowed from the grounds of the office onto Diponegoro Street, where her supporters stood twenty deep. She said, "I am the lawful, legal and constitutional chairperson of the PDI for the 1993–98 period. That which called itself a 'congress' in Medan is in violation of the party's rules and the constitution." She then linked her struggle and that of her supporters to the 1945 constitution and, by implication, to her father as one of its chief authors: "Remember that what we are fighting for now is defending the sovereignty that is in the hands of the people and to redress the democracy given to us under the 1945 constitution," she said to "roars of approval" from the crowd.[30] Inspired by Megawati's stand, prodemocracy activists, students, and members of NGOs brought their respective organizations into a loose federation that they called the Indonesian People's Assembly (Majelis Rakyat Indonesia) and rallied to her cause. By July, "democracy forums" had sprung up in the grounds of the PDI building, and large crowds, spilling out onto the street, gathered to hear members of the radical People's Democratic Party and others—such as the outspoken PDI legislator Aberson Marle Sihaloho—offer fundamental criticism of the Soeharto regime.[31] A number of people took heart from these developments—for instance, Bambang Widjojanto of the Legal Aid Foundation saw in Megawati's defiance of the government an opportunity to promote people's power in Indonesia.[32] But, as Aspinall observed, "it was difficult for . . . [Megawati] to appear as the embodiment of the whole of society against the regime like, say, Corazon Aquino had in the more homogeneous culture of the Philippines" because she "lacked significant (modernist) Muslim support." As Aspinall also noted, this state of affairs was a measure of Soeharto's success in co-opting prominent figures from this stream of Islam by permitting the establishment of ICMI in 1990 under Habibie's leadership and by adopting a receptive stance to their various demands.[33] There were some exceptions to this trend—most notably, Sri Bintang Pamungkas and Ridwan Saidi (who claimed that "that modernist Muslims . . . [were] poorly positioned to intervene in the process of democratisation and regime transition when it eventually began"[34])—and their number would grow in the following months, partly as a result of the government's treatment of Megawati. However, in general terms, it is true to say that in July 1996 the leaders of modernist Islam were unsympathetic to Megawati's struggle against the Soeharto government.

Such freedom could not last. Summarizing a special report carried in *Tempo* magazine three years later, Aspinall wrote, "Suharto gave a verbal command to [Feisal] Tanjung, Yogie [Memet] and Coordinating Minister for Political and Security Affairs, Soesilo Soedarman, to take over the . . . [PDI headquarters]. The Director General for Social and Political Affairs of the Interior Ministry, Sutoyo N.K. and Syarwan Hamid were the chief planners of the operation, while the Commander of the Greater Jakarta . . . [military region], Major General Sutiyoso, held primary responsibility for coordinating operations in the field."[35] Thus, it was that on July 27, some of her loyalists who had taken up guard duty there, having declared their willingness to die for Mbak Megawati, proved as good as their word as they sought unsuccessfully to fend off an attack on the party building by thugs dressed as Soerjadi supporters and reinforced by police and army personnel. The government admitted that five died and 146 were injured in the attack and subsequent rioting, but three months after the event, the Indonesian Commission on Human Rights declared that an additional twenty-three people were still missing and quite possibly were dead.[36]

The expression "government thugs" was in danger of becoming a tautology in late New Order Indonesia. It reminds one of a remark made by Aung San Suu Kyi on July 8, 1989, which was not without applicability to Indonesia and which revealed in the starkest terms what Megawati had been up against: "She declared that the NLD [National League for Democracy] wanted 'the [Burmese] army to realize that they have been made to play the role of thugs, to make sure that a few old men [principally Ne Win] can remain in power.' "[37] The thuggish role imposed on the Indonesian armed forces on July 27 was designed to secure the same outcome that Soeharto had enjoyed in previous presidential elections: the unanimous endorsement of a further term by the members of the People's Consultative Assembly. His pride would settle for nothing less; certainly, it could not brook an electoral contest with the daughter of the man he had deposed in 1966–1967.[38]

LEGAL CHALLENGE

If Megawati was angered by the Soeharto government's removal of her from the party leadership in May, she was deeply shocked and saddened by its murderous attack on her party office in July. This was evident from a talk she gave one hundred days later at a *selamatan*-like commemoration of the event.[39] According to a journalist from *Jawa Pos*,

> Her voice choked up when she touched on the event . . . which then became known as "Grey Saturday." Mega said . . . "it does not feel like it but evidently it is already 100 days since the 27 July affair. We can count one hundred days since the take over (Mega wept and stopped speaking for almost three minutes) of the office of the Central Leadership Council of the PDI at Diponegoro Street No. 58 (tears again prevented Mega from continuing). This is a troubling experience for PDI members, and a troubling experience for the Indonesian people."[40]

In this state of mind, Megawati considered her choices. If she had ever felt tempted by the idea of forming a people's power–movement, then it was probably this demonstration of the ruthlessness with which Soeharto and his military loyalists were prepared to defend his presidency that persuaded her to resist risking the safety and well-being of her supporters. But nor was she prepared to accept the advice of those who urged her to lie low; such was her sense of outrage and indignation. She had filed a lawsuit in early July against sixteen functionaries of Soerjadi's faction of the PDI, against the home affairs minister Yogie Memet, against the armed forces chief Feisal Tanjung, and against the chief of police—challenging the result of the congress that ousted her as chair and demanding the award of damages. In the wake of Grey Saturday she resolved to make legal challenges such as this the centerpiece of her strategy. Accordingly, she filed another suit against the General Election Institute, which rejected her list of the PDI's candidates for the 1997 election in favor of one provided by Soerjadi.[41] Throughout the following months, she filed hundreds of other suits in Jakarta and in the regions, employing a veritable army of lawyers in the process.

It was a shrewd step: by winning, she would expose the illegal acts of the government; by losing—which was, of course, far more likely—the judiciary's lack of independence would be glaringly obvious. Either way, she would make it clear that what existed in Indonesia was not the rule of law. Her commitment and seriousness of purpose in this matter could not be doubted; indeed, she persisted in it despite a warning from her friend and supporter Abdurrahman Wahid, who urged her to drop her lawsuit against the armed forces commander, the police chief, and the minister for home affairs.[42] She never missed an opportunity to affirm her strong commitment to the *negara hukum*, the state based on the rule of law, as demonstrated, for example, in the following remark, from late September: "Again I want it to be apparent in the record of my life that I am making a serious effort . . . to remind people again that this state was established as a law state that has to be obeyed by everyone who considers themselves Indonesians."[43]

But in taking this firm stand in defense of the *negara hukum*, Megawati placed herself in a paradoxical position, for it was her father who undermined the *negara hukum* by "explicitly rejecting the *trias politika* (separation of powers) [of Montesquieu] for Indonesia" and by appointing the chairman of the Supreme Court to his cabinet;[44] not Soeharto, who was merely a later beneficiary of his actions. No less paradoxical was the fact that while she was engaged in this struggle on behalf of the *negara hukum* in the aftermath of Grey Saturday, a number of the people who had associated themselves with her struggle in June and July—including Muchtar Pakpahan and fifteen members of the People's Democratic Party—were arrested and charged under her father's antisubversion law.[45] As noted in chapter 2, this law was first issued as a presidential decree by Sukarno in 1963; and as noted in chapter 6, Soeharto's New Order government incorporated it into Indonesian law by statute in 1969, taking advantage of its catchall phrasing but redefining the ideological principles that it was designed to protect.[46] Eventually, even the New Order government became embarrassed by it, although this did not stop them from invoking its clauses in the aftermath of July 27.[47]

Indeed, Megawati herself came close to being hoist with her father's petard. After celebrating the anniversary of the PDI at her home in January 1997 (at which she "appealed to all the leaders of the nation . . . to throw off the hypocrisy which constricts the Indonesian nation at this time"[48]), the police claimed she was in violation of law 5 of 1969, which states that no political meeting can be held without a police permit.[49] Like the antisubversion law, this law had its origins in a presidential decree issued by Sukarno in 1963 and was later incorporated into Indonesian law by statute.[50]

Most paradoxical of all is the fact that Megawati appeared to regard her father as a democrat and proponent of the *negara hukum*, based on the strength of his role as one of the principal authors of the 1945 constitution. Consider her exhortation of June 23, 1996, "Remember that what we are fighting for now is defending the sovereignty that is in the hands of the people and to redress the democracy given to us under the 1945 constitution"; and her statement from late September, "I am making a serious effort . . . to remind people again that this state was established as a law state." Perhaps she had taken at face value the official explication of the 1945 constitution, which proclaimed Indonesia to be a "state which is based on Law (Rechtsstaat)." She was also no doubt familiar with his frequent assertions of love for the people and his no-less-frequent claims to be uniquely able to give voice to their aspirations. It is quite possible that she misconstrued this populist strand in his thinking as a democratic one.[51] This assessment would be in keeping with the tendency of many Indonesian leaders from the democratic era to associate democracy not with, say, liberty or the means to guarantee it but rather with the people, "seen as an undifferentiated mass, whose interests were overwhelmingly common rather than mutually antagonistic," and with their participation in government.[52] This is a disturbing conclusion to reach, for its implication is that Megawati's commitment to the *negara hukum* had not extended to thinking through the conditions necessary for its survival.

Such skepticism may seem churlish, for Megawati showed no sign of abandoning her legal vigil. One of her colleagues, Haryanto Taslam, was declared a suspect by the police in the case of the allegedly illegal gathering held at her house in January 1997; in fact, Megawati herself was summoned to the South Jakarta police station as a witness. She was interrogated at length on February 20 and March 3, and on each occasion she was accompanied by several thousand of her supporters fearlessly shouting, "If Megawati is allowed to participate, we say 'yes' to the 1997 Elections!" But although she complied with the summons, she queried the legality of the procedure. Indeed, she filed a law suit in the administrative court against Soeharto himself, the attorney general, and the chief of the South Jakarta police, on the grounds that as a member of parliament her investigation by the police required the written permission of the president, whereas he had only provided spoken permission.[53]

In early April, R. O. Tambunan, the head of Megawati's legal team (called "the Indonesian Democracy Defence Team"),[54] reported that the Jakarta Administrative Court had rejected Megawati's lawsuit on the grounds that "it could not interfere in a criminal case that was under investigation."[55] By this time approximately thirty of her lawsuits had been rejected by the courts, usually on the grounds that they did not have the authority to sit in judgment on internal party matters. It was this outcome that led R. O. Tambunan and about forty members of his legal team to approach the Supreme Court directly with a letter expressing concern about government interference in judicial decisions. He later declared to a journalist that "the throwing out of the accusations of the DPP [Dewan Pimpinan Pusat, "Central Leadership Council"] PDI of Megawati Sukarnoputri leads one to suspect a connection between the Supreme Court and an external party which has asked the judges to reject Megawati's claims."[56] In the late New Order period, this conclusion would have surprised very few; nevertheless, its public utterance by a well-known lawyer helped to make abundantly clear to all that the judiciary in Indonesia had been reduced to a mere extension of the government.

THE 1997 ELECTIONS

Growing signs of anger and resentment were evident in Indonesian society at this time. Apart from the increasing boldness and outspokenness of Megawati's supporters, Moslems vented their feelings on Christians and Chinese in Situbondo, Tasikmalaja, and Rengasdengklok in October, December, and January 1997, respectively. Consequently, a nervous government banned all outdoor election campaigning for the elections of May 29. This election had already been rendered more meaningless than previous ones by the government's rejection of Megawati's list of election candidates in favor of one proffered by Soerjadi. As a result, many citizens—Megawati's supporters in particular—wondered whether there was any point at all in voting. Refusing to exercise one's right to vote was not illegal but could lead to sanctions from the authorities. Far more dangerous was to call on others not to vote. As we shall see, this is what the modernist Islamic leader Sri Bintang Pamungkas did. A final possibility was to vote informally by piercing all three party symbols or none. These approaches were regarded in Indonesia as a way of registering a protest against the government and are known collectively as *Golput*.[57] But, as the outspoken General Theo Syafei acknowledged, a voter who did not pierce any party symbol ran the risk of having his or her ballot paper used by an official to record a vote for the government party.[58]

In February, the Indonesian Bishops Conference in its pre-Easter pastoral letter—which was signed by Cardinal Julius Darmaatmadja—offered guidance to those of its flock who were wondering what to do in these difficult circumstances:

> If you truly feel unrepresented and are convinced in good conscience that your sovereignty has no channel for expression, we can understand that you will give expression to your sense of responsibility and freedom by not choosing, and you do not commit a sin by not voting. Conversely, if you face very strong pressure, you may conform to local direction rather than be made to suffer a disproportionate loss at a later date. What is important is that you are able to justify your choice morally.[59]

While Catholics were considering their position, modernist Moslems in ICMI were forced to rethink theirs in light of the harsh treatment meted out to two of their most prominent colleagues by the regime. Sri Bintang Pamungkas was ejected from this organization and lost his position as a parliamentarian from the Islamic Unity Development Party (Partai Persatuan Pembangunan; PPP) after he made a speech in Germany in 1995. The president was also visiting Germany at the time, and in the speech Sri Bintang allegedly referred to Soeharto as "a dictator." Deprived of his parliamentary immunity, he was then convicted under the lese-majesty clause of the Indonesian criminal code (article 134) of having engaged in "deliberate disrespect for the President" and, on May 8, 1996, was sentenced to thirty-four months' jail. Released from jail pending the outcome of his appeal, he resumed his political activities. Just three weeks later, on May 29, 1996, he launched the Indonesian Democratic Union Party (Partai Uni Demokrasi Indonesia).[60] Furthermore, early in the following year he sent Lebaran greeting cards to all the senior officials of the Indonesian government, including Soeharto himself. The cards contained the aims of his new party: to boycott the general elections of 1997 and to reject the nomination of Soeharto for president for the term 1998–2003. Consequently, he was arrested and jailed on March 5 and charged under the familiar antisubversion law.[61]

Amien Rais's initial protest was more muted than Sri Bintang's but was perhaps more significant, as he was not only a member of ICMI but also the leader of the large, modernist Islamic educational organization Muhammadiyah. It seems that his principal crime, in Soeharto's eyes, was to describe as "unconstitutional" the high level of foreign involvement in Freeport and the other mining ventures in Indonesia.[62] At the president's instigation, Habibie removed him from ICMI on February 24, thereby confirming that his organization was not one for the expression of Islamic aspirations but rather a corporatist-style body that Soeharto used to control the *ummat*.[63]

While modernists such as Amien Rais were learning that membership of ICMI did not exempt them from the regime's insistence on total compliance, traditionalists such as the leader of the Nahdlatul Ulama (NU), Abdurrahman Wahid, were being made to pay for their independence. In recent years Abdurrahman had made critical remarks about Soeharto and had refused to endorse his renomination for president in 1993. Consequently, the aggrieved president encouraged the activities of Abdurrahman's rivals at NU's 1994 congress, at which the latter just managed to hang on to his position, and in the following period. He was aided in this activity by his daughter Siti Hadijanti Rukmana, Habibie, Feisal Tanjung, and Hartono—all of whom distributed money and other resources to the NU leader's main opponents in 1995.[64] Finally, after seeing what happened to Megawati in 1996, Abdurrahman signaled to Soeharto that he was ready to abandon his critical stance. As noted, he did so by urging Megawati to drop her lawsuit against the armed forces commander, the police chief, and the minister for home affairs.[65] A formal reconciliation between Abdurrahman and Soeharto took place on November 2, 1996, and the following day he declared that NU would support Soeharto's reelection as president at the meeting of the People's Consultative Assembly in March 1998.[66] In the months preceding the election, he went even further by taking Siti Hadijanti Rukmana on a tour of *pesantren* in Central and East Java. She was, it will be recalled, a vice chairperson on Golkar's executive board, with responsibility for coordinating the party's election campaign in East and Central Java. By taking this step, Abdurrahman was, in effect, encouraging members of Nahdlatul Ulama to vote for the government party.[67]

Soeharto issued a threat on February 28 that gave the lie to the regime's characteristic *negara hukum* rhetoric: "If the people want Suharto to step down, I'll say thank you. I'll accept the decision. But if they do it by means other than the MPR . . . I'll clobber them because they are violating the constitution."[68] The hollowness of this rhetoric was even more evident in Feisal Tanjung's assertion two days earlier that during the election campaign "troops would be under orders to 'shoot on sight' anyone who 'violates the law.'"[69] But the many opponents of the regime had grown bolder, and with this boldness came an enhanced ability to see the *negara hukum* for what it was: a smoke screen, behind which lay the reality of the *negara kekuasaan,* or power state.[70] Indeed, one is sometimes left with the impression that the leaders themselves were the last ones to be inhabited by the myths and lies by which they ruled.

On April 15, approximately two thousand PDI members loyal to Megawati kept her cause before the public eye by staging a rally outside the parliament, crying out remarks such as "This is the house of the people" and "Soerjadi is not a representative of the people." Some of them handed to officials a petition entitled "A Statement of Concern over the Implementation of the 1997 Elections." It urged the People's Consultative Assembly "to admonish the government: in order that they . . . restore the leadership of Megawati Sukarnoputri, who was chosen in a democratic and legitimate way according to law; and in order that the law, democracy and morality is not deformed nor violations of human rights occur in the running of the elections." Twenty members of parliament from the PDI signed it, including Taufik Kiemas, Guruh Sukarnoputra, Aberson Marle Sihaloho, Sophan Sophiaan, and Mangara M. Siahaan.[71] Two days later Megawati herself issued a bleak assessment of the state of Indonesian society and politics, in an English-language document intended to demonstrate to her foreign constituency of journalists, members of the United States Congress, and officials of the State Department that she stood for more than simple opposition to Soerjadi and his faction in the PDI. She wrote, "There is a strong impression that we cannot hold ourselves together as a nation living within a . . . [law state]. There is a strong impression that we are disintegrating as a pluralistic society, and that we are heading towards a society dominated by social jealousy and mutual distrust." By way of solution, she called for the restoration of Indonesian democracy and an independent judiciary.[72]

Then, on April 23, she declared that the PDI under her leadership would not take part in the election campaign.[73] Although this decision was greeted with relief by hard-pressed government security officials, it caused a degree of confusion among her supporters, some of whom visited her at her home in South Jakarta to ask what she meant by her directive.[74] Furthermore, it did not stop many of them, especially in Solo and Yogyakarta, from joining the campaign of the PPP and even declaring their willingness to vote for it on May 29, in light of the exclusion of the PDI from the elections. Although the national leadership of the PPP viewed this development with apprehension, the chairperson of the PPP in Solo, Moedrick Setiawan Sangidoe, welcomed followers of Megawati with open arms. Before long, this new, enthusiastic, and growing alliance of nominal and devout Moslems acquired the name Mega-Bintang, or Mega-Star (where "star" refers to the emblem of the PPP). Needless to say, the government, which had managed to co-opt a section of the devout, was alarmed to see its divide-and-rule approach partly undone by the popularity of this broad cultural alliance. It subsequently attempted to ban pictures or banners that contained the words Mega-Bintang or otherwise suggested an alliance of Megawati's supporters with the Unity Development Party.[75]

Megawati finally declared her intentions for polling day in a short speech from her house on May 22. First she expressed her sympathy for the large number of people who had lost their lives during the campaign; then she stated that the sovereignty of the people found no place in the manner in which these elections were being implemented. Afterward, she declared that "I will not use my political right as a citizen in the elections scheduled for 29 May 1997."[76]

By stating that she would not be voting, Megawati may have been hoping that members and supporters of her party would follow suit, thereby swelling the Golput ranks.[77] But clearly her minimum expectation of her followers was that they would not vote for the PDI (Soerjadi), for she also said, "As the General Chairperson of the DPP PDI which is valid and constitutional, I am of the opinion that what some are pleased to call 'the Medan Congress PDI' is invalid and unconstitutional, and therefore to choose it on 29 May 1997 is also invalid and unconstitutional."[78] Given this frame of mind, she would have been pleased with the collapse in the PDI vote, from 15 percent in 1992 to 3.07 percent in 1997. However, she would not have been pleased to see the timidly led and conformist PPP benefit from her political misfortune by gaining an additional 5 percent of the vote, from 17 percent in 1992 to 22.76 percent in 1997, largely as a result of the Mega-Bintang phenomenon. Although it is impossible to calculate the Golput vote accurately, we can certainly estimate it. If we start with the decline in the PDI vote of approximately 12 percent and subtract the 5 percent that went to the PPP, then it is reasonable to speculate that the remaining 7 percent of voters who were lost to the PDI either refused to vote or deliberately spoiled their ballot paper, which is to say they voted Golput. Soeharto also had reason to be pleased. Golkar's vote, boosted perhaps by Abdurrahman's opening the Nahdlatul Ulama constituency to the government party, jumped from 68 percent in 1992 to 74.54 percent in 1997.[79] This result clearly made up for Golkar's humiliating loss of votes to the PDI in 1992, but it was only achieved after Soeharto had wreaked destruction on the PDI in 1996—and it was this act, of course, that did so much to damage the legitimacy of his regime.

NOTES

1. See Robison, "Indonesian Politics in 1993/94," 53.
2. Patrick Walters, "Poll Rival," *Australian*, January 23, 1995, 14.
3. For the details, see John McBeth, "Mediating or Meddling?" *Far Eastern Economic Review*, January 26, 1995, 24.
4. John McBeth, "Father Knows Best," *Far Eastern Economic Review*, November 25, 1993, 25–26; John McBeth, "Containment Strategy," *Far Eastern Economic Review*, June 8, 1995, 18–19.
5. Patrick Walters, "Suharto Ensures His Succession," *Australian*, February 14, 1995, 13.
6. See Aspinall, "Political Opposition," 221–22.
7. Hartono, quoted in Fealy, "Indonesian Politics," 24. See also Patrick Walters, "Golkar Campaigners See Yellow on Election Trail," *Weekend Australian*, March 16–17, 1996, 15.
8. Fealy, "Indonesian Politics," 3.
9. Abdurrahman Wahid interviewed by Diane Martin on the Australian Broadcasting Corporation's *Indian Pacific* radio program, October 26, 1996. Compare the similar remark of another supporter of Megawati, Laksamana Sukardi, the treasurer of the PDI: "Having the courage to say 'no' is the only requirement for a PDI leader" (Patrick Walters, "Big Names Battle for Crucial East Java," *Australian*, June 1, 1995).
10. My argument here owes a good deal to Anderson, "Cartoons and Monuments," 282–321.
11. "Support for Megawati 'against' Establishment," *Jakarta Post*, October 21, 1995.
12. See Fealy, "Indonesian Politics," 30–31.
13. "Who's Afraid of Mega?" *Jakarta Post*, February 1, 1996.
14. I am drawing here on David Gutmann's theory of postparental women who "can discover in themselves an executive and 'political' capacity that had hitherto lain fallow and unrecognized" and which has its origins in aggressive qualities assigned to their partners during the "chronic emergency" of parenthood but subsequently reclaimed.

Gutmann's conclusions are based on the observation of trends across cultures—urban American, Mayan, Navajo, and Druze—and cannot, therefore, be dismissed as an artifact of this or that particular culture. See his *Reclaimed Powers*. A summary of his work may be found in McIntyre, "Introduction," 7–9.

15. Readers may wish to consult this statement in the original Indonesian: "Dia orang kuat. Inilah satu-satunya betina yang jantan" ("Mencari Presiden lewat Sejumlah Formulir," *Forum Keadilan*, February 12, 1966, 100).

16. "Mayoritas Rakyat Indonesia belum merdeka dari Rasa Takut," *Kompas*, September 30, 1995, www.library.ohiou.edu/indopubs/1995/09/30/0008.html.

17. Aspinall, interview with Megawati Sukarnoputri, December 11, 1995, in his "Political Opposition," 223n119.

18. "Wawancara Aung San Suu Kyi," *Tempo Online*, November 29, 1996, www.library.ohiou.edu/indopubs/1996/11/29/0104.html.

19. Aung San Suu Kyi, *Freedom from Fear*, 180–81.

20. See Aspinall, "Political Opposition," 241.

21. Laksamana Sukardi was a banker who had occupied senior positions at Citibank in Indonesia and at Lippobank. Like Sophan Sophiaan, Kwik Kian Gie, and Mangara Siahaan, he joined the PDI in the early 1990s. He is the nephew of Wachdiat Sukardi, a member of the former Indonesian National Party who, in May 1980, was one of fifty signatories of a Statement of Concern that accused President Soeharto of appropriating the state ideology of *Panca Sila* for his own purposes and of behaving in an unconstitutional manner. He subsequently served on the Petition of Fifty working group (Aspinall, "Political Opposition," 202, 202n24, 235n162; *Meluruskan Perjalanan Orde Baru*).

22. Patrick Walters, "Jakarta Pressure on Leader to Resign," *Australian*, June 6, 1996, 9.

23. "Mega: Saya akan tetap Maju terus," *Jawa Pos*, June 6, 1996, and personal observation.

24. "Ministers Back Breakaways to Oust PDI Chief Megawati," *Jakarta Post*, June 6, 1996; "Kader PDI Bali dukung Mega, Kantor DPP dijaga Arus Bawah," *Bisnis Indonesia*, June 7, 1996.

25. See Willner, *Spellbinders*, 3–8.

26. "Ribuan Warga PDI Jatim akan 'long-march' Surabaya-Jakarta," *Kompas*, June 15, 1996.

27. See "PDI Rebels Call on Megawati to Defend Herself," *Jakarta Post*, June 19, 1996.

28. "Megawati Fires 16 Dissenters from PDI Board," *Jakarta Post*, June 20, 1996.

29. "Megawati Rally Erupts," *Australian*, June 21, 1996, 1. See also "Kongres Dibuka, Long March Berdarah," *Bernas*, June 21, 1996, for a detailed chronology.

30. Patrick Walters, "Sukarno's Daughter Confronts the Generals," *Australian*, June 24, 1996, 1–2. See also John McBeth, "Political Engineering," *Far Eastern Economic Review*, July 4, 1996, 14–15.

31. See Aspinall, "Political Opposition," 253.

32. Margot Cohen, "New Zeal," *Far Eastern Economic Review*, July 11, 1996, 19–20; "Sebuah Pertarungan Banteng Berkepala Dua," *Forum Keadilan*, July 15, 1996, 19.

33. Aspinall, "Political Opposition," 263.
34. Ridwan Saidi made this remark to Edward Aspinall on November 27, 1996 ("Political Opposition," 260n90). See also, Hefner, *Civil Islam,* 184.
35. Aspinall, "Political Opposition," 257n79.
36. Louise Williams, "Riot Report Damns Regime," *Sydney Morning Herald,* October 14, 1996.
37. Aung San Suu Kyi, *Freedom from Fear,* 313.
38. See Harold Crouch, "All to Placate a Proud Sultan," *Australian Financial Review,* July 30, 1996, www.library.ohiou.edu/indopubs/1996/07/31/0049.html; see also, Goenawan Mohamad, "Jalan Mega, Perkuat Oposisi di Luar Sistem," *Suara Independen,* July 1996, 30.
39. Javanese nominal Moslems such as Megawati, whose principal religious allegiance is to an essentially syncretist complex of beliefs, commemorate death by holding a *selamatan,* or communal feast. It is held on the death and then "three, seven, forty and one hundred days after death, on the first and second anniversaries of the death, and on the thousandth day after death" (Geertz, *Religion of Java,* 71–72).
40. "Peringati 27 Juli, Mega Menangis," *Jawa Pos,* November 4, 1996.
41. "Gugatan Megawati Diserahkan ke Pengadilan Negeri Jakpus," *Suara Pembaruan,* July 4, 1996; "Mega Resmi Gugat LPU," *Bernas,* October 9, 1996.
42. *Suara Pembaruan,* October 4, 1996.
43. "Megawati Sukarnoputri: Pintu Ditutup, Dinding Dibuka," *Tiras,* September 28, 1996, www.library.ohiou.edu/indopubs/1996/09/29/0008.html.
44. Lev, "Judicial Institutions," 268.
45. A. Made Tony Supriatma, *1996: Tahun Kekerasan,* 38.
46. Zifcak, "'But a Shadow of Justice,'" 356–57.
47. "Ancaman Bom di Jakarta," *Kabar dari Pijar,* July 30, 1996, www.library.ohiou.edu/indopubs/1996/07/30/0012.html; *Forum Keadilan,* February 3, 1994, 10; "Hidang–UU Subversi," *Apakabar,* February 3, 1996, www.library.ohiou.edu/indopubs/1996/02/03/0029.html.
48. "Pidato Politik Megawati: Stop Ketidakberesan dan Lepaskan Kemunafikan," *Waspada,* January 11, 1997, www.library.ohiou.edu/indopubs/1997/01/11/0064.html.
49. "Keterangan Megawati Akan Diminta Polres Jaksel," *Suara Pembaruan,* January 18, 1997.
50. Zifcak, "Political Trials in Indonesia," 356–57.
51. I am grateful to the late Herb Feith for this suggestion.
52. Feith, *Decline of Constitutional Democracy,* 40.
53. "Akhirnya: Mega Gugat Soeharto," *Suara Independen* 4, no. 3 (February 1997): 3–5, www.library.ohiou.edu/indopubs/1997/03/24/0069.html; "Tak Semudah Mengusir Mega di Angkasa," *Suara Independen* 4, no. 3 (February 1997): 6, www.library.ohiou.edu/indopubs/1997/03/22/0088.html.
54. "R. O. Tambunan: Saya tidak Bisa Menyetir Ibu Mega," *Suara Merdeka,* October 13, 1996; Aspinall, "Political Opposition," 266n117.
55. "Indonesian Court Rejects Appeal by Ousted Politician," *Wall Street Interactive Edition,* April 11, 1997, www.library.ohiou.edu/indopubs/1997/04/14/0046.html.
56. "40 Pengacara 'Demo' ke MA," *Bernas,* March 12, 1997. Speaking at a press conference at the end of 1997, R. O. Tambunan said that 95 percent of the sixty-five

lawsuits that his Indonesian Democracy Defence Team filed for Megawati and her supporters had been rejected in courts across the country ("RI's Legal System Not Independent: Megawati's Lawyers," *Jakarta Post,* December 30, 1997, 1).

57. According to Dwight Y. King, "Golput or *golongan putih* (lit. white group) . . . refers to . . . non-cooperation in the electoral process . . . . The term is also rich in connotation. 'White' symbolizes pure-minded and also blank ballots. Golput also has historical significance, reviving a movement started by Arief Budiman at the time of the first New Order election in 1971. Thirdly, it functions as political humour, since Golput mirrors Golkar (Golongan Karya, lit. functional groups), the party closest to the government" (*"White Book,"* 2). See also "Dr Arief Budiman, Dosen did Melbourne University, Aktivis Golput: 'Jangan Bikin Pemilu Bohong-Bohongan,'" *Suara Independen* 7, no. 3 (May 1997).

58. James Balowski, "Growing Support for Indonesian Election Boycott," *Green Left Weekly,* March 9, 1997, 1, www.library.ohiou.edu/indopubs/1997/03/09/0021 .html; Tapol, *Briefing Paper,* 3–5; "Giliran Theo di 'Recall'?" *Forum Keadilan* 4, no. 6 (June 2, 1997): 26; Patrick Walters, "Indonesian Poll Violence Worsens as Stakes Rise," *Weekend Australian,* May 17–18, 1997, 13.

59. Quoted in "Ancaman Golput dan 'Dagangan Politik' Tiga Orsopol Pemilu 1997," *Tempo,* March 16, 1997, www.library.ohiou.edu/indopubs/1997/03/16/0038.html.

60. "Sri Bintang Establishes New Party," *Kompas* [in translation], May 30, 1996, www.library.ohiou.edu/indopubs/1996/05/29/0049.html; Schwartz, *Nation in Waiting,* 321, 324; Zifcak, "Political Trials in Indonesia," 357n6.

61. *Kompas Cyber Media,* March 6, 1997, www.kompas.com. See also, the section on Sri Bintang Pamungkas contained in Human Rights Watch, *Human Rights Watch World Report 1998,* www.hrw.org/worldreport/Asia-07htm#P652_167139.

62. Presumably Amien Rais had in mind article 33.3, which states that "the Land, the water, and the natural resources contained therein shall be controlled by the state and exploited for the greatest prosperity of the people" (Lev, *Transition to Guided Democracy,* 297).

63. John McBeth, "Line in the Sand," *Far Eastern Economic Review,* March 27, 1997, 14–15; John Leahy, "Muslim Leader Forced Out for Radical Views," *South China Morning Post,* February 26, 1997, www.library/ohiou.edu/indopubs/1997/02/26/0030.html; "Soeharto Marah Amien Didepak," *Suara Independen* 4, no. 3 (February 1997): 14, www.library.ohiou.edu/indopubs/1997/03/22/0087.html.

64. Fealy, "1994 NU Congress and Aftermath," 266–75.

65. Aspinall, "Political Opposition," 267–68; Hefner, *Civil Islam,* 193–96.

66. Hefner, *Civil Islam,* 194.

67. "President's Daughter in Bid to Woo Muslim Vote," *South China Morning Post,* April 1, 1997, www.library.ohiou.edu/indopubs/1997/03/31/0075.html; Mietzner, "Between *Pesantren* and Palace," 181–82.

68. "Suharto Alert Seen as Threat to Separatists," *South China Morning Post,* March 8, 1997, www.library.ohiou.edu/indopubs/1997/03/08/0025.html.

69. Quoted in Tapol, *Briefing Paper,* 3.

70. In February an observer was moved to comment on the absence of fear among Megawati's supporters in the PDI: "PDI members have turned out to have a quite ex-

traordinary militancy. They appear absolutely free of trauma relating to the 27 July Affair which made victims of their friends, five of whom were killed and twenty of whom have gone missing. They also seem to ignore the fury of high ranking officers in the Armed Forces, including the commander, Feisal Tanjung, who repeatedly threatens to take firm action against them" ("Mega dan Sejumlah Tanda," *Suara Independen* 4, no. 3 [February 1997]: 7, www.library.ohiou.edu/indopubs/1997/03/23/0004.html).

71. "Wawancara Alex Litaay: Sebuah Aksi unjuk Gigi," *Tempo Interaktif* 7, no. 2 (April 19, 1997): 2. See also, "'Semut Merah' Beraksi, Megawati Kembali?" *Forum Keadilan* 2, no. 6 (May 5, 1997), 12–13.

72. Megawati Soekarnoputri, "Restoring Democracy," 1, 2; Patrick Walters, "Megawati Cautions on Break up of Indonesia," *Australian,* April 18, 1997, 9; "Manifesto Mega, Untuk atau tidak untuk Pemilu," *D&R,* April 26, 1997, via *Indonesia Daily News Online*.

73. "Megawati: Massa PDI Tidak Usah Kampanye," *Bernas,* April 24, 1997, 2.

74. "Megawati's Vote Directives Hailed," *Jakarta Post,* April 25, 1997, 1; "Megawati Warns Supporters of Provocation," *Jakarta Post,* April 28, 1997, 1.

75. "Lagi, Warga PDI 'Lompat' ke PPP," *Bernas,* April 19, 1997, 1; "'Mega-Bintang' Muncul di Jateng," *Suara Pembaruan,* May 6, 1997, 2; "'Mega-Bintang' Banners Banned," *Jakarta Post,* May 13, 1997, 1; "Ancaman Mega-Bintang," *Forum Keadilan* 4, no. 6 (June 2, 1997): 16. Moedrick is linked to Megawati by marriage. His wife is a niece of Megawati's first husband, Surindro Supjarso, who, it will be recalled, died in a plane crash in West Irian (as it was then called) in January 1971 ("Moedrick: Megawati-PPP Alliance Broker," *Jakarta Post,* May 15, 1997, 1). See also, Aspinall, "Political Opposition," 270–71. Personal communication, Arief Budiman, March 16, 2001.

76. "Tulisan Tangan Megawati," *Indonesia Daily News Online*, May 25, 1997.

77. Patrick Walters, "Muslim Supporters Rally in Defiance of Anti-march Decree," *Weekend Australian,* May 24–25, 1997, 13.

78. "Megawati tidak akan Nyoblos," *Suara Pembaruan,* May 23, 1997, 1.

79. The election results may be found in *Kompas,* June 23, 1997.

12

The Fall of Soeharto

A sudden deterioration in the economy in the second half of 1997 added to the damage already done to the standing of the New Order and its leader. The rupiah came under pressure about three weeks after the Thai baht was floated on July 2. Consequently, on August 14, the government floated the rupiah; in September, it postponed some major government projects; and in early October, it sought the assistance of the IMF. This setback for the economy was exacerbated by a severe drought that showed every sign of cutting deeply into the coming rice harvest.[1]

In this time of economic uncertainty, Golkar general chairperson Harmoko declared that his organization would nominate Soeharto as president for the 1998–2003 period because the input that it had received from society showed that "the wishes of the people coalesce around the Soeharto name."[2] This announcement was made formal at a leadership meeting of the party convened between October 16 and 19. Soeharto responded to this nomination on October 19 with a display of modesty designed either to appease opponents or flush them out. "Has *Golonan Karya* accurately picked up on the aspirations of the people when it says that they trust me. Possibly I will be accused of being a Golkar cadre who is arrogant because, after having already been President six times, I still want to accept for a seventh."[3] He invited party members to check again whether the people still believed in him. If they did not, the president declared, it would not be a problem, because "he would 'place himself within the succession philosophy of the Javanese shadow theatre.' He said that philosophy was *lengser keprabon, madeg pandito,* meaning to step down as king and become a priest."[4]

Amid the widespread comment that these remarks provoked, a journalist asked Megawati for her reaction. She was clearly not taken in, for she replied by telling a story about her opposition to her father's designation as president for life by the Interim People's Consultative Assembly, a story that also reveals something of the intimate nature of her relationship with her father, as she recalled it thirty-four years later:

> At that time, in the State Palace in 1964 [read: 1963], he, as was usual after work, took off his official jacket and replaced it with a pyjama coat. Usually, he would come directly to my room and lie down while asking me to massage him. Then suddenly he said to me that the MPRS wanted to promote him to President for Life. "So I want to get your evaluation in this matter," he said to me at that time. The answer I gave, well it did not constitute an answer but took the form of another question. I still remember precisely the question I put to him: "Is there no one else in your view, Father, who can be nominated for this position?" Then he said, "Why do you have thoughts like that?" I replied, "surely it is easy for you to understand why I as a child put forward a question like that." It was because he had already begun to enter his twilight years. And we all wanted him to experience life in a normal fashion. . . . I said that "in my opinion . . . you have tried to create cadres who could be prepared to lead this nation in the future." . . . Father said that this was correct. Then he added: "But what can one do if the people want me to become president for life." I replied . . . "but if I may make a proposal, whether we like it or not, we have to have the courage to bring forward the various candidates for leader." Then Father questioned me as follows: "where did you get the courage to make a proposal like that." Then I said, "you are getting on, Father." And then there were those matters of which I had some experience myself and to which I had given a great deal of thought; in particular, concerning the damage done to his health by his life-long struggle both in and out of jail. He had chronic kidney disease. It was most disruptive so that he was no longer able to give his best for the nation.[5]

In the following weeks the economic situation rapidly deteriorated. The IMF's assistance package of October 31 was ill-conceived, and its support for the closing of sixteen private banks on November 1 only succeeded in producing a run on the remaining ones. At the same time, Soeharto restarted those government projects in which his family had interests, thereby causing an additional loss of confidence by foreign investors in the management of the Indonesian economy. Then, in early December, Soeharto fell ill, giving rise to fears that the economic crisis would be exacerbated by a political one over the presidential succession. Consequently, the rupiah sunk to 5,600 to the U.S. dollar on December 16, whereas it had traded at 2,400 the previous May and at 4,000 in late October.[6]

Exactly a week later, on the fourth anniversary of her election as leader of the PDI, Megawati issued an end-of-year message in which she returned to the theme of the old and ill leader who was no longer able to give his best for the country. On this occasion, however, her remarks had lost their previous obliqueness:

> Efforts to build a personality cult around President Soeharto are already well advanced.... As a consequence, all aspects of the life of the nation and the state in Indonesia have become unhealthy because they depend completely on the one individual, President Soeharto.... To again nominate Soeharto, who has already been President of Indonesia for more than thirty years, as the sole candidate to become President for a seventh time, and in the troubled physical condition that we can all observe, will only add to the crisis of confidence concerning Indonesia.[7]

On January 6, 1998, Amien Rais, who had become increasingly outspoken in his criticisms of the government, announced that he wanted to work with Megawati and Abdurrahman Wahid in addressing the country's growing problems. He said that cooperation between the three of them would make a lot of sense because each of them represented one of the groupings within society—Megawati, the national group; Abdurrahman, traditional Islam; and Amien himself, modernist Islam—and together they would enjoy considerable influence. Megawati responded postively to Amien Rais's proposal, but nothing was heard from Abdurrahman.[8]

On the same day, the president unveiled a budget that was unrealistic in its assumptions—namely, a rupiah trading at 4,000 to the U.S. dollar, 4 percent growth, and 9 percent inflation.[9] Consequently, domestic and foreign investors, "convinced that Soeharto neither understood the magnitude of the problem Indonesia faced nor was capable of overcoming it," "abandoned rupiah-denominated assets."[10] The rupiah dropped to 10,000 to the U.S. dollar on January 8, prompting panic-buying in supermarkets by middle-class shoppers while a number of anti-Chinese, food riots flared up in various parts of the country.[11]

Despite police threats to break it up, Megawati went ahead with a celebration of the twenty-fifth anniversary of the PDI at her home on January 10.[12] In front of a large crowd of supporters, domestic and foreign press, foreign diplomats and opposition figures, she built on the theme of her recent remarks in a brave, defiant, and at times bitterly ironic speech:

> At this opportunity I appeal to all the people of Indonesia:... Do not nominate retired General Soeharto again to become president for a seventh time. Because to grant him a term of office as president in excess of thirty years amounts to an effort to make him, President Soeharto, president for life. The Indonesian nation must not make this mistake for a second time....
>
> We possess a number of names which are often mentioned as the best sons of Indonesia who are capable of becoming the next President of the Republic of Indonesia. One might mention Try Sutrisno, R. Hartono, Wiranto, B.J. Habibie,

Ginanjar Kartasasmita, Soedharmono, Rudini, and many more prominent figures in society.

However, if our brothers whose names I have just mentioned cannot find the courage within themselves to nominate and be nominated in an open fashion as Indonesian president to replace retired General Soeharto then this matter constitutes an event of the utmost concern in the life of the nation and the state.

Therefore, if it appears that they are without courage, then on this occasion I declare with honesty and in a straightforward fashion that I am not unwilling to lead this country and nation provided that is, of course, the wish and demand of the People.[13]

Amien Rais, who had himself declared his willingness to be nominated for the presidency the previous September, greeted Megawati's speech with enthusiasm.[14] On January 15, they met at the house of PNI member Mrs Supeni and signed a joint statement that expressed concern about recent events in Indonesia and underlined the preparedness of the two signatories to be nominated for the presidency for the 1998–2003 period.[15] Also expected at this meeting was Abdurrahman Wahid, who had offered a cautious remark in support of Megawati's speech: "The brave heart Megawati has shown represents the people's courage. It is now escalating."[16] But he failed to show up, suggesting that his suspicion of the modernists, aggravated by a personal antipathy for Amien, was still greater than his desire to get rid of Soeharto.[17] And four days later he suffered a massive stroke.[18]

Megawati and Amien Rais met again on January 25 at the Indonesian Islamic University in Yogyakarta, by which time Soeharto had made it clear that not only did he intend to stand again for the presidency but that he also wanted B. J. Habibie as his running mate. Added to investors' misgivings about Soeharto were their severe doubts about Habibie, who was well-known for his unorthodox economic views and extravagant attempt to develop an Indonesian aircraft industry.[19] The result was a precipitous drop in the rupiah on January 21 to 17,000 to the U.S. dollar.[20] In her speech to the students, Megawati, mindful of a film she had seen recently, said that Indonesia in her present condition "was like the *Titanic* sinking while the members of the crew and their officers were busy meeting in a closed room . . . . At this moment concrete steps are required in order to save the ship which has millions of people on board, not a lengthy discussion without clear purpose."[21] She declared her willingness to work with Amien, and he in turn expressed his support for her.[22]

But for these two to cooperate meaningfully, many fears and suspicions would have to be overcome. They came from opposite sides of one of the deepest social and cultural divisions in Indonesia, that between devout Moslems of a modernist persuasion on the one hand and the nominally Islamic syncretists whose deeper allegiance is to a complex mixture of animist, Hindu, and Buddhist beliefs, on the other.[23] Furthermore, the politicians representing the two streams had a long history of conflict. Most recently, modernists in the government-linked ICMI, including Amien Rais himself, had given a degree of support to Soeharto's actions against Megawati and her supporters in the PDI in 1996.[24] But if she and her supporters were bitter about this, the modernists asked what had she ever done for Islam, especially when troops under the ultimate command of her close Christian acquaintance General Moerdani were gunning down the devout in Tanjung Priok in 1984.[25]

At approximately the same time as Amien and Megawati were exploring the possibilities of cooperation, President Soeharto began to speak rather ominously of "we Muslims." His daughter Siti Hadijanti attempted to blame the Sino-Indonesians for the failure of her "I Love the Rupiah" campaign. Armed forces chief Feisal Tanjung called the conglomerates "unpatriotic" and threatened them with further action if they did not return their capital to Indonesia.[26] On February 3, Syarwan Hamid plumbed the depths of New Order cravenness by speaking at a large mosque in Jakarta of "these rats who take away the fruits of our national development and work for their own self interest. Don't think the people don't know who these rats are. It's time to eradicate these rats."[27]

Megawati and Amien Rais could at least agree on opposition to this scapegoating, although Amien had to discard the anti-Chinese and anti-Christian perspectives of his past to do so. But this he did in a most emphatic way: "Soeharto thinks only of his and his family's interests," he said. "He is willing to make every other group a scapegoat. We must not victimize people. We should blame the government for this crisis, not the Chinese."[28] Megawati likewise responded on February 9 in an *Idul Fitri* message to the Indonesian people in which she said that responsibility for the bankruptcy of the state should be sheeted home to those who are truly at fault and not to those who have been wrongly accused.[29]

When the one thousand members of the People's Consultative Assembly met on March 1, they seemed oblivious to the fact that the rupiah was trading at around 10,000 to the U.S. dollar and that the economy was experiencing a massive contraction.[30] Nor, indeed, did they seem aware that most large businesses, unable to repay their foreign currency–denominated loans, were technically bankrupt; that the banking sector was in disarray; that millions of people had been thrown out of work; and that there were widespread shortages of basic commodities.[31] With barely a murmur, the members listened to Soeharto's accountability speech, in which he made only brief mention of the economic crisis; and on March 10, they unanimously elected him and Habibie president and vice president. Of course, they could not have been altogether unaware of what was going on around them, for they also passed a decree that gave the president extensive emergency powers.[32]

Megawati and the secretary-general of her party, Alex Litaay, sought to remind members of the assembly of the formidable constitutional powers that the body actually possessed if only they had had the courage to exercise them. To do so, the two issued a statement on March 3 on behalf of the central leadership council of the PDI that rejected the accountability speech of the "President/Mandatory of the MPR for the period 1993–1998" and insisted that he give "an accounting which is more complete, honest, and objective, and which has to be in keeping with . . . the mandate and guidelines for the implementation of the constitution."[33]

Megawati's bold stand in her opposition to Soeharto's renomination for the presidency, even going so far as to declare her own willingness to stand, earned her the respect of many, including Amien Rais. But after releasing the statement, she appeared to step back from the political struggle against the president—and at the very moment it began to acquire momentum. Students demonstrating against Soeharto had been growing in number since mid-February, and by mid-March the military was experiencing considerable difficulty in confining them to their campuses. The president's new cabinet was announced on March 14, and among notable appointments were his daughter Siti Hadijanti, as minister for social affairs, and one of his most prominent cronies, Bob Hasan, as minister for trade—all of which crystallized the students' opposition to him and his circle on the grounds of *korupsi, kolusi, dan nepotisme* (corruption, collusion, and nepotism). Yet Megawati remained in the background, turning down invitations from student leaders to join in their struggle and leaving the running to Amien.

The reason for her sudden withdrawal was apparently a growing anxiety on her part concerning the well-being of her followers. Her sensitivity in this area was acute in the aftermath of Grey Saturday, in which a number of her supporters lost their lives. She was clearly afraid that others could experience a similar fate, especially those who were not students but members of the urban poor with no campuses on which to vent their anti-Soeharto feelings. Furthermore, one of the members of her leadership council, Haryanto Taslam, had been "disappeared" by the security forces on March 2, and she probably feared that any precipitate action on her part would only reduce his chances of survival.[34]

Thus, she relegated herself and her organization to the role of onlooker, witnessing a remarkable increase in the number, size, and geographical spread of student demonstrations against Soeharto in March and April. Then, on May 4, the president, acting in compliance with one of the requirements of the IMF agreement, removed the subsidy on petrol. This step caused a 70 percent jump in the price of fuel and led to increases of a lesser but still substantial nature in bus fares. He was under considerable pressure to take this action but, according to his government's latest agreement with the IMF, was not required to do so until the end of October.[35] It was therefore surprising that Soeharto went ahead when he did, evidently not considering the likely exacerbating effect of this move on the rising tide of protest and dissent, nor even recalling how the government's raising the price of petrol and cooking oil in January 1966 galvanized the students' opposition to Sukarno, thereby strengthening his own challenge to the incumbent president.[36]

Rioting, accompanied by looting and burning in ethnic Chinese areas of the city, immediately broke out in Medan, North Sumatra, and continued for three days. Increasingly militant students clashed violently with the security forces in Jakarta, Yogyakarta, Ujung Pandang, and Solo, where approximately four hundred people were injured on May 8. The president, seemingly quite out of touch, left Jakarta on May 9 to attend a summit meeting of developing nations in Cairo. Three days later, on May 12, four students were shot dead at the private Trisakti University in Jakarta by unidentified assassins, widely assumed to be special forces under the command of the president's son-in-law, General Prabowo Subianto.[37]

Both Amien Rais and Megawati were among the many mourners who attended the funeral service on the university grounds the following day. In a powerful speech, Amien "put forward a choice for the leadership of the armed forces: defend either the interests of the people or the interests of a particular family."[38] Megawati, who only spoke at the insistence of the students present, was more cautious. No doubt she was thinking of Grey Saturday, but perhaps she was also thinking of the more distant past. We have observed her responding to the leadership crisis of recent months in the light of her remembering her father's behavior at an equivalent point in his presidency. It would be in keeping with this reflective cast of mind if she had recalled not only those who had died here the day before but also those who had suffered in this very same spot thirty-three years before. The students present were, of course, too young to remember, and their parents may have preferred to forget that Trisakti University was built on the gutted ruins of Res Publica University, which had been put to the torch by anticommunist demonstrators on October 15, 1965, owing to the Communist Party associations of its Sino-Indonesian owners.[39] She may have also recalled Arief Rahman Hakim, a medical student at the University of Indonesia who was shot dead by the palace guard while demonstrating against her father on February 24, 1966.[40] Activism and sadness can pull in opposite directions, and it was perhaps difficult for Megawati to make a bold appeal in the manner of Amien. Instead, she spoke apprehensively, urging caution on her listeners: "It is said that we are a state that is opposed to violence, that we are a state that loves peace and considers freedom important. But the reality on the contrary is like this." She then "appealed to students, society at large, and the armed forces to work from this time on to build unity."[41]

Megawati's words of caution had little impact. Shortly after she uttered them, rioting broke out in the area around Trisakti University, quickly spread to other areas of Jakarta, and raged until May 15. By the end of that period, 1,189 people had lost their lives, some of whom were ethnic Chinese whereas others were "residents of poor neighbourhoods who joined in the looting and died while trapped in burning shopping centres." Also, hundreds of Chinese were physically attacked. Among this last category of victims were many women who were either raped or subject to other forms of sexual violence. Property damage was also extensive: 4,083 shops and 1,026 private homes, mostly owned by Chinese, were burned. Forty shopping malls were destroyed.[42] At first glance, this extraordinary paroxysm of anti-Chinese violence appeared to be spontaneous in its origins, triggered by the shootings of the Trisakti students; but on further inspection, it proved to have been instigated by the familiar government thugs exploiting anti-Chinese sentiment with appalling effectiveness. It is still impossible to say with certainty which particular government thugs they were—most suspicion fell on General Prabowo—or what precisely their motive was in starting the riots, though it does seem safe to conclude that they did not intend what they in fact achieved: the inflicting of grievous damage on the reputation of the armed forces and the complete destruction of Soeharto's legitimacy, already weakened by the economic crisis.[43] If he was to remain in office beyond this point, it could only be by the constant application of force by a military then held in low esteem by the populace.

Having cut short his stay in Cairo, the president returned to Jakarta on May 15. The following day he declared his willingness to reshuffle the cabinet. Amien Rais called on him to step down within the week, and a prominent member of the government party and former cabinet minister, Mien Sugandhi, called on him to resign. On May 18, students occupied the parliament building. While this was happening, Harmoko, the speaker of parliament and a hitherto obsequious supporter of Soeharto, surprised everyone by calling on the president to step down. That evening the president invited several Moslem leaders to meet him at the palace the following morning. They included Nurcolish Madjid and a fragile Abdurrahman Wahid, largely blind as a result of the stroke he had suffered the previous January and unable to walk without assistance. Nurcolish suggested that Amien also be invited, but Soeharto refused.[44]

Abdurrahman, it will be recalled, had patched up his differences with Soeharto in November 1996 and had even assisted Soeharto's daughter in her campaign on behalf of Golkar in the months preceding the 1997 elections. Unwilling to abandon this alliance and distrustful of the modernist Moslems, especially Amien Rais, he resisted the offers of the latter in January 1998 to join him and Megawati in a broad anti-Soeharto alliance. While resting at home after his stroke, he made sure that Nahdlatul Ulama did not object to Soeharto's reelection as president in early March. He also expressed his satisfaction with the new cabinet, despite its having no prominent NU figure included. In mid-April he alienated the students opposed to the president by claiming that they were in the pay of certain parties. A week later the leadership council of NU repudiated this claim and belatedly sought to align their organization with the reform movement.[45]

When the meeting took place early in the morning of May 19, Abdurrahman lent his support to Soeharto, who proposed forming a new cabinet, establishing a committee that would oversee political reform and a fresh national election, and then stepping down as president. A week before, this would have seemed a radical proposal, but Soeharto's position had deteriorated so rapidly in the intervening days that it now appeared to most of those present as quite inadequate. Thus, Nurcolish Madjid told him that nothing less than his immediate resignation would be acceptable to the people. Abdurrahman came to Soeharto's defense, "saying that he was surprised that Nurcholish now wanted to demolish the president."[46] Needless to say, Soeharto resisted, implying that the person who would succeed him if he resigned, vice president B. J. Habibie, was not up to the job. "There is a question of whether he is capable," Soeharto said. At the conclusion of the meeting, Soeharto spelled out his proposal on national television. But it left people completely unmoved, and Abdurrahman's subsequent appeal to the students to stop protesting and allow Soeharto a chance to implement his promises earned him criticism not only from Amien and the students but also from his colleague in the Democracy Forum, Marsillam Simanjuntak, who said that Abdurrahman "abandoned his chance to play a key role in history."[47]

Early the next day, Amien Rais called off a large protest march to the National Monument after being warned that the military was prepared to use lethal force against it. But large anti-Soeharto demonstrations took place in other centers around the country: it was estimated that one million people took to the streets of Yogyakarta. Speaker of the parliament Harmoko hardened his stance of just two days by threatening the president with impeachment by the People's Consultative Assembly if he did not resign by May 23. During the course of the day, Soeharto tried, largely unsuccessfully, to fill the positions on his reform committee; and at about eleven o'clock that night he received a letter from the coordinating minister of the economy, Ginandjar Kartasasmita, and thirteen other cabinet ministers, saying that "they would refuse to join a new cabinet." It seems at this point that Soeharto decided to resign. At a brief ceremony at the palace at nine o'clock the following morning, Soeharto read a brief resignation speech, and Habibie took the oath of office.[48]

NOTES

1. Hill, *Indonesian Economy in Crisis,* 11, 15, 81; Schwarz, *Nation in Waiting,* 338.
2. "Ketika Bola Suksesi Mengempis Lagi," *Forum Keadilan* 15, no. 6 (November 3, 1997): 12.
3. "Pak Harto Bersedia Dipilih Lagi?" *Forum Keadilan* 16, no. 6 (November 17, 1997): 100.
4. Ben Abel talks with Ben Anderson, "A Javanese King Talks of His End," *Inside Indonesia* 54 (April–June 1998): 16–17.
5. "Mega pernah beri Pertimbangan pada Bung Karno," *Jawa Pos*, October 23, 1997.
6. Hill, *Indonesian Economy in Crisis,* 15, 19; Schwarz, *Nation in Waiting,* 338–40; Aspinall and van Klinken, "Chronology of Crisis," 159.
7. Megawati Soekarnoputri, "Pesan Akhir Tahun 1997: Hanya ada Satu Jalan: Perubahan dan Perbaikan," *SiaR,* January 7, 1998, at www.library.ohiou.edu/indopubs/1998/01/07/0018html.
8. "Amien Rais siap Bergandengan dengan Gus Dur dan Megawati," *Kompas Cyber Media*, January 7, 1998; "Mega-Amien Minta Dialog Dipercepat," *Jawa Pos*, January 8, 1998.
9. Hill, *Indonesian Economy in Crisis,* 12.
10. Schwarz, *Nation in Waiting,* 340.
11. Aspinall and van Klinken, "Chronology of Crisis," 159–60; Greg Earl and Michael Dwyer, "Jakarta Dumps $10bn Projects," *Australian Financial Review*, January 12, 1998.
12. "Polda Larang Mega Rayakan HUT PDI," *Bernas*, January 8, 1998; "Megawati Free to Hold Private Functions: ABRI," *Jakarta Post*, January 9, 1998.
13. "Pidato Ketua Umum DPP PDI Megawati Soekarnoputri Menyambut HUT ke XXV PDI," *SiaR,* January 11, 1998. It is possible that Eros Djarot, a film director, newspaper proprietor, and friend of Megawati at that time, had a hand in the writing of this speech.
14. "Amien, Gus Dur Back Megawati's Presidency Bid," *Jakarta Post*, January 12, 1998.
15. "Amien Rais dan Megawati Bertemu," *Kompas Cyber Media,* January 16, 1998.
16. "Megawati's Nomination 'Up to the People,'" *Jakarta Post*, January 13, 1998.
17. See Mietzner, "Between *Pesantren* and Palace," 188.
18. Mietzner, "Between *Pesantren* and Palace," 189.

19. The second IMF agreement, signed in Jakarta on January 15, required the Indonesian government to cease all budget and off-budget funding to Habibie's aircraft manufacturer, Nusantara Aircraft Industry (Industri Pesawat Terbang Nusantara, IPTN). See John Bresnan, "United States," 94.

20. Aspinall and van Klinken, "Chronology of Crisis," 160.

21. "Mega: Kondisi Indonesia Bagai Kapal 'Titanic,'" *Bernas*, January 26, 1998.

22. "Mega: Kondisi Indonesia Bagai Kapal 'Titanic,'" *Bernas*, January 26, 1998.

23. Liddle, "Coercion," 275–76.

24. See Hefner, *Civil Islam*, 187.

25. On September 12, 1984, the military fired on a demonstration of Moslems in the port area of Jakarta known as Tanjung Priok, killing "at least 28 people, and perhaps over a hundred" (Ricklefs, *History of Modern Indonesia*, 381). They were protesting, among other things, a government decision of that year requiring all political and social organizations to replace their various political and religious credos and symbols with the state ideology of Pancasila, which would serve as their sole ideological basis. See also, Schwarz, who estimates that "dozens" of demonstrators were killed by the soldiers on this occasion (*Nation in Waiting*, 172–73).

26. Schwarz, *Nation in Waiting*, 345–46; Liddle, "Indonesia's Unexpected Failure," 18.

27. Quoted in Hefner, *Civil Islam*, 205.

28. Quoted in Schwarz, *Nation in Waiting*, 346.

29. "Pesan Idul Fitri dari Megawati," *XPOS*, February 16, 1998, www.library.ohiou.edu/indopubs/1998/02/16/0001.html; "Mega Sedih dan Takut," *Bernas*, February 10, 1998.

30. Indonesia's economy contracted by 13.6 percent in 1998 (see Hill, *Indonesian Economy*, 264).

31. Liddle, "Failure of Leadership," 17.

32. Schwarz, *Nation in Waiting*, 350.

33. "Indonesia's Megawati Seeks Economic Plan Details," *Reuters*, March 3, 1998, www.library.ohiou.edu/indopubs/1998/03/04/0006.html; "Megawati Tolak Pertanggung-jawaban Soeharto," *AJI News*, March 3, 1998, www.library.ohiou.edu/indopubs/1998/03/04/0038.html; "Pernyataan Politik . . . Dewn Pimpinan Pusat Partai Demokrasi Indonesia," *AJI News*, March 3, 1998.

34. In fact, he survived the ordeal, being released on April 17. See Aspinall and van Klinken, "Chronology of Events," 161; "DPP PDI pro-Megawati akui kehilangan Haryanto Taslam," *SiaR*, March 31, 1998, www.library.ohiou.edu/indopubs/1998/04/07/0028.html; David Jenkins, "'Kidnapped' Activist Turns Up as Government Tries to Calm Students," *Sydney Morning Herald*, April 20, 1998.

35. Schwarz, *Nation in Waiting*, 354.

36. Crouch, *Army and Politics in Indonesia*, 165.

37. Aspinall and van Klinken, "Chronology of Crisis," 163–65.

38. "Amien Rais tentang Gugurnya Mahasiswa: Jadikan Semangat Perjuangan Reformasi," *Republika Online*, May 14, 1998, www.republika.co.id.

39. See Coppel, *Indonesian Chinese in Crisis*, 55.

40. Crouch, *Army and Politics in Indonesia*, 182–83.

41. "Amien Rais tentang Gugurnya Mahasiswa," *Republika Online*, May 14, 1998.
42. Human Rights Watch, "Indonesia: The Damaging Debate," at www.hrw.org/reports98/indonesia3/index.htm.
43. Edward Aspinall wrote of the "implied social contract" between the government and the middle classes whereby the latter "ceded their political rights in exchange for social stability and economic growth." He added that it was "the collapse of the economy from late 1997 which finally destroyed . . . [this] social contract." One might add that the government's failure to provide social stability, most notably on May 13–15 in Jakarta, delivered the coup de grâce (Aspinall, "Opposition," 141–42).
44. Schwarz, *Nation in Waiting,* 358–59; Aspinall and van Klinken, "Chronology of Crisis," 165–66; Mietzner, "Between *Pesantren* and Palace," 193–94.
45. Mietzner, "Between *Pesantren* and Palace," 187–92.
46. Mietzner, "Between *Pesantren* and Palace," 194.
47. Schwarz, *Nation in Waiting,* 360–62; "Pak Harto: 'Saya ini Kapok Jadi Presiden,'" *Kompas Cyber Media*, May 20, 1998.
48. Schwarz, *Nation in Waiting,* 364–66.

13

Democracy Returns

THE REBIRTH OF DEMOCRACY

B. J. Habibie, the New Order *wunderkind*, brilliant in everything except his choice of mentor, learned of Soeharto's contempt for him on the eve of his appointment as president.[1] This awful discovery appeared to encourage him to embrace democracy rather than attempt to perpetuate the old dispensation and serve out the remainder of his predecessor's term.[2] But he had little choice in the matter if he was to survive politically; such was the strength of the *reformasi* wave washing through the political system. Half-Gorbachev and half–Egon Krenz, he visited the parliament on May 28, only one week after his swearing in, and agreed with its leadership that a special session of the People's Consultative Assembly would be held at the end of the year to provide a new, liberal framework for the calling of fresh parliamentary elections in the middle of 1999 and a presidential one at the end of the year.[3] The following day he declared that "anyone at all may form a political party."[4]

Even before Habibie made his announcement, new political parties had started to spring up alongside Golkar, PPP, and PDI. Just a few days after Soeharto's resignation, a number of Islamic religious teachers, or *kiai,* called for the establishment of a political party based on the Nahdlatul Ulama. After initially refusing, Abdurrahman Wahid changed his mind but, in keeping with his essentially nationalist orientation, insisted that there should be no reference to Islam in the name of the new party. Eventually, those involved in its setting up decided on the name National Awakening Party (Partai Kebangkitan Bangsa). It was formally launched on July 23 with Abdurrahman appealing on that occasion to all Nahdlatul Ulama members to vote for it in the coming elections.[5]

Amien Rais was at first undecided as to the ideological orientation of the party he proposed to establish. Either he could capitalize on his standing as the chairperson of Muhammadiyah and set up a modernist Islamic political party; or, consistent with his presidential ambitions, he could seek a wider constituency of liberal-minded modernists and more secular nationalist and even Christian supporters. Finally, he decided on the latter alternative and in late August presented his National Mandate Party (Partai Amanat Nasional) to the public as "a modern, broad-based organization open to all social, religious and ethnic groups" and declared that he favored a coalition with Megawati's PDI.[6]

Amien's bold attempt to bridge the various divisions within Indonesian society left the Islamic modernists without a dominant figure to lead them into the elections. Consequently, a half-dozen small modernist political parties sprung up, the most prominent of which being the Crescent and Star Party (Partai Bulan Bintang), which declared itself to be the successor organization to Masjumi—the large, modernist political party banned by Sukarno in 1960. Amien's decision to form a pan-religious party also gave Habibie an opportunity to represent a Golkar dominated by his associates from ICMI and from other modernist organizations, as indeed it became after its congress in July, as a last bulwark against another secularly inclined Sukarno taking over the presidency.[7]

Megawati had every reason to be skeptical of President Habibie. As a loyal member of Soeharto's government, Habibie had helped undermine her (and Abdurrahman) in the preceding years. He now claimed to be a democrat, but it did not stop him from appointing to his cabinet two experienced exponents of state terror who bore a direct responsibility for her removal from the PDI leadership at the contrived Medan congress of the party in May 1996 and for Grey Saturday itself, including the murder of her supporters that day. They were General Feisal Tanjung, to whom he entrusted the coordinating ministry for security and political matters, and General Syarwan Hamid, whom he made minister for home affairs. The head of Megawati's legal team, R. O. Tambunan, urged the latter to stand down from his ministerial post, but he refused, claiming in his own defense "that what he did as the head of the social and political staff of the armed forces was done as 'a soldier carrying out orders.'"[8] And Megawati would not have been reassured to discover that the only PDI member in the cabinet—Panangian Siregar, the minister for the environment—was a supporter of Soerjadi. It is therefore understandable that when Habibie invited her to his office for talks on June 15, she failed to respond to his invitation.[9] Nevertheless, it was stubborn of her not to try to bring their two political ambitions into harmony at this very fluid point in Indonesia's emerging democracy. The two political leaders may not have made much progress, but at least she would not have wounded his fragile vanity, as she almost certainly did by refusing his invitation.[10] Whether for this reason or out of fear of Megawati's bright electoral prospects, Habibie and his ministers reverted to the disingenuous style of the New Order by repeating its legal fiction that the only valid PDI leadership council was the one headed by Soerjadi, which had been chosen at the Medan congress. They lent strong support to this leadership council in its convening of a party congress in Palu, Central Sulawesi, in late August. Syarwan Hamid addressed the opening session amid clashes between supporters of rival groups. Finally, the government formally accepted the newly elected leadership council headed by Budi Hardjono.[11]

Clearly annoyed by Habibie's sleight of hand, Megawati declared her intention to convene a party congress in Yogyakarta or Bali in October and threatened demonstrations against the government if its members attempted to disrupt it. She then called on her supporters to prepare for elections in the following year.[12] Megawati and other members of her party leadership settled on Bali after four PDI leaders from her national and Balinese regional councils enjoyed a productive discussion with the governor of Bali, Drs Dewa Made Beratha, on the possibility of convening the congress in his province.[13] They recognized that without the support of his regional representative, minister for home affairs Syarwan Hamid would not be able to imitate the dirty tricks of his predecessor, Yogie Memet, at the 1993 PDI congress (not to mention the 1996 Medan one). As an additional precaution, they decided to hold the congress, not in Den Pasar as originally intended, but in Sanur at the five-star Grand Bali Beach Hotel, built by Sukarno with Japanese war reparations money and opened in 1966.[14] The minister would surely hesitate before inviting dissident party members from the Budi Hardjono faction or thugs posing as dissident party members to disrupt a PDI congress at this location, let alone condone the smashing of a jeep through the front doors.

Once Megawati's leadership council had settled on Bali as the venue for the congress, they it made it plain that they would not allow themselves to be subject to the usual New Order manipulations. They did not seek police permission to hold the congress, and they ignored the hypocritical remark of police chief General Roesmanhadi about "valuing legality." One of their members flatly declared, "The decision to hold the congress in Bali cannot be challenged. We are not moving it anywhere else."[15]

Before this trial of wills was resolved, the research office of Megawati's PDI convened a one-day seminar on September 28 in the ballroom of the Gran Melia Hotel in Jakarta. It was entitled "The Concept and Program of the PDI *Perjuangan*: Law, Politics, Education and the Economy," and it attracted a large number of middle-class participants (newspaper estimates varied between one thousand and two thousand), including civil servants in the process of reconsidering their Golkar affiliation, each paying an entry fee of 25,000 rupiahs.[16]

In her welcoming address, Megawati sought to rescue from recent criticism the 1945 constitution—in particular, its first article, which proclaims Indonesia to be a unitary state. She claimed that article 1 had been given a bad name by the confused practices of the previous regime, which favored the center, downgraded the regions, and suppressed diversity. She implied that an opposite approach would give the regions substantial autonomy, could still be implemented within the framework of the unitary state, and certainly did not require a shift to a federal system of government. She then made it plain that the unitary state did not imply centralism, nor did it imply authoritarianism. Reverting to a familiar argument, she said that this defect was simply a consequence of the Soeharto regime's deviations, which could be overcome if the country returned to the values expressed in the ideology of *Pancasila* and the 1945 constitution. For good measure, she endorsed the contents of article 28—the very article that was introduced over her father's objections—by saying that "the right to associate and express opinions has to be guaranteed by law." Finally, in sharp distinction to her socialist father, she spoke in favor of a market economy, though not an unfettered one: "Via a democratic political system, the people have the sovereignty to manage the market economy so that besides growth, national economic development also brings about justice and an even distribution of wealth."[17]

On September 29, the day following the seminar, defense minister and armed forces commander General Wiranto declared that he had no objection to Megawati's PDI convening a congress on Bali.[18] His remarks reflected a belated recognition on the part of the government that in the new democratic environment there was little it could do to stop her without causing damage to its standing at home and abroad and, ultimately, to President Habibie's own election prospects.

The congress opened on the morning of October 8 with a rally at the Kapten Japa field, one to two kilometers to the north of Sanur, where attendance numbered thirty thousand, comprising conference delegates, party members, and supporters. Signs and banners were numerous. One declared, "Mega embodies the suffering of the people" and seemed suggestive of her strong appeal among the disadvantaged members of the community. Some youthful admirers offered their explanations for her popularity, mentioning "the achievements of her father" and that she was "outside the system of KKN" (*korupsi, kolusi, dan nepotisme*; corruption, collusion and nepotism). She addressed the gathering in a manner quite unlike her father, whose grave she had visited on her way to Bali.[19] He had captivated audiences with his flamboyance and extemporaneous oratory, whereas she appeared modest and down-to-earth as she read from the text of her speech in a clear, plain voice.

Some of the remarks she made at the Kapten Japa field that morning lend weight to the view that her political thinking has a collectivist, or populist, strand to it, although one quite unlike the radical populism of her father in his later years, who envisaged the Indonesian people as both the bearers and the beneficiaries of socialism. She spoke of her party not as a vehicle for the representation of diverse groups and interests within the community but as an instrument of her leadership of the Indonesian People (always with a capital *P*), whom she regards as a single entity who speak, or should speak, with only one voice and who willingly acknowledge her as their leader:

> The Congress this time is the People's Congress, and if the People have the desire and are united then there is nothing which they cannot reach for and achieve! That is the spirit of struggle of the PDI which I lead. . . . The capital which I possess above all is the trust of the People and their conviction that the ideals of the PDI are congruent with their aspirations and aims. . . . That is why they come in their droves and extend their hands while shouting "Mbak Mega, I will follow you."[20]

This same strand in her political thinking was quite evident in the advice she later offered to the Habibie government; and consistent with such populism elsewhere, one noticed elements of solicitousness and condescension in her remarks about "the People":

> Speak honestly to the People about the real condition of our economy! . . . The People have to really know so that the People can really help. Trust in your own People, and never ever again make the People uncomprehending and afraid, because they have too often been intimidated, and had their dignity and self worth undermined.[21]

Finally, she has some advice for all leaders in Indonesia, in which one can hear not only the strains of populism—in her emphasizing collective uniqueness, rather than individual diversity—but also a muffled echo of her father's voice: "Listen to the voice of the People, feel the heart beat of the People, give voice to the aspirations of the People. For the voice of the People constitutes a Mandate."[22]

Megawati's emphasis on leadership rather than representation was also apparent in her actual management of the congress. As noted, she had been obliged to accept dissident party members onto her central leadership council at the national consultation of December 1993. These dissidents had then used their positions of authority within the party to disrupt her leadership.

Mindful of this adverse experience, she appealed to congress delegates to give whomever they chose as leader of the PDI the authority to determine alone the composition of the party's leadership council.[23] Of course, she and everyone else expected her to be chosen for that position, as she was the only candidate and an overwhelmingly popular one at that. Thus, she was in effect asking delegates to give her the power to be sole *formateur* of the council. This was an understandable request in light of the party's recent history, and the majority of delegates were willing to go along with it. Others, however, saw it as undemocratic. Haryanto Taslam for one, a member of her leadership council who had been kidnapped by the security forces between March 2 and April 17, 1998, expressed an objection.[24]

In the event, Megawati was reelected general chairperson by acclamation and declared the party's presidential candidate. When the leader of a plenary session of the congress invited the 1,026 delegates to stand if they supported her election as leader, they all rose to their feet and burst into the song "Mega Will Definitely Win," which had become popular among her supporters in the struggle against Soeharto. Furthermore, the delegates gave her the authority she had sought to determine the composition of her leadership council, and in a break with previous practice, it even allowed her to appoint new members of the party directly to this council.[25] Exercising this extraordinary authority, Megawati appointed fifteen people to the leadership council and announced its composition to the final plenary session of the congress, on October 10: as chairpersons, Sutardjo Suryoguritno, I Gusti Ngurah Sara, Kwik Kian Gie, Theo Syafei, K. H. Hasyim Wahid, Suparlan, P. B. Da Costa, Dimyati Hartono, and Mochtar Buchori; as secretary-general, Alexander Litaay; as deputy secretary-generals, Mangara Siahaan, Haryanto Taslam, and Tarto Sudiro; as treasurer, Laksamana Sukardi; as deputy treasurers, Mailana Suwondo and Novianti Nasution.[26]

Of these, many were familiar as longtime supporters of Megawati within the PDI, but three were new members: Hasyim Wahid, Mailana Suwondo, and Theo Syafei.[27] Hasyim Wahid is a younger brother of Abdurrahman Wahid, and Megawati said that she had made this appointment "to honour Gus Dur" (as Abdurrahman was also called). Suwondo is a businessman, and Theo Syafei is a retired general who was withdrawn from the armed forces parliamentary fraction just before the 1997 elections after publicly defending Golput as a legitimate way of registering a protest against an electoral process that offered no meaningful choice.[28]

Theo Syafei was not the only senior military figure to join the PDI at this time. Among the others were retired army generals Raja Kami Sembiring Meliala and Sunarso Djajusman as well as a large number of former naval and marine officers.[29] The navy and marines were considered sympathetic to

President Sukarno in the past, so it was therefore not surprising that some of their former members would join the political party led by his daughter. But it is especially noteworthy that retired officers from the army found Megawati a reassuring leader and joined her party, given that it was the army who overthrew her father in 1966. "Don't blame us," Theo Syafei said, "if we choose the PDI because it is the only party which accommodates our aspirations. There's no badmouthing in the PDI about military doctrines or ideals"[30]

Theo Syafei's comment was largely accurate. Megawati had welcomed these former soldiers into the ranks of the PDI, and her remarks concerning the armed forces in her opening address to the congress were broadly supportive of its attempts to undertake reform.[31] Certainly, this behavior was remarkable, especially coming from one who had suffered a number of bitter experiences at the hands of the armed forces; in particular, the attack on her party headquarters on July 27, 1996. But it seems that this event did not deflect her from the view that the unity and well-being of Indonesian society depended on close cooperation between the military and the people at large. That she continued to adhere to such a view was an indication of the conservative nature of her populism and the degree to which her thinking in this area had been shaped by the very similar rhetoric of the New Order, despite her opposition to Soeharto. However, it was perhaps also a measure of the anxiety she had felt at the widespread rioting triggered by the attack on her party headquarters, not to mention the Trisakti killings—recall her appealing on the following day for "students, society at large and the armed forces to work from this time on to build unity"—and the anti-Chinese rioting that immediately followed. Perhaps these events stirred up traumatic memories of even worse ones: the mass murder of Communist Party members in late 1965 and the student demonstrations against her father in early 1966. Was it this background that gave Megawati's populism such a tentative quality and prevented her from envisaging any relationship with the people to which the military was not also party? Whatever the case, some PDI members—including Laksamana Sukardi, Sophan Sophiaan, and Aberson Marle Sihaloho—were troubled by the entry of retired generals into the PDI, fearing that they would use the organization to safeguard the doctrine proclaiming a dual function for the armed forces as both a security and a social–political force, which was at the time under fierce attack from students and reform-minded groups.[32]

By the time the congress came to an end, there was a strong feeling among delegates and nondelegates that Megawati was well placed to become the next president of Indonesia. She had survived her forcible removal from the party leadership by the Soeharto government and had stared down Habibie's attempt to continue the policy of his predecessor and mentor by denying the legality of her claim to the PDI leadership. Now that the Sanur Congress had done its work, she was the elected leader of a political party whose organizational structure was largely intact, despite the Soeharto regime's continued interference in its affairs. Moreover, she continued to enjoy a large and, in some quarters, devoted following among the Indonesian people. Her only rival in terms of organization and resources was Golkar, but it was now widely reviled for its coercive and corrupt role in providing the New Order regime with a veneer of popular support. Thus, few would have quarreled with the comment of one observer that "she was a major contender [for the presidency] before this congress, and after this [congress], she is the front runner."[33]

NOTES

1. Schwarz, *Nation in Waiting*, 361–63.
2. See O'Rourke, *Reformasi*, 144.
3. "Sidang Istimewa MPR Akhir 1998, Pemilu 1999," *Kompas Cyber Media*, May 29, 1998.
4. "Habibie: Siapa Saja boleh bentuk Partai," *Kompas Cyber Media*, May 30, 1998, www.library.ohiou.edu/indopubs/1998/05/29/0088.html.
5. Mietzner, "Nationalism and Islamic Politics," 174–77; "Partai Kebangkitan Bangsa Berdiri," *Kompas Cyber Media*, July 24, 1998.
6. Mietzner, "Nationalism and Islamic Politics," 86–189.
7. Mietzner, "Nationalism and Islamic Politics," 192–95.
8. "TPDI: Terlibat 27 Juli, Syarwan Harap Mundur," *Kompas Cyber Media*, May 29, 1998.
9. "Tolak Habibie, Megawati Terima Wakil Bank Dunia," *SiaR,* June 17, 1998, www.library.ohiou.edu/1998/06/19/0031.html.
10. Compare "Kapan Mega Lepas Beban Sejarah?" *XPOS* 26, no. 1 (June 27–July 3, 1998), www.library.ohiou.edu/1998/07/01/0007.html.
11. "Budi Hardjono, Ketua Umum DPP PDI," *Kompas Cyber Media*, August 27, 1998; "Susunan DPP PDI Hasil Kongres Palu," *Detikcom*, August 18, 1998.
12. "Megawati Vows to Hold Congress, Contest Election," *Tempo Interaktif*, September 2, 1998.
13. "PDI Megawati Rayu Gubernur Bali untuk Izin Kongres," *Republika Online*, September 16, 1998.
14. Vickers, *Bali,* 184–85; Masashi Nishihara, *Japanese and Sukarno's Indonesia*, 104.
15. "310 Cabang PDI Siap ke Bali," *Detikcom*, September 25, 1998, http://detik.com. Also "Blih, Mbak Mega Jadi Kongres!" *Forum Keadilan* 14, no. 7 (October 19, 1998): 22.
16. "Suara Keras Mega di depan 1000 Peserta Sarasehan," *Detikcom*, September 28, 1998. See also, Saur Hutabarat, "PDI Perjuangan Dan Suara Kelas Menengah," *Suara Pembaruan Daily,* October 7, 1998, www.suarapembaruan.com.

17. "Sambutan Ketua Umum DPP PDI Megawati Sukarnoputri pada Seminar Sehari Balitbang DPP PDI, Hotel Gran Melia, Jakarta, 28 September 1998," www.library.ohiou.edu/indopubs/1998/10/06/0004.html.

18. "Asal tidak Rusuh ABRI tak Keberatan Kongres PDI," *Detikcom*, September 29, 1998.

19. "Kongres PDI Perjuangan dibuka Hari ini," *Kompas Cyber Media*, October 8, 1998.

20. "Pidato Pembukaan Kongres," 5, www.library.ohiou.edu/indopubs/1998/10/10/0007.html.

21. "Pidato Pembukaan Kongres," 9–10.

22. "Pidato Pembukaan Kongres," 20.

23. "Pidato Pembukaan Kongres," 22–23.

24. "PDI Perjuangan Retak?" *Detikcom,* September 28, 1998.

25. "Alex Litaay Sekjen PDI," *Media Minggu,* October 11, 1998.

26. "Jalan Panjang dari Sanur," *Tempo*, October 19, 1998, 23.

27. "Megawati Lantik 164 Purnawirawan sebagai Anggota Baru," *Kompas Cyber Media*, October 4, 1998.

28. "Giliran Theo di 'Recall'?" *Forum Keadilan* 4, no. 6 (June 2, 1997): 26.

29. "Megawati Lantik 164 Purnawirawan," *Kompas Cyber Media*, October 4, 1998.

30. Greg Earl, "Sukarno's Daughter Marshalls Her Forces," *Australian Financial Review*, October 7, 1998, 12.

31. "Pidato Pembukaan Kongres," 19.

32. "Masuknya Mantan Jendral Bisa Rusak Citra PDI," *SiaR,* October 10, 1998, www.library.ohiou.edu/indopubs/1998/10/12/0017.html; "Usai Pesta, Debat pun Tiba," *Forum Keadilan* 15, no. 7 (November 2, 1998): 22–23.

33. Jeffrey Winters, quoted in "Analysis: Megawati Eyes Indonesia Presidency," *Reuters*, October 11, 1998.

14

A Female President?

No sooner had Megawati emerged as front-runner for the presidency than political opponents and *santri* queried her suitability on the grounds of religion and gender. On October 14, AM Saefuddin, the minister for food and horticulture in the Habibie government and a candidate for the leadership of the PPP, declared to journalists that he was prepared to nominate himself for the presidency. Commenting on the candidate of the PDI, he said, "I am capable of defeating her. Her religion is Hinduism. I am a Moslem. Are the Indonesian people willing to have a president of the Hindu religion?" When challenged on the accuracy of this claim, he replied, "I have seen [a picture of] her praying in a Balinese temple."[1] He later added, "we hold women in high esteem and believe that heaven is the sole of a woman's foot, but the President and Vice President of the Republic of Indonesia must be Moslems and not women."[2] Although Saefuddin was defeated for the leadership of the PPP by Hamzah Haz of the Nahdlatul Ulama, Hamzah Haz shared his view that only a Moslem male was eligible to become the president of Indonesia.[3]

The Congress of Indonesian Moslems (Kongres Umat Islam Indonesia) followed suit, passing a recommendation to that effect on November 6.[4] This action was opposed by both Abdurrahman Wahid, who said that "the People could get angry with the *ulama* who make a recommendation that the next president be a male," and his NU colleague Said Aqiel Siradj, who described it as a step backward for Moslems.[5] Amien Rais also entered the debate, offering the view that a woman may become president but only if there is no man who is capable of assuming the job.[6] This remark was unlikely to improve his chances of forming a coalition with Megawati "to manage national stability," in keeping with a proposal that he had made only a few weeks previously, and it is very possible that the insult gave her considerable offense.[7]

But Megawati was already feeling offended (probably by Saefuddin's original comment) and was struggling to regain her emotional equanimity, as suggested by her remarks to supporters on October 28:

> In front of cadres, sympathizers and members of the PDI *Perjuangan* Megawati said that whoever attacks and discredits her will be faced with a smile because that is the best way in politics. Previously, she also expressed the wish that PDI members would not react. "Why must you react? Just let things be. What is important is that we continue to cultivate our inner worth."[8]

To judge by this comment, Megawati responded to personal adversity by presenting an impervious exterior to the world while withdrawing into the self, and she gave this manner of behavior even clearer expression when she advised the much-criticized soldiers of the special forces unit Kopassus in September 2000: "Self-confidence is not inspired by other people, but emanates from deep down in your hearts."[9] Indeed, it suggests a later version of her defensive pride, acquired as a response to the complex mixture of privilege and neglect that marked her childhood years, and it stands in sharp contrast to her father's vanity. Whereas Sukarno derived a degree of sustenance by preening himself in public and by attracting admiring looks from a large circle of admirers, she achieved the same result by self-absorption and by regarding others with a certain indifference.[10] It should not be concluded from this comparison that only Sukarno was fully involved with the Indonesian people. He certainly gave the appearance of involvement, with his charm and gregariousness, but he also was remote and detached from their daily concerns.

Megawati's pride was well suited to the late Soeharto years in that it gave her the wherewithal to stand up to him and enjoined a style of politics that was dignified and self-contained; but it did not seem well suited to the open and competitive form of electoral politics that emerged in Indonesia in the latter half of 1998. In addition to limiting her ability to respond effectively to the likes of the aggressive and extroverted Saefuddin, it led people to regard her as aloof and to find her long, smiling silences no longer eloquent but simply exasperating.

PARLIAMENTARY ELECTIONS

President Habibie and the leadership of parliament decided that fresh parliamentary elections would be called in the middle of 1999 and would be followed by another presidential election toward the end of the year. Immediately afterward, the president appointed a team of experts—the Team of Seven, as they became called—under the leadership of Professor Ryaas Rasyid, the director general of general administration and regional autonomy within the ministry of home affairs, to draft appropriate laws for the consideration of parliament. Within a short space of time, they produced draft laws on political parties, the system of election, and the composition of the People's Representative Council and the People's Consultative Assembly. The latter two provided for a parliament of 495 elected members, consisting of 420 members elected by a single-member district system weighted in favor of the outer islands and 75 members elected by a proportional representation (PR) system from a national pool comprising the votes for the unsuccessful candidates in the various districts. An additional 55 members would be appointed from the ranks of the armed services, resulting in a parliament with an overall membership of 550 individuals, who would be joined by 81 regional delegates and 69 group delegates to constitute a People's Consultative Assembly of 700 members.[11]

The election law had much to recommend it. Its district component would bring parliamentarians into close and continual contact with their diverse constituents and thereby counter the chief disadvantage of the PR system, as experienced by Indonesia in its last free elections in 1955. This was its tendency to place a great distance between electors (who voted for parties) and their representatives (who were chosen by the leadership of the parties).

Golkar became the party that most energetically lobbied the Team of Seven on the advantages of a district system of election. Its reasoning on this matter was that its lengthy prominence at the national and local levels of government would hand their candidates an advantage in such a system. Certainly this is what Alex Litaay, the secretary-general of Megawati's PDI, was worried about when he pointed to the former military commanders, governors, bupatis, and mayors that Golkar could select as its candidates in the districts.[12] Consequently he opposed the district system on behalf of his party, calling for a PR one instead. He was not alone in this stand, which was echoed within the parliament by the PPP and the PDI (Budi Hardjono). Indeed, this was one thing that the two PDIs could agree on.

The students who had played such an important role in forcing Soeharto's retirement were outraged no only by these draft laws, which they saw as "preserving the privileges that Golkar and the Armed Forces had enjoyed for so long under the New Order," but also by the failure of the Habibie government to bring charges of corruption against Soeharto. Consequently, they demonstrated in front of the special session of the People's Consultative Assembly, which had convened in early November 1998 to provide a new legal framework for parliamentary and presidential elections. The students demanded that Habibie transfer power to a transitional government to be headed by

Megawati, Abdurrahman Wahid, Amien Rais, Bishop Carlos Belo of Dili, and Sultan Hamengkubuwono X of Yogyakarta. The leaders resisted the students' attempt to cast them in such a radical role, but they felt the need to offer them something. So on November 11 they met in Jakarta and issued a statement calling for the abolition of the armed forces' dual function within six years and an investigation into the wealth of Soeharto and his cronies.[13]

The three laws on parties, elections, and the composition of the DPR and MPR were finally passed on January 28, 1999, and President Habibie signed them into law on February 1. Their content reflected a strained compromise between the views of the interested parties. Instead of 55 seats in a DPR of 550 members, as advanced in the original legislation, the armed forces were assigned 38 seats in a DPR of 500. In turn, the MPR was to comprise the 500 members of parliament, 135 regional representatives, and 65 group representatives. Also, instead of a district system mixed with elements of PR, the final version provided for a fundamentally PR system tempered by a mild district component. The National Democratic Institute for International Affairs described the working of this "election system apparently without exact precedent or parallel anywhere else in the world":

> Each party will assign its candidates to individual districts [*kabupaten*]. Voters will cast ballots for a party, rather than a candidate. Ballots will include only the names and logos of the eligible parties. But at the same time, the lists of which candidates have been assigned by the parties to given districts will be made public and will be posted at the polling stations. Although candidates will be matched to districts, there are no provincial or district residency requirements.[14]

Both the PDI (Budi Hardjono) and the PDI (Megawati) were able to meet the eligibility requirements of the new laws for participation in the elections, although the latter was obliged to modify its name and emblem to do so—it became the Indonesian Democracy Party of Struggle (Partai Demokrasi Indonesia Perjuangan; PDIP). Thus, it seemed likely that the elections scheduled for June 7 would finally determine the relative strengths and future viability of the two parties. Overall, six of the forty-eight parties that were declared eligible to contest the elections claimed to be descendants of the Indonesian National Party (PNI), established in 1946, and its preindependence namesake, established by Sukarno himself on July 4, 1927. These six parties included the two PDIs; the Partai Nasional Indonesia, chaired by Mrs Supeni, who had served as an ambassador in the Guided Democracy period; the Partai Nasional Indonesia Front Marhaenis, led by Soeharto's wealthy half-brother Probosutedjo, who had defeated Megawati's sister Rachmawati for the chairpersonship in an election that some claimed was tainted by money politics; the Partai Nasional Indonesia Massa Marhaen of Bachtar Oscha Chatik; and the Partai Nasional Demokrat of Edwin H. Soekowati.[15]

Having finally achieved official recognition for her party and the right to compete in the elections, Megawati looked forward to them with high hopes. Speaking in Singapore in March 1999 to the Institute of Defence and Strategic Studies, she confidently declared that "we will get the largest share of the vote." Her optimism seemed well based. Not only was she widely regarded as the front-runner, but she also had good reason to feel secure in the friendship of Abdurrahman Wahid who, by strongly criticizing the recommendation of the Congress of Indonesian Moslems that the president of Indonesia be both male and Moslem, gave the appearance of being strongly behind her presidential bid. Indeed, in the same Singapore speech, she described Abdurrahman as "my best friend."[16]

Ten days later, Megawati's "best friend" followed her to Singapore and, on March 24, addressed the same body that she had spoken to. Singapore's former ambassador to the United States S. R. Nathan introduced Abdurrahman as "a beacon for calm and order in these tumultuous times in Indonesia." However, Abdurrahman certainly gave the lie to his introducer, as he declared that members of the National Awakening Party who won seats in the elections—and he confidently predicted that his party would win the most seats—would not vote for Megawati in the election for president in the People's Consultative Assembly.[17] He said that many of its members still clung to the idea of Islamic law that barred a woman from becoming president, adding

> I am close to Megawati, she is like a sister to me, but the most important thing is that we should abide by democracy . . . by the rule of the majority, and the majority I don't think will elect Megawati. This I say in good faith because I know the situation is like that . . . Maybe she can become vice president [or speaker of parliament].[18]

His other remarks were no less surprising. "If my eyesight returns, I'll be the president," he declared.[19] He then went on to mention some of the people he would appoint to his cabinet, including Kwik Kian Gie as coordinating minister for the economy, and East Timorese resistance leader Xanana Gusmao as foreign minister.[20] Referring to the communal violence between Dayaks and Madurese transmigrants in West Kalimantan and between Christians and Moslems in Maluku, he declared with breathtaking confidence that he would "take care" of it in "approximately one month." "Everything will be safe for us. Please believe me."[21]

Wahid left his audience in Singapore and in Indonesia with much to puzzle over, and one Indonesian confessed to being deeply disconcerted—Said Aqiel Siradj, one of Abdurrahman's close allies in the Nahdlatul Ulama:

> This amazed me . . . because when the *Kongres Umat Islam Indonesia* put out a declaration some time ago which rejected the idea of a woman becoming president, Gus Dur was among those who reacted most vigorously. At that time I saw how Gus Dur defended Megawati vehemently with all the propositions and verses from the Yellow Books which he had studied.[22]

Although Abdurrahman had previously contradicted the belief strongly held in some Islamic quarters that the Indonesian president should be a Moslem male—basing his position on feminist principles as well as in defense of Megawati—he was now prepared to exploit it to advance his presidential prospects at Megawati's expense.[23] This was a shocking conclusion, and Megawati and her supporters were naturally reluctant to reach it—so much so that to discount it they seized on his remarks made on his return from Singapore to the effect that he was still supporting her. They also took comfort from the fact that he visited her at her home on March 29.[24]

It is clear from the foregoing that the anxiety among some devout Moslem leaders concerning Megawati's presidential candidacy was not confined to her gender. Equally disturbing for them was her secular outlook and only nominal commitment to Islam. Their anxiety deepened when they read the list of the PDIP's parliamentary candidates, for they came to the conclusion that as many as half of them were non-Moslem. Although this estimate overstates the case, an examination of those PDIP members actually elected to the 1999–2004 parliament reveals that 37 percent were indeed non-Moslems.[25] This pronounced overrepresentation of non-Moslems, who formed only 13.1 percent of the population in 1985,[26] did not seem to be the result of deliberate action, but little was done to rectify it (although the electoral law did provide party leadership boards with some scope to revise their candidate lists).[27]

This extraordinary carelessness on the part of Megawati and other members of the PDIP leadership was not without its consequences. On June 2, the Religous Scholars, Council of Indonesia (Majelis Ulama Indonesia; MUI), a semiofficial body appointed by and, in the Soeharto years, tightly controlled by the national government,[28] urged Moslems "to vote for political parties which represent their community, field Moslem legislative candidates of 'noble conduct,' and campaign for reform."[29] It seems that this proposal was intended to dissuade Moslems from voting for the PDIP, but other parties objected to it. Amien Rais of the National Mandate Party, Sri Bintang Pamungkas of the Indonesian Democratic Union Party, and Abdurrahman Wahid of the National Awakening Party, feared that this directive would sharpen differences between Moslems and non-Moslems. As the leaders of broad-based parties that hoped to attract largely Moslem support in the elections, they were no doubt worried about the consequences of such polarization for their own electoral prospects.[30]

Although it is impossible to gauge the precise impact of the MUI recommendation on the intentions of Islamic voters, one can conclude that its influence was minimal. Megawati's party obtained the largest number of votes, by far, in the June 7 elections: 35,434,607 votes, or 33.78 percent of the total vote (104,887,309); with Golkar next, at 23,389,394 votes, or 22.30 percent.[31] Of note is that a sizable number of those votes came from *santri* strongholds, such as the island of Madura. J. Soedjati Djiwandono, writing in the *Jakarta Post* concluded, "The ruling of the Indonesian Council of Ulama (MUI) and warnings by various Muslim leaders on the gender issue seem to have been ignored by many Muslims."[32] It seems that one reason for this flouting of the MUI was the strong personal appeal of Megawati herself, who was widely admired for her courageous stand against Soeharto in the late New Order years. According to Greg Fealy, "in 1999, Megawati enjoyed widespread public sympathy and good will. More than any other political leader, she symbolized resistance to the oppression of the Soeharto era. As a result, Islamic parties found many Muslim voters unmoved by or disapproving of their attacks on Megawati."[33]

FROM PARLIAMENTARY TO PRESIDENTIAL ELECTIONS

Early counting of ballots soon revealed that Megawati's PDIP had won a substantial victory. As noted, emotional distress and social privilege during her childhood years had combined to produce an adult who was proud and aloof, and it seems that her remarkable achievement at the polls reinforced these character traits. Instead of responding to an overture by Amien Rais on June 16 as a first step toward building majority support in the People's Consultative Assembly for her presidential bid, she ignored him.[34] And instead of making sure that Abdurrahman Wahid was firmly in her camp—he had given her many reasons to doubt this in recent months—she began to treat him with a certain amount of disdain, although this may have been partly related to his recent public claim that "Mega is stupid but she is honest with the people."[35] She also began to formulate the view that, as the winner of the elections, she was entitled to the presidency. The view that the leader of the party which obtained the largest number of votes had a just claim on the presidency had much to recommend it on democratic grounds. Such a view was enunciated by Amien Rais on the eve of election day, when he was still hopeful that that person would be him, and the view was even conceded by incumbent president Habibie after the results became known.³⁶ Nevertheless, it has no standing in the 1945 constitution, which simply states that the president and vice president are chosen by a majority vote in the People's Consultative Assembly, and it certainly did not stop Habibie from planning to run as the Golkar candidate. Megawati was being unrealistic in continuing to adhere to this position, especially as her party controlled only 185 seats in the 700-seat assembly: 153 parliamentary members plus 32 regional representatives from the PDIP.³⁷ Indeed, her stand showed that it was not only her long silences that were poorly adapted to the new, open politics; likewise, her strong sense of entitlement did not serve her well in the period between the parliamentary and presidential elections, when wheeling and dealing was at a premium.

Circumstances also worked against Megawati. She was unwilling to proclaim an election victory and, on that basis, her right to the presidency until the final results were announced, which did not take place until July 26.³⁸ Had the final results been announced earlier, she would have been able to stake her claim to the presidency sooner, and it is possible that her campaign for that high office would have quickly gained momentum before her disillusioned suitors and erstwhile supporters had time to work against her. But by waiting and remaining largely quiet for the seven weeks from election day on June 7 until July 26, she gave Amien Rais and Abdurrahman Wahid, now fearful of being consigned to minor roles in a Megawati government, ample opportunity to try to thwart her.³⁹

Both leaders made as much as they could of opposition in some Islamic quarters to a female president. Amien exaggerated the differences between Habibie as the presidential candidate of the Golkar Party and Megawati as the candidate of the PDIP to justify running a compromise candidate who would bridge the gap between these two.⁴⁰ In a shrewd calculation, he proposed that this candidate should be Abdurrahman himself, for only he had the authority to draw the National Awakening Party away from Megawati. This party had originally supported him for the presidency but had shifted its allegiance to Megawati after her election victory, on the grounds that the election winner was entitled to become president. Amien Rais believed that Abdurrahman could bring the National Awakening Party into an alliance with his National Mandate Party and the two Islamic parties most strenuously opposed to her presidency on gender grounds: the Crescent and Star Party and the Unity Development Party.⁴¹ When asked why he himself was not going to stand as the presidential candidate of this grouping—which he called the Central Axis— Amien replied that it would be inappropriate for him to take such a step in light of National Mandate Party's modest 7.5 percent of the vote (actually 7.12 percent).⁴² However, these democratic scruples did not stop him from proposing Abdurrahman for the job, despite the National Awakening Party's not much less modest 12.61 percent, and Abdurrahman displayed no such scruples himself in readily accepting the proposal.

This was not the only attempt to block the winner of the parliamentary polls from becoming president. The Habibie government considered introducing legislation requiring a university degree of presidential candidates, and the indefatigable Amien proposed that presidential candidates be obliged to give a one-hour speech before the members of the People's Consultative Assembly before the ultimate vote.[43] "To many of Megawati's supporters," as Karen Strassler has written, these attempts to deny her the presidency "seemed patently unjust, a betrayal of the people's will manifested in the election results." Consequently, "groups of mostly young men began taking an 'oath' to fight for her victory which culminated in pricking one's thumb and making a thumbprint in blood on a white sheet that could be displayed and then sent to Parliament."[44] Anxious remarks in elite circles about the primitive and criminal nature of this behavior prompted Guruh, Megawati's younger brother, to comment that "a thumb print in blood is not a manifestation of a criminal attitude but constitutes an oath of loyalty of the people to their leader . . . and is taken precisely because the people are infuriated by the obscenity of elite politics at the present time."[45]

By the time Megawati finally delivered her victory speech—on July 29, three days after the final results were announced—her prospects of winning the presidency had been reduced by the emergence of the Central Axis, formed essentially of Islamic parties, with Abdurrahman Wahid as its candidate. However, these matters probably did not present themselves to Megawati in such clear terms at the time, for Abdurrahman frequently insisted that he was still supporting her for the presidency and she certainly wanted to believe him.[46] She also had many other matters to reflect on, as she claimed an outstanding election victory exactly three years and two days since the Soeharto government ordered thugs to attack her party headquarters in Jakarta, and three years and two months since it established a rival leadership board for the PDI at a manipulated congress in Medan. She doubtlessly felt vindicated by the poor showing of this PDI in the elections—that is, the PDI led by Soerjadi and then Budi Hardjono. It obtained a mere 345,720 votes, which yielded two seats, insufficient to reach the threshold for participation in the 2004 elections.[47]

In her speech, which was broadcast by the private television channels, Megawati clearly spelled out her view that the leader of the winning party in the parliamentary elections had a just claim on the presidency:[48] "As the leader of the victorious party in the elections, I have obtained a mandate and commission from the electors to form a new government which is in keeping with the wishes and aspirations of the people."[49] She then expressed gratitude

> to all the people of Indonesia who have rejected all deviations from the democratic process in defending the *Negara Hukum* and protecting Basic Human Rights by giving the most votes to the PDI *Perjuangan*. This decision of the people reflects how strong the aspiration of our people is to live in harmony and peace in a world of democracy which guarantees the freedom of each member of society not only in attitude and affiliation but also to exchange ideas and differ in opinion.[50]

Megawati had touched on these themes before. Her brave defense of the *negara hukum* (state based on the rule of law) goes back to the late Soeharto years, but her explicit appeal to basic human rights and her call for freedom of association and expression are more recent, both dating back to her speech at the Gran Melia Hotel in Jakarta on September 28, 1998. In this speech, however, they are advanced somewhat more insistently and with a stronger emphasis on the fact that the rights in question are rights that belong to individuals.

This comparatively new emphasis in her thinking is more compatible with her commitment to the *negara hukum* than it is with the populism with which it coexists. Indeed, one may observe Megawati struggling to reconcile her father's hostility to Montesquieu's *trias politica* and her own dawning recognition that the *negara hukum* depends for its very existence on a separation of powers. This conflict is clearly expressed in a remark she made in her speech to the Institute of Defence and Strategic Studies in Singapore in March 1999:

> Although Indonesia does not adhere to Montesquieu's Trias Politika system, PDI Perjuangan still holds strongly to the position that there must be a clear and transparent division between the legislative, judicial and executive powers and that this must be applied to our future political system. This division is necessary to prevent the intervention of the executive in the legislative and even judicial branches, as has been the case so far.[51]

Megawati then addressed the role of the military in society. Consistent with the more insistently liberal tone in the quoted passage, her first observation was sharper and more to the point than were her comments on this topic in her opening speech to the PDI congress the previous October, where she was broadly supportive of the military's attempts to reform itself. She said, "Concerning my attitude towards the role of the military in a society which practices democracy, I firmly adhere to the principle of civilian supremacy."[52] But if this assertion was reassuring from a democratic point of view, her next remark was less so. She continued, "I firmly declare that our archipelagic state which takes the form of a unitary state very much requires an effective and professional military."[53] It may be, of course, that she was merely referring to the need for a capable military to defend the country from external threats; however, it is more likely that she had internal threats in mind, in which case it is obvious that she was prepared to resort to military force to maintain the *negara kesatuan* (unitary republic). Not only does this standpoint make little sense from a practical point of view, given the tendency of the military to exacerbate disaffection at the local level, but it is also likely to come into conflict with her commitment to the rule of law. Preservation of the *negara kesatuan* as a voluntary association is one thing; its maintenance by force is another and is certainly not conducive to the continued existence of the *negara hukum*. Her subsequent reassurance was cold comfort at best: "This affirmation does not subtract from my attitude which is very clearly anti-militarism."[54]

We have so far recorded Megawati's stance in favor of the unitary republic; we have heard her give expression to an authoritarian populism that was more conservative than her father's radical version; and we have noted her repeating his hostility to Montesquieu's *trias politica*. But we have also noted her advocacy of substantial regional autonomy; freedom of association and assembly, not to mention other basic rights; an independent judiciary; and the rule of law, *negara hukum*. Such ambivalence is evidence of a mind in conflict, divided between aspects of her father's political beliefs and style and her new, apparent commitment to liberal and democratic values. A similar ambivalence also characterized her thinking on East Timor, which was, of course, very much on her mind when she delivered this speech. One month later the people of East Timor were scheduled to have a referendum to choose between a wide autonomy for their province or a rejection of that autonomy, leading to independence in keeping with an agreement struck between the Republic of Indonesia and Portugal on May 5, 1999.

At first, Megawati did not dispute the justification of the Soeharto regime for the incorporation of East Timor into Indonesia. For example, on November 23, 1997, the Antara news agency reported her as saying that "the integration of East Timor into Indonesia was the wish of the inhabitants of East Timor themselves. Therefore we have to defend our territory in keeping with our self respect as a nation."[55] However, after she and Abdurrahman met Bishop Belo in Jakarta on July 17, 1998, she appeared less certain on the subject of the aspirations of the East Timorese, saying, "We have to listen to what the East Timorese community actually wants."[56]

But she reverted to her previous position in response to President Habibie's announcement of January 27, 1999. He declared that he would allow the East

Timorese to vote on an autonomy proposal for their province and, if they rejected it, would recommend to the People's Consultative Assembly that they be granted their independence.[57] After claiming that the Habibie administration was a transitional one without the right to make such a fundamental decision, bearing as it did on the territorial integrity of the nation, she added,

> The political and constitutional integration of the territory of East Timor into the Unitary State of the Republic of Indonesia is valid because it amounts to a realization of the wish of the East Timorese people which has been accommodated by the People's Representative Council (DPR) in Law No. 7/1976 which itself was reinforced by Decision No. VI/1987 of the People's Consultative Assembly.[58]

This stance produced a surprised response from Xanana Gusmao, who struggled to reconcile her position on East Timor with her brave stance against the Soeharto dictatorship: "I cannot imagine why the leader of a party who persevered in her struggle in the New Order period is not able to respect the fundamental rights of people as embodied in the principles of democracy."[59] It is indeed puzzling that Megawati's insight into and experience of the Soeharto regime's lawlessness did not enable her to see either the brutal annexation of East Timor in 1975 or the subsequent suppression and murder of its people for what they were. She was not alone, however. Abdurrahman Wahid had also experienced the hostility of Soeharto, though not to the same degree as Megawati, and was familiar with Soeharto's authoritarian ways; yet he too opposed Habibie's initiative. He declared that Indonesia had already made the decision to make East Timor a part of Indonesia: "That has to be respected so that for me East Timor has to remain a part of our state."[60]

It is tempting to attribute such attitudes to the shortcomings of a successor generation of independent Indonesians who, forgetting the anticolonial message of their forebears, began to acquire the political attitudes and dull moral sensibility of imperialists. By calling Gusmao the Sukarno of East Timor, Jose Ramos Horta was trying to tell the Indonesian epigones that their imperialist behavior constituted a violation of the principles of their preeminent founding father. Some Indonesian opponents of Soeharto also subscribed to this viewpoint, but as noted in chapter 1, the imperialism really began with Sukarno himself and his colleague Muhammad Yamin in the debate on the territorial extent of the Republic of Indonesia within the Japanese-sponsored Committee for the Study of Preparation for Independence in May and July 1945. The majority vote in the investigating committee, one supporting Yamin's fatherland, suggests that interpretations of Indonesian nationalism in terms of an emancipatory, anti-Dutch colonial impulse alone miss much of its true nature and consequently fail to make sense of the widespread, ready acceptance of Soeharto's incorporation of Portuguese East Timor into Indonesia, even by individuals otherwise critical of him, such as Abdurrahman Wahid and Megawati. Commentators noting the remarks of Megawati on East Timor have called her "a conservative nationalist," but in this respect it seems that she resembles not only many members of her own generation, including Abdurrahman, but also a sizable number of the founding generation, including her father.

It is all the more remarkable that in her speech of July 29 she expressed significantly different views on East Timor. Apart from repeating her criticism of Habibie for exceeding his mandate by offering the East Timorese a referendum on his autonomy proposal, she said that the agreement between Indonesia and Portugal must nevertheless be honored, as must the decision that the East Timorese take on their future by means of the referendum. Touching on the issue of human rights violations, she elaborated as follows:

> We have to acknowledge as a reality that is difficult to deny that violations of basic human rights frequently occurred in East Timor while the New Order regime was in power. Because of that the conduct of the referendum has to be seen as a means of achieving a peaceful solution; and at the same time of giving back the basic human right of the people of East Timor to determine their own destiny.[61]

To note the liberal stand that Megawati took on East Timor in her July speech is not to say that this was her final position or that she would not revert to her previous one. On this matter, as on the others discussed earlier, one senses a struggle within her, the outcome of which remained uncertain.

She then moved from the issue of East Timor to the problems besetting Aceh. Building on the popular perception of herself as a maternal figure who embodies the suffering of all Indonesians, she addressed the people of Aceh as follows:

> Especially to my brothers and sisters in Aceh, I say, "Be patient." Later when your *Cut* [Acehnese term for "female leader"] is running this country, she will not allow one drop of blood to be spilled of the people whose achievements were so great in the struggle for Indonesian independence. To you I will give my love, I will distribute the proceeds from your Arun [liquid natural gas refinery] so that the people can relish the beauty enjoyed by the Verandah of Mecca as a consequence of it being developed with love and responsibility by fellow Indonesian citizens.[62]

We see here evidence of a desire by Megawati to approach national leadership in Indonesia differently, by replacing the security approach of her predecessor with care and respect. In her reference to the proceeds from the Arun refinery, we observe a practical application of her claim that the unitary state does not preclude a measure of regional autonomy. But we also recognize the familiar, authoritarian populism in her emphasis on a personal style of leadership in which her proclaimed love is considered sufficient guarantee of her honesty of purpose.

Most populist leaders have, of course, been males—her father, for one—so it is interesting to see the difference that Megawati's gender made as she continued to define her relationship to the citizens of Indonesia in maternal terms. On a visit to East Timor ten days later, undertaken to persuade the local inhabitants to remain part of Indonesia, she declared, "I am always mindful; indeed, I never forget the land of East Timor which I love. Although you are distant, I hold you close in my heart. I am your mother."[63] Megawati's claim may have resonated among inhabitants of the Indonesian heartland, who perhaps did not object to the New Order–style infantilizing that it implied, but it must have appeared appallingly inappropriate, not to say offensive, to the East Timorese who were about to vote in the referendum on August 30.

In that referendum, 78.50 percent of them rejected Indonesian rule, and it must be said in Megawati's favor that she accepted the result with good grace. It was announced on the morning of September 4, and within hours the Indonesian armed forces and their militia proxies had instigated massive violence and destruction in the province. On September 6, Megawati read a statement that surprised analysts, although it was consistent with her remarks on East Timor in her speech of July 30. It "called on all Indonesians to accept the result and offered a personal apology for violence committed against the East Timorese since Jakarta's 1975 invasion."[64]

The result of the referendum in East Timor caused distress and humiliation within the Indonesian heartland, and the consequent widespread anger with President Habibie for initiating this test of local opinion severely damaged his electoral prospects. Nevertheless, as the session of the People's Consultative Assembly that would elect a president and vice president approached, Megawati seemed unable to improve her prospects of being chosen for the top job. She felt such pride in the aftermath of her victory in the parliamentary elections that she had trouble concealing her disdain for some of her would-be partners, saying on one occasion that "it was difficult to imagine the PDI *Perjuangan* having to form a coalition with a party whose vote was minimal."[65]

She continued to assert that she was entitled to the presidency on the basis of her victory in the parliamentary elections. "I am amazed that a fuss is made over the issue of the presidential candidate. Logically, the general chairperson of the winning party can become president," she said on September 20.[66] Consequently, Megawati and her party entered the assembly, which convened on October 1, enjoying the clear support of only one other organization, the

National Awakening Party (Partai Kebangkitan Bangsa; PKB), led by Matori Abdul Djalil, which had obtained fifty-one seats in the parliamentary elections. Recall that this party was established by Abdurrahman in 1998 as an electoral offshoot of the Nahdlatul Ulama. It had originally nominated him as its presidential candidate but switched to Megawati in August after her victory in the parliamentary elections.[67] When Matori was asked at that time whether the support of the PKB for Megawati did not imply a rejection of Abdurrahman's nomination for the presidency by the Central Axis, he replied that "the Central Axis was not serious in nominating Gus Dur."[68]

In keeping with this alliance, the PDIP agreed to support Matori for the chair of the People's Consultative Assembly in return for the PKB's support for Megawati in the presidential election. But Abdurrahman opposed this agreement, ordering Matori to bring the PKB behind the candidate of the Central Axis, Amien Rais. When Matori refused, Abdurrahman became enraged and, showing a scant regard for the truth, accused the PKB leader of accepting large sums of money from Megawati.[69] Not only did Amien enjoy the support of the Central Axis, but Golkar backed him as well, based on the understanding that the Central Axis would support the Golkar chair, Akbar Tanjung, for the position of chairperson of parliament.[70] Thus, when the vote was taken on October 3, Amien Rais won comfortably, 305 to 279, only adding to Matori's humiliation at Abdurrahman's hands. The significance of these events was not lost on commentators. Not only had Abdurrahman shown himself to be a serious, indeed a ruthless, rival of Megawati for the presidency, but he could possibly prevail if the Central Axis–Golkar coalition was resurrected for the presidential election. For this to happen, Golkar would have to withdraw its support for Habibie, or Habibie would have to withdraw from the presidential race. Neither prospect was unimaginable, as the president's support within his own party was highly qualified, and it was possible that he would withdraw his candidacy if his accountability speech was rejected by the assembly. Iclasul Amal, rector of the University of Gadjah Mada, opined that in a race between Megawati and Abdurrahman without Habibie, Abdurrahman "would edge out Megawati."[71]

The Central Axis therefore had every reason to honor its agreement with Golkar over the election of the parliamentary chair on October 5 and duly supported Akbar Tanjung. When it became clear that he would win, the PDIP and PKB tried unsuccessfully to make his election a consensus decision of the entire parliament to conceal the fact that they had been outvoted once again.[72] This second failure of Megawati and the PDIP, caused largely by their failure to lobby widely, exasperated the PKB, which came to fear that if it continued to support her party, it would leave the general session of the People's Consultative Assembly empty-handed.[73] It also caused alarm among observers pondering the implications and consequences for Indonesian democracy if the political party enjoying the largest public support failed to win not only the chairs of the assembly and parliament but also the presidency, as now seemed possible. Former editor of *Tempo* Goenawan Mohamad told *Kompas*,

> Although the elections did not produce an outright victory for the PDI *Perjuangan*, nevertheless the garnering of 35 per cent of the vote can not be ignored just like that. "Fascism or militarism will arise if the trust of the people in elections disappears. And this is not to mention the anxiety over the emergence of a new tension between the Islamic grouping and the nationalists." . . . The key to all these problems, Goenawan said, is Abdurrahman Wahid. . . . All that anxiety will disappear if Gus Dur does not wish to be nominated as president. Besides Gus Dur has had a commitment all this time to nominate Megawati as president. "I do not like the idea of Megawati becoming president, but I appeal to Gus Dur and the members of the People's Consultative Assembly to give Megawati an opportunity to lead this Republic. . . . I very much hope that Gus Dur will be generous, and not merely advance his own interests."[74]

On October 6, the *reformasi* fraction in the assembly—comprising two Central Axis parties, the National Mandate Party, and the Justice Party (Partai Keadilan)—formally nominated Abdurrahman for the presidency.[75] The National Awakening Party (PKB) abandoned Megawati at this point, declaring its support for Abdurrahman's candidacy. Alwi Shihab, who appeared to have taken over the running of the PKB from Matori, declared, "It is not that we have abandoned Mbak Mega, but we have been dictated to by circumstances, and we cannot do otherwise."[76]

But PDIP officials still seemed unwilling to grasp the fact that Abdurrahman was a serious presidential contender in his own right and not simply a stalking-horse for Megawati. Kwik Kian Gie responded, "I don't know . . . but I hope this is his [Abdurrahman's] strategy for a political manoeuver to, at the right time, lend his support for Megawati in the presidential election." Sutjipto commented in a similarly wishful vein: "We believe Gus Dur will not run for the presidential race, because he himself supports Megawati."[77] The woman herself was equally reluctant to see things as they were. Despite Abdurrahman's various attacks on her in the week leading up to the presidential vote—on one occasion he claimed that the PDIP had no understanding of Islam, and on another he insisted that the Nahdlatul Ulama would not accept a female leader—she continued to believe that he would make way for her in the end.[78] On October 18, just two days before the presidential election was scheduled to take place, she reverted to her previous claim that she was entitled to the presidency on the basis of the victory of her party in the parliamentary elections the previous June. She said, "The nation's political elite must put the interest of the people first. After all, who holds the sovereignty? The people or the MPR?"[79]

Megawati's expectation that others should come to her—as the PKB had done in August—and her misplaced trust in Abdurrahman Wahid left her in a vulnerable but not hopeless position. A survey of the various alignments within the People's Consultative Assembly on the eve of the presidential election revealed that in a three-way race between President Habibie, Abdurrahman, and Megawati, Habibie would obtain the majority of Golkar votes as well as attract the support of the sizable number of Central Axis members who had misgivings about Abdurrahman. Indeed, in such a contest it seemed likely that Abdurrahman would drop out first. But if Habibie failed to run, then his Golkar votes would flow to Abdurrahman. The errant Central Axis voters, who preferred Habibie to their own candidate, would then return to the fold and support Abdurrahman. Although they held Habibie in higher esteem than they did him, they would certainly choose the latter ahead of the seemingly secular Megawati.[80] It was therefore very much in the interests of Megawati and her supporters that Habibie not be excluded from the presidential contest.

Nevertheless, the PDIP fraction reacted coolly when Habibie read his accountability speech before the assembly on October 14. In a vote taken on October 19, they rejected the speech, knowing full well that if a majority of the assembly followed suit, then Habibie might withdraw from the presidential election. But in fact, his speech was rejected narrowly, by a vote of 355 to 322, and in the early hours of October 20, he did indeed withdraw from the presidential race.[81]

Megawati and her party now reaped the reward of their series of political failures: a presidential competition that she would need a miracle to win, given that Abdurrahman now enjoyed the support of most of Golkar (owing to Habibie's withdrawal), all the parties in the Central Axis, and the PKB. No miracle was forthcoming. At about 2:30 PM on the same day, Abdurrahman Wahid was elected president in the assembly by 373 votes to Megawati's 313.[82]

Immediately, the result was known, Megawati's disappointed supporters rioted in Jakarta, Solo, and Bali despite an appeal by her to all Indonesians "to accept this situation." In these circumstances she did not feel that she could refuse Abdurrahman's request that she run for vice president, bitterly angry though she was at what she believed to be his stealing the presidency, which was rightly hers. The following day she defeated Hamzah Haz of the PPP for this position by 396 votes to 284.[83] In her acceptance speech, which was televised live, she addressed herself to her supporters, some of whom had continued to riot on the Thursday:

> I ask my children throughout the fatherland to resume your activities with an honest heart, and because you can see your mother [*Ibu*] standing at this podium there is no need for you to behave emotionally.[84]

This appeal, with her election as vice president, was sufficient to settle even her most agitated supporters—they did not seem to be offended by her condescendingly maternal stance—and calm soon returned to the streets.[85]

This session of the People's Consultative Assembly came to an end with the election of a president and vice president, but this had not been its only task or perhaps even its most important. Invigorated by its parliamentary members who had been elected directly—that is, in a free election—it resolved to reverse the situation of the New Order period, in which it had provided a paper-thin veneer of democratic respectability to the authoritarian President Soeharto. On October 19, a plenary session of the assembly passed amendments to nine of the constitution's thirty-seven articles. These were referred to collectively as the first amendment, and their effect was to strengthen the position of the legislative and judicial branches of government at the expense of the executive. Finally, the MPR issued a decree requiring the president to present reports to annual sessions of the assembly as well as give the customary accountability speech at the end of the presidential term.[86]

Thus, as Abdurrahman embarked on his term of office, he faced a more assertive and more powerful legislature than any that had existed since 1960, when, after it rejected his budget, Sukarno dismissed the parliament elected in the democratic elections of 1955.[87] Abdurrahman's difficulty was compounded by the fact that the position of his own party, the PKB, in the DPR was quite weak, occupying only 51 of the 462 elected seats. Getting his way would not be easy and would clearly require all the flexibility and persuasiveness that he had demonstrated in his successful bid for the presidency.

NOTES

1. "Saefuddin Menghadang Mega, Bali yang Berang," *Tempo*, November 2, 1998, 18. As stated in chapter 4, Sukarno's mother, Ni Njoman Rai Siremben (Megawati's grandmother), was a member of an old *pasek* ("elevated commoner") family from Boeleleng, Bali, and the photograph to which Saefuddin refers is one of Megawati praying with members of the Balinese side of her family.

2. "Gus Dur dan Amien Tanggapi Masalah Wanita Presiden," *Media Indonesia Online*, November 9, 1998, www.mediaindo.co.id.

3. Mietzner, "Nationalism and Islamic Politics," 183–84.

4. "Rekomendasi Kongres Umat Islam: Presiden dan Wakil Presiden Harus Pria," *Kompas Cyber Media*, November 7, 1998.

5. *Media Indonesia Online*, November 9, 1998; "Keputusan KUII Kemunduran bagi Umat Islam," *Solo Pos*, November 9, 1998, reprinted in Nur Hidayah, *Kontroversi Presiden Wanita*, 81.

6. "KUI Tolak Wanita jadi Presiden," *Bali Pos*, November 8, 1998, reprinted in Nur Hidayah, *Kontroversi Presiden Wanita*, 44–45.

7. "PDI Megawati Sambut Ajakan Amien Rais," *Detikcom*, October 23, 1998.

8. *Media Indonesia Online,* October 29, 2000, quoted in Angus McIntyre, "Megawati's Political Views," *Jakarta Post Online*, August 15, 2001.

9. Quoted in McIntyre, "Megawati's Political Views."

10. The distinction between vanity and pride is explored in Little, "Two Narcissisms," 16–27.

11. Bourchier, "Habibie's Interregnum," 17; Kevin Evans, "Ballot Ballet," *Inside Indonesia* 56 (1998): 6–7; *Kompas Cyber Media*, July 21, 1998; John McBeth, "Dawn of a New Age," *Far Eastern Economic Review*, September 17, 1998, 24–27.

12. "PDI Perjuangan Takuti Paku dan Kuku dalam Pemilu," *Kompas Cyber Media*, October 30, 1998.

13. Bishop Belo was unable to attend the meeting of November 11. Bourchier, "Habibie's Interregnum," 19; "Suara Ragu-Ragu dari Ciganjur," *Tempo*, November 23, 1998, 29.

14. National Democratic Institute for International Affairs, *New Legal Framework*.

15. "Perebutan di Tubuh PNI," *Republika Online*, October 15, 1998; "Probosutedjo Pimpin PNI," *Suara Merdeka Cyber News*, February 1, 1999, www.suaramerdeka.com; "Sudah 321 Parpol ke Depkeh," *Kompas Cyber Media*, February 6, 1999; "Daftar 48 Partai Peserta Pemilu," *Detikcom*, March 12, 1999.

16. Richard Borsuk, "Opposition Leader Megawati Says Postelection Coalition Plan is Unclear," *Asian Wall Street Journal Interactive Edition*, March 16, 1999, www.library.ohiou.edu/indopubs/1999/03/16/0020.html.

17. Jay Solomon, "Islamic Leader's Ambitions Point to Rifts in Indonesia," *Asian Wall Street Journal Interactive Edition*, March 25, 1999, www.library.ohiou.edu/indopubs/1999/03/24/0113.html.

18. Quoted in "Gus Dur: Indonesia Can't Have Woman President," *Agence France Presse,* March 24, 1999.

19. Solomon, "Islamic Leader's Ambitions."

20. "Abdurrahman Wahid's Comments in Singapore," *Business Times* [Singapore] March 25, 1999, www.library.ohiou.edu/indopubs/1999/03/28/0016html.

21. Solomon, "Islamic Leader's Ambitions."

22. "Peluang Mega setelah Pernyataan Gus Dur," *Suara Merdeka*, April 3, 1999, www.library.ohiou.edu/indopubs/1999/04/02/0075.html. The "Yellow Books" are "Arab language works . . . which are studied in the pesantren and together set the standards and paradigms for the graduates of those schools. The works cover the subject of jurisprudence (fikih), nature of God (tauhid), Traditions of the Prophet (hadis), mystical practice (tasawuf), and the Arab language" (Federspiel, *Dictionary of Indonesian Islam*, 133).

23. Mietzner, "1999 General Session," 41. Mietzner also points out that "leaders of Islamic boarding schools (*kiai*) had already prepared a set of theological arguments to legitimise a female president at a PKB gathering in late February" (41). For further detail and incisive commentary on Abdurrahman's behaviour toward Megawati at this time, see Fealy, "Abdurrahman Wahid," 9–12.

24. "Peluang Mega"; "Gus Dur Ngobrol dengan Mega," *Suara Merdeka*, April 3, 1999, www.library.ohiou.edu/indopubs/1999/04/02/0070.html.

25. Yayasan Untuk Indonesia, *Tragedi Megawati*, 71–75; H. A. Sumargono, "Isu Agama dan Sekulerisme Politik: Catatan untuk Denny J. A," www.library.ohiou.edu/1999/06/14/0089.html; "PDI-P No Threat to Islam," *Jakarta Post Online*, June 28, 1999. According to the National Democratic Institute (NDI), the religious affiliation of those members of the PDI-P who were actually elected to the 1999–2004 parliament is as follows: Moslems, 63 percent; Protestants, 25 percent; Catholics, 7 percent; and Hindus, 5 percent. The comparable figures for the Golkar Party are 86 percent, 9 percent, 4 percent, and 1 percent (see the NDI's *1999 Presidential Election*, appendix 8). See also, Leo Suryadinata, *Elections and Politics in Indonesia*, 142.

26. Liddle, "Management of Ethnic Relations," 275.

27. Mietzner, "1999 General Session," 49.

28. Federspiel, *Dictionary of Indonesian Islam*, 150; personal communication, Greg Fealy, May 17, 2001.

29. "MUI sets 'Guidelines' for Muslims to Vote," *Jakarta Post Online*, June 3, 1999.

30. "MUI Jalankan Skenario Jegal Mega," *SiaR,* June 4, 1999, www.library.ohiou.edu/indopubs/1999/06/04/0042.html; "Parties against MUI Call for Vote Support," *Jakarta Post Online*, June 3, 1999; "Gus Dur Blasts MUI Directive," *Jakarta Post Online*, June 4, 1999.

31. Aris Ananta, Evi Nurvidya Arifin, and Leo Suryadinata, *Indonesian Electoral Behaviour,* 274–75.

32. J. Soedjati Djiwandono, "Learning to Lose with Dignity," *Jakarta Post Online*, July 1, 1999.

33. Fealy, "Islamic Politics," 128.

34. "Amien Rais: Aneh, kalau Saya tetap Berjuang jadi Presiden," *Kompas Cyber Media*, June 17, 1999.

35. "Wawancara Abdurrahman Wahid: 'Megawati paling pantas jadi Presiden,'" *Tempo*, June 6, 1999, 26.

36. "Partai dengan Suara Terbanyak Berhak Dapatkan Kursi Presiden," *Kompas Cyber Media*, June 5, 1999; "Pengakuan Habibie: Mandat Rakyat bagi Megawati Lebih Besar," *Kompas Cyber Media*, August 5, 1999.

37. International Crisis Group, *Indonesia's Presidential Crisis*, appendix A.

38. See the comments of Laksamana Sukardi quoted in "PDI-P Bahas Caleg yang akan ke Senayan," *Kompas Cyber Media*, July 20, 1999.

39. Mietzner, "1999 General Session," 42.

40. "NU-Muhammadiyah Sepakat soal Presiden," *Jawa Pos Online,* June 27, 1999, www.jawapos.com; "Megawati's Bid Suffers Setback," *Jakarta Post Online*, June 27, 1999.

41. Fealy, "Islamic Politics," 131; Mietzner, "1999 General Session," 43.

42. "Amien Rais: Gus Dur Calon Presiden," *Kompas Cyber Media*, July 21, 1999.

43. "Amien Rais: Presiden Perempuan tak Soal," *Detikcom*, July 6, 1999; "Drunk on Power," *Jakarta Post Online*, July 6, 1999; "Expert Queries 'Sudden' Drafting of Presidency Bill," *Jakarta Post Online*, July 8, 1999.

44. Strassler, "Currency and Fingerprints," 79.

45. "Guruh Minta Mega tak Hentikan Cap Jempol Darah," *SiaR*, July 16, 1999, www.library.ohiou.edu/indopubs/1999/07/16/0021.html; Strassler, "Currency and Fingerprints," 79–82.

46. See "Amien Rais: Gus Dur calon Presiden Alternatif," *Kompas Cyber Media*, July 21, 1999.

47. "Hasil Pemilu 1999," *Museum-KPU.com*, http://kpu.go.id. The National Democratic Institute for International Affairs summarized the threshold provision of the elections law as follows: "A party must gain 2 percent of the seats in the DPR [national parliament] (10 seats)—or 3 percent of the seats in the provincial and district assemblies distributed in half of the provinces and half of the districts in Indonesia—to be eligible to run in the future" (*New Legal Framework*).

48. "Megawati Siap Gantikan Habibie," *Kompas Cyber Media*, July 30, 1999.

49. "Pidato Politik Ketua Umum PDI Perjuangan Megawati Soekarnoputri dalam rangka Menyambut Kemenangan Rakyat pada Pemilu 1999," *Kompas Cyber Media*, July 30, 1999.

50. "Pidato Politik dalam Rangka Kemenangan."

51. "Text of Speech by Megawati in Singapore," March 15, 1999, www.library.ohiou.edu/indopubs/1999/03/19/0022.html.

52. "Pidato Politik dalam Rangka Kemenangan."

53. "Pidato Politik dalam Rangka Kemenangan."

54. "Pidato Politik dalam Rangka Kemenangan."

55. "Mega Diatas Timor Timur," PRD International Office Sydney, www.library.ohiou.edu/indopubs/1997/12/02/0029.html.

56. "Gus Dur-Belo-Megawati: Harus segera lakukan Konsensus Nasional," *Kompas Cyber Media*, July 18, 1998.

57. Lowry, "East Timor," 92.

58. "Gus Dur dan Megawati Tolak Pelepasan Timtim," *Kompas Cyber Media*, January 30, 1999.

59. Quoted by Tri Agus S. Siswowiharjo, "Bung Karno, Megawati dan Xanana Gusmao," Solidamor, www.library.ohiou.edu/indopubs/1999/03/13/0024.html.

60. "Tolak Pelepasan Timtim," *Kompas Cyber Media*, January 30, 1999.

61. "Pidato Politik dalam Rangka Kemenangan."

62. "Pidato Politik dalam Rangka Kemenangan." Megawati also made passing reference to the people of Irian Jaya and Ambon.

63. "Megawati kepada Warga Timtim: Pilih sesuai Nurani," *Kompas CyberMedia*, August 10, 1999.

64. Amy Chew, *Reuters,* September 6, 1999. See also, Hamish McDonald, "Megawati Blames Chaos on Habibie," *Sydney Morning Herald Online,* September 8, 1999. See also Megawati, "Blame It on Habibie, and Suharto," *Newsweek International*, September 20, 1999, www.library.ohiou.edu/indopubs/1999/09/14/0189.html.

65. "Megawati Siap Berdialog," *Kompas Online*, August 11, 1999.

66. Quoted in "Pokok dan Tokoh," *Tempo*, October 3, 1999.

67. "Pertemuan Matori-Megawati: 'Besanan' PKB dan PDI-P," *Kompas Cyber Media*, August 18, 1999; Fealy, "Islamic Politics," 131.

68. "Pertemuan," *Kompas Cyber Media*, August 18, 1999.
69. Mietzner, "1999 General Session," 44.
70. National Democratic Institute, *1999 Presidential Election,* 22.
71. Quoted in "PDI-P's Political Prowess Comes under Question," *Jakarta Post Online*, October 5, 1999.
72. National Democratic Institute, *1999 Presidential Election*, 22; "Akbar Tanjung Ketua DPR," *Kompas Cyber Media*, October 6, 1999.
73. Mietzner, "1999 General Session," 44.
74. "Goenawan Mohamad: PDI Perjuangan jangan Diasingkan," *Kompas Cyber Media*, October 6, 1999.
75. "Fraksi Reformasi Calonkan Gus Dur," *Kompas Cyber Media*, October 7, 1999.
76. "Fraksi Reformasi."
77. "PKB Reverses Field, Backs Gus Dur," *Jakarta Post Online*, October 8, 1999.
78. Mietzner, "1999 General Session," 44–45.
79. "Megawati Tells MPR to Heed Voters," *Jakarta Post Online*, October 19, 1999.
80. Mietzner, "1999 General Session," 45–46.
81. National Democratic Institute, *1999 Presidential Election,* 23.
82. National Democratic Institute, *1999 Presidential Election*, 23; Mietzner, "1999 General Session," 46–47.
83. Mietzner, "1999 General Session," 51; National Democratic Institute, *1999 Presidential Election,* 23–24.
84. "Pidato Pelantikan Wakil Presiden Republik Indonesia," October 22, 1999, 3, http://mpr.wasantara.net.id.
85. National Democratic Institute, *1999 Presidential Election,* 23–24; "Kenapa Massa Mengamuk Saat Mega Kalah?" *Tempo*, October 31, 1999, 16–17; "Amuk Massa karena Ibu," *Tempo,* October 31, 1999, 29.
86. National Democratic Institute, *1999 Presidential Election,* 6, 18, 20; "UUD 1945, Perubahan Pertama dan Perubahan Kedua," *Kompas Cyber Media*, August 21, 2000, 30–32.
87. Feith, "Dynamics of Guided Democracy," 343–44.

15

Megawati Sukarnoputri as Vice President

Almost from the very moment Abdurrahman Wahid gained office he displayed contempt for the coalition that had brought him to power and for the parliament itself. In November, he dismissed Hamzah Haz, the chairperson of the Unity Development Party and a key figure in the Central Axis, from his cabinet position as coordinating minister for people's prosperity. When the parliament exercised its power of interpellation for the first time in over thirty years to obtain an explanation from the president regarding why he had closed the departments of information and social security, he referred to its members as "kindergarden students."[1]

It took only a month or so for leading figures in the Central Axis—such as Amien Rais and, of course, Hamzah Haz himself—to regret their support of Abdurrahman for the presidency and to even entertain the idea of replacing him at some time in the future. But if they were having second thoughts about him, many maintained their negative view of Megawati. She did nothing to challenge it by holidaying with her family in Hong Kong over the Christmas period at the very time a new wave of communal violence broke out in the troubled province of Maluku.[2] In this frame of mind, they considered the possibility of revising article 8 of the constitution, which deals with the issue of presidential succession, at the annual session of the People's Consultative Assembly scheduled for August.[3] Rather than have the vice president serve out the remainder of the president's term in the event of his "death, resignation, removal from office, or inability to exercise his duties," the Central Axis figures proposed that the vice president serve only until the next annual session of the MPR, which would be entrusted with the task of choosing a new president.[4]

Megawati had indeed got off to a hesitant start as vice president, still embittered as she was by what she saw as Abdurrahman's betrayal and the failure of the MPR to recognize her democratic claim on the presidency. Nevertheless, she was still capable of drawing lessons from her setback of the previous year, and one of these was the need to improve her standing among devout Moslems. In early March 2000, she undertook the pilgrimage to Mecca.[5] It is noteworthy that in the very same month that she was reaching out to the devout, Abdurrahman was giving them offense by proposing the revocation of decision 25/1966 of the Interim People's Consultative Assembly (MPRS), which banned Marxism and Communism.[6]

But if it is possible to date Megawati's newfound piety from this time, it is not possible to be definitive on other matters relating to her politics and political beliefs: their inconsistencies continued to abound. For example, in her opening address to the first congress of the PDIP, which convened in Semarang at the end of March, she reiterated her protest against the undemocratic outcome of the presidential election. According to *Jakarta Post Online*, Megawati said that "Indonesian people are not yet prepared to support democratic ideas because the current political system fails to give a party that won the popular vote a chance to assume power."[7] As her new secretary-general, Sutjipto, explained to the press after the congress, "Megawati did not denounce the indirect election system which cost her the presidency last October, but instead condemned the lack of morality of the other factions for depriving her of her claim to the nation's top job."[8] It was as if she believed in democracy for herself alone. As David Bourchier has pointed out, she presided over the Semarang congress

> in true New Order style, forcing other contenders for the position of party chair [including her former speech writer, Eros Djarot] to withdraw in order that she could be elected by acclamation—avoiding the need for a vote. Observers at the congress noted the lack of expression of dissenting opinion, leading the *Jakarta Post* to editorialise that "the party's democratic credentials have now been destroyed."[9]

Within weeks of the conclusion of the PDIP congress, President Abdurrahman dismissed two members of his cabinet—minister for investment and state enterprises Laksamana Sukardi and minister for industry and trade Jusuf Kalla—and justified his action by claiming to the parliamentary leadership in a confidential briefing that they were both involved in corruption. It was this allegation as much as the dismissals themselves that angered the parliament, the political parties from which the ministers came (the PDIP and Golkar), and Megawati, who had not been consulted by Abdurrahman before he took this action, despite her being both vice president and chairperson of the PDIP.

Indeed, she and legislators from her party were particularly annoyed, as the claim was plainly false in the case of Laksamana Sukardi, whose record was impeccable.[10]

Indeed, they suspected his dismissal was related to his action earlier in the year in exposing the actions of Marimutu Sinivasan, the owner of the Texmaco conglomerate, who violated banking regulations in late 1997 by using his influence with President Soeharto to obtain a loan of US$1.2 billion from a state bank, Bank Negara Indonesia—well in excess of the legal lending limit.[11] Certainly, there were stories that Sinivasan had ingratiated himself with Abdurrahman by donating a large sum of money to Nahdlatul Ulama.[12] Whatever the case, Abdurrahman had already given offense to the parties who formed the Central Axis and, by sacking these two ministers, now antagonized the two largest parties in the parliament, who occupied 273 of its 500 seats.

Consequently, on June 29, the parliament decided by a large majority—332 out of 431 members present—to exercise its interpellation right to obtain a full explanation from the president for his sacking of the ministers.[13] As the day on which Abdurrahman was due to appear before the house approached, it was announced that Megawati would read out the prepared statement of the blind president to the assembled members. Apparently he had asked her to do so in the hope that her presence would oblige her party members to soften the tone of their questions. In the end, she decided not to do it, saying, "This is Mas Dur's problem, not mine," and the task was entrusted to state secretary Djohan Effendy.[14] Nevertheless, she urged PDIP legislators to behave with restraint. "I ask PDI perjuangan members at the House to behave normally and properly during the hearing," she said.[15] She herself was behaving with remarkable restraint. Still embittered by Abdurrahman's undermining of her presidential bid in the previous year, she also had to cope with his frequent remarks to palace visitors that not only belittled her abilities but also contained mischievous speculation regarding the nature of her private life.[16] Megawati had withstood adverse comments in the past—most notably from A. M. Saefuddin in October 1998—but not of such an intrusive nature; and one can imagine her drawing on all the resources of her defensive pride to maintain her equanimity in the face of such provocation.

Abdurrahman appeared before the house on July 20 and struck a combative tone in his prepared statement and in his unrehearsed remarks. He refused to answer questions concerning the dismissal of the ministers and asserted that the parliament had acted unconstitutionally in claiming a right of interpellation. He said, "This is a presidential system of Government. . . . The President is not accountable to the House. The President will give his account at the end of his term to the People's Consultative Assembly."[17] The following day, Abdurrahman sent a letter of apology to the house, saying that he did not deny the right of the house to question the president. He later provided some documents to support his dismissing of the ministers. But, as Greg Fealy has explained, little new light was shed on the matter by this action; indeed, the main outcome of the interpellation session was "to heighten tensions between the executive and the legislature regarding the DPR's right to demand accountability from the president."[18]

When the MPR convened on August 7 for its first annual session, some of its members talked of reconstituting the annual session as a special session to impeach the president. Megawati again refused to take on the task of reader, so the job of reading out the president's report to the assembly fell to cabinet secretary Marsillam Simanjuntak. The members were highly critical of the report delivered to them, and the vice president's action suggested that she, too, was not satisfied with its defense of his stewardship.[19] Certainly, she shared with members of the assembly their expressions of deep dissatisfaction with Abdurrahman's erratic leadership style, not to mention his failure to reduce conflict in society, restore the economy, and combat corruption. Like them as well, she was impatient with his open and tolerant attitude to separatist movements in Aceh and Irian Jaya. Furthermore, there can be no doubt that she fully supported the assembly's instruction to Abdurrahman to implement special autonomy in Aceh and West Irian and take decisive action against the separatist movements in these two provinces.[20]

Under heavy pressure from the main political parties, the president reluctantly agreed "to delegate to the vice-president the tasks of carrying out the day-to-day technical details of running the government, preparing the cabinet's working agenda and determining the focus and priority of the government."[21] The president's August 10 announcement of this transfer to the assembly was well received by legislators and the public alike—it even led to a modest strengthening of the rupiah on currency markets.[22] But he later qualified his remarks, saying that he was transferring to the vice president only "tasks," not "authority."[23]

This favorable response may be interpreted as a sign of Megawati's growing stature among those who were formerly skeptical of her. She could claim no outstanding successes as vice president; in fact, she seemed at a loss in dealing with the continuing communal violence in Maluku. But what contrasted favorably with Abdurrahman's widely perceived waywardness was her steady and predictable approach, her repeated appeals to maintain the unity of the nation, and her firm line against Papuan nationalists—in December 1999, she repeated her father's claim that "without Irian, Indonesia is not complete."[24] Of course, the chief stumbling block to her acceptance by the devout in 1999 had been her apparent secularism. Since then, she had reached out to the Moslems by going on the pilgrimage to Mecca, whereas Abdurrahman had given offense, especially to the modernists, by proposing that the ban on Marxism and communism be revoked. Thus, by August 2000, members of the Central Axis had come to view Megawati with new respect and to offer her their support, and the earlier proposals to revise article 8 of the constitution were quite forgotten.[25] Indeed, the annual session of the People's Consultative Assembly decided that "in the event that a Special Session of the Assembly dismisses the President . . . [then] the Assembly will appoint the Vice President as President until the end of his term of office."[26]

It did not take the president long to break his commitment to work more closely with Megawati, by allowing her very little, if any, say in the composition of his new cabinet. The final list contained no senior PDIP leaders and no Golkar member whatsoever. In response, she boycotted the announcement of its membership on August 23.[27] Consequently, he antagonized her and the parliament, thereby disturbing the relative calm that had prevailed between the legislative and executive branches of government since he made his commitment earlier in the month. A week after the announcement of the new cabinet, the parliament returned to the fray, further strengthened by the second amendment, which gave constitutional force to the parliament's power of investigation.[28] It decided by an overwhelming majority (356 to 4, with 45 abstentions) "to establish a Special Inquiry into the so-called Bulog-gate and Brunei-gate scandals."[29] In the case of the former, the parliament claimed that the president's masseur had obtained a loan of 35 billion rupiah from an official of the price-stabilizing body Bulog, who appears to have thought that he was acting on the president's behalf; and the latter referred to a gift of US$2 million, which Abdurrahman received from the Sultan of Brunei and for which there had been no clear accounting.[30]

In September, Megawati attended a celebration in Port Morseby marking the twenty-fifth anniversary of Papua New Guinea. On her return to Jakarta, she stopped off in Irian, where she turned a stony face to Papuan aspirations for independence. "It is sad," she said, "that after all this pain and struggle to be part of Indonesia then you emotionally declare your independence." She added that they should learn from "the East Timor experience": "Look at what is happening now in East Timor. One year after they decided to separate from their brothers and sisters, they are still facing several internal problems."[31] With sentiments such as these, it is not surprising that from November onward she helped push Abdurrahman's government toward a far more repressive approach in Irian Jaya.[32] And she was fully implicated—as, of course, was Abdurrahman Wahid himself—in a toughening of government policy toward the Free Aceh Movement (Gerakan Aceh Merdeka) in April 2001 after the expiry of the so-called "Humanitarian Pause" in January of the same year.[33] Presidential instruction number 4 of April 11, 2001, having noted the failure of the government to settle the dispute through dialogue, authorized military operations in the province.³⁴

As mentioned, there was another aspect of government policy toward Irian Jaya and Aceh. The October 1999 session of the People's Consultative Assembly, hoping to draw the sting of the separatist movements in the two provinces, had obliged Abdurrahman's government to grant the provinces special autonomy, and in August 2000 it recommended to the government and the parliament that the appropriate legislation be passed before May 1, 2001.³⁵ This deadline, however, was not met; nevertheless, the parliament began its deliberations on this matter in April. Moreover, it distinguished itself by choosing to consider the more radical draft bills that emanated from the provinces themselves, rather than the bland offerings of the central government. Despite some foot-dragging from the PDIP, which professed concern for the future of the unitary state, the legislature approached these two drafts open-mindedly, giving hope to many who saw their passing into law as the best hope for the survival of the Republic of Indonesia as a voluntary association.³⁶ But this was a busy time for the Indonesian parliament. It was unable to give the draft laws its undivided attention, preoccupied as it was with its struggle with the president.

Parliament's special inquiry into "Bulog-gate" and "Brunei-gate" filled the press in the last months of 2000, especially with news of the testimony given by the former police commander Lieutenant-General Rusdihardjo, who asserted that the president had admitted to issuing a Bulog check worth 5 billion rupiah (US$500,000) "to a young businesswoman in Semarang who was the daughter of a local NU leader."³⁷ Finally, it reported to parliament at the end of January 2001 that it was "'reasonable to suspect' that the president had been involved in the Bulog affair. It also noted that the contradictions between his various explanations of what happened to the Sultan of Brunei's gift indicated that not all were true."³⁸ On February 1, the parliament, with the support of all the major parties within it (except Abdurrahman's National Awakening Party), voted to accept the report and then voted in favor of a memorandum declaring that the president "had 'truly violated the Constitution and the National Will' in two respects. Firstly he had violated his oath of office 'to hold firmly to the Constitution and fully implement all Laws and Regulations,' and secondly, he had failed to implement MPR decree XI/1998 on clean government, free of corruption, collusion and nepotism."³⁹

By issuing this memorandum the parliament had taken the first step in a constitutional process that could end in the dismissal of the president.⁴⁰ According to the constitution, its elucidation, and two decrees of the People's Consultative Assembly, if the parliament "considers that the President has truly (*sungguh*) violated the . . . National Will (sometimes translated as National Policy) as fixed either by the Constitution or by the MPR . . . [People's Consultative Assembly]" or is responsible for "the violation of the constitution," then the DPR can issue a memorandum of censure. In the absence of a satisfactory response from the president within three months, the parliament can issue a second memorandum. If this memorandum does not elicit an appropriate response within one month, the DPR can then "call the MPR into session in a special sitting to ask the President to account for his actions." The aforementioned sources of law are silent on the matter of impeachment; however, the constitution does declare that "the MPR is the repository of Indonesian sovereignty," that "the President is appointed by it," and that "it is therefore usually accepted that if the MPR rejects the President's account of his actions it can dismiss the President."[41]

Presumably to forestall the issuing of this memorandum, Abdurrahman proposed on January 28 to declare a state of emergency and dissolve parliament. In the face of strong opposition from the leaders of the armed forces, he did not proceed. Nevertheless, the fact that he was willing to contemplate such a measure only hardened his opposition from parliament and significantly added to the distrust that members had felt for him since his failure to keep his word in August 2000 over the promised job sharing with Megawati. In this environment there was very little prospect of a last-minute compromise being struck between the contending parties. Abdurrahman may have enjoyed more success in shoring up his presidency had he sought to appease Megawati as well as offer senior cabinet positions to the political parties that he had previously antagonized. However, he no longer seemed capable of this degree of flexibility, so the stage seemed set for a final, bitter struggle between president and parliament.

Immediately following the parliament's vote on February 1 in favor of the memorandum, violence broke out in East Java, the home province of Abdurrahman and the Nahdlatul Ulama. Youth from Nahdlatul Ulama–affiliated organizations spared the PDIP but attacked the property of two other organizations implicated in the passage of the memorandum: Golkar, whose parliamentary representatives had voted for it; and the modernist Islamic association Muhammadiyah, led until recently by Amien Rais, who had strongly supported Abdurrahman for the presidency in 1999 but was now just as intent on his removal.[42] If the president did not lend support to these actions, then nor did he condemn them either; it was possibly Megawati's anger at such ambivalence that led her to take an oblique swipe at him by declaring, "This anarchy doesn't show maturity on the part of their leaders."[43]

Abdurrahman did not improve his standing later in the month when he refused to vary his overseas travel plans despite an explosion of ethnic violence in Cental Kalimantan. In mid-February, Dayaks massacred at least five hundred

Madurese in the town of Sampit causing a massive flight of Madurese to safer locations. But while *Bapak* president was absent and seemingly indifferent to the intense suffering of the survivors, *Ibu* was present in the provincial capital of Palangkaraya on March 1, doing what she could.[44] Indeed, television viewers in Jakarta were treated to and touched by news film of her hugging a Madurese woman who was grieving over the death of her husband.[45]

The following day, leaders of Golkar, PDIP, and Moslem parties met in Jakarta. All were increasingly inclined to see Megawati as a worthy replacement for Abdurrahman. Heard no more were the previous insistences of Hamzah Haz and Saefuddin that the Indonesian president must be Moslem and male, as well as Amien's earlier assertion that a female president would only be acceptable if there was no competent male available. Indeed, Hamzah Haz and Amien Rais now came out in support of Megawati, and Hidayat Nur Wahid of the Justice Party said that "since Mega is a true Moslem, we do not see any problem in supporting her to replace Gus Dur."[46] Also, after a meeting with Megawati on March 28, chairperson of the Muhammadiyah Syafii Ma'arif declared that his organization "never questioned a woman becoming president. That is an outdated piece of jurisprudence."[47]

The president responded to parliament's memorandum on March 28. He denied involvement in the Bulog affair and asserted that he had not handled the gift provided by the sultan of Brunei, which, in any case, was not public money. He also argued that the finding of the special inquiry—that it was "reasonable to suspect" that he had been involved in the Bulog affair—failed to demonstrate that he had "truly violated" the constitution or the national will.[48]

This was a telling point, but the leaders of the main parties failed to respond to it directly, simply asserting that the president had not addressed the specific allegations against him. The speakers in the debate in parliament over whether to issue another memorandum shifted the gravamen of their censure from the specific claims contained in the first memorandum to the more general issue of what they regarded as his policy and leadership failures. In objecting to this questionable procedure and in making the point that the general quality of his leadership could not be made the basis for his dismissal, Abdurrahman stood on firm legal ground.[49] But, as Lindsey has pointed out, what he did not take into account was that the People's Consultative Assembly, where his fate would eventually be decided, "can amend and reverse its own procedures, including those for impeachment, or act retrospectively to validate or nullify any act or legal event"—such is its power, which "is constitutionally expressed to be without limit."[50] In these circumstances, as Fealy observed at the time, it is clear that "the majority opinion of the MPR counts for more than the finer points of legal interpretation."[51]

The parliament passed its second memorandum of censure on April 30 with the support of all the major groupings—except Abdurrahman's National Awakening Party, which opposed it, and the military/police faction, which abstained. Having "concluded that 'President Abdurrahman Wahid, over the past three months, failed to heed the first memorandum,' it 'called on him to heed the second . . . within one month.'"[52] In his desperation, Abdurrahman began to think again of declaring a state of emergency, disbanding the parliament and the People's Consultative Assembly, and holding new elections; in fact, he proposed as much to the army and police chiefs on May 5. They refused to countenance such a course of action, with the former, General Endriartono Sutarto, advising the president "not to plan, or even consider, declaring a state of emergency, which is only used for the dissolution of the House."[53]

At this low point in his political fortunes, Abdurrahman turned for help to Megawati's younger, outspoken sister Rachmawati, a most energetic guardian of their father's legacy. Sukarno had expressed the hope in 1965 that his teachings would last a thousand years, and it was as if his second daughter was determined to do everything that she could within the span of her life to realize this wish.[54] He had hoped to petrify history in the image of his final achievements, but when he was overthrown in 1966, it was Rachmawati who turned into stone. Sukarno died in 1970, but for her he has remained more alive than all the living, and she has devoted her entire adult life to a detailed, literal, and precise perpetuation of his legacy and defense of his good name. Consequently, she bluntly criticized Megawati when she joined the PDI in 1987 for failing to follow Sukarno's example and remain above the political parties, especially ones that would only seek to exploit his name.

However, in May 2001, Rachmawati's concern ran deeper than it did in 1987. She began to fear that history was about to repeat itself. Public discussion of Abdurrahman's strokes and their possible impact on his behavior reminded her of similar speculation about Sukarno's kidney disease in 1965. The possibility that the parliament would call a special session of the People's Consultative Assembly to demand an accounting from Abdurrahman reminded her of the special session that had removed her father from office in March 1967.[55] Consequently, she rushed to Abdurrahman's defense, and, on the same day that he had proposed declaring a state of emergency, she told the press that if the vice president could not work with the president, then she should resign as former Vice President Hatta had resigned in 1956 when he found himself in disagreement with Sukarno.[56] Megawati endured her sister's intervention with characteristic stoicism, but it only served to harden her heart against the man who had instigated it. As this outcome was entirely predictable, one wonders what he had in mind when he approached Rachmawati.

She was an isolated figure without political influence, and there was very little she could offer him—certainly nothing that would outweigh the consequences of her elder sister's anger.

This was not the only area where the president's behavior seemed self-defeating. As his one-month deadline approached, his thoughts again turned to the declaration of a state of emergency, and on May 26 he threatened to make such a declaration.[57] Thus far, the president had pointed to some weaknesses in the parliament's case against him, but if he were actually to declare a state of emergency and seek on that basis to disband the parliament and the People's Consultative Assembly, as seemed likely, then he would give the latter body a solid case in favor of his dismissal. For although the constitution states that "the President may declare a state of emergency," it does not give him the power to override it, as would be required to freeze or disband these two bodies; and no lesser legal instrument could give him that power (Abdurrahman seemed to have in mind government regulation 23 of 1959). Thus, although the special inquiry's finding that it was "reasonable to suspect" that he had been involved in the Bulog affair might not constitute strong grounds for asserting that he had violated the constitution, the declaration of a state of emergency certainly would.[58]

Whether for this reason or some other, the president decided against such drastic action, for the time being at least, issuing instead an executive order on May 28 that ordered "the Coordinating Minister for Political, Social and Security Affairs to take the necessary special actions and steps, by coordinating with all elements of the security forces, to overcome the crisis and uphold order, security and the law as quickly as possible."[59] At first, this order and its legal standing caused some confusion in political circles, but then the president's opponents pooh-poohed it while the coordinating minister in question, Susilo Bambang Yudhoyono, made it plain that he served not only the president but the vice president.[60] On May 30, the parliament voted overwhelmingly to call for a special session of the People's Consultative Assembly, having taken the view that the president's response to the memoranda was unsatisfactory and having disregarded a report from the attorney general's office that cleared Abdurrahman of corruption allegations. In keeping with assembly standing orders that require that two months' notice be given of a special session, the working body of the assembly fixed August 1 as the date on which it would begin.[61]

Two days later, on June 1, the president took everyone by surprise by announcing a cabinet reshuffle. He dismissed Susilo Bambang Yudhoyono, whom only a few days earlier he had entrusted with the task of upholding law and order, and replaced him with minister for transportation and communications Agum Gumelar on the grounds that he wanted "someone who can foster ties with Megawati." It is true that Agum was regarded as close to Megawati—he was a former special forces commander who had given a degree of support to Megawati at the "national consultation" of December 1993, where she was elected PDI chairperson. And it is possible that Megawati was still making up her mind about Susilo Bambang Yudhoyono, as he must have played some role in the attack on PDI headquaters in July 1996, being chief of staff of the Fifth (Jakarta) Military Command at the time. However, there were other, more direct ways than this for the president to improve relations with his deputy. Abdurrahman also dismissed attorney general Marzuki Darusman and minister for maritime affairs and fisheries Sarwono Kusumaatmadja, replacing them with justice minister Baharuddin Lopa and Rochim Dahuri, respectively.[62] He also attempted to dismiss the national police chief, General Surojo Bimantoro, but the latter refused to step down, pointing to MPR decree 4/2000, which "requires the president to seek DPR approval before appointing or dismissing the chiefs of the armed services and the police."[63] The parliament continued to recognize Bimantoro as the national police chief, zealously guarding the new power derived from the aforementioned MPR decree and fearful that Abdurrahman wanted to remove him to clear the way for a more tractable officer who would be prepared to implement a state of emergency.[64]

One week later, on June 6, the one hundredth anniversary of the birth of Sukarno and the second anniversary of the establishment of Rachmawati's Bung Karno University, Rachmawati returned to the fray. In an article in the daily newspaper *Kompas,* she criticized "the party which had won the most votes in the 1999 elections" for taking advantage of Sukarno's name while failing to perpetuate his teachings or inculcate his original ideals in the Indonesian people. She also repeated her former suggestion that if Megawati could not work with the president, then she should resign as former Vice President Hatta had done in 1956. In a later address on the same day, one commemorating the founding of her university, she returned to her earlier apprehension that Abdurrahman was in danger of experiencing her father's fate—that is, being overthrown by people claiming to act in the name of democracy and the constitution.[65]

The celebration of Sukarno's birth was followed a fortnight later in Blitar by the commemoration of his death. Both Rachmawati and Megawati attended, as did the president. In her speech, Rachmawati dwelt on the suffering that Sukarno had endured in the final years of his life and called for the revoking of Interim People's Consultative Assembly decree 33/1967. This was the order by which the Interim People's Consultative Assembly dismissed him from office in 1967. Abdurrahman responded sympathetically, expressing the hope that the People's Consultative Assembly would see fit to replace this decree with another, one that acknowledges Sukarno's standing as father of the nation. Then, having claimed to have studied Sukarno's teachings since childhood, he declared, "Although I am not able to see, it has been my destiny to lead this country." But some young men in the audience, who interpreted the workings of fate in an altogether different way, shouted out, "Mega is our president." Very irritated, Abdurrahman told them to stop calling out. "If you continue to do so you will only lower the esteem in which *Bu Mega* is held. Is that what you want? Let us show respect for the Vice President by behaving in an orderly fashion at this meeting."[66]

With the approach of August 1, the day on which the special session of the People's Consultative Assembly was scheduled to begin, the struggle between the various protagonists assumed an increasingly acrimonious and desperate character. At the beginning of July, the president tried again to dismiss police chief General Bimantoro. Fearful that this move was the prelude to the declaration of a state of emergency, the working body of the People's Consultative Assembly prepared to summon its parent body to a plenary session, which would then bring forward the starting date of the special session.[67] Abdurrahman responded by saying that he would declare a state of emergency on July 20 at 6 PM. On July 9—the same day that the MPR's working body met—Megawati made her position clear, saying that convening a special session was the only way to resolve the political crisis. Six days later, Rachmawati accused her sister of betraying their father's legacy, claiming that she does no more than continue Bung Karno's biological line, having failed altogether to perpetuate his ideology or carry on his ideals.[68] Then, on the day that the alleged state of emergency was to be declared, she expressed her support for such a move.[69]

At 5:30 that afternoon, the president, determined to circumvent the MPR's decree requiring him to seek the approval of parliament "before appointing or dismissing the chiefs of the armed services and the police," appointed General Chaeruddin Ismail as acting police chief. Then, at 6 PM, he said that he would delay the declaration of the state of emergency until 6 PM of July 31 in the hope that a political compromise would be reached before that date. But the assembly leaders were in no mood for compromise. Disturbed by the appointment of an acting police chief, they met at 8:30 PM and decided to convene a plenary session of the assembly on the following day.[70]

At this plenary session, members of the assembly criticized the president for creating division within the ranks of the police force, and some alleged that he was in violation of the constitution. Finally, they voted 592–5 (with 4 abstentions) to bring forward the opening of the special session, from August 1 to that very day—July 21. Once opened, it voted in favor of meeting again on July 23 at 9 AM.[71] Abdurrahman said that the calling of the special session was illegal, and he resolved not to comply with its request that he attend on

July 23 to present an accountability speech.[72] Moreover, in the early hours of July 23, he finally issued his declaration of a state of emergency. It provided for the suspension of parliament, the People's Consultative Assembly, and the former government political party Golkar, as well as for the calling of fresh elections within a year. Akbar Tanjung, the speaker of parliament and chairperson of Golkar, asked the Supreme Court for an opinion on the legality of the president's decree. At 7 AM, a weary chief justice suggested that the move was unconstitutional, for the president did not have the power to suspend the parliament or the assembly, whereas the holding of elections was a matter for the legislature and the legal standing of Golkar was a matter for the courts.[73]

Thus, far from saving his presidency, the only thing Abdurrahman achieved by issuing his decree was to provide the assembly with incontrovertible grounds for his dismissal. At its meeting that day members overwhelmingly decided to reject his decree (599 in favor; 2 abstentions) and, on the basis of his having issued it, to dismiss him from office and replace him with the vice president (591 to 0). Megawati was sworn in as president at approximately 5 PM.[74]

There were five candidates for the position of vice president, and two rounds of voting in the MPR boiled it down to a choice between two: Akbar Tanjung, the speaker of the DPR and chairperson of Golkar, and Hamzah Haz, the leader of the PPP. This was the same Hamzah Haz who had claimed in late 1998 that only a Moslem male was eligible to become the president of Indonesia and who had been defeated by Megawati in the vice presidential election in 1999. He now declared that he was willing to serve as the deputy to a female president. For her part, Megawati saw some advantages in having him as vice president. His presence at the peak of her government would either win it the support of devout Moslems or at the very least make it harder for them to criticize her. He was also less likely to pose a political threat to her than the more formidable Akbar Tanjung. Accordingly, Megawati ordered her party members in the MPR to support Hamzah Haz in the third round, which they did, thereby enabling him to win by 340 votes to Akbar Tanjung's 237.[75]

NOTES

1. Mietzner, "First 100 Days," 337n19; Fealy, "Parties and Parliaments," 105.
2. Mietzner, "First 100 Days," 338; "Ketua DPR: Wapres Seharusnya Tidak ke Hongkong," *Antara Online*, December 30, 1999.
3. Amien Rais told a Japanese newspaper at the end of January, "We are debating and considering revising article eight in the constitution in August" ("Amien Rais

Threatens Constitution Revision on Succession," *AFX-ASIA*, January 31, 2000, www.library.ohiou.edu/indopubs/2000/01/0193.html).

4. "Menangkal Mega, Menyiasati UUD," *Tempo*, March 12, 2000, 42–43; "Yusril: Paling Krusial Amandemen Pasal 8 UUD 1945," *Kompas Cyber Media*, March 13, 2000, www.library.ohiou.edu/indopubs/2000/03/12/0045.html.

5. "Wapres akan Ibadah Haji," *Kompas Cyber Media*, March 9, 2000, www.library.ohiou.edu/indopubs/2000/01/1643.html.

6. *Kompas Online*, March 26, 2000.

7. *Jakarta Post Online*, March 28, 2000.

8. "PDI Perjuangan Opposes Direct Presidential Election," *Jakarta Post Online*, April 12, 2000, www.library.ohiou.edu/indopubs/2000/04/11/0064.html.

9. Bourchier, "Conservative Political Ideology," 121.

10. "Graft Rumours Swirl after Reshuffle," *Jakarta Post Online*, April 28, 2000; "Dibalik Pencopotan Itu," *Tempo*, May 7, 2000, 19–21; "Langit Kuning dibawah Mega," *Gatra Online* Nomor 27/VI, May 20, 2000.

11. International Crisis Group, *Bad Debt*, 21; "Laksamana Blasts Decision to Halt Texmaco Inquiry," *Jakarta Post Online*, May 22, 2000, www.library.ohiou.edu/indopubs/2000/05/22/0033.html.

12. Louis Kraar, "The Corrupt Archipelago," *Fortune Online*, July 10, 2000. I am indebted to Tim Lindsey for bringing this article to my attention.

13. "Indonesian Parliament Votes in Favor of Questioning President," *Agence France Presse*, June 29, 2000.

14. "Megawati to Read Gus Dur's Statement," *Jakarta Post Online*, July 19, 2000; "Luka yang Digarami, Awan yang Menggantung," *Tempo*, July 30, 2000, 21.

15. "Megawati to PDI-P: Go Easy on Gus Dur," *Jakarta Post Online*, July 19, 2000.

16. See David Jenkins, "In the Name of the Father," *Sydney Morning Herald*, July 21, 2001, 21.

17. "President Strikes Back," *Jakarta Post Online*, July 21, 2000.

18. Fealy, "Parties and Parliament," 107.

19. "Megawati Refuses to Read Progress Report," *Jakarta Post Online*, August 8, 2000.

20. International Crisis Group, *Indonesia: Ending Repression in Irian Jaya*, 18.

21. International Crisis Group, *Indonesia's Presidential Crisis*, 6.

22. Jay Solomon, "Power Shift Brings Momentary Relief, New Doubts," *Asian Wall Street Journal Interactive Edition*, August 11, 2000, www.library.ohiou.edu/indopubs/2000/08/11/0078.html.

23. International Crisis Group, *Indonesia's Presidential Crisis*, 6.

24. "Wapres: Tanpa Irian Indonesia tidak Komplet," *Suara Pembaruan Online*, December 14, 1999, www.library.ohiou.edu/indopubs/1999/12/15/0101.html.

25. "Saatnya Megawati Memimpin?" *Tempo*, August 20, 2000, 15.

26. Lindsey, "Constitutional Law," 2; *Ketetapan-Ketetapan Majelis Permusyawaratan Rakyat Republik Indonesia Hasil Sidang Umum Tahunan MPR RI Tahun 2000 (7 s/d 18 Agustus 2000) Beserta Perubahan Kedua Undang-Undang Dasar Negara Republik Indonesia Tahun 1945*, 19.

27. John McBeth, "Choosing Sides," *Far Eastern Economic Review*, September 7, 2000, 26–28.

28. The Second Amendment was approved by the MPR on August 18. It further strengthened the legislature at the expense of the executive by, among other things, giving "constitutional force" to the parliament's "powers of interpellation . . . and investigation . . . into government activities." (Fealy, "Parties and Parliament," 105).

29. International Crisis Group, *Indonesia's Presidential Crisis*, 7.

30. International Crisis Group, *Indonesia's Presidential Crisis*, 4–5.

31. "VP Advises Irianese to Rethink Freedom Calls," *Jakarta Post Online*, September 18, 2000.

32. Richard Chauvel, "Indonesia's Dead End in Papua," *Age Online*, December 26, 2000.

33. The "Humanitarian Pause" was agreed to by the government of Indonesia and the Free Aceh Movement on May 12, 2000, and came into effect in June 2000. The Henry Dunant Centre, which was established by the Red Cross Movement in January 1999, assisted in the negotiation of the agreement (International Crisis Group, *Aceh: A Fragile Peace*, 2); Reid, "War, Peace," 11).

34. "Instruksi Presiden No 4 Tahun 2001 tentang Langkah-Langkah Komprehensif dalam Rangka Penyelesaian Masalah Aceh," www.library.ohiou.edu/indopubs/ 2001/08/02/0098.html; John Haseman, "Jakarta Hardens Aceh Policy," *Jane's Defence Weekly*, May 2, 2001, www.library.ohiou.edu/indopubs/200105/02/0083.html.

35. "Ketetapan Majelis Permusyawaratan Rakyat Republik Indonesia Nomor IV/MPR/2000 tentang Rekomendasi Kebijakan Dalam Penyelenggaraan Otonomi Daerah," *Ketetapan-Ketetapan Majelis Permusyawaratan Rakyat Republik Indonesia Hasil Sidang Umum Tahunan MPR RI Tahun 2000 (7 s/d 18 Agustus 2000)*, 37; National Democratic Institute for International Affairs, *Indonesia's Road to Constitutional Reform*, 12.

36. International Crisis Group, *Aceh: Can Autonomy Stem the Conflict?* 6–7; International Crisis Group, *Indonesia: Ending Repression in Irian Jaya*, 22–24.

37. International Crisis Group, *Indonesia's Presidential Crisis*, 7.

38. International Crisis Group, *Indonesia's Presidential Crisis*, 7.

39. International Crisis Group, *Indonesia's Presidential Crisis*, 7.

40. International Crisis Group, *Indonesia's Presidential Crisis*, 1.

41. Lindsey, "Constitutional Law and the Presidential Crisis," 1–2.

42. International Crisis Group, *Indonesia's Presidential Crisis*, 9.

43. "Nation Is in Worst Condition since 1945, Says Megawati," *Jakarta Post Online*, February 10, 2001.

44. "Megawati tak Terbendung lagi," *Detikcom*, March 8, 2001; International Crisis Group, *Communal Violence in Indonesia*, 2, 12.

45. I am indebted to Douglas Ramage for this vignette.

46. "Megawati Backed to Be President," *Jakarta Post Online*, March 3, 2001.

47. *Detikcom*, March 8, 2001.

48. International Crisis Group, *Indonesia's Presidential Crisis: The Second Round*, 2.

49. International Crisis Group, *Indonesia's Presidential Crisis: The Second Round*, 2, 4.

50. Lindsey, "Constitutional Law and the Presidential Crisis," 2.

51. Greg Fealy, "Wahid Set on Living Dangerously," *Australian Financial Review*, June 5, 2001.

52. International Crisis Group, *Indonesia's Presidential Crisis: The Second Round*, 2, 3–4.

53. See International Crisis Group, *Indonesia's Presidential Crisis: The Second Round*, 6.

54. See Rachmawati Sukarnoputri, "Sukarnoism Is to Kill Sukarno," *Kompas Cyber Media*, June 6, 2001, where she states, "In his speech on 17 August 1965, Bung Karno prayed that his ideas and teachings would last for a thousand years. That prayer of his is an instruction for the nation and for us who are his children."

55. See Rachmawati Sukarnoputri, "Persis Skenario 1965, Penyebarluasan Sakitnya Presiden," *Kompas Cyber Media*, May 15, 2001.

56. "Karena Mendukung Memorandum II Rachmawati Sukarnoputri Nilai Mega Ambivalen," *Tempo Interaktif*, May 5, 2001. To the dismay of many, Hatta submitted his resignation as vice president on July 20, 1956, and vacated the office on December 1 of the same year (see Feith, *Decline of Constitutional Democracy*, 524).

57. "Gus Dur and Megawati Engage in War of Words," *Jakarta Post Online*, May 27, 2001.

58. Lindsey, "Constitutional Law and the Presidential Crisis," 4–8.

59. "Full Text of President's Executive Order," *Jakarta Post Online*, May 29, 2001.

60. "Susilo Announces Three-Point Agenda," *Jakarta Post Online,* May 29, 2001.

61. "I Won't Resign, Gus Dur Says," *Jakarta Post Online*, June 1, 2001.; Anon, "Events of July 2001," 1.

62. "President Fires Five Ministers, Attorney General," *Jakarta Post Online*, June 1, 2001.

63. "Police Chief Rejects Gus Dur's Order to Quit," *Jakarta Post Online*, June 2, 2001; Fealy, "Parties and Parliament," 104–5.

64. "Bimantoro Still National Police Chief," *Jakarta Post Online*, June 3, 2001.

65. Rachmawati Sukarnoputri, "Sukarnoism," *Kompas Cyber Media*, June 6, 2001; "Rachma sindir PDI-P Manipulasi Bung Karno," *Suara Merdeka Online*, June 7, 2001; "Megawati's Sister Brands Moves to Oust Wahid a Coup d'Etat," *Agence France Presse*, June 6, 2001, www.library.ohiou.edu/indopubs/2001/06/06/0006.html.

66. "Haul Bung Karno: Rachmawati Usul Tap MPRS No 33/1967 Segara Dicabut," *Kompas Cyber Media*, June 21, 2001; "I Take After Sukarno, Claims Abdurrahman," *Jakarta Post Online*, June 21, 2001; Dewi Fortuna Anwar, "Tragic Ending," 2.

67. The fact that this procedure is not to be found in the standing orders of the MPR is of little consequence, for this body certainly has the constitutional power to ratify irregularities after the event (Lindsey, "Constitutional Law and the Presidential Crisis," 2; see also, Anon, "Events of July 2001," 1–2).

68. "Megawati: SI satu-satunya Jalan atasi Konflik Politik," *Kompas Cyber Media*, July 11, 2001; "Rachma: Mega bersama Orang Status Quo," *Riau Pos*, July 16, 2001.

69. "Rachmawati Soal Kompromi: 'Crucial Point' ada di tangan PDI Perjuangan," *Tempo Interaktif*, July 20, 2001.
70. "Special Session, Not State of Emergency," *Jakarta Post Online*, July 21, 2001.
71. Anon, "Events of July 2001," 2.
72. "Presiden tidak akan Mundur," *Kompas Cyber Media*, July 22, 2001.
73. Anon, "Events of July 2001," 3.
74. Anon, "Events of July 2001," 3–4; "MPR Rejects Presidential Decree," *Jakarta Post Online*, July 23, 2001.
75. National Democratic Institute for International Affairs, *Indonesia's Change of President*, 17–19; Leo Suryadinata, *Elections and Politics in Indonesia*, 193–97; Harold Crouch, "Drifting Along: Megawati's Indonesia," *Australian Financial Review*, May 10, 2002.

16

President Megawati Sukarnoputri

Megawati did not revive her father's practice of reporting to the nation on Independence Day. Rather, she followed Soeharto's habit of delivering a state of the nation address to the Indonesian parliament the day before. In her first such speech, on August 16, 2001, she broached the topic of corruption in a direct and personal way:

> Unlike a feudalistic society which does not tend to see KKN (Corruption, Collusion, Nepotism) as a big mistake, a democratic society sees this as a tremendous problem. Regardless of how trivial they may be, KKN practices will transgress public trust and at the same time violate one's official oath. In this context, allow me to humbly report to this august gathering that I have privately gathered all members of my immediate family, requesting them to solemnly pledge not to open the slightest window of opportunity for the recurrence of KKN in my family. They have given me their solemn pledge, and I hope that they will be able to resist the many temptations around them. . . . I have also requested all my Cabinet ministers to report their wealth and as soon as possible submit their report to the Public Servants' Wealth Audit Commission.[1]

What Megawati is suggesting here is that at least she, if not perhaps all members of her family, was untainted by the various practices of the New Order. This view of things is certainly consistent with the widespread perception of her that took hold in the 1990s as being "outside the system of KKN," to quote again one of her admirers at the PDI congress at Sanur in October 1998. If suspicion fell on her family, it was invariably her husband, Taufik Kiemas, who was its object. The two, however, are not so easily separated. Not only did he manage the petrol pump business on her behalf, but her own wealth audit report reveals that husband and wife certainly prospered during the late

Soeharto years.² The point is not that there was a discrepancy between her public image and reality but rather that her position as a beneficiary of the New Order throws additional light on the tentative nature of her populism, which prevented her from picturing a relationship with the people to which the military was not also party. Being the joint owner of numerous dwellings, automobiles, and luxury items popular with the middle class of Jakarta may not have stifled Megawati's concern for the poor, but it did give her reason to fear them, thereby making her empathy with their concerns more difficult to achieve.

JAKARTA GUBERNATORIAL ELECTION

Megawati's favorable view of the military as a unifier of society whom she involved in her relationship with the people influenced the stance she adopted to provincial governors. She instructed members of her party in provincial legislatures to ignore their own party aspirants and vote instead for candidates chosen by her and the central party leadership. Most of these were retired army officers and former appointees of Soeharto who were seeking a second term, such as Sutiyoso in Jakarta, Mardiyanto in Central Java, and Imam Utomo in East Java. Megawati's husband justified this practice by saying,

> We do not have leadership candidates who have experience in leading 35 million people in East Java, 30 million people in Central Java. It is only the military who have experience in leading the tens of millions of people in Java. Therefore, we make a winner of the unitary state presiding over a diverse society and not the PDIP.³

The most striking example of Megawati's behavior in this regard was her support for Sutiyoso, the governor of the special region of Jakarta, which culminated in his gaining a second term of office, beginning September 2002. Recall that Major General Sutiyoso was the commander of the Jakarta military region who was given the task of coordinating the attack on the PDI headquarters on July 27, 1996, in which 5 Megawati loyalists were killed, 146 injured, and an additional 23 went missing. Despite these casualties and the widespread rioting to which the attack gave rise, Soeharto must have been pleased with Sutiyoso's conduct at the time, for he promoted him to lieutenant general and appointed him governor of Jakarta for the October 1997–October 2002 period.⁴

Megawati had appeared deeply shocked by this event and, at a *selamatan*-like commemoration of it a hundred days later, wept copiously. Unwilling to risk further casualties but unwilling to submit to *force majeure*, she decided to challenge various arbitrary acts of the government on legal grounds, and to this end appointed R. O. Tambunan as the head of her Indonesian Democracy Defence Team. No progress was made with these challenges while Soeharto remained president, but a year after his resignation the police did show an interest in investigating the events of July 27, 1996 (Grey Saturday). Evidence of army involvement led to an expansion of the police inquiry into a combined military/national police investigation. But by February 2001, aggrieved members of the public were complaining over the stalling of this investigation. Nevertheless, they probably took some comfort from the likely prospect of Megawati's soon becoming president and her doing something about this unsatisfactory state of affairs.

She did become president on July 23 of that year, but she failed to attend the commemoration of Grey Saturday's dead and missing four days afterward. In January 2002, Haryanto Taslam and Panda Nababan, both members of the PDIP fraction in the national parliament, raised the matter of the stalled inquiry with the police, but nothing appeared to come of their efforts.[5] As the 2002 anniversary approached, R. O. Tambunan spoke out at a public meeting: "Formerly we defended 27 July. After she became President it was her responsibility to pursue the matter. But we see signs that Mega herself does not wish this matter to be brought before a court."[6] He also noted that the victims of July 27, including the families of those who had been killed or who had gone missing, had been offered 10 million rupiah and asked to sign a document declaring that they would not pursue the matter further. According to one member of a victim's family contacted by *Kompas*, the money was handed out by Agung Imam Soemanto, the chairperson of the PDIP fraction in the Jakarta parliament, who claimed that the money came from the Jakarta regional office of the party and was intended as compensation. Another informant told the newspaper that Agung also promised to introduce victims or their families to Megawati, but this never happened. Tambunan concluded his remarks by declaring that President Megawati was considered by the Indonesian Democracy Defence Team to have deviated from her promise to uphold justice and the law.[7] Another one of her discarded allies, film director Eros Djarot, arrived at a similar conclusion, describing her willingness to forget the July 27 case as a manifestation of an antidemocratic attitude.[8]

If observers, let alone supporters, of Megawati's presidency were surprised by her unwillingness to take legal action against the instigators of the July 27 affair—even going so far as to participate in buying off the victims—then they were simply amazed when she declared in late June 2002 that the PDIP's central leadership council supported Sutiyoso's election for a second term as governor of Jakarta. Sutjipto, Megawati's PDIP spokesperson, offered the following reason for the decision of the party's leaders. He said that they believed that Sutiyoso was the best person available to maintain security in the capital city in the leadup to the 2004 elections.[9] This explanation beggared belief: the commander in the field for the attack on the PDI headquarters, which resulted in heavy casualties and triggered the largest riots in Jakarta for over twenty years, recommended himself to the PDIP leadership on these grounds? The same man who was already governor during the worse rioting of May 1998, when over one thousand people died and many Sino-Indonesian women were raped, presented himself to Megawati as the law-and-order candidate for governor of Jakarta? Not surprisingly, speculation was rife regarding the real reason: could it be that her support for Sutiyoso was the payoff for her husband's alleged success in winning contracts from the city?[10] Although this motive or a similar one could not be ruled out, Megawati actually seemed to believe that this man was the best equipped to maintain security in Jakarta. This standpoint was the most telling sign of the degree to which her populism was qualified, indeed diluted, by what can only be described as her New Order way of looking at things, right down to its "security approach" to government and including even the wariness of the urban poor, which was one of its components.

Members of the PDIP's six Jakarta branches showed signs of revolt against the decision of the central leadership council. They had presented eleven nominations for governor, but Sutiyoso was not on their list. They began staging regular demonstrations against the incumbent in front of the Jakarta parliament building, where they were joined by student groups and representatives of the Betawi people.[11] One assumes that these demonstrations enjoyed widespread community support because the governor was so universally disliked. According to one commentator, "Sutiyoso is a deeply unpopular figure in Jakarta who is held responsible for the city's many urban problems and is widely reviled for his luxurious life style."[12] In the face of such resistance, the leadership council threatened sanctions against members of the PDIP fraction in the Jakarta parliament if they did not vote for Sutiyoso.[13] A former PDIP member of the national parliament, Indira Damayanti, summarized well the mood within the party at this time:

> I think *Ibu* Megawati has gone too far in issuing a directive to City Council members to re-elect Sutiyoso as Jakarta Governor ... The July 27 incident was a tragedy for the PDI Perjuangan. So it's not surprising that the victims of the incident are disappointed with Megawati's decision to nominate someone who is implicated in the case.[14]

The eighty-four members of the Jakarta parliament gathered in the parliament building on September 11 to cast their votes. Demonstrators from a range of groups massed outside, forcing frequent adjournments in the election process. The fence surrounding the building was pushed over, leading the security forces to resort to tear gas, water cannons, and rubber bullets. The vote was eventually taken, and Sutiyoso and his running partner for the position of deputy governor, Fauzi Bowo, emerged as victors, gaining 47, or 56 percent, of the 84 votes cast.[15]

Afterward, Megawati made disingenuous comments on the outcome: "If he was reelected as governor, it was not because of me. Never relate it to me."[16] Her comments and the manner in which the outcome was achieved leads one to reflect again on the nature of Megawati's relationship with the people of Jakarta, who had offered her such strong support in the past. What a mismatch it was, really. Fondly believing that she embodied their suffering and their hopes for a better life, the people had given her their votes; their love; and, in the case of those who had defended her party headquarters, their lives. But she returned this love with a New Order political approach based on a lively apprehension of them.

SEPARATIST MOVEMENTS

Aceh

The constitutional crisis of the first half of 2001 delayed the passing into law of the draft legislation that provided special autonomy to the province of Aceh. The resolution of this crisis cleared the way for Megawati to sign this law, which she did on August 9, 2001. While on a short visit to the province in early September, she apologized to the Acehnese for the past mistakes of the Indonesian government, but she then gave the appearance of being indifferent to their suffering by adding brusquely, "If we only look to the past, we will never make progress in our lives."[17] Also, she did not seem to acknowledge that this legislation, enlightened though it was in many respects, had very little prospect of gaining acceptance in the aftermath of presidential instruction 4/2001, which, as noted, was issued in April and authorized new military operations in the province.

Her evident belief that military force would be effective in maintaining the territorial integrity of the Republic of Indonesia (*negara kesatuan*) had its origins in her more general view that the cohesion and welfare of Indonesian society required close cooperation between the military and civilians. This position was cognate with her conservative populism, which, as noted, envisaged the armed forces presiding as guardian of her relationship with the people. She gave expression to it in her speech of July 29, 1999, in which she declared, "I firmly declare that our archipelagic state which takes the form of a unitary state very much requires an effective and professional military." It was also apparent in her previous support as vice president for this presidential instruction and in her remarks in Washington on September 19, 2001, that "as did Lincoln in the United States, we will defend the integrity of Indonesia no matter how long it will take."[18] Megawati maintained this position despite an increase in civilian fatalities at the hands of an often lawless military: the death toll for 2001 reached thirteen hundred by September.[19] Thus, she not only gave the lie to the promise she had made in the same July 1999 speech that as president she would "not allow one drop of blood to be spilled of the people" of Aceh, but she also further damaged the *negara hukum* in that province and placed it in an increasingly precarious position in the others.

Although Megawati maintained this hardline posture in her first months as president, she did not repudiate the overlapping efforts of foreign governments, the Henry Dunant Centre, and pragmatic members of her cabinet (including coordinating minister for security affairs Susilo Bambang Yudhoyono) to bring about a negotiated resolution to the conflict with the Free Aceh Movement (Gerakan Aceh Merdeka; GAM). In May 2002, GAM accepted the special autonomy law for Aceh as a starting point for negotiation. Megawati declared it to be "the main pillar for conflict resolution," and on December 9 both parties signed a Cessation of Hostilities Agreement.[20] This agreement, however, quickly came undone; and, on May 18, 2003, Megawati issued a presidential decree proclaiming a state of emergency in Aceh and placing the province under martial law.[21] She later commented, "I refused to disregard the founding father's wish just to meet the demands of a number of separatist members who were led by foreign nationals."[22]

It is, of course, understandable that Megawati was anxious to preserve the territorial integrity of the Republic of Indonesia. Yet, on this occasion, it was her sister Rachmawati who, though certainly no less anxious, appeared to have the better grasp of what would help to achieve this goal. Having noted tellingly that GAM's demand for independence was not unrelated to the province's previous status as an area of military operations, she declared that the conflict between the opposing parties could only be resolved by dialogue between them.[23]

Papua

The special autonomy bill for Papua, as the province was called in this draft legislation, was signed into law on October 23, 2001. Like the Aceh law, it was a substantial piece of legislation; and like the Aceh law also, the likelihood of its gaining acceptance among the people to whom it was directed was severely limited by continuing military repression. It will be recalled that in the latter part of 2000 Megawati had supported a hardening of the military response to independence activists in the province. Over the following year, the arrests, tortures, and murders to which this change of policy gave rise proved inhospitable soil for the new law to take root. As one scholar commented, "It is difficult to imagine how Special Autonomy can be successfully 'socialised' and accepted by broad sections of the society in political circumstances of great tension, uncertainty and fear created by the security forces."[24]

The law's prospects of acceptance were only made worse when Papuan leader Theys Eluay, who "personified more than any other . . . the belief that Papuan aspirations could be achieved by non-violent means," was found murdered outside Jayapura on November 11.[25] He had dined the previous night at the local headquarters of the special forces, and Papuans immediately suspected them of being responsible. Members of this military unit were subsequently charged with the killing, and in April 2003, six were convicted and sentenced to prison terms ranging only from two years to three-and-a-half years.[26] The thuggish and simplistic response to these sentences by army chief of staff General Ryamizard Ryacudu offers some insight into the military's talent for exacerbating separatist sentiment: "I don't know. People say they were wrong and broke the law; okay, we are a law state and they have to be sentenced. But for me they are heroes because they murdered a man who was a rebel, the leader of rebels."[27]

It might be protested that the president's confidence in the military surely did not extend to this particular, outspoken general, and yet such evidence as there is suggests that he was her preferred candidate for the position of chief of staff in which he was installed in June 2002.[28] This hapless biographer has tried hard to explain Megawati's regard for the military but as he contemplates her willingness to entrust the territorial integrity of the Republic of Indonesia to such generals as Ryamizard Ryacudu, he is struck by the incompleteness of his previous formulations.

Terrorism

The terrorist attacks in the United States on September 11, 2001, and their aftermath—in particular, the Bali bombings of October 2002—placed additional pressure on Indonesia's nascent democracy. The explosion of two bombs on the night of October 12, 2002, in an area particularly popular among foreign tourists—Jalan Legian in Kuta—killed 202 people.[29] Its consequences were far-reaching. The president, shaken by the event and under considerable pressure from countries whose citizens had been injured or killed in the bomb blasts, felt unable to wait on the processes of the parliament, where an antiterrorism bill had been stalled for months. Consequently, she issued two government regulations in lieu of law that not only gave officials considerable scope to arrest and detain individuals suspected of terrorist activity but also explicitly provided for the retrospective prosecution of those who had carried out the bombings in Bali.[30] In March 2003, the parliament transformed these two regulations into laws 15/2003 and 16/2003. The people at large, confronted with this unmistakable evidence of terrorism in their midst, appeared to tolerate this hardening of policy but not without misgivings. The retrospective nature of these laws—in this respect they resembled law 26/2000 on human rights courts—was a source of concern, and some small Moslem parties, believing them to be unconstitutional, voted against them. There was also the plausible fear among sections of the population that these laws, though less draconian than the Internal Security Acts of Singapore and Malaysia, might at some time be used against them by a president already well disposed toward the military and inclined to see things their way. Observers of the separatist struggles in Aceh and Papua believed it was only a matter of time before they were applied in these two provinces. Indeed, in September 2002, Indonesian foreign minister Hasan Wirajuda called the Free Papua Movement a terrorist organization, whereas Susilo Bambang Yudhoyono, the coordinating minister for political and security affairs, claimed that the Free Aceh Movement was carrying out acts of terrorism.[31] Following the bombing of the Marriott Hotel in Jakarta on August 5, 2003, Susilo Bambang Yudhoyono urged the case for more stringent antiterrorism measures than that allowed for by these laws: "Those who criticize about human rights being breached must understand that all the bombing victims are more important than any human rights issue."[32] Defense minister Matori Abdul Djalil later proposed new legislation on the Internal Security Acts model.[33]

INSULTING THE PRESIDENT

It is difficult to escape the impression that Megawati has changed in recent years. I have suggested that her substantial victory in the parliamentary elections of 1999 reinforced her pride and aloofness, which had their origins in the emotional distress and social privilege of her childhood years; but it is possible that this was not the end of the process. Certainly by combining the roles of head of government and head of state into one position, the office of president offers good reason for the pride of its incumbent to expand; and it seems that Megawati has proved all too human in this regard, to judge by her reaction to those protestors who expressed their hostility to government policy by defacing her portrait.

In the first year of Megawati's presidency a number of protesters were arrested and charged under Indonesia's lese-majesty law—articles 134, 136, and 137 of the criminal code—which "makes it an offence punishable by a maximum of six years gaol to engage in 'deliberate disrespect for the President or Vice-President'" and derives from the more repressive elements of the colonial legal system.[34] Although this frequency cannot be attributed directly to Megawati, her angry denunciation on July 8, 2002, of demonstrators who allegedly disfigured photos of her and the vice president encouraged police and prosecutors to continue applying the law. She said at that time,

> It is not me or Hamzah Haz in a personal capacity but as symbols of the state. I was chosen by the MPR to implement the mandate of the state. If the society and those activists do not value the symbols of the state, what will become of us. . . . If I meet directly with them I will invite them to adopt the citizenship of another country.[35]

Six months later Megawati again responded to demonstrators who had personalized their protests against her policies by treating her portrait with disrespect. Indeed, one may observe her struggling not very successfully to apply the advice she had offered to members of her party in October 1998 when her Islamic faith and ability to be president were being questioned: "Why must you react? Just let things be. What is important is that we continue to cultivate our inner worth." She declared,

> When I see my photo, although I look pretty in it, being trodden on and then burnt, I think that I might erupt like volcanic lava or boiling mud. And I also think that I will note down the people who carried it out. But then I quickly enter into a dialogue with myself . . . how low I will sink and how abject I will become if I allow myself to be dragged down by those people.[36]

Nevertheless, the prosecutions proceeded, and by September 2003 fourteen people had been sentenced to prison terms "ranging from a few months up to three years" under the lese-majesty provisions of the criminal code.[37] That these laws were not repealed on the achievement of independence is testimony to the etatist nature of Indonesian nationalism and might be seen as something of an indictment of Sukarno and others of his generation. That his daughter should then turn to them is evidence, if not of hubris, then of a process common in leaders upon their achieving high office: the expansion of self-regard matched by a corresponding shrinking of ideals. For it is surely a parody of her former brave defense of the *negara hukum* that Megawati should encourage the use of these laws to stifle political dissent and punish those whose manner of protest offended her dignity.

NOTES

1. "State of the Nation Address," *Jakarta Post Online*, February 5, 2002.

2. Compare Krishna Sen, "Mega Factor," 21–22; "KPKN Umumkan Harta Kekayaan Pejabat Negara: Megawati Terkaya," *Kompas Cyber Media*, April 18, 2001; "Kekayaan Gus Dur Rp 3, 5 Miliar, Mega Rp 60, 2 Miliar," *Tempo Interaktif*, April 18, 2001.

3. "PDI-P Ingin Tiru Orba untuk Menangi Pemilu," *Suara Merdeka Online*, July 31, 2003.

4. O'Rourke, *Reformasi*, 15; *Indonesian Governments Guide 2002* (Jakarta: Masindo, 2002), 400.

5. "Penanganan Kasus 27 Juli Dinilai Makin Tak Jelas," *Suara Pembaruan Online*, January 30, 2002.

6. "Tim Pembela Demokrasi Indonesia: Usut Tuntas Kasus 27 Juli," *Kompas Cyber Media*, July 23, 2002.

7. "Tim Pembela Demokrasi Indonesia."

8. "Presiden Megawati tidak boleh lupakan Kasus 27 Juli," *Kompas Cyber Media*, July 23, 2002.

9. "Internal Rifts in PDI Perjuangan Getting Worse," *Jakarta Post Online*, July 17, 2002.

10. "Mega Man: A Look at Taufik Kiemas," *Laksamana.Net*, November 2, 2001, www.laksamana.net.

11. "Mega Backs Sutiyoso, Angry with City Chapters," *Jakarta Post Online*, June 26, 2002.

12. Tim Dodd, "Too Close for Comfort," *Australian Financial Review*, July 24, 2002, 69.

13. "Internal Rifts in PDI Perjuangan Getting Worse," *Jakarta Post Online*, July 17, 2002.

14. "Internal Rifts in PDI Perjuangan."

15. "Sutiyoso terpilih lagi," *Media Indonesia Online*, September 12, 2002: "Aku masih yang dulu," *Media Indonesia Online*, September 12, 2002; "Sutiyoso Gubernur DKI Lagi," *Detikcom*, September 11, 2002.

16. "Megawati Says Her Support Had Nothing to Do with Sutiyoso's Win," *Jakarta Post Online*, September 14, 2002.

17. "Megawati Asks for Aceh's Forgiveness," *Jakarta Post Online*, September 9, 2001.

18. Quoted in Aspinall, "Downfall of President Abdurrahman Wahid," 37.

19. Human Rights Watch, *Human Rights Watch World Report 2002: Indonesia*. This report adds that "while most of the deaths were civilians killed in the course of military operations, the rebel Free Aceh Movement (*Gerakan Aceh Merdeka* or GAM) was also responsible for serious abuses."

20. Reid, "War, Peace," 12–13; Michelle Ann Miller, "The Life and Death of Aceh's Peace Process," *Inside Indonesia* (July–September 2003), 30.

21. "Pemerintah Berlakukan Status Darurat Militer di Aceh," *Media Indonesia Online*, May 19, 2003; Miller, "Life and Death," 29.

22. "Megawati Seeks Support for Aceh War," *Jakarta Post Online*, May 21, 2003. Megawati's comment about foreign nationals was a reference to the alleged Swedish citizenship of the GAM leader Hasan Tiro.

23. "Rachmawati: Penyelesaian konflik Aceh harus Kedepankan Dialog," *Media Indonesia Online*, May 22, 2003, www.mediaindo.co.id.

24. Chauvel, *Land of Papua*, 2:43; "Malam ini Provinsi Irian Jaya Disahkan Menjadi Provinsi Papua," *Kompas Cyber Media*, October 22, 2001.

25. Chauvel, *Land of Papua*, 40.

26. "Theys Meninggal, Irian Berduka," *Kompas Cyber Media*, November 12, 2001; Human Rights Watch, "Indonesia: Investigate Death of Papuan Leader"; Human Rights Watch, "Indonesia: Investigate Shootings in Papua, No Reprisals"; "'Gelar Pahlawan' bagi Pelanggar HAM," *Sinar Harapan Online*, April 29, 2003, www.sinarharapan.co.id.

27. "'Gelar Pahlawan' bagi Pelanggar HAM," *Sinar Harapan Online*, April 29, 2003.

28. "Ryamizard Hari Ini KSAD," *Suara Merdeka Online*, June 4, 2002; "Ryamizard Dilantik sebagai KSAD," *Tempo Interaktif*, June 4, 2002.

29. See Human Rights Watch, "Indonesia: Bali Attack Should Not Undermine Civil Liberties."

30. International Crisis Group, *Impact of the Bali Bombings,* 3; Lindsey, "Indonesia's New Anti-terrorism Law"; Tapol, *Indonesia's Anti-terrorism Decree a Threat to Basic Rights*; Clarke, "Retrospectivity," 18–19.

31. International Crisis Group, *Impact of the Bali Bombings*, 3, 8; Human Rights Watch, *In the Name of Counter-terrorism,* 7.

32. "Indonesia Bombing Kills at least 10 in Midday Attack," *New York Times Online*, August 6, 2003, http://query.nytimes.com/search/restricted/article?res=F30C12FE3D550C758CDDA10894DB404482.

33. "Opposition Grows to Government-Proposed Draconian Security Law," *Jakarta Post Online*, August 13, 2003.

34. Zifcak, "'But a Shadow of Justice,'" 357n6; Amnesty International, *Indonesia: Old Laws—New Prisoners,* 2. See also, Human Rights Watch, *A Return to the New Order?*

35. "Megawati kecam Penginjak Foto Presiden dan Wapres," *Kompas Cyber Media*, July 9, 2002.

36. "Presiden Kritik Aksi Mahasiswa yang Bakar Ban," *Kompas Cyber Media*, January 29, 2003.

37. Amnesty International, *Indonesia: Old Laws—New Prisoners*, 7.

Conclusion

There can be no doubt that the 1957–1959 period was a turning point away from the parliamentary democracy of the previous period and toward the personal rule of first Sukarno and then Soeharto. To interpret Indonesian history in these terms is to group together two leaders who are usually contrasted in terms of their ideological orientations and to see in their personalities a partial explanation for the nature of Guided Democracy and the New Order. The question is whether the shift in political behavior (described in detail in chapters 9–16) amounts to evidence of a turning point away from personal and toward constitutional rule. It is risky attempting to write the "history of the present," not least because one is hostage to tomorrow's headlines and therefore liable to endure the fate described by Walter Raleigh: "who-so-euer in writing a modern Historie shall follow truth too neare the heeles, it may happily strike out his teeth."[1] Nevertheless, constitutional rule does show signs of taking hold in Indonesia, as the following summary testifies.

A disorderly and delayed leadership succession is a likely result of personal rule, whereas one that is orderly and reasonably frequent is a good indication of functioning constitutional rule.[2] The trend from personal rule to constitutional rule in Indonesia may be observed, first of all, in the shift from succession of the first type toward succession of the second. President-for-life Sukarno, as noted in chapters 2–5, built a system of rule so focused on himself that it was immediately evident to rival political forces that it could not possibly outlive him. In the end, a mere apprehension that he might die proved quite sufficient to trigger a series of events that resulted in the murder of approximately a half-million members and supporters of the Communist Party, the overthrow of his presidency, and the collapse of Guided Democracy.

The economic crisis that undermined Soeharto's thirty-year presidency occurred only months before the quinquennial session of the MPR, which would hear the president's accountability speech and choose the occupant of the office for the next five years. The institutional machinery was there to implement a peaceful transition of authority to a new president, but Soeharto had so manipulated circumstances that such an outcome was impossible. He made sure, as he had on every previous occasion, that there were no alternative candidates—we have noted the lengths to which he went to sideline Megawati—and, as a second line of defense, that all the members of the MPR were loyal to him. Consequently, they accepted his accountability speech and on March 10, 1998, voted him into another term as president without a single voice being raised in opposition. It was only after his abandonment by his political allies two months later that he resigned, but in the meantime over a thousand people were murdered, died, or suffered intensely as a result of actions instigated by people close to him.

The end of Habibie's interim term as president in October 1999 also coincided with an adverse event of major proportions for the Republic of Indonesia—the loss of East Timor. But the similarity with the Soeharto succession goes no further than this. First, the MPR presiding over the presidential election consisted largely of members elected directly by the people; second, there were two other candidates for the office. Moreover, the assembly rejected Habibie's accountability speech, and although he was under no constitutional obligation to do so, he withdrew from the presidential race, thereby facilitating the emergence of a new officeholder.

Habibie's withdrawal from the presidential contest led many MPR members who were disturbed by Megawati's secularism to vote for Abdurrahman Wahid despite having misgivings about the effect on him of two recent strokes. It was obvious from his demeanor that the motor area of his brain had been damaged. And as he set about insulting those figures in the parliament on whom his political survival depended—recall that the form of government at this time (before the third amendment) was described as "presidential with parliamentary characteristics"—the suspicion arose that the cognitive area had not been spared either. When this institution attempted to assert its authority over him, his response revealed that he had not noticed how a free election had breathed new life into the parliament and correspondingly weakened the presidential power. He said, "This is a presidential system of Government." As noted in chapter 12, this conflict between the parliament and president was eventually resolved by the MPR's dismissing him.

The assembly acted within its powers in taking this action; nevertheless, one aspect of the process occasioned misgivings: the finding of the special parliamentary inquiry—namely, that it was "reasonable to suspect" that the president had been involved in the Bulog affair, which was then used by the parliament as the rationale for instigating his dismissal proceedings. As Abdurrahman himself argued, this finding fell far short of proof that he had indeed violated the constitution or the national will. This may appear to be a minor consideration in light of the fact that the president was eventually dismissed for other behavior—in particular, declaring a state of emergency to suspend the parliament and the People's Consultative Assembly, which was undeniably in violation of the constitution. However, it appears that he may have been panicked into this drastic step by the previous, questionable action of the parliament. It is interesting to note that the third amendment to the constitution, introduced in November 2001, not only provided for a conventional presidential democracy but also tightened the requirements concerning the president's dismissal by, among other things, involving the new constitutional court in the process.

With this change from postponed and chaotic succession to comparatively orderly and frequent succession, there remains the question about how this still-basic constitutional order was able to acquit itself so well on the most intractable of issues. Conventional theoretical wisdom asserts that the "constitutional hypocrisy" of sultanistic regimes in manipulating constitutional and electoral processes impairs the prospects for a subsequent shift to democratic rule. In contrast, Soeharto's taking advantage of the loose formulation of the 1945 constitution to justify his personal rule appeared only to discredit him and not the document itself, as Liddle has argued (although it was obvious to many that it needed substantial revision so that it could not be so used again).[3] Furthermore, the managed elections of the New Order, far from devaluing democratic elections, actually enhanced their standing in the popular mind. Indeed, managed elections as part of Soeharto's democratic charade had required an administrative apparatus no less complex than that needed in a substantial democracy, and this apparatus was inherited by the new government, enabling them to hold free elections only four months after the necessary legislation had been passed. Finally, these elections of June 1999 proved a remarkable tonic, invigorating the DPR and MPR, which then implemented a genuinely democratic reading of the constitution, one more in keeping with the intentions of Hatta than those of Sukarno.

The ready availability of a workable and respected constitution together with functioning electoral machinery enabled a sudden mobilization of members of the middle class and students largely in response to Soeharto's failure to respond adequately to the economic crisis of 1997 to be set in a democratic mold before the ambivalence of that class reasserted itself and the urban poor became disillusioned with their new, supposed champions.

Even as constitutional rule showed signs of taking hold, it was substantially redefined and in some respects deepened by four amendments to the 1945 constitution and by the introduction of laws 22 and 25 of 1999. As noted in chapter 1, the two laws embodied the aspirations of the long-abandoned law 1/1957 by providing for the democratization of government in the province, *kabupaten* and municipality, and village, as well as bestowing substantial autonomy and corresponding fiscal powers on *kabupatens* and municipalities. Although these two laws were conceived in haste by the Habibie government, which had hoped to draw the sting of regional disaffection, although they were passed by the parliament without much discussion in April 1999, and although they were activated amid considerable confusion in 2001, their passage satisfied an established principle of constitutionalism that the government of a vast territory must be decentralized to be democratic.[4]

Nevertheless, constitutional rule in Indonesia is struggling to establish itself within a still-impaired economy. There has been some improvement since the sharp contraction in economic activity and the sudden inflation of 1997–1998. By 2003 the country was experiencing its fourth year of growth, at 3.5–4.5 percent per annum, and inflation had declined to 7 percent. However, in the absence of new foreign direct investment, this rate of growth has been generated by domestic demand and is insufficient to contain, let alone reverse, the expansion in unemployment since the crisis.[5] This situation is doubly disturbing: many people continue to suffer severe economic hardship, and given the well-established threat that poverty poses to the durability of democracy, it calls into question this form of government in Indonesia.[6]

Even more daunting for Indonesian constitutionalism than the still-low levels of economic activity are the egregious practices that are the legacy of thirty-nine years of personal rule. Although the military has been separated from the police, the behavior of both—in Aceh and Papua in particular—justifies the characterization of the Indonesian state as, in some respects, lawless.[7] The independence, integrity, and effectiveness of the judiciary have not yet been restored to their pre-1959 levels, despite the energetic efforts of reformers. Rent taking and other forms of corruption remain rampant, mimicking and mocking the emerging constitutional trend. Soeharto, their chief exponent, has left, but as a result of democratization and decentralization, thousands of small-frog Soehartos have appeared in the municipalities and *kabupaten* and their respective parliaments that now make up the principal tier of regional government in Indonesia.[8]

Furthermore, the presidents since 1998 have displayed only a limited value commitment to constitutional democracy. Certainly, the practices and ideology of personal rule were not an effective school for democratic ideas. Nevertheless, Megawati had proved able to resist them at the time of the New Order's ascendency. It was therefore surprising to observe her succumbing to them after she became vice president and then president and to discern in her stance a wariness and even fear of the people at large. This state of mind, reminiscent of nineteenth-century liberals' anxiously contemplating the newly enfranchised "lower classes," does not seem confined to Megawati. Indeed, observation suggests that it is widespread among politicians and members of the middle class.[9]

It remains to be seen what effect the amended 1945 constitution—at first glance, the jewel in the crown of Indonesia's emergent constitutionalism—will have on this fragile order. This book begins with a consideration of how this constitution had provided an opening for personal rule, had facilitated the shift toward constitutional rule, and via a process of extensive amendment reconfigured presidential democracy in Indonesia. We conclude with an assessment of how the amended document will likely affect the country's constitutional prospects.

Once Ad Hoc Committee 1 of the MPR placed direct presidential elections on the constitutional reform agenda, speculation rose about its likely effects. Clearly, such elections would restore authority to the presidency that was lost to the assertiveness of the DPR elected in 1999 and strengthened by two amendments to the constitution in 1999–2000. Given the winner-take-all character of presidential elections, in which candidates compete to occupy a one-person office where all executive power is concentrated, there was also anxiety that such elections in Indonesia would widen the various divisions in society. Indeed, some argued specifically that presidential elections would exacerbate tensions between *santri* and non-*santri*.[10] Conceivably, it was these concerns that led the authors of the amendment to attach high-threshold requirements to the provision for direct election: first, the president and vice president had to be nominated by political parties (or coalitions of political parties) and had to be placed on joint tickets; second, the winning pair had to win not only more than 50 percent of the total votes cast but also 20 percent of the vote in more than half the total number of provinces.

Their calculation must have been that as no single political party was likely to reach this threshold on its own, they would be obliged to form an electoral alliance—recall that Megawati and the PDIP only polled 33.7 percent of the parliamentary vote in 1999 when she was at the height of her popularity. For the sake of social harmony, the most desirable combination would presumably be one that brought together a *santri* party and a non-*santri* party, as had already occurred when President Abdurrahman chose Megawati as his vice president and Megawati chose Hamzah Haz as hers. However, it is also possible that the winning combination will come from roughly the same social segment of society.[11] Thus, these requirements, though designed to induce consociational or consensual electoral behavior in Indonesia's political leaders, may fail in their purpose. Indonesia's presidential democracy will be left not quite as majoritarian as some other governments of this type, thanks to its proportional representation election system and a markedly decentralized form of government; however, it may be majoritarian enough to raise doubts about its suitability for Indonesia's plural society, owing to the direct election of the president in whom executive power is concentrated.[12] It would certainly appear less suitable than would the form of parliamentary democracy that existed in Indonesia before 1957, which contained significant consensual elements, such as broadly based coalition cabinets and the titular duumvirate, or *dwitunggal,* of Sukarno and Hatta.

The attributes that give presidential democracy its majoritarian tendency are the concentration of executive power in one person and the selection of that person by popular election. As such, they also give the office its personal quality and by so doing subject its occupant to the temptations of vanity and pride. For example, the president may claim a superior democratic legitimacy on the grounds that he or she was chosen by the whole people. In the case of Indonesia, as in the case of other presidential democracies, this would be a dubious argument. As institutions, the DPR and the new Council of Regional Representation (Dewan Perwakilan Daerah) are also elected by the whole people and may therefore be said to enjoy the same democratic legitimacy as the one-person presidency. Nevertheless, if practice in other presidential democracies serves as an accurate guide, then the successful Indonesian candidate will lay claim to such legitimacy even when that success is based on a modest vote in the first round.[13]

A second factor making for overconfidence, pride, and even hubris in a democratically elected president is the fact that the person becomes not only head of government but also head of state. This fusion of roles will certainly raise the standing of the officeholder in the eyes of the community and, in all probability, in his or her own eyes as well. The existence of a lese-majesty law, which "makes it an offence punishable by a maximum of six years gaol to engage in 'Deliberate' disrespect for the President or Vice-President,"[14] would further augment the narcissism of the president in Indonesia, as evidently happened in the case of Megawati.

We have encountered disproportionate pride and hubris and their immensely damaging consequences in the personal rule of Sukarno, whereby he achieved a result terribly unlike the one he intended. It is, therefore, disconcerting to note the opportunities that presidential democracy gives for it to flourish. It is customary to view constitutional rule as the opposite of personal rule, but where constitutional rule takes the form of presidential democracy, it is the personal nature of the presidential office in both cases that is striking.[15] One's fear in this regard is that presidential democracy, by enabling the narcissism of its leaders to proliferate, will eventually make itself hostage to the officeholder's resulting hubris. Such a situation is less likely to develop in a consensual democracy in which the prime minister is only *primus inter pares* in a cabinet based on a broad coalition of political parties who together command a majority in the parliament. Perhaps exacerbating the situation is the rigidity of presidential constitutions, evident in the fact that presidents are elected for a fixed term—five years in the Indonesian case. This form of government, having promoted the overconfidence of the president, then obliges the citizenry to live with its consequences for a lengthy period without redress. By contrast, if a consensual democracy does not induce an appropriate modesty in its prime minister to begin with, then its ability to replace the leader at any time will oblige him or her to pay a heavy price for overconfidence.[16]

We are left with a system of government that seems less than ideal for Indonesia. It is perhaps too majoritarian for its plural society, and although the election thresholds may encourage consensual behavior among the leaders of the political parties, they offer no guarantee. The inclusive functioning of the government will in large part depend on the wisdom of its party leaders and, in particular, its successful presidential candidates. Yet, the personal nature of the office promotes qualities—overconfidence, pride, hubris—that work against wisdom. Furthermore, this situation is made worse by the constitutional prohibition on the president's serving more than two terms. This prohibition offers some protection against another Soeharto-like figure's occupying the presidency for an extraordinary length of time, but in the process, it may create other difficulties. Under this arrangement, a president in his or her second term can no longer be held accountable by the voters.[17] One thinks of constitutional rule as having the capacity to engender better behavior in leaders than they would prove capable of if left to their own devices. It is therefore remarkable that the authors of this amendment, by releasing the second-term president from the discipline imposed by voters' deciding on his or her third term, were prepared to surrender this corrective power at such a critical juncture.

Against these imperfections in the amended 1945 constitution, it is important to acknowledge the document's unrivaled strength: nationalist legitimacy, which it can claim for the form of government it prescribes on account of its derivation from the Constitution of the Proclamation of Independence.[18] Indonesia's new presidential democracy may share the shortcomings inherent in this form of government, but they pale beside the benefit to be derived from its incorporation into the Indonesian nationalist tradition. Were such a naturalization of presidentialism, with the liberal democratic values that inform it, to take place, then one would have confidence in finally proclaiming 1998 as the turning point from personal to constitutional rule.

NOTES

1. Ash, *History of the Present,* xviii–xix.
2. "One of the major functions of a constitution is to solve in an orderly and peaceful manner the problem of succession for societies which do not believe in an inherited right to rule" (Shils, "Fortunes of Constitutional Government," 458).
3. Liddle, "Suharto's Indonesia," 29; Chehabi and Linz, "Theory of Sultanism: 1," 17ff.
4. Friedrich, *Constitutional Government and Democracy,* 594–95.
5. MacIntyre and Budy P. Resosudarmo, "Survey of Recent Developments," 137–38; Ray, "Survey of Recent Developments," 245–48, 251.
6. Przeworski, *Democracy and Development,* 137.
7. The notion of the "lawless state" is clarified by Lindsey, "Criminal State," 287–88.
8. The expression "small-frog Soehartos" is derived from Geertz, "Person, Time, and Conduct," 409.
9. For discussion of a similar state of mind in Thailand, see Anek Laothamatas, "Tale of Two Democracies," 220–23.
10. R. William Liddle, "Pemilihan Presiden dan Primordialisme," *Tempo,* August 27, 2000, 52; Lijphart, "Presidentialism and Majoritarian Democracy," 1:97.
11. Linz points to this "dysfunctional" consequence of runoff presidential elections in his "Presidential or Parliamentary Democracy," 1:21.
12. The consensus model of democracy "does not differ from the majoritarian model in accepting that majority rule is better than minority rule, but it accepts majority rule only as a *minimum* requirement: instead of being satisfied with narrow decision-making majorities, it seeks to maximize the size of these majorities. Its rules and institutions aim at broad participation in government and broad agreement on the policies that the government should pursue" (Lijphart, *Patterns of Democracy,* 2). Lijphart argues elsewhere that "while the separation of power exerts some pressure toward consensus democracy, the popular election of the president and the concentration of executive power in one person are strong influences in the direction of majoritarianism." His conclusion is that "presidentialism spells majoritarianism" ("Presidentialism and Majoritarian Democracy," 1:98–99, 101).
13. Linz, "Presidential or Parliamentary Democracy," 1:6–8; Lijphart, "Presidentialism and Majoritarian Democracy," 1:102–3.
14. Zifcak, "'But a Shadow of Justice,'" 357n6.
15. Compare Guenther Roth's discussion of personal rulership in the case of the American presidency, in his "Personal Rulership," 198.
16. For a discussion of the rigidity of presidentialism, see Linz, "Presidential or Parliamentary Democracy," 1:8–10.

17. Linz, "Presidential or Parliamentary Democracy," 1:12.

18. Andrew Ellis and Etsi Yudhini write that "within the MPR (and indeed outside) there are many people who attach importance to the 1945 Constitution as a symbol of Indonesia's independence, while being prepared to amend its substance to meet the requirements of times that have changed" (National Democratic Institute for International Affairs, *Indonesia's New State Institutions*).

Postscript: The Indonesian Parliamentary Elections of 2004

The Indonesian elections of 2004 were the first to be held under the amended 1945 constitution and the legislation derived from it relating to political parties and to the method of election of parliament and the president. As noted in chapter 8, the amended 1945 constitution requires that all members of the national parliament and regional parliaments be chosen via general elections; creates a new Council of Regional Representation, comprising four nonparty representatives from each province; and provides for the direct election of the president and vice president, replacing the previous system of indirect election by the members of the People's Consultative Assembly. This postscript provides a description and analysis of the parliamentary elections only. An account of the following presidential election may be found on the home page of Rowman & Littlefield (www.rowmanlittlefield.com).

The legislation stemming from the amended constitution (laws 12/2003 and 22/2003) stipulates a national parliament of 550 members. As means of selecting candidates, it designates a form of open-list proportional representation in new electoral districts for the national and regional parliaments and the single nontransferable vote for the Council of Regional Representation. The former method of election allocates seats to parties in proportion to the number of votes their candidate lists have attracted. It also gives voters some say in the particular persons who will occupy these seats. By so doing, it overcomes in part at least the shortcomings of the electoral charades of the Soeharto era and the essentially closed-list proportional representation systems used in the 1999 and 1955 elections, in which the composition of the electoral lists was largely the prerogative of party leaders.[1] The nontransferable vote method of election, which requires voters to vote for only one candidate in multimember electoral districts, was judged appropriate for selecting the four representatives of each province to sit in the Council of Regional Representation.[2]

There was one aspect of law 12/2003 that attracted the attention of the newly formed constitutional court, which was created by the amended constitution. In response to representations from thirteen persons who had been members of the Communist Party before its banning in 1966, the court ruled that article 60g was unconstitutional. This article prohibited "former members of the banned Indonesian Communist Party" from standing for legislatures at both the national and regional levels. In the court's view, it "denied their rights as citizens to express their political beliefs and was in conflict with basic human rights which are guaranteed by the [amended] 1945 Constitution."[3] But this extraordinary ruling was made too late—February 24, 2004—to have any effect on the conduct of the elections scheduled to be held only ten days later.

On April 5, 2004, 83 percent of the 148,000,369 registered voters (124,449,083 persons) peacefully filled in four ballot papers: one the size of a broadsheet newspaper, for the national parliament; two for provincial and district parliaments; and a final one, for the Council of Regional Representation. In the light of the complexity of the task, it is perhaps not surprising that almost eleven million voters, or 8.81 percent of the total, spoiled their ballot for the national parliament. The remaining 113,498,755 voted validly, and also shrewdly, unaffected by traditional habits of deference.[4] Although only half availed themselves of the opportunity to select not only a party but also a particular candidate from that party, they nevertheless voted, as Ricklefs observed, "in a way that showed that many of them know what democracy is and intend to turn it to their advantage. A good many politicians who might have assumed the masses were rather naive and easy to manipulate now have cause to reconsider."[5]

Not least among these is Ir Soetjipto, the secretary-general of the Indonesian Democracy Party (PDIP). On February 16, he told the editors of the *Jakarta Post,* "We just need to show her [Megawati's] . . . picture. That will be enough and most people are still taken by big names like hers."[6] Nothing could have been further from the truth.

Concerned about high prices, job shortages, and corruption, voters turned their backs on her in large numbers.[7] The proportion of the vote enjoyed by her party dropped by almost half, from 33.8 percent in 1999 to 18.53 percent in 2004 (a difference of −45.15 percent). Even greater declines in the PDIP's fortunes occurred in the provinces of Aceh (−67.75 percent) and Papua (−75.28 percent), where as vice president and president, Megawati had adopted a hard line against separatists. The drop in Jakarta was of similar proportions (−64.45 percent) and presumably related to her support for its deeply disliked governor, retired general Sutiyoso.

The near halving of the PDIP's electoral strength enabled Golkar, the former government party of the Soeharto era, to win a plurality of votes, with 21.58 percent of the whole, although this result was also down on its 1999 total of 22.3 percent (−3.24 percent). The other major parties also suffered declines: the National Awakening Party (PKB) of Abdurrahman Wahid received 10.57 percent (−16.69 percent); the Islamic Unity Development Party, 8.15 percent (−24.12 percent); and the National Mandate Party of Amien Rais 6.44 percent (−8.29 percent). By contrast, two other parties made striking gains. The Democrat Party, which was created in 2002 as a vehicle for the presidential aspirations of Susilo Bambang Yudhoyono, garnered 7.45 percent of the vote (remarkable in view of its short history); and the devoutly Islamic Justice and Prosperity Party jumped from 1.36 percent in 1999 to 7.34 percent in 2004 (439.41 percent).[8] An exit poll suggests that the Democrat Party drew considerable support from disaffected PDIP and Golkar supporters, whereas the Justice and Prosperity Party drew voters away from Unity Development Party, the National Mandate Party, the Crescent and Star Party, and the National Awakening Party.[9]

What light do these results throw on the relationship between Islam and politics in Indonesia? In 2004, "formalist Islamic parties," which want Islamic law to be formally acknowledged by the state, won 21.94 percent of the vote (in 1999, the proportion was 16 percent); "pluralist Islamic parties," which have accepted the religiously neutral *Pancasila* as their ideological basis, obtained 17.01 percent (1999, 22.16 percent); their combined votes amounted to approximately 38.95 percent (1999, 37.91 percent) of the total. This vote for formalist Islamic parties is a much smaller proportion of the total vote than the 43.9 percent they obtained in the elections of 1955, despite the fact that Indonesia has become a more devoutly Islamic country in the intervening years. Even the combined vote for both types of Islamic parties falls short of the 1955 figure. This election result and, indeed, the 1999 result before it have led some students of Indonesian politics to conclude that the link has been severed between devout adherence to Islam and support for avowedly Islamic political parties evident in the 1950s and early 1960s. They conclude that there has since been a fundamental change in the attitudes of Moslems, and they point to survey research that has over 51 percent of devout Moslems, or *santri*, declaring their intention to vote for secular parties such as Golkar and PDIP in 2004 "while [only] 21.4 percent preferred parties that are steadfast in struggling for *sharia*, namely the Unity Development Party (PPP), the Crescent and Star Party (PBB) and the Justice and Prosperity Party (PKS)."[10]

Fealy, who developed the two categories of Islamic parties described here, has argued against this viewpoint, asserting that on the basis of the 1999 results, "political Islam might not be as weak as many commentators suggest." Certainly, it is hard to dispute his claim that the National Mandate Party "would have done better in the 1999 election had they been more Islamic" in light of the leakage of National Mandate Party votes to PKS in 2004.[11] Additional factors that lend weight to his argument against dismissing political Islam are the fourfold increase in support for the Justice and Prosperity Party between 1999 (when it was known as the Justice Party) and 2004 and the related growth in the strength of the formalist Islamic parties as compared to their pluralist counterparts. The matter is further complicated, as Ricklefs and Fealy have pointed out, by anecdotal evidence which suggests that many voters were attracted to the PKS not by its Islamism but rather by its strong stand against corruption and by its leaders and parliamentary members' reputation for honesty. In this respect it resembles the Communist Party, whose strong electoral support in the 1950s was based in part on its reputation for incorruptability. And, like the Communist Party then, a question now hangs over the PKS about whether its electoral success is matched by a corresponding value commitment to democracy. Ricklefs reflects this concern in his remark that one should not "underestimate . . . what PKS would seek to do if, over time, it fulfils its promises, wins greater support and eventually becomes able to wield a determining influence over public policy."[12]

Whatever the fate of the PKS, the foregoing account shows that it has managed to accommodate Moslems of all varieties. Even extremists in the Javanese city of Solo found a party to vote for in the PKS without, one assumes, suffering undue cognitive dissonance.[13] Indeed, they might even become less extreme as a result of participating in the democratic process. However, the electoral law's ban on regional parties, requiring political parties participating in the parliamentary elections to have a substantial administrative presence in two-thirds of the provinces,[14] has disenfranchised the numerous inhabitants of Papua and Aceh, who suffer under repressive policies of the central government and, in their misery, embrace separatism. The framers of the electoral law were clearly afraid that regional parties would threaten the country's unity, yet the very opposite may be true: such parties, by effectively representing the grievances of the Papuans and the Acehnese in the national parliament, might very well contribute to a lessening of separatist sentiment.[15]

Nevertheless, the parliamentary elections taken as a whole were a remarkable success. On the one hand, there was the extraordinary administrative achievement of the Indonesian Electoral Commission in successfully conducting simultaneous elections for four parliaments (national, provincial, district or municipal, and the new Council of Regional Representation) and in deploying two electoral systems in the process, one of which had never been used in Indonesia before. On the other, the voters distinguished themselves by turning out in large numbers, voting peacefully and accepting the results.

But Indonesia's first free and successful elections in 1955 could not save its then-parliamentary democracy, which was brought down only eighteen months later, in March 1957. There are many differences between 1955 and 2004, but one deserves our particular attention, as it helps to explain the demise of 1957 and throw light on the present success of democracy in Indonesia. As Ricklefs and others have observed, voter alignments in 1955 reflected and indeed exacerbated divisions between devout Moslems (*santri*) and nominal Moslems (non-*santri*).[16] At its most extreme, this division found its political counterpart in a struggle between the Communist and Islamic parties and to some extent between Java and the outer islands. The results of the 1999 and 2004 elections suggest that this debilitating overlap of sociocultural and political divisions was evident in comparatively fewer voters. Voter alignments now cut across this old fault line to a large extent, as substantial numbers of the devout vote for pluralist Islamic parties or even secular parties. There are a number of explanations for this change, ranging from Soeharto's depoliticization of Islam to the triumph of the neomodernist school, with its catch-cry "Islam yes; Islamic parties no."[17] But these explanations, whether taken individually or together, do not tell the whole story. At its most stark, it is impossible to imagine the *santri* making these new connections across the *santri*–non-*santri* divide in the continued presence of the Indonesian Communist Party. It has been plausible to view Indonesia's new constitutional order as the antithesis of the arbitrary and personal rule of Sukarno, which made possible the destruction of the Communist Party in 1965 by the *santri* and their non-*santri* allies, with the encouragement and support of the army. But this consideration invites the conclusion that without this destruction the severing of the link between devout Moslems and formalist Islamic political parties beneficial to Indonesian democracy would not have occurred. To that extent, Indonesians who are now enjoying their newfound rights and freedoms are, to paraphrase Marx, drinking nectar from the skulls of the slain.

NOTES

1. Lijphart, *Patterns of Democracy,* 147–48; Alan Wall, "Some Questions about the Electoral System for the 2004 Indonesian General Election," www.infid.be/faq.html.

2. Lijphart, *Patterns of Democracy*, 149; Wall, "Some Questions."

3. "Mahkamah Konstitusi: Bekas PKI boleh Memilih dan Dipilih," *Tempo Interaktif*, February 24, 2004; Muninggar Sri Saraswati, "Ex-PKI Members regain Rights," *Jakarta*

Post Online, February 25, 2004; *Undang-Undang Republik Indonesia Nomor 12 Tahun 2003 tentang Pemilihan Umum Anggota Dewan Perwakilan Rakyat, Dewan Perwakilan Daerah, dan Dewan Perwakilan Rakyat Daerah*, www.kpu.go.id/peraturan_uu/UU_PEMILU.htm.

4. The figures for registered voters, actual voters, and those who cast valid and invalid votes for the national parliament came from "KPU Decision on the Result of the 2004 Legislative Elections: Valid Votes 113,498,755," *KPU.GO.ID*, May 14, 2004, www.kpu.go.id/english/berita/lihat-dalam.php?ID=506&cat=Berita.

5. Merle Ricklefs, "Demokrasi in Indonesia," *Australian Financial Review*, April 16, 2004. In sum, 59,310,274 persons, or 52.26 percent of those casting valid votes for the national parliament, selected both a party and a candidate from that party ("KPU Decision").

6. Fabiola Desy Unidjaja, "PDI-P Campaign Again to Rely on Megawati's Fame," *Jakarta Post Online*, February 17, 2004.

7. See International Foundation for Election Systems, *National Public Opinion Survey 2003*, 18, www.ifes.org/reg_activities/docs/national_public_opinion_survey_FINAL.pdf; International Foundation for Election Systems, *Results from Waves I through IV of Tracking Survey*, March 1, 2004, www.ifes.org/reg_activities/docs/2004_Tracking_Survey_Analysis_Report_I_IV.pdf.

8. The 2004 parliamentary election results quoted here were obtained from the webpage of the Indonesian Election Commission, www.kpu.go.id/suara/hasilsuara_dpr_sah.php. The 1999 results came from Aris Ananta, Evi Nuruidya Arifin, and Leo Suryadinata, *Indonesian Electoral Behaviour*, 259. I am most grateful to Marthin Nanere, for doing the calculations of difference, and to Joanne Peck, for clarifying some mathematical points for me.

9. According to this poll, as many as 8 percent of those who voted for the PDIP in 1999 shifted to the Democrat Party in 2004, whereas another 7 percent moved to Golkar. Golkar in turn lost 4 percent of those who voted for it in 1999 to the Democrat Party. And transferring their support to the PKS in 2004 were 9 percent of those who voted for the PPP in 1999, 16 percent of those who chose PAN, 22 percent of PBB voters, and 4 percent of PKB voters. See Lembaga Penelitian, Pendidikan dan Penerangan Ekonomi dan Sosial (LP3ES), *Pemilih PDIP beralih ke Partai Demokrat, Suara PPP dan PAN bocor ke PKS*, Jakarta, April 7, 2004, www.ndi.org/worldwide/asia/indonesia/Survey_Pemilih_Release_1.pdf.

10. Moch. N. Kurniawan, "Survey Finds Muslim Voters Favor Pluralism," *Jakarta Post Online*, November 19, 2003.

11. Fealy, "Islamic Politics," 122–23, 125, 127, 129. Also, Mujani and Liddle, "Indonesia's Approaching Elections," 109–23.

12. Greg Fealy, personal communication, July 8, 2004; Ricklefs, "Demokrasi in Indonesia."

13. Ricklefs, "Demokrasi in Indonesia."

14. *Undang-Undang Republik Indonesia Nomor 12 Tahun 2003*, section 7.

15. See Sherlock, *2004 Indonesian Elections*, 7.

16. Ricklefs, "Demokrasi in Indonesia."

17. For the details, see Fealy, "Islamic Politics."

Bibliography

NEWSPAPERS, NEWS OUTLETS, AND NEWS MAGAZINES

In the notes, online versions are distinguished from their hard copy counterparts by distinctive titles—for example, *Kompas Cyber Media*—and accompanying URLs.

Age
Agence France Presse
AJI [Aliansi Jurnalis Independen] News
Asian Wall Street Journal
Australian
Australian Broadcasting Corporation
Australian Financial Review
Australian Women's Weekly
Bernas
Bintang Timur
Bisnis Indonesia
D&R
Detikcom
Editor
Far Eastern Economic Review
Fortune
Forum Keadilan
Green Left Weekly
Inside Indonesia
Jakarta-Jakarta
Jakarta Post
Jawa Pos
Kabar dari Pijar

Kompas
Media Indonesia
Medika
Merdeka
Mimbar Indonesia
New York Times
Pelita
Pikiran Rakyat
Pos Kota
Republika
SiaR
Sinar Harapan
South China Morning Post
Suara Independen
Suara Merdeka
Suara Pembaruan
Sydney Morning Herald
Tempo
Tempo Interaktif
Waspada
XPOS
Zaman

PUBLICATIONS OF NONGOVERNMENT ORGANIZATIONS

Amnesty International. *Indonesia: Old Laws—New Prisoners of Conscience.* July 10, 2003. http://web.amnesty.org/library/Index/ENGASA210272003?open&of=ENG-IDN.

Human Rights Watch. *Human Rights Watch World Report 1998.* www.hrw.org/worldreport/Asia-07htm#P652_167139.

———. *Human Rights Watch World Report 2002: Indonesia.* www.hwr.org/wr2k2/asia7.html.

———. "Indonesia: Bali Attack Should Not Undermine Civil Liberties." October 18, 2002. www.hrw.org/press/2002/10/bali1018htm.

———. *Indonesia: The Damaging Debate on Rapes of Ethnic Chinese Women.* www.hwr.org/reports98/indonesia3/index.htm.

———. "Indonesia: Investigate Death of Papuan Leader." November 11, 2001. www.hrw.org/press/2001/11/indonesia1111.htm.

———. "Indonesia: Investigate Shootings in Papua, No Reprisals." September 5, 2002. www.hrw.org/press/2002/09/papua0905.htm.

———. *In the Name of Counter-terrorism: Human Rights Abuses Worldwide.* Briefing paper for the Fifty-ninth Session of the United Nations Commission on Human Rights, March 25, 2003. http://hrw.org/un/chr59/counter-terrorism-bck4.htm#P271_58375.

———. *A Return to the New Order? Political Prisoners in Megawati's Indonesia.* July 2003. http://hrw.org/reports/2003/indon0703/.

International Crisis Group. *Aceh: Can Autonomy Stem the Conflict?* Asia Report 18. June 27, 2001. www.crisisweb.org//library/docments/report_archive/A400331_27062001.pdf.

———. *Aceh: A Fragile Peace.* Asia Report 47. February 27, 2003. www.crisisweb.org/library/documents/report-archive/A400907_27022003.pdf.

———. *Bad Debt: The Politics of Financial Reform in Indonesia.* Asia Report 15. March 13, 2001. www.crisisweb.org//library/documents/report_archive/A400253_13032001.pdf.

———. *Communal Violence in Indonesia: Lessons from Kalimantan.* Asia Report 19. June 27, 2001. www.crisisweb.org/library/documents/report_archive/A400332_27062001.pdf.

———. *Impact of the Bali Bombings.* Indonesia briefing. October 24, 2002. www.crisisweb.org//library/documents/report_archive/A400804_24102002.pdf.

———. *Indonesia: Ending Repression in Irian Jaya.* Asia Report 23. September 20, 2001. www.crisisweb.org//library/documents/report_archive/A400414_20092001.pdf.

———. *Indonesia's Presidential Crisis.* February 21, 2001. www.crisisweb.org/library/documents/report_archive/A400243_21022001.pdf.

———. *Indonesia's Presidential Crisis: The Second Round.* May 21, 2001. www.crisisweb.org/library/documents/report_archive/A400296_21052001.pdf.

National Democratic Institute for International Affairs. *The Fundamental Changes That Nobody Noticed: The MPR Annual Session, November 2001.* January 2002. www.accessdemocracy.org/library/1378_id_gov_112002.pdf.

———. *Indonesia's Change of President and Prospects for Constitutional Reform: A Report on the July 2001 Special Session of the People's Consultative Assembly and the Presidential Impeachment Process.* October 2001. www.accessdemocracy.org/library/1319_id_presconstref102001.pdf.

———. *Indonesia's New State Institutions: The Constitution Completed, Now for the Detail: The MPR Annual Session.* November 2002.

———. *Indonesia's Road to Constitutional Reform: The 2000 MPR Annual Session.* Assessment report. October 2000. www.accessdemocracy.org/library/1077_id_constireform.pdf.

———. *The New Legal Framework for Elections in Indonesia: A Report of an NDI Assessment Team.* February 23, 1999. www.accessdemocracy.org/library/215_id_framework.pdf.

———. *The 1999 Presidential Election and Post-election Developments in Indonesia: A Post-election Assessment Report, November 28, 1999.* www.accessdemocracy.org/library/1079_id_preselect.pdf.

Tapol: Indonesian Human Rights Campaign. *Briefing Paper: The 1997 General Elections in Indonesia.* April 1997. http://tapol.gn.apc.org/.

———. *Indonesia's Anti-terrorism Decree a Threat to Basic Rights.* October 2002. http://tapol.gn.apc.org/pr021028.htm.

ARTICLES, BOOKS, AND SPEECHES BY SUKARNO

Amalkan Ilmu daripada Kehidupan Sehari-hari (The School of Life): Amanat Presiden Sukarno pada Peringatan Hari Sardjana ke-IV, 30 September 1963 di Istana Olahraga Gelora Bung Karno, Senajan, Djakarta. Departemen Penerangan R.I.

"Amanat PJM Presiden pada Peringatan 4 Windu Hari Sumpah Pemuda di Istana Negara Djakarta pada Tanggal 28 Oktober 1960." Sekretariat Negara Kabinet Presiden.

"Amanat PJM Presiden Sukarno Kepada Ikatan Penerbit Indonesia (IKAPI) di Istana Bogor, 26 Pebruari 1966." Sekretariat Negara Kabinet Presiden.

"Amanat PJM Presiden Sukarno pada Pelantikan/Penjumpahan Major Djendral KKO Ali Sadikin Mendjadi Gubernur/Kepala Daerah Chusus Ibu Kota Djakarta Raya, Istana Negara, Djakarta, 28 April 1966." Sekretariat Negara Kabinet Presiden.

"Amanat PJM Presiden Sukarno pada Pembukaan Sidang Pimpinan MPRS ke-X di Istana Negara, Djakarta, 6 Desember 1965." Sekretariat Negara Kabinet Presiden.

"Amanat PJM Presiden Sukarno pada Peringatan 'Hari Sumpah Pemuda' Tanggal 28 Oktober 1962 jang diutjapkan di Istana Olah Raga Senajan Gelora Bung Karno, Djakarta, 30 Oktober 1962." Sekretariat Negara Kabinet Presiden.

"Amanat PJM Presiden Sukarno pada Peringatan Hari Ulang Tahun PNI ke-38 di Stadion Utama Gelora Bung Karno, Senajan, Djakarta, 25 Djuli 1965." Sekretariat Negara Kabinet Presiden.

"Amanat PJM Presiden Sukarno pada Rapat CGMI di Istora, Senajan, Djakarta, 29 September 1965." Sekretariat Negara Kabinet Presiden.

"Amanat PJM Presiden Sukarno pada Sidang Kabinet Paripurna di Istana Negara, Djakarta, 11 March 1966." Sekretariat Negara Kabinet Presiden.

"Amanat PJM Presiden Sukarno pada Upatjara Peringatan Tri Pantjawarsa Universitas Gadjah Mada di Siti Hinggil, Jogjakarta, 20 Desember 1964." Sekretariat Negara Kabinet Presiden.

Amanat Presiden Sukarno pada Konperensi Besar IPPI: Djer Basuki Mawa Beja! Disampaikan dalam Pertemuan Besar di Istana Olahraga Gelora Bung Karno, Senajan, Djakarta, pada tanggal 25 Maret 1963. Departemen Penerangan R.I., penerbitan chusus 269.

Amanat Presiden Sukarno pada Rapat Raksasa Front Nasional "Mengganjang Malaysia" di Istora Olahraga Gelora Bung Karno, Senajan, Djakarta, pada Tanggal 27 Djuli 1963. Departemen Penerangan R.I., penerbitan chusus 278.

Apa Sebab Negara Republik Indonesia Berdasarkan Pantja-Sila? Amanat PJM Presiden Soekarno pada tgl. 24 September 1955 di Soerabaja. Kementerian Penerangan R.I.

"Batu Udjian Sedjarah [1941]." In *Dibawah Bendera Revolusi,* edited by H. Mualliff Nasution, 1:521–31. Jakarta: Panitya Penerbit, 1965.

Berdiri diata Kaki Sendiri (Berdikari): Amanat Politik Presiden/Pemimpin Besar Revolusi/Mandataris MPRS pada Pembukaan Sidang Umum ke-III Madjelis Pemusjawaratan Rakjat Sementara, tanggal 11 April 1965. MPRS dan Departemen Penerangan R.I.

"Berilah Isi kepada Hidupmu! Amanat Presiden Sukarno pada Ulang Tahun Proklamsi Kemerdekaan Indonesia, 17 Agustus 1956 di Djakarta." In *Dibawah*

Bendera Revolusi, edited by H. Mualliff Nasution, 2:251–79. Jakarta: Panitya Penerbit, 1965.

"Berirama Dengan Kodrat: Amanat Presiden Sukarno pada Ulang Tahun Proklamasi Kemerdekaan Indonesia 17 Agustus 1954 di Djakarta." In *Dibawah Bendera Revolusi,* edited by H. Mualliff Nasution, 2:195–217. Jakarta: Panitya Penerbit, 1965.

Bertjita-tjitalah Setinggi Bintang Dilangit! Amanat Presiden Sukarno pada peringatan Hari Pendidikan Nasional di Istana Olahraga Gelora Bung Karno, Senajan, Djakarta pada Tanggal 2 Mei 1964. Departemen Penerangan R.I.

"Capailah Bintang-Bintang di Langit (Tahun Berdikari): Amanat Presiden Republik Indonesia Sukarno Pada Ulang Tahun Proklamasi Kemerdekaan Indonesia 17 Agustus 1965 di Jakarta." In *Amanat Proklamasi: Pidato pada Ulang Tahun Proklamasi Kemerdekaan Indonesia,* 4:159–95. Jakarta: Inti Idayu Press and Yayasan Pendidikan Soekarno, 1986.

"Dari Sabang Sampai Merauke! Amanat Presiden Sukarno pada Ulang Tahun Proklamasi Kemerdekaan Indonesia, 17 Agustus 1950 di Djakarta." In *Dibawah Bendera Revolusi,* edited by H. Mualliff Nasution, 2:99–121. Jakarta: Panitya Penerbit, 1965.

"Djadilah Alat Sedjarah! Amanat Presiden Sukarno pada Ulang Tahun Proklamasi Kemerdekaan Indonesia, 17 Agustus 1953 di Djakarta." In *Dibawah Bendera Revolusi,* edited by H. Mualliff Nasution, 2:171–91. Jakarta: Panitya Penerbit, 1965.

Djadilah Kader Bangsa dan Kader Revolusi: Amanat Presiden Sukarno pada rapat umum pembukaan Kongres ke-VII Ikatan Pemuda Peladjar Indonesia (IPPI) di Istora Gelora "Bung Karno," Senajan, Djakarta, pada tanggal 25 Djuli 1964. Departemen Penerangan R.I.

"Djerit-Kegemparan [1928]." In *Dibawah Bendera Revolusi,* edited by H. Mualliff Nasution, 1:51–55. Jakarta: Panitya Penerbit, 1965.

From Non-alignment to Coordinated Accumulation of Moral Force toward Friendship, Peace, and Social Justice among Nations: An Address by Sukarno before the Belgrade Summit Conference of Non-aligned Countries on 1st September 1961. Department of Information, Republic of Indonesia, special issue.

"Genta Suara Republik Indonesia: Amanat Presiden Sukarno pada Ulang Tahun Proklamasi Kemerdekaan Indonesia, 17 Agustus 1963 di Djakarta." In *Dibawah Bendera Revolusi,* edited by H. Mualliff Nasution, 2:521–53. Jakarta: Panitya Penerbit, 1965.

Go Ahead! Pidato PJM Presiden Sukarno pada Penutupan Kongres Nasional ke VII PKI di Djakarta pada tanggal 30 April 1962. Djakarta: Jajasan Pembaruan, 1965.

Hantjurkan Kontra Revolusi: Amanat PJM Sukarno pada Resepsi Pembukaan Kongres Wanita Indonesia di Djakarta, tgl. 19 Mei 1963. Djakarta: Partindo, 1963.

Indonesia Tetap Tegak Berdiri sampai Achir Zaman: Amanat Presiden Sukarno pada Peringatan Peristiwa Merah-Putih (14-2-46 di Minahasa) pada Tanggal 11 Maret 1965 di Istana Negara, Djakarta. Departemen Penerangan R.I., penerbitan chusus 363.

"Indonesianisme dan Pan-Asiatisme [1928]." In *Dibawah Bendera Revolusi,* edited by H. Mualliff Nasution, 1:73–77. Jakarta: Panitya Penerbit, 1965.

"Jangan sekali-kali Meninggalkan Sejarah!" In *Amanat Proklamasi: Pidato pada Ulang Tahun Proklamasi Kemerdekaan Indonesia,* 4:197–226. Jakarta: Inti Idayu Press and Yayasan Pendidikan Soekarno, 1986.

Komando Presiden: Adakan Gerakan Sukarelawan Indonesia untuk Mempertinggi Ketahanan Revolusi Kita! Amanat Presiden Sukarno pada penutupan Konperensi Presidium Kabinet-kerdja dengan Tjatur-Tunggal seluruh Indonesia, pada tanggal 16 Maret 1964 di Istana Negara. Departemen Penerangan R.I., penerbitan chusus 305.

Komando Presiden Soekarno Pemimpin Besar Revolusi kepada Angkatan 45: Diutjapkan pada Pembukaan Musjawarah Besar Angkatan 45 seluruh Indonesia, tanggal 15 Maret 1960. Departemen Penerangan R.I., penerbitan chusus 98.

Kuliah Umum Presiden Soekarno pada Pembukaan "Studium Generale" bagi Gabungan Mahasiswa2 Bandung, 11 Oktober 1959. Departemen Penerangan R.I., penerbitan chusus 72.

Kumpulkan Ilmu Pengetahuan untuk Pembangunan: Amanat Presiden Sukarno pada Hari Sardjana di Istana OlahRaga "Bung Karno," Senajan, Djakarta, tanggal 29 September 1962. Departemen Penerangan R.I., penerbitan chusus 235.

Laksanakan Pantja-Logi: Irigasi-Edukasi-Emigrasi-Industrialisasi-Indoktrinasi: Amanat Presiden Sukarno pada hari peringatan Twiwarsa Departemen Perguruan Tinggi dan Ilmu Pengetahuan di Istana Olahraga Gelora Bung Karno, Senajan, Djakarta, pada tanggal 13 April 1964. Departemen Penerangan R.I.

Madju Terus Pantang Mundur Sampai "Malaysia" Hantjur Lebur! Amanat Presiden Sukarno pada Pembukaan Penggemblengan Kader Revolusi Angkatan "Dwikora" pada tanggal 31 Agustus 1964 di Istana Negara, Djakarta. Departemen Penerangan R.I.

Membangun Sosialisme Indonesia dengan Konsepsi Sendiri! Amanat Presiden Sukarno pada Peringatan Hari Bank dan Pembukaan Mubes Sardjana Ekonomi Indonesia di Istora Gelora "Bung Karno," Senajan, Djakarta, pada tanggal 6 Djuli 1964. Departemen Penerangan R.I., penerbitan chusus 327.

"Me-'Muda'-Kan Pengertian Islam [1940]." In *Dibawah Bendera Revolusi,* edited by H. Mualliff Nasution, 1:369–402. Jakarta: Panitya Penerbit, 1965.

"Mendjadi Pembantu 'Pemandangan': Sukarno, oleh . . . Sukarno Sendiri [1941]." In *Dibawah Bendera Revolusi,* edited by H. Mualliff Nasution, 1:507–13. Jakarta: Panitya Penerbit, 1965.

Menjelamatkan Republik Proklamasi: Tjatatan Stenografis dari Pidato Presiden Soekarno tgl. 21 Pebr. 1957 Djam 20.05 di Istana Merdeka. Kementerian Penerangan R.I.

Nationalism, Islam, and Marxism. Translated by Karel H. Warouw and Peter Weldon. Introduction by Ruth T. McVey. Modern Indonesia Project Translation Series. Ithaca, N.Y.: Cornell University, 1970.

Nawa Aksara (Nawa Aksara): Amanat Presiden Sukarno didepan Sidang Umum Madjelis Permusjawaratan Rakjat Sementara Ke-IV/1966, pada tanggal 22 Djuni 1966 di Istana Olah Raga "Bung Karno" Senajan, Djakarta. Kementerian Penerangan R.I.

"Never Leave History! Address by the President of the Republic of Indonesia on the Twenty-first Anniversary of Independence 17 August 1966." Department of Information, Republic of Indonesia.

Pamong Desa Salah Satu Sokoguru Revolusi Indonesia: Amanat Presiden Sukarno kepada para peserta Kongres Persatuan Pamong Desa Indonesia (PPDI) di Istana Negara, pada tanggal 12 May 1964. Departmen Penerangan R.I.

Persatuan Total dengan Poros Nasakom: Amanat Presiden Sukarno pada Kongres Gerwani ke-IV di Gedung Wanita, Djakarta, 14 Desember 1961. Departemen Penerangan R.I., penerbitan chusus 207.

Persembahkan Hidupmu kepada Tanah Air dan Bangsa: Tjeramah Presiden Sukarno didepan Para Mahasiswa Universitas Gadjah Mada di Sitinghinggil Jogjakarta, 22 Oktober 1962.

"Pidato disampaikan dalam Pertemuan dengan para Pelajar dan Pemuda di 'Atjeh Bioskop,' June 16, 1948, 8:30 pm." In *Untuk Apa Kita Merdeka: Amanat dan Kursus Politik Bung Karno di Sumatera dalam Masa Perang Kemerdekaan 1945–1949*, edited by M. Hasan Basry. Jakarta: Kopkar Pip, 1995.

"[Pidato] disampaikan dalam rapat samudera di Bukittinggi, bertetapan dengan peringatan Israk dan Mikraj, dipancarluaskan RRI Bukit Tinggi, Sabtu 5 Juni, tahun 1948." In *Untuk Apa Kita Merdeka: Amanat dan Kursus Politik Bung Karno di Sumatera dalam Masa Perang Kemerdekaan 1945–1949*, edited by M. Hasan Basry, 2–15. Jakarta: Kopkar Pip, 1995.

"Pidato PJM Presiden pada Rapat Umum di Saparua pada Tanggal 8 Nopember 1958." Sekretariat Negara Kabinet Presiden.

"Pidato PJM Presiden Sukarno pada Rapat Raksasa berkenaan dengan Peringatan Hari Pahlawan di Semarang, 10 Nopember 1961." Sekretariat Negara Kabinet Presiden.

Pidato Presiden Soekarno pada Pembukaan Kongres Pemuda Seluruh Indonesia tanggal 15 Pebruari 1960 di Bandung. Departemen Penerangan R.I.

Pidato President Sukarno pada Hari Sumpah Pemuda tgl. 28 Oktober 1956 di Djakarta. Kementrian Penerangan R.I.

PWI Benar-Benar Mendjadi Alat Revolusi: Amanat Presiden Sukarno pada rapat-umum "Madju Tak Gentar" memperingati ulang-tahun ke-19 Persatuan Wartawan Indonesia (PWI) di Istora "Bung Karno," Senajan, Djakarta, pada tanggal 23 Pebruari 1965. Departemen Penerangan R.I., penerbitan chusus 368.

Rapatkan Barisanmu dengan Pemerintah dan Sukseskan Triprogram Gaja Baru: Amanat Presiden Sukarno pada Peringatan Hari Ibu di Istana Negara, Djakarta, tanggal 21 Desember 1963. Departemen Penerangan R.I., penerbitan chusus 301.

Sarinah: Kewajiban Wanita dalam Perjuangan Republik Indonesia. 1947. Jakarta: Inti Idayu Press and Yayasan Pendidikan Soekarno, 1984.

Suatu Bangsa jang Besar tidak akan Tenggelam, ketjuali djikalau Robek-robek Petjah dirinja sendiri dari dalam: Amanat Presiden pada Peringatan Isra' dan Mir'radj pada Tanggal 21 Nopember 1965 di Istana Negara, Djakarta. Departemen Penerangan R.I.

Susunlah Konstitusi jang Benar-Benar Konstitusi Res Publica: Pidato Presiden Republik Indonesia pada waktu membuka Konstituante 10 Nopember 1956. Kementerian Penerangan R.I.

"Tabir adalah Lambang Perbudakan [1939]." In *Dibawah Bendera Revolusi*, edited by H. Mualliff Nasution, 1:349–51. Jakarta: Panitya Penerbit, 1965.

"Tahun Kemenangan: Amanat Presiden Sukarno pada Ulang Tahun Proklamasi Kemerdekaan Indonesia 17 Agustus 1962 di Djakarta." In *Dibawah Bendera Revolusi,* edited by H. Mualliff Nasution, 2:485–517. Jakarta: Panitya Penerbit, 1965.

"Tahun Vivere Pericoloso: Amanat Presiden Sukarno pada Ulang Tahun Proklamasi Kemerdekaan Indonesia, 17 Agustus 1964 di Djakarta." In *Dibawah Bendera Revolusi,* edited by H. Mualliff Nasution, 2:559–598. Jakarta: Panitya Penerbit, 1965.

Tenaga Gadungan lebih Berbahaja daripada Imperialis: Amanat Presiden Sukarno pada Rapat Raksasa peringatan Ulang-Tahun ke-45 PKI, tanggal 23 Mei 1965 di Stadion Utama Gelora "Bung Karno," Senajan, Djakarta. Departemen Penerangan R.I., penerbitan chusus 371.

Tidak ada Bangsa jang Besar tanpa Perbuatan: Amanat Presiden Sukarno pada Hari Ibu tgl. 22 Desember 1961 di Istana Negara. Departemen Penerangan R.I., penerbitan chusus 193.

Tjeramah Presiden Soekarno kepada Peladjar-Peladjar di Surakarta Tanggal 26 Djuli 1960. Departemen Penerangan R.I., penerbitan chusus 137.

To Build the World Anew: President Sukarno's Address before the Fifteenth General Assembly of the United Nations on Friday 30 September 1960. Department of Information, Republic of Indonesia, special issue 68.

DOCUMENTS, AUTOBIOGRAPHIES, ALLIED MATERIAL

Adams, Cindy. *Sukarno: An Autobiography As Told to Cindy Adams.* Hong Kong: Gunung Agung, 1966.

———. *Sukarno My Friend.* Singapore: Gunung Agung, 1970.

Bahar, Saafroedin, Ananda B. Kusuma, and Nannie Hudawati, eds. *Risalah Sidang Badan Penyelidik Usaha-Usaha Persiapan Kemerdekaan Indonesia (BPUPKI) Panitia Persiapan Kemerdekaan Indonesia (PPKI), 29 Mei 1945–22 Agustus 1945.* Jakarta: Sekretariat Negara Republik Indonesia, 1995.

Bendera Sudah Saya Kibarkan! Pokok-Pokok Pikiran Megawati Soekarnoputri. Jakarta: Pustaka Sinar Harapan, 1993.

Gerovital H3: Original Product of Prof. Dr. Ana Aslan: Neurotropic, Antidepressive, Vitaminic, Eutrophic and Regenerative factor[s] in the Treatment of Ageing and Trophic Disturbances. Bucharest: National Institute of Gerontology and Geriatrics, 1977.

Ketetapan-Ketetapan Majelis Permusyawaratan Rakyat Republik Indonesia Hasil Sidang Umum Tahunan MPR RI Tahun 2000 (7 s/d 18 Agustus 2000) Beserta Perubahan Kedua Undang-Undang Dasar Negara Republik Indonesia Tahun 1945. Jakarta: BP Panca Usaha, 2000.

Lubis, Mochtar, ed. *Hati Nurani Melawan Kezaliman: Surat-Surat Bung Hatta kepada Presiden Soekarno 1957–1965.* Jakarta: Pustaka Sinar Harapan, 1986.

Martowidjojo, H. Mangil. *Kesaksian tentang Bung Karno 1945–1967.* Jakarta: Grasindo, 1999.

Meluruskan Perjalanan Orde Baru: Pertanggung-Jawaban Petisi 50 kepada Rakyat Indonesia. Kelompok Kerja Petisi 50/Pernyataan Keprihatinan, n.d.

Nababan, Panda, ed. *Gerak dan Langkah Megawati Soekarnoputri.* Jakarta: n.p., 1999.
Nasution, A. H. *Memenuhi Panggilan Tugas.* Vol. 2A, *Kenangan Masa Gerilya.* Jakarta: CV Haji Masagung, 1989.
Nasution, A. H. *Memenuhi Panggilan Tugas.* Vol. 5, *Kenangan Masa Orde Lama.* Jakarta: CV Haji Masagung, 1989.
"Pernyataan Politik Partai Demokrasi Indonesia." *AJI News.* March 3, 1998. www.library.ohiou.edu/indopubs/1998/03/04/0038.html.
"Pidato Ketua Umum DPP PDI Megawati Soekarnoputri Menyambut HUT ke XXV PDI." *SiaR.* January 11, 1998. www.library.ohiou.edu/indopubs/1998/01/11/0047.html.
"Pidato Pembukaan Kongres Perjuangan Ketua Umum DPP-PDI, Megawati Sukarnoputri." Dewan Pimpinan Pusat Partai Demokrasi Indonesia. www.library.ohiou.edu/indopubs/1998/10/10/0007.html.
"Pidato Politik Ketua Umum PDI Perjuangan Megawati Soekarnoputri dalam rangka Menyambut Kemenangan Rakyat pada Pemilu 1999," *Kompas Cyber Media*, July 30, 1999. www.kompas.com.
Pour, Julius. *Benny Moerdani: Profil Prajurit Negarawan.* Jakarta: 1993.
Ramadhan, K. H. *Kuantar Ke Gerbang: Kisah Cinta Ibu Inggit Dengan Bung Karno.* Jakarta: Penerbit Sinar Harapan, 1981.
Roeder, O. G. *Anak Desa: Biografi Presiden Soeharto.* Jakarta: CV Haji Masagung, 1990.
———. *The Smiling General: President Soeharto of Indonesia.* Jakarta: Gunung Agung, 1969.
Sadli, Mohammad. "Recollections of My Career." *Bulletin of Indonesian Economic Studies* 29, no. 1 (April 1993): 35–51.
"Sambutan Ketua Umum DPP PDI Megawati Sukarnoputri pada Seminar Sehari Balitbang DPP PDI, Hotel Grand Melia, Jakarta, 28 September 1998." www.library.ohiou.edu/indopubs/1998/10/06/0004.html.
Sjahrir, Sutan. *Our Struggle.* Translated and introduced by Benedict R. O'G. Anderson. Modern Indonesia Project Translation Series. Ithaca, N.Y.: Cornell University, 1968.
Soeharto (seperti dipaparkan kepada G. Dwipayana dan Ramadhan K. H.). *Pikiran, Ucapan dan Tindakan Saya: Otobiografi.* Jakarta: P.T. Citra Lamtoro Gung Persada, 1988.
Soeharto, R. *Saksi Sejarah: Mengikut Perjuangan Dwitunggal.* Jakarta: Gunung Agung, 1984.
Soekarno, Guntur. "Granat Maut (Peristiwa Cikini 1957)." In *Bung Karno: Bapakku, Kawanku, Guruku.* Jakarta: PT Dela-Rohita, 1977.
Soekarno, Rachmawati. *Bapakku Ibuku.* Jakarta: Garuda Metropolitan Press, 1984.
Soekarnoputri, Megawati. "An Agenda for Reform [April 1997]." In *Indonesian Politics and Society: A Reader,* edited by David Bourchier and Vedi Hadiz, 203–7. London: RoutledgeCurzon, 2003.
———. "Pesan Akhir Tahun 1997: 'Hanya Ada Satu Jalan: Perubahan dan Perbaikan." *SiaR.* January 7, 1998. www.library.ohiou.edu/indopubs/1998/01/07/0018html.

———. "Restoring Democracy, Justice, and Order in Indonesia: An Agenda for Reform."
Yamin, Muhammad. *Naskah-Persiapan Undang-Undang Dasar 1945.* Jakarta: Jajasan Prapantja, 1959.

BOOKS AND ARTICLES

Abel, Ben, and Ben Anderson. "A Javanese King Talks of His End." *Inside Indonesia* 54 (April–June 1998).
Ananta, Aris, Evi Nurvidya Arifin, and Leo Suryadinata. *Indonesian Electoral Behaviour: A Statistical Perspective.* Singapore: Institute of Southeast Asian Studies, 2004.
Anderson, Benedict R. O'G. "Cartoons and Monuments: The Evolution of Political Communication under the New Order." In *Political Power and Communications in Indonesia,* edited by Karl D. Jackson and Lucian W. Pye, 282–321. Berkeley: University of California Press, 1978.
———. *Java in a Time of Revolution: Occupation and Resistance, 1944–1946.* Ithaca, N.Y.: Cornell University Press, 1972.
———. *Mythology and the Tolerance of the Javanese.* Modern Indonesia Project Monograph Series. Ithaca, N.Y.: Cornell University, 1965.
———. "Old State, New Society: Indonesia's New Order in Comparative Historical Perspective." *Journal of Asian Studies* 42, no. 3 (May 1983): 477–96.
———. "A Time of Darkness and a Time of Light: Transposition in Early Indonesian Nationalist Thought." In *Perceptions of the Past in Southeast Asia,* edited by Anthony Reid and David Marr, 219–248. Singapore: Heinemann, 1979.
Antlov, Hans. "Not Enough Politics! Power, Participation, and the New Democratic Polity in Indonesia." In *Local Power and Politics in Indonesia: Decentralisation and Democratisation,* edited by Edward Aspinall and Greg Fealy, 72–86. Singapore: Institute of Southeast Asian Studies, 2003.
———. "Village Government and Rural Development in Indonesia: The New Democratic Framework." *Bulletin of Indonesian Economic Studies* 39, no. 2 (2003): 193–214.
Anwar, Dewi Fortuna. "The Tragic Ending of Abdurrahman Wahid's Presidency." Paper presented to the conference celebrating the thirty-fourth anniversary of the Indonesian Institute of Sciences, Jakarta, July 26, 2001.
Anwar, H. Rosihan. "Perbedaan Analisa Politik Antara Sukarno dengan Hatta." *Kompas,* September 15, 1980, iv–v.
Aris, Michael. Introduction to *Freedom from Fear and Other Writings,* by Aung San Suu Kyi, edited by Michael Aris. London: Penguin Books, 1991.
Ash, Timothy Garton. *History of the Present: Essays, Sketches and Despatches from Europe in the 1990s.* London: Penguin Books, 2000.
Aspinall, Edward. "The Downfall of President Abdurrahman Wahid: A Return to Authoritarianism?" In *Women in Indonesia: Gender, Equity and Development,* edited by Kathryn Robinson and Sharon Bessell, 28–40. Singapore: Institute of Southeast Asian Studies, 2002.

———. "Opposition and Elite Conflict in the Fall of Soeharto." In *The Fall of Soeharto,* edited by Geoff Forrester and R. J. May, 130–153. Singapore: Select Books, 1999.

———. "Political Opposition and the Transition from Authoritarian Rule: The Case of Indonesia." Ph.D. diss., Australian National University, 2000.

Aspinall, Edward, and Greg Fealy. "Introduction: Decentralisation, Democratisation and the Rise of the Local." In *Local Power and Politics in Indonesia: Decentralisation and Democratisation,* edited by Edward Aspinall and Greg Fealy, 1–11. Singapore: Institute of Southeast Asian Studies, 2003.

Aspinall, Edward, and Gerry van Klinken. "Chronology of Crisis." In *The Last Days of President Soeharto,* edited by Edward Aspinall, Herb Feith, and Gerry van Klinken, 159–66. Clayton, Vic.: Monash Asia Institute, 1999.

Auden, W. H. *The Dyer's Hand and Other Essays.* New York: Random House, 1962.

Aveling, Harry. *A Thematic History of Indonesian Poetry: 1920 to 1974.* Special Report 9. DeKalb, Ill.: Northern Illinois University, Center for Southeast Asian Studies, 1974.

Barton, Greg. *Abdurrahman Wahid: Muslim Democrat, Indonesian President: A View from the Inside.* Sydney: UNSW Press, 2002.

Barton, Greg. *Gus Dur: The Authorized Biography of Abdurrahman Wahid.* Jakarta: Equinox Publishing, 2002.

Bauman, Zygmunt. *Mortality, Immortality, and Other Life Strategies.* Stanford, Calif.: Stanford University Press, 1992.

Berman, Marshall. *All That Is Solid Melts into Air: The Experience of Modernity.* New York: Verso, 1995.

Bourchier, David. "Conservative Political Ideology in Indonesia: A Fourth Wave?" In *Indonesia Today: Challenges of History,* edited by Grayson Lloyd and Shannon Smith, 112–25. Singapore: Institute of Southeast Asian Studies, 2001.

———. "Crime, Law and State Authority in Indonesia." In *State and Civil Society in Indonesia,* edited by Arief Budiman, 177–212. Monash Papers on Southeast Asia 22. Clayton, Vic.: Monash University, Centre of Southeast Asian Studies, 1990.

———. "Habibie's Interregnum: *Reformasi,* Elections, Regionalism and the Struggle for Power." In *Indonesia in Transition: Social Aspects of Reformasi and Crisis,* edited by Cris Manning and Peter Van Dierman, 15–38. Singapore: Institute of Southeast Asian Studies, 2000.

———. "Lineages of Organicist Political Thought in Indonesia." Ph.D diss., Monash University, Clayton, Victoria, 1996.

———. "The 1950s in New Order Ideology and Politics." In *Democracy in Indonesia: 1950s and 1990s,* edited by David Bourchier and John Legge, 50–62. Monash Papers on Southeast Asia 31. Clayton, Vic.: Monash University, Centre of Southeast Asian Studies, 1994.

Bowlby, John. *Attachment and Loss.* Vol. 3, *Loss: Sadness and Depression.* Harmondsworth, Eng.: Penguin Books, 1981.

Bradley, A. C. *Shakespearean Tragedy: Lectures on Hamlet, Othello, King Lear, Macbeth.* London: MacMillan, 1961.

Bresnan, John. *Managing Indonesia: The Modern Political Economy.* New York: Columbia University Press, 1993.

———. "The United States, the IMF, and the Indonesian Financial Crisis." In *The Politics of Post-Suharto Indonesia,* edited by Adam Schwarz and Jonathan Paris, 87–112. New York: Council on Foreign Relations Press, 1999.

Brooks, Karen. "The Rustle of Ghosts: Bung Karno in the New Order." *Indonesia* 60 (October 1995): 61–99.

Brown, Colin. *A Short History of Indonesia: The Unlikely Nation?* Sydney: Allen & Unwin, 2003.

———. "Sukarno on the Role of Women in the Nationalist Movement." *Review of Indonesian and Malayan Affairs* 15, no. 1 (1981): 68–92.

Carr, E. H. *What Is History?* edited by R. W. Davies. London: Penguin Books, 1990.

Carrere d'Encausse, Helene, and Stuart R. Schram. *Marxism and Asia: An Introduction with Readings.* London: Allen Lane/Penguin Press, 1969.

Chauvel, Richard. *The Land of Papua and the Indonesian State: Essays on West Papua.* 2 vols. Clayton, Vic.: Monash Asia Institute, 2003.

Chehabi, H. E., and Juan J. Linz. "A Theory of Sultanism: 1. A Type of Nondemocratic Rule." In *Sultanistic Regimes,* edited by H. E. Chehabi and J. J. Linz, 3–25. Baltimore: Johns Hopkins University Press, 1998.

———. "A Theory of Sultanism: 2. Genesis and Demise of Sultanistic Regimes." In *Sultanistic Regimes,* edited by H. E. Chehabi and J. J. Linz, 26–48. Baltimore: Johns Hopkins University Press, 1998.

Chowdhury, Najma. "Bangladesh: Gender Issues and Politics in a Patriarchy." In *Women and Politics Worldwide,* edited by Barbara J. Nelson and Najma Chowdhury, 94–113. New Haven, Conn.: Yale University Press, 1994.

Clarke, Ross. "Retrospectivity and the Constitutional Validity of the Bali Bombing and East Timor Trials." *Australian Journal of Asian Law* 5, no. 2 (2003): 1–32. www.law.unimelb.edu.au/alc/assets/ajal_clarke_bali.pdf.

Clarke, William, ed. *Essays: Selected from the Writings, Literary, Political, and Religious, of Joseph Mazzini.* London: Walter Scott, n.d.

Coppel, Charles A. *Indonesian Chinese in Crisis.* Kuala Lumpur: Oxford University Press, 1983.

Crouch, Harold. "All to Placate a Proud Sultan." *Australian Financial Review,* July 30, 1996. www.library.ohiou.edu/indopubs/1996/07/31/0049.html.

———. *The Army and Politics in Indonesia.* Ithaca, N.Y.: Cornell University Press, 1988.

———. "Democratic Prospects in Indonesia." In *Democracy in Indonesia: 1950s and 1990s,* edited by David Bourchier and John Legge, 115–127. Monash Papers on Southeast Asia 31. Clayton, Vic.: Monash University, Centre of South East Asian Studies, 1994.

———. "Patrimonialism and Military Rule in Indonesia." *World Politics* 31, no. 4 (July 1979): 571–87.

———. "Political Update 2002: Megawati's Holding Operation." In *Local Power and Politics in Indonesia: Decentralisation and Democratisation,* edited by Edward Aspinall and Greg Fealy, 15–34. Singapore: Institute of Southeast Asian Studies, 2003.

Dahm, Bernhard. *Sukarno and the Struggle for Indonesian Independence,* translated by Mary Somers Heidhues. Ithaca, N.Y.: Cornell University Press, 1969.
Davies, A. F. *The Human Element: Three Essays in Political Psychology.* Melbourne: McPhee Gribble/Penguin Books, 1988.
———. *Skills, Outlooks, and Passions: A Psychoanalytic Contribution to the Study of Politics.* Cambridge: Cambridge University Press, 1980.
Dick, H. W. "The Rise of a Middle Class and the Changing Concept of Equity in Indonesia: An Interpretation." *Indonesia* 39 (April 1985): 71–92.
Donald, David Herbert. *Lincoln.* London: Jonathan Cape, 1995.
Eccleston, Bernard, Michael Dawson, and Deborah McNamara, ed. *The Asia-Pacific Profile.* London: Routledge, 1998.
Echols, John M., and Hassan Shadily. *An Indonesian–English Dictionary.* Ithaca, N.Y.: Cornell University Press, 1989.
Edel, Leon. "Biography: A Manifesto." *Biography: An Interdisciplinary Quarterly* 1, no. 1 (Winter 1978): 1–3.
Ellis, Andrew. "The Indonesian Constitutional Transition: Conservatism or Fundamental Change?" *Singapore Journal of International & Comparative Law* 6 (2002): 116–53.
———. "MPR Annual Session 2002: An Initial Note." National Democratic Institute for International Affairs, Washington, D.C., August 12, 2002.
Elson, R. E. *Suharto: A Political Biography.* Cambridge: Cambridge University Press, 2001.
Fealy, Gregory John. "Abdurrahman Wahid and the al-Khidr Question." In *The Presidency of Abdurrahman Wahid: An Assessment after the First Year,* edited by Damien Kingsbury, 5–14. Annual Indonesia Lecture Series 23. Clayton, Vic.: Monash Asia Institute, 2001.
———. "Indonesian Politics, 1995–96: The Makings of a Crisis." In *Indonesia Assessment: Population and Human Resources,* edited by Gavin W. Jones and Terence H. Hull, 19–38. Singapore: Institute of Southeast Asian Studies, 1997.
———. "Islamic Politics: A Rising or Declining Force?" In *Indonesia: The Uncertain Transition,* edited by Damien Kingsbury and Arief Budiman, 119–36. Adelaide, Austral.: Crawford House, 2001.
———. "The 1994 NU Congress and Aftermath: Abdurrahman Wahid, *Suksesi,* and the Battle for Control of NU." In *Nahdlatul Ulama, Traditional Islam and Modernity in Indonesia,* edited by Greg Fealy and Greg Barton, 257–77. Clayton, Vic.: Monash Asia Institute, 1996.
———. "Parties and Parliament: Serving Whose Interests?" In *Indonesia Today: Challenges of History,* edited by Grayson Lloyd and Shannon Smith, 97–111. Singapore: Institute of Southeast Asian Studies, 2001.
———. "Ulama and Politics in Indonesia: A History of Nahdlatul Ulama, 1952–1967." Ph.D. diss., Monash University, Clayton, Victoria, 1998.
Federspiel, Howard M. *A Dictionary of Indonesian Islam.* Monographs in International Studies. Athens: Ohio University, Center for International Studies, 1995.
Feith, Herbert. *The Decline of Constitutional Democracy in Indonesia.* Ithaca, N.Y.: Cornell University Press, 1962.

———. "Dynamics of Guided Democracy." In *Indonesia,* edited by Ruth T. McVey, 309–409. New Haven, Conn.: Human Relations Area Files Press, 1967.

———. *The Indonesian Elections of 1955.* Modern Indonesia Project, Southeast Asia Program, Department of Far Eastern Studies. Ithaca, N.Y.: Cornell University, 1957.

Feith, Herbert, and Lance Castles, eds. *Indonesian Political Thinking, 1945–1965.* Ithaca, N.Y.: Cornell University Press, 1970.

Fischer, Louis. *The Story of Indonesia.* New York: Harper & Brothers, 1959.

Friedrich, Carl J. *Constitutional Government and Democracy: Theory and Practice in Europe and America.* Waltham, Mass.: Blaisdell Publishing, 1968.

Geertz, Clifford. "Person, Time, and Conduct in Bali." In *The Interpretation of Cultures: Selected Essays by Clifford Geertz,* 360–411. London: Hutchinson, 1975.

———. *The Religion of Java.* Chicago: University of Chicago Press, 1976.

Goodnow, Frank J. *Principles of Constitutional Government.* New York: Harper & Brothers, 1916. Quoted in Jackson and Rosberg, *Personal Rule in Black Africa.*

Greenstein, Fred I. "Can Personality and Politics Be Studied Systematically?" *Political Psychology* 13, no. 1 (1992): 105–28.

———. "The Impact of Personality on the End of the Cold War: A Counterfactual Analysis." *Political Psychology* 19, no. 1 (1998): 1–16.

Gutmann, David. *Reclaimed Powers: Toward a New Psychology of Men and Women in Later Life.* New York: Basic Books, 1987.

Hardjowirogo, Pak. *Sedjarah Wayang Purwa.* Djakarta: Balai Pustaka, 1965.

Harvey, Barbara S. *Permesta: Half a Rebellion.* Modern Indonesia Project, Southeast Asia Program, Department of Far Eastern Studies. Ithaca, N.Y.: Cornell University, 1977.

Hatta, Mohammad. "A Dictatorship Supported by Certain Groups." In *Indonesian Political Thinking 1945–1965*, edited by Herbert Feith and Lance Castles, 138–41. Ithaca, N.Y.: Cornell University Press, 1970.

Hauswedell, Peter Christian. "Sukarno: Radical or Conservative? Indonesian Politics 1964–5." *Indonesia* 15 (April 1973): 109–43.

Hefner, Robert W. *Civil Islam: Muslims and Democratization in Indonesia.* Princeton, N.J.: Princeton University Press, 2000.

Heine-Geldern, Robert. *Conceptions of State and Kingship in Southeast Asia.* Data Paper 18. Ithaca, N.Y.: Cornell University, Southeast Asia Program, 1956.

Hering, B. B. "Once More the Four Letters of Ir. Sukarno." In *Sukarno's Mentjapai Indonesia Merdeka,* edited and translated by B. B. Hering, v–xii. South East Asian Monograph Series 1. Townsville, Queensland: James Cook University, 1991.

Hering, Bob. *Mohammad Hoesni Thamrin and His Quest for Indonesian Nationhood, 1917–1941.* Stein, Neth.: Yayasan Kabar Seberang, 1996.

———. *Soekarno: Founding Father of Indonesia, 1901–1945.* Leiden, Neth.: KITLV Press, 2002.

Hidayah, Nur, ed. *Kontroversi Presiden Wanita.* Jakarta: PT Pabelan, 1998.

Hill, Hal. *The Indonesian Economy.* 2nd ed. Cambridge: Cambridge University Press, 2000.

———. *The Indonesian Economy in Crisis: Causes, Consequences and Lessons.* Sydney: Allen & Unwin, 1999.

Holmes, Richard. "Biographer's Footsteps." *International Review of Psycho-Analysis* 19 (1992): 1–8.
Ingleson, John. *Road to Exile: The Indonesian Nationalist Movement, 1927–1934.* Singapore: Heinemann, 1979.
Izarman, ed. *Bung Karno: Saya Berdarah Bali.* Denpasar, Bali: Penerbit Harian Umum Nusa Tenggara, 1998.
Jackson, Robert H., and Carl G. Rosberg. *Personal Rule in Black Africa: Prince, Autocrat, Prophet, Tyrant.* Berkeley: University of California Press, 1982.
Jalal, Ayesha. *Democracy and Authoritarianism in South Asia: A Contemporary and Historical Perspective.* Cambridge University Press, 1995.
Jaya, Wihana Kirana, and Howard Dick. "The Latest Crisis of Regional Autonomy in Historical Perspective." In *Indonesia Today: Challenges of History,* edited by Grayson Lloyd and Shannon Smith, 216–28. Singapore: Institute of Southeast Asian Studies, 2001.
Jenkins, David. *Suharto and His Generals: Indonesian Military Politics, 1975–1983.* Modern Indonesia Project Monograph Series. Ithaca, N.Y.: Cornell University, 1984.
Jones, Howard Palfrey. *Indonesia: The Possible Dream.* New York: Harcourt, Brace Jovanovich, 1971.
Kahin, Audrey R., and George McT. Kahin. *Subversion as Foreign Policy: The Secret Eisenhower and Dulles Debacle in Indonesia.* New York: New Press, 1995.
Kapuscinski, Ryszard. *The Emperor.* London: Pan Books, 1984.
Kaufmann, Walter, ed. *The Portable Nietzsche.* London: Penguin Books, 1976.
Keeler, Ward. *Javanese Shadow Plays, Javanese Selves.* Princeton, N.J.: Princeton University Press, 1987.
Kerrigan, William. "Life's Iamb: The Scansion of Late Creativity in the Culture of the Renaissance." In *Memory and Desire: Aging–Literature–Psychoanalysis,* edited by Kathleen Woodward and Murray M. Schwartz, 168–91. Bloomington: Indiana University Press, 1986.
King, Dwight Y. Introduction to *"White Book" on the 1992 General Election in Indonesia: Body for the Protection of the People's Political Rights Facing the 1992 General Election (BPHPR),* translated and introduced by Dwight Y. King. Modern Indonesia Project. Ithaca, N.Y.: Cornell University, 1994.
Labrousse, Pierre. "The Second Life of Bung Karno: Analysis of the Myth (1978–1981)." *Indonesia* 57 (April 1993): 175–96.
Laothamatas, Anek. "A Tale of Two Democracies: Conflicting Perceptions of Elections and Democracy in Thailand." In *The Politics of Elections in Southeast Asia,* edited by R. H. Taylor, 201–223. Washington, D.C.: Woodrow Wilson Center Press/Cambridge University Press, 1996.
Lasswell, Harold D. *Psychopathology and Politics.* New York: Viking Press, 1966.
Legge, J. D. *Central Authority and Regional Autonomy in Indonesia.* Itheca, N.Y.: Cornell University Press, 1961.
———. *Sukarno: A Political Biography.* 2nd ed. Sydney: Allen & Unwin, 1984.
Lejeune, Philippe. *On Autobiography,* edited by Paul John Eakin and translated by Katherine Leary. Minneapolis: University of Minnesota Press, 1989.

Lev, Daniel S. "Judicial Institutions and Legal Culture in Indonesia." In *Culture and Politics in Indonesia,* edited by Claire Holt, 246–318. Ithaca, N.Y.: Cornell University Press, 1972.

———. *The Transition to Guided Democracy: Indonesian Politics, 1957–1959.* Cornell University Modern Indonesia Project, Southeast Asia Program, Department of Far Eastern Studies. Ithaca, N.Y.: Cornell University, 1966.

Lichtheim, George. *Marxism: An Historical and Critical Study.* New York: Frederick A. Praeger, 1967.

Liddle, R. William. "Coercion, Co-optation, and the Management of Ethnic Relations in Indonesia." In *Government Policies and Ethnic Relations in Asia and the Pacific,* edited by Michael E. Brown and Sumit Ganguly, 273–319. Cambridge, Mass.: MIT Press, 1997.

———. "Indonesia's Democratic Opening." *Government and Opposition* 34, no. 1 (Winter 1999): 94–99.

———. "Indonesia's Democratic Transition: Playing by the Rules." In *The Architecture of Democracy,* edited by Andrew Reynolds, 373–99. Oxford: Oxford University Press, 2001.

———. "Indonesia in 1987: The New Order at the Height of Its Power." *Asian Survey* 28, no. 2 (February 1988): 180–91.

———. "Indonesia's Unexpected Failure of Leadership." In *The Politics of Post-Suharto Indonesia,* edited by Adam Schwarz and Jonathan Paris, 16–39. New York: Council of Foreign Relations Press, 1999.

———. "The Middle Class and New Order Legitimacy: A Response to Dan Lev." In *The Politics of Middle Class Indonesia,* edited by Richard Tanter and Kenneth Young, 49–52. Clayton, Vic.: Monash University, Centre of South East Asian Studies, 1990.

———. "Soeharto's Indonesia: Personal Rule and Political Institutions." In *Leadership and Culture in Indonesian Politics,* 15–36. Sydney: Allen & Unwin, 1996.

Lijphart, Arend. *Democracy in Plural Societies: A Comparative Exploration.* New Haven, Conn.: Yale University Press, 1980.

———. "Introduction." In *Parliamentary versus Presidential Government,* edited by Arend Lijphart, 1–27. Oxford: Oxford University Press, 1992.

———. *Patterns of Democracy: Government Forms and Performance in Thirty-six Countries.* New Haven, Conn.: Yale University Press, 1999.

———. "Presidentialism and Majoritarian Democracy: Theoretical Observations." In *The Failure of Presidential Democracy: Comparative Perspectives,* edited by Juan J. Linz and Arturo Valenzuela, 1:91–105. Baltimore: Johns Hopkins University Press, 1994.

Lindsey, Timothy. "Constitutional Law and the Presidential Crisis in Jakarta: Some Preliminary Observations." Work in Progress paper, Asian Law Centre, University of Melbourne, 2001.

———. "The Criminal State: *Premanisme* and the New Indonesia." In *Indonesia Today,* ed. Grayson Lloyd and Shannon Smith, 283–97. Singapore: Institute of Southeast Asian Studies, 2001.

———. "From Rule of Law to Law of Rulers—to Reformation?" In *Indonesia: Law and Society,* edited by Timothy Lindsey, 11–20. Sydney: Federation Press, 1999.

———. "Indonesian Constitutional Reform: Muddling Towards Democracy." *Singapore Journal of International & Comparative Law* 6 (2002): 244–301.

———. "Indonesia's *Negara Hukum*: Walking the Tightrope to the Rule of Law." In *Reformasi: Crisis and Change in Indonesia,* edited by Arief Budiman, Barbara Hatley, and Damien Kingsbury, 363–83. Clayton, Vic.: Monash Asia Institute, 1999.

———. "Indonesia's New Anti-terrorism Law: Damned If You Do, Damned If You Don't." Work in Progress paper, Asia Law Centre, University of Melbourne.

———. "An Overview of Indonesian Law." In *Indonesia: Law and Society,* edited by Timothy Lindsey, 1–10. Sydney: Federation Press, 1999.

Lintner, Bertil. *Aung San Suu Kyi and Burma's Unfinished Renaissance*. Working Paper 64, Centre of Southeast Asian Studies, Monash University. Clayton, Vic.: Monash University, 1990.

Linz, Juan J. "Presidential or Parliamentary Democracy: Does It Make a Difference?" In *Failure of Presidential Democracy,* edited by Juan J. Linz and Arturo Valenzuela, 1: 3–87. Baltimore: Johns Hopkins University Press, 1994.

Little, Graham. "On Followers and Friends." In *Friendship: Being Ourselves with Others.* Melbourne: Text Publishing, 1993.

———. "The Two Narcissisms: Comparing Hawke and Keating." In *Political Lives,* edited by Judith Brett, 16–27. Sydney: Allen & Unwin, 1997.

Lowry, Bob. "East Timor: An Overview of Political Developments." In *Indonesia in Transition: Social Aspects of Reformasi and Crisis,* edited by Chris Manning and Peter van Diermen, 91–108. Singapore: Institute of Southeast Asian Studies, 2000.

Mackie, Jamie. "Inevitable or Avoidable? Interpretations of the Collapse of Parliamentary Democracy." In *Democracy in Indonesia: 1950s and 1990s,* edited by David Bourchier and John Legge, 26–38. Monash Papers on Southeast Asia 31. Clayton, Vic.: Monash University, Centre of Southeast Asian Studies, 1994.

Mackie, J. A. C. *Konfrontasi: The Indonesia–Malaysia Dispute, 1963–1966.* Kuala Lumpur: Oxford University Press, 1974.

Mackie, Jamie, and Andrew MacIntyre. "Politics." In *Indonesia's New Order: The Dynamics of Socio-economic Transformation,* edited by Hal Hill, 1–53. Sydney: Allen & Unwin, 1994.

MacIntyre, Andrew. *Business and Politics in Indonesia.* Sydney: Allen & Unwin, 1991.

MacIntyre, Andrew, and Budy P. Resosudarmo. "Survey of Recent Developments." *Bulletin of Indonesian Economic Studies* 39, no. 2 (2003): 133–56.

McDonald, Hamish. *Suharto's Indonesia.* Melbourne: Fontana Books, 1980.

McIntyre, Angus. "The 'Greater Indonesia' Idea of Nationalism in Malaya and Indonesia." *Modern Asian Studies* 7, no. 1 (1973): 75–83.

———. *In Search of Megawati Sukarnoputri.* Working paper. Clayton, Vic.: Monash Asia Institute, 1997.

———. "In Sukarno's Time: An Exploration of His View of History." In *Sukarno,* edited by John Legge, 24–29. Annual Indonesia Lecture Series 24. Clayton, Vic.: Monash Asia Institute, 2002.

———. "Introduction." In *Aging and Political Leadership,* edited by Angus McIntyre, 1–12. Melbourne: Oxford University Press, 1988.

———. *Soeharto's Composure: Considering the Biographical and Autobiographical Accounts*. Working paper. Clayton, Vic.: Monash Asia Institute, 1996.

———. "Sukarno Kesepian: His Desolation and the Politics of Being Central." Paper presented at the Biennial Conference of the Asian Studies Association of Australia, University of Melbourne, July 3–5, 2000.

McLeod, Ross H. "Government–Business Relations in Soeharto's Indonesia." In *Reform and Recovery in East Asia: The Role of the State and Economic Enterprises*, edited by Peter Drysdale, 146–68. London: Routledge, 2000.

McVey, Ruth T. "The Beamtenstaat in Indonesia." In *Interpreting Indonesian Politics: Thirteen Contributions to the Debate*, edited by Benedict Anderson and Audrey Kahin, 84–91. Modern Indonesia Project, Southeast Asia Program, Department of Far Eastern Studies. Ithaca, N.Y.: Cornell University, 1982.

Mietzner, Marcus. "Between *Pesantren* and Palace: Nahdlatul Ulama and Its Role in the Transition." In *The Fall of Soeharto,* edited by Geoff Forrester and R. J. May, 179–99. Singapore: Select Books, 1999.

———. "The First 100 Days of the Abdurrahman Presidency: An Evaluation." In *Indonesia: The Uncertain Transition,* edited by Damien Kingsbury and Arief Budiman, 329–48. Adelaide, Austral.: Crawford House Publishing, 2001.

———. "Nationalism and Islamic Politics: Political Islam in the Post-Suharto Era." In *Reformasi: Crisis and Change in Indonesia,* edited by Arief Budiman, Barbara Hatley, and Damien Kingsbury, 173–99. Clayton, Vic.: Monash Asia Institute, 1999.

———. "The 1999 General Session: Wahid, Megawati and the Fight for the Presidency." In *Indonesia in Transition: Social Aspects of Reformasi and Crisis*, edited by Chris Manning and Peter van Diermen, 39–57. Singapore: Institute of Southeast Asian Studies, 2000.

Miller, John. *Mikhail Gorbachev and the End of Soviet Power.* London: MacMillan, 1993.

Modelski, George, ed. *The New Emerging Forces: Documents on the Ideology of Indonesian Foreign Policy.* Canberra: Australian National University, Research School of Pacific Studies, Department of International Relations, 1963.

Mohamad, Goenawan. "Bung Karno." In *Sidelines: Writings from Tempo,* translated by Jennifer Lindsey, 185–87. Melbourne: Hyland House, in association with Monash Asia Institute, 1994.

Mortimer, Rex. *Indonesian Communism under Sukarno: Ideology and Politics, 1959–1965.* Ithaca, N.Y.: Cornell University Press, 1974.

Mrazek, Rudolf. *Sjahrir: Politics and Exile in Indonesia.* Ithaca, N.Y.: Cornell University, Studies on Southeast Asia, 1994.

Mujani, Saiful, and R. William Liddle. "Indonesia's Approaching Elections: Politics, Islam, and Public Opinion." *Journal of Democracy* 15, no. 1 (2004): 109–23, http://0-muse.jhu.edu.alpha2.latrobe.edu.au/journals/journal_of_democracy/v015/15.1mujani.pdf.

Mulder, Neils. *Mysticism and Everyday Life in Contemporary Java: Cultural Persistence and Change.* Singapore: Singapore University Press, 1980.

Nasution, Adnan Buyung. *The Aspiration for Constitutional Government in Indonesia: A Socio-legal Study of the Indonesian Konstituante, 1956–1959.* Jakarta: Pustaka Sinar Harapan, 1992.

———. "Human Rights and the Konstituante Debates of 1956–59." In *Democracy in Indonesia: 1950s and 1990s,* edited by David Bourchier and John Legge, 43–49. Monash Papers on Southeast Asia 31. Clayton, Vic.: Monash University, Centre of Southeast Asian Studies, 1994.

Nishihara, Masashi. *The Japanese and Sukarno's Indonesia: Tokyo–Jakarta Relations, 1951–1966.* Honolulu: University Press of Hawaii, 1976.

O'Rourke, Kevin. *Reformasi: The Struggle for Power in Post-Soeharto Indonesia.* Sydney: Allen & Unwin, 2002.

Paget, Roger K. "Introduction." In *Indonesia Accuses! Soekarno's Defence Oration in the Political Trial of 1930,* edited and translated by Roger K. Paget, xvii–lxxx. Kuala Lumpur: Oxford University Press, 1975.

Palfrey Jones, Howard. *Indonesia: The Possible Dream.* New York: Harcourt Brace Jovanovich, 1971.

Phillips, Adam. "On Composure." In *On Kissing, Tickling, and Being Bored,* 40–45. London: Faber and Faber, 1993.

Pringgodigdo, A. K. *The Office of President in Indonesia as Defined in the Three Constitutions in Theory and Practice,* translated by Alexander Brotherton. Modern Indonesia Project Translation Series, Ithaca, N.Y.: Cornell University 1957.

Przeworski, Adam, Michael E. Alvarez, Jose Antonio Cheibub, and Fernando Limongi. *Democracy and Development: Political Institutions and Well-Being in the World, 1950–1990.* Cambridge: Cambridge University Press, 2000.

Ray, David J. "Survey of Recent Developments." *Bulletin of Indonesian Economic Studies* 39, no. 3 (2003): 245–70.

Reeve, David. *Golkar of Indonesia: An Alternative to the Party System.* Singapore: Oxford University Press, 1985.

Reid, Anthony. *The Indonesian National Revolution: 1945–1950.* Melbourne: Longman, 1974.

———. "War, Peace and the Burden of History in Aceh." Working Paper 1, Asia Research Institute, National University of Singapore, June 2003. www.ari.nus.edu.sg/docs/wps/wps03_001.pdf.

Ricklefs, M. C. *A History of Modern Indonesia Since c. 1200.* 3rd ed. London: Palgrave, 2001.

Robison, Richard. "Organising the Transition: Indonesian Politics in 1993/94." In *Indonesia Assessment 1994: Finance as a Key Sector in Indonesia's Development,* edited by Ross H. McLeod, 49–74. Singapore: Institute of Southeast Asian Studies, 1995.

Robson, Stuart. *Javanese Grammar for Students.* Monash Papers on Southeast Asia 26. Clayton, Vic.: Monash University, 1992.

Roth, Guenther. "Personal Rulership, Patrimonialism, and Empire-Building in the New States." *World Politics* 20 (January 1968): 194–206.

Sahgal, Nayantara. *Indira Gandhi: Her Road to Power.* London: MacDonald, 1983.

Sartori, Giovanni. *Democratic Theory.* New York: Frederick A. Praeger, 1967.
Schram, Stuart. *Mao Tse-tung.* Harmondsworth, Eng.: Penguin Books, 1968.
Schwarz, Adam. *A Nation in Waiting: Indonesia in the 1990s.* Sydney: Allen & Unwin, 1994.
——. *A Nation in Waiting*: *Indonesia's Search for Stability.* Boulder: Westview Press, 2000.
Sen, Krishna. "The Mega Factor in Indonesian Politics: A New President or a New Kind of Presidency." In *Women in Indonesia: Gender, Equity and Development,* edited by Kathryn Robinson and Sharon Bessell, 13–27. Singapore: Institute of Southeast Asian Studies, 2002.
Seth, Sanjay. "'Nehruvian Socialism,' 1927–1937: Nationalism, Marxism and the Pursuit of Modernity." *Alternatives* 18 (1993): 453–73.
Sherlock, Stephen. *The 2004 Indonesian Elections: How the System Works and What the Parties Stand For* (Canberra: Centre for Democratic Institutions, 2004), 7, www.cdi.anu.edu.au/indonesia/indonesia_downloads/Sherlock_Election%202004.pdf.
Shils, Edward. "The Fortunes of Constitutional Government in the Political Development of the New States." In his *Center and Periphery: Essays in Macrosociology.* Chicago: University of Chicago Press, 1975.
Shore, Miles F. "Henry VIII and the Crisis of Generativity." *Journal of Interdisciplinary History* 2 (1972): 359–90.
Siegel, James T. *A New Criminal Type in Jakarta: Counter-revolution Today.* Durham, N.C.: Duke University Press, 1998.
Smith, Denis Mack. *Mussolini.* New York: Alfred A. Knopf, 1982.
Smith, Martin. *Burma: Insurgency and the Politics of Ethnicity.* London: Zed Books, 1991.
Sneddon, James Neil. *Indonesian Reference Grammar.* Sydney: Allen & Unwin, 1996.
Stange, Paul. "The Logic of Rasa in Java." *Indonesia* 38 (October 1984): 113–34.
Strassler, Karen. "Currency and Fingerprints: Authentic Reproductions and Political Communication in Indonesia's 'Reform Era.'" *Indonesia* 70 (October 2000): 71–82.
Sukatmo, Adriana Elisabeth, Ganewati Wuryandari, and M. Riza Sihbudi. *PDI dan Prospek Pembangunan Politik.* Jakarta: PT Gramedia Widiasarana Indonesia, 1991.
Supriatma, A. Made Tony, ed. *1996: Tahun Kekerasan Potret Pelanggaran HAM di Indonesia.* Jakarta: Yayasan Lembaga Bantuan Hukum Indonesia, 1997.
Suripto. *Bung Karno: Hari-Hari Terakhirnya.* Surabaya, Indon.: PT "Grip," 1978.
Suryadinata, Leo. *Elections and Politics in Indonesia.* Singapore: Institute of Southeast Asian Studies, 2002.
Suu Kyi, Aung San. *Freedom from Fear and Other Writings,* edited by Michael Aris. London: Penguin Books, 1991.
Tanter, Richard. "The Totalitarian Ambition: Intelligence and Security Agencies in Indonesia." In *State and Civil Society in Indonesia,* edited by Arief Budiman, 213–88. Papers on Southeast Asia 22. Clayton, Vic.: Monash University, Centre of Southeast Asian Studies, 1990.
Teeuw, A. *Modern Indonesian Literature.* The Hague: Martinus Nijhoff, 1979.

van Dijk, Kees. *A Country in Despair: Indonesia between 1997 and 2000.* Leiden: KITLV Press, 2002.
van Klinken, Gerry. "Sukarno's Daughter Takes Over Indonesia's Democrats." *Inside Indonesia* (March 1994): 2–4.
Vatikiotis, Michael R. J. *Indonesian Politics under Suharto: Order, Development, and Pressure for Change.* New York: Routledge, 1993.
Vickers, Adrian. *Bali: A Paradise Created.* Melbourne: Penguin Books, 1989.
Walicki, Andrzej. *Marxism and the Leap to the Kingdom of Freedom: The Rise and Fall of the Communist Utopia.* Stanford, Calif.: Stanford University Press, 1995.
Ward, Ken. *The 1971 Election in Indonesia: An East Java Case Study.* Papers on Southeast Asia 2. Clayton, Vic.: Monash University, Centre of Southeast Asian Studies, 1974.
Warren, Carol. *The Bureaucratisation of Local Government in Indonesia.* Working Paper. Centre of Southeast Asian Studies. Clayton, Vic.: Monash University, 1990.
Willner, Ann Ruth. *The Spellbinders: Charismatic Political Leadership.* New Haven, Conn.: Yale University Press, 1984.
Winnicott, D. W. "The Capacity to Be Alone." *International Journal of Psycho-Analysis* 39 (1958): 416–20.
Wolpert, Stanley. *Zulfi Bhutto of Pakistan: His Life and Times.* New York: Oxford University Press, 1993.
Yayasan Untuk Indonesia. *Tragedi Megawati: Revisi Politik Massa di Indonesia.* Yogyakarta: Tarawang, 2000.
Zhisui, Li. *The Private Life of Chairman Mao: The Memoirs of Mao's Personal Physician.* London: Chatto & Windus, 1994.
Zifcak, Spencer. "'But a Shadow of Justice': Political Trials in Indonesia." In *Indonesia: Law and Society,* edited by Timothy Lindsey, 355–66. Sydney: Federation Press, 1999.

Index

Abdulgani, Roeslan, 156
Abdullah, Taufik, 38–40
Abdul Rahman, Tunku, 26
Aceh: attitude of Megawati toward, 213–14, 226; and Free Aceh Movement, 227, 245, 247; and "Humanitarian Pause," 227; PDIP vote drops in, 262; presidential instruction authorizing military operations in, 227–28, 244; regional parties absent in, 264; special autonomy legislation and, 228, 244; and state of emergency, 245; Adams, Cindy, 104, 105, 106, 111, 112, 119
Agung, Anak Agung Gde, 47; arrest of, 46
Aidit, D. N., 49, 52
Ali, Maulana Mohamed, 72
Ali, Shaukat, 72
Amat Idris, Mbok, 110
Anak Desa: Biografi Presiden Soeharto (Roeder), 110, 111, 118
Anti-Duhring (Frederick Engels), 81, 89n5
Anwar, Rosihan, 36–38, 47
Aquino, Corazon, 141, 166
Arismunandar, Wismoyo, 162
Army Staff and Command College, 116, 122n67

Aslan, Ana: treats Sukarno, 66
Aspinall, Edward, 96, 166, 167
Association of Indonesian Islamic Intellectuals, 156, 162; and Golkar, 193; Habibie's leadership of, 167; 171, 172, 184
Atmopawiro, 110, 114
Auden, W. H., 61
Aung San Oo, U, 141
Aung San Suu Kyi, 139–41; attitude to fear of, 164; and criticism of Ne Win, 167; introduction of to President Sukarno, 164
Aung San, U, 139
Autobiography (Otobiografi) as Related to G. Dwipayana and Ramadhan K. H. (Soeharto), 104, 110, 115, 117, 118
Awami League, 139–40

Badan Pendukung Sukarnoisme (BPS). *See* Body of Support for Sukarnoism
Badan Penyelidik Usaha Persiapan Kemerdekaan Indonesia (BPKI). *See* Committee for the Study of Preparation for Independence
Bangladesh, 139–40
Bank Negara Indonesia. *See* Indonesian State Bank

Bantjeuj Prison, 40
Belo, Carlos, 204
Bendera Sudah Saya Kibarkan (Megawati), 156
Beratha, Dewa Made, 194
Bhutto, Benazir, 140–41
Bhutto, Murtaza, 141
Bhutto, Shah Nawaz, 141
Bhutto, Zulfikar Ali, 140
Bimantoro, Surojo, 233, 234
biography, political: of founding fathers, 36–40; and history, 4; interior time in, 5n9; life and times tradition in, 3; thematic approach to, 3
Body of Support for Sukarnoism, 45
Bondan, Molly, 90n33
Bourchier, David, 8, 100, 224
Bowo, Fauzi, 244
British Embassy: burning of, 27–28
Brunei Revolt, 26
Bucho Cabinet, 10
Buchori, Mochtar, 197
Bulog, 97, 227, 228
bureaucracy, 94, 95

Catholic Party, 152
Central Axis, 208–9, 215–17, 223, 225, 227
Central Indonesian National Committee, 10, 11; working committee of, 11–12
Charter of Total Struggle, 16
Chatik, Bachtar Oscha, 205
Chehabi, H. E., 101
Chiang, Kai-shek: and massacre of Shanghai workers, 72
Chowdhury, Najma, 140
Cikini Affair, 142–43
Citra Lamtoro Gung Persada, 111
Cohen, Margot, 154
Committee for the Preparation of Indonesian Independence, 9–10; and election of Sukarno and Hatta president and vice-president, 10
Committee for the Study of Preparation for Independence, 6, 7, 8, 10

Congress of Indonesian Moslems, 201, 206
Congress Party, 139
Constituent Assembly, 14, 15, 130; and request to adopt 1945 Constitution, 18; dissolution of, 19; and Jakarta Charter, 134
Constitution, 1945, 3, 6–12 130, 166, 257, 259n18; and adoption by decree, 1, 18–19; article 8 of, 223, 227; article 28 of, 8; as false friend to constitutional rule, 95; first amendment of, 1, 4, 130–31, 218; flexible nature of, 30; form of government envisaged by, 6; fourth amendment of, 133, 134; infamous loophole of, 128; official elucidation of, 8; second amendment of, 131–32, 227; third amendment of, 132–33; transitional provisions in, 9–10
Constitution, 1949: federal character of, 12–13; human rights provisions in, 13
Constitution, 1950: abrogation of, 19; human rights provisions in, 13; and provision for unitary state, 13; and relationship between cabinet and parliament, 13; Supomo's contribution to, 13
Constitutional Court, 133; and finding legislation unconstitutional, 262
constitutional rule, 1, 127, 130; and damaging legacy of personal rule, 254; defined, 2–3; Habibie's contribution to, 135; and limited value commitment of recent presidents, 254–55; prospects for, 4; and succession, 128, 129, 251–53, 258n2; taking hold of, 254; threatening of by weak economy, 254; underpinning of by amended 1945 Constitution, 255
Council of Regional Representation, 132, 133, 256, 261, 262, 264
Crescent and Star Party, 193, 208, 263

criminal code: and lese-majesty law, 172, 248, 256
Crouch, Harold, 68, 93, 96, 97, 100

Da Costa, P. B., 197
Dahuri, Rochim, 233
Damayanti, Indira, 243
Darmaatmadja, Julius, 171
Darusman, Marzuki, 233
Daryanto, Nico, 152, 153
Daryatmo, 108
Davies, A. F., 57n29
Dekon. *See* Economic Declaration
democracy. *See* middle class, democracy
Democrat Party, 263
Dewan Perwakilan Daerah (DPD). *See* Council of Regional Representation
Dewan Perwakilan Rakyat (DPR). *See* People's Representative Council.
Dewi, Ratna Sari, 54, 146, 147
Dick, Howard, 98
district (administrative unit), 15, 129, 254
Djajusman, Sunarso, 197
Djalil, Matori Abdul, 215, 247
Djarot, Eros, 189n13, 224, 242
Djiwandono, J. Soedjati, 207
Djuanda, Ir: death of, 28; and the economy, 26, 27; as leader of business cabinet, 16, 17;
Djunaedi, H. Mahbub, 37–38
Dullah, 143
Dwipayana, G., 112, 119
Dwitunggal. *See* leadership, political

East Timor: referendum on, 211–13; result in, 214
Economic Declaration, 26
economy: under Guided Democracy, 48–49; under the New Order, 98–99; and severe downturn of 1997, 127, 180–84; since 2000, 127, 254
Effendy, Djohan, 225

elections: of 1971, 94; of 1977, 94; of 1982, 94; of 1987, 94, 151, 154; of 1992, 94, 154–55; of 1997, 171–75; of 1999, 129,130, 202–7; of 2004, 261–65; and electoral systems, 203, 204, 261–62; and *Golput*, 171, 174, 175, 178n57; for governor of Jakarta, 241–44; for parliament and constituent assembly (1955), 14; for president (1998), 184; for president (1999), 214–18; for regional parliaments (1957), 18
Ellis, Andrew, 132
Elson, R. E., 97
"Europe: Its Condition" (Mazzini), 66

Fals, Iwan, 154
Fatimah, 107, 110
Fatmawati, 141–42, 148
Fealy, Greg, 74, 207, 226, 263, 264
Feith, Herbert, 13, 14, 44
Fellinger, Dr., 51
Fischer, Louis, 66
"Freedom from Fear" (Aung San Suu Kyi), 164

Gandhi, Indira, 139
Gandhi, Mahatma, 72
Garcia Lorca, Federico, 112
Geertz, Clifford, 114
generation of 1945, 95; as all *brengsek* (rotten), 113
Gerakan Aceh Merdeka (GAM). *See* Aceh
Gie, Kwik Kian, 176n21, 197, 205, 216
Godean, 107
Golkar, 94, 152, 154, 155, 157, 158, 162, 175, 180, 192, 203, 217, 224, 227, 229, 235; and 1999 election results, 207; and vote drops in 2004, 263
Golongan Karya. *See* Golkar
Gombong, 108
gotong rojong cabinet. *See* Sukarno, mutual help cabinet of

Gotta, Salvatore, 67
Goulart, Joao, 86
"Grey Saturday," 168, 185, 186, 193; and stalled investigation, 242; victims of paid off, 242; Guided Democracy: as authoritarian system, 25; and centrifugal forces, 44; and the economy, 26, 48–49; and NASAKOM, 76; as system of personal rule, 2, 29–31
Gumelar, Agum, 158, 161, 232–33
Gusmao, Xanana, 205, 212
Gutmann, David, 77n2, 175n14

Habibie, B. J., 1, 4, 158, 162, 172, 182, 209; ability of queried by Soeharto, 188; and his accountability speech, 217; and allowing referendum to East Timorese, 211–12, 214; comparison with Gorbachev, 135, 192; and Golkar, 193; and high opinion of Soeharto, 122n65; as New Order *wunderkind*, 192; and succession, 252; as vice-president, 128; as vice-presidential candidate, 183; withdrawal of from presidential race, 129
Hakim, Arief Rahman, 186
Hamengku Buwono II, Sultan, 108
Hamengku Buwono IX, Sultan, 117; and misgivings about Soeharto, 124n77; as vice-president, 128
Hamengku Buwono X, Sultan, 204
Hamid, Sultan: arrest of, 46
Hamid, Syarwan, 164, 167, 194; cravenness of, 184; as minister in Habibie cabinet, 193
Hamka, 148
Hanafi, A. M., 65
Hardjono, Budi, 156, 157, 194, 203, 204, 209
Hardjowijono, Pak, 108
Harmoko, 162, 180; and calling on Soeharto to step down, 187; and threatening president with impeachment, 188

Hartini, 54, 142, 146, 147, 156
Hartogh, C., 81
Hartono, 162, 172, 182
Hartono, Dimyati, 197
Hasan, Bob, 185
Hasina, Sheikh, 139–40
Hasjim, Kiai Haji Abdul Wahid, 157
Hassan, Hassan Gamal Ahmad, 148
Hatta, Mohammad: and announcement of Proclamation X, 11; as constitutionalist, 7; formation of presidential cabinets of, 12; and kidnapping by youth, 64; letter of to Sukarno, 46–47; and opposition to Yamin's fatherland concept, 9; and permitting formation of political parties, 12; as RUSI premier, 12; support of by regionalists, 15; as vice-president, 14
Haz, Hamzah, 134, 217, 230, 248; dismissal of from cabinet, 223; election of as vice-president, 235; and saying only Moslem male eligible to be president, 201
Hegel, Georg Wilhelm Friedrich, 87, 88
Hendropriyono, 158, 161
Henry Dunant Centre, 245
Horta, Jose Ramos, 212
Humardani, Sudjono, 117
Hussein, Colonel, 45

Ikatan Cendiakawan Muslimin Indonesia (ICMI). *See* Association of Indonesian Islamic Intellectuals
Indonesia Muda. *See Young Indonesia*.
Indonesian Communist Party, 14, 49, 65, 262; attitude to Malaysia of, 27; in Guided Democracy, 25; and Land Reform and Crop Sharing Laws, 74–75; massacre of members of, 2, 53, 88, 99, 101; and NASAKOM, 72–76; pressuring Sukarno of, 26; student front of, 75
Indonesian Democracy Party, 94, 151–52, 154, 161, 162, 173, 174,

175, 192; attack on headquarters of, 167; election candidates rejected by, 168; government interference in; 155–58; and Medan Congress (1993), 155–56; and Medan Congress (1996), 166; and rejection of Soeharto's accountability speech, 185; and Sanur Congress, 194–99; twenty-fifth anniversary of, 182. *See also* Indonesian Democracy Party of Struggle

Indonesian Democracy Party of Struggle, 194, 204, 215, 217, 224, 225, 227; rebellion of Jakarta branches of, 243; and over-representation of non-Moslem candidates, 206; and Semarang Congress, 224; and victory in 1999 parliamentary elections, 207; and vote drops in 2004, 262–63

Indonesian Democratic Union Party, 172

Indonesian Electoral Commission, 264

Indonesian history: concept of historical necessity in, 33, 81–82; "history of the present" in, 3, 251; ironies of, 130, 135; role of individuals in, 135; from Sukarno's perspective, 81–89; turning points of, 2, 18, 251, 258

Indonesian Moslems' Party, 94

Indonesian National Party, 14, 43, 72, 94, 151, 152

Indonesian National Party of the Marhaen Masses, 205

Indonesian Party, 43

Indonesian People's Assembly, 166

Indonesian Publishers' Association, 106

Indonesian Socialist Party, 14, 46

Indonesian State Bank: and Texmaco, 225

Indonesian Workers' Welfare Union, 165

Ingleson, John, 36–38

Interim People's Consultative Assembly, 26, 30, 53, 93, 146, 181

International Monetary Fund (IMF), 26, 181, 185–86

Irian Jaya: Megawati opposes separatists of, 226, 227; and special autonomy legislation, 228. *See also* Irian, West; Papua

Irian, West: incorporation of, 44, 83–85; vote in UN on, 17; Islam: and attitudes of modernists to Megawati, 167, 184; and boarding schools, 162–63, 172–73; and Central Axis, 208–9; and devout Moslems, 152, 201, 207, 255, 263, 265; and division between modernists and syncretists, 183–84; and female president, 201; and Megawati as syncretist, 144–45; 177n39, 206; and modernist Islam and Amien Rais, 182; and anger vented at Christians and Chinese, 171; and 1999 parliamentary elections, 202–7; and 2004 parliamentary elections, 263–65; and Sukarno, 144–45; and traditionalist Islam and Abdurrahman Wahid, 182; and under-representation of Moslems on PDIP candidate lists, 206

Ismail, Chaeruddin, 234

Italian Fascist Party, 67

Jakarta Charter, 7, 18–19, 133–34

Jakarta Post, 207, 224, 262

Jenkins, David, 118

Jones, Howard, 104, 105

Justice Party, 216. *See also* Justice and Prosperity Party

Justice and Prosperity Party, 263–64; and resemblance to Communist Party, 264

kabupaten. *See* second-level region; district

Kakiailatu, Toeti, 150n49

Kalimantan, Central: and massacre in Sampit, 229–30

Kalimantan, West: Dayaks and Madurese in, 205; Kalla, M. Jusuf: dismissed from cabinet, 224
Kartasasmita, Ginanjar, 183
Kartoredjo, 107, 108, 110
Kautsky, Karl, 82
Keibuho, 116
Kemusuk, 107, 108, 111
Kertorejo, 108
Kertosudiro, 110, 114
kesepian. *See* Sukarno
Kiemas, Taufik, 173; and alleged links to Communist Party, 161; management of petrol stations of, 151; and running for parliament, 152, 155; and suspicion of corruption, 240
KKN (Korupsi, Kolusi, Nepotisme; Corruption, Collusion, Nepotism), 240
Komite Nasional Indonesia Pusat (KNIP). *See* Central Indonesian National Committee
Kompas, 38, 216
Kongres Umat Islam Indonesia. *See* Congress of Indonesian Moslems
Konstituante. See Constituent Assembly
Kopkamtib (Komando Operasi Keamanan dan Ketertiban). *See* Operations Command to Restore Security and Order
kotamadya. *See* municipality
Krenz, Egon, 135, 192
Kromodiryo, Mbah, 110, 114
Kuomintang, 72
Kusumaatmadja, Sarwono, 233

Labrousse, Pierre, 147
Lasswell, Harold D., 57n34
laws: 1/1957, 15, 29, 129, 254; 19/1964, 30; 13/1965, 30; 5/1969, 30, 169; 5/1979, 129; 22/1999, 129, 254; 25/1999, 129, 254; 26/2000, 247; 12 and 22/2003, 261, 262; 15 and 16/2003, 247

leadership, political: as *dwitunggal* (two-in-one), 14; as female, 139–41, 214; nostalgia for, 4; as strong, 4
Lenin, V. I., 82, 83, 89
lese-majesty law. *See* criminal code
Lev, Daniel, 16, 48
Liddle, R. William, 98, 99, 130, 253
Lincoln, Abraham, 84, 88
Lindsey, Timothy, 8, 132, 134, 230
Linz, Juan J., 101
Litaay, Alex, 185, 197, 203
London Agreeement, 27
Lopa, Baharuddin, 233; Lorca, Gabriel Garcia, 112
Lubis, Colonel Zulkifli, 45

Ma'arif, Syafii, 230
MacIntyre, Andrew, 94, 95, 96, 103, 113
Mackie, Jamie, 16, 18, 25, 27, 49, 68, 94, 95, 96, 103, 113
Madjid, Nurcolish: and urging of Soeharto to resign, 187–88
Maharani, Puan, 151
Majelis Permusyawaratan Rakyat (MPR). *See* People's Consultative Assembly
Majelis Rakyat Indonesia. *See* Indonesian People's Assembly
Majelis Ulama Indonesia. *See* Religious Scholars' Council of Indonesia
Malaysia: as British neocolonial project, 85; breaking commercial and financial relations with, 28; confrontation toward, 26, 44; and landings at Pontian and Labis, 68
Malik, Adam, 38; as vice-president, 128
Maluku: violence between Christians and Moslems in, 205; Megawati at a loss on, 226
Mangunkusumo, Tjipto, 41, 43
Manila Accord, 27
Manila Conference, 85
Marriot Hotel, 247
Martov, L., 89
Marx, Karl, 82

Marzuki, Tommy, 147
Masagung, 107
Masjumi, 14, 45, 46; banning of, 29,
May 26 Decrees, 26
Mazzini, Giuseppe, 66–67
Memet, Yogie, 155, 157–58, 161, 164, 167, 168, 194
Merdeka, 38
middle class: as beneficiaries of destruction of Communist Party, 265; changing fortunes of, 98; and democracy, 127, 135, 253; and "pariah entrepreneurs", 99; and pribumi businesses, 99; and Sino-Indonesian cronies, 98
Moerdani, General Benny: as minister of defense, 155; relationship with Soeharto of, 123n73; and Sukarno, 144
Mohamad, Goenawan, 36, 150n49, 216
Mortimer, Rex, 68
Muhammadiyah, 134, 172, 229
Mujibur Rahman, Sheikh, 139–40
municipality, 15, 29, 129, 254
Murba Party, 45
murders, state-sponsored, 119
Murtopo, Lieutenant General Ali, 108, 109
Mussolini, Benito, 67
My Friend the Dictator (Adams), 104

Nababan, Panda, 242
Nahdlatul Ulama, 14, 72, 74, 76, 94, 134, 172–73, 175, 188, 192, 216, 225, 229; paramilitary corps of, Banser, 74,76
NASAKOM. *See* unity of nationalist, religious, and communist forces
Nasser, Gamal Abdel, 84
Nasution, Adnan Bujung, 156
Nasution, A. H., 16, 46, 51; role of in Guided Democracy, 25, 31; and being kicked upstairs, 31
Nasution, Novianti, 197
Nathan, S. R., 205

National Awakening Party, 192, 208, 215, 216, 217, 218, 228, 231, 263
National Democratic Institute for International Affairs, 204
National Mandate Party, 193, 216, 263, 264
"Nationalism, Islam and Marxism" (Sukarno), 72, 73
Natsir, Mohammad, 14, 118
negara hukum. *See* rule of law
negara kekuasaan. *See* power state
negara kesatuan. *See* unitary state
Nehru, Jawaharlal, 139
Ne Win, U, 139
New Order: origins of, 93; and patrimonialism, 93–94; as personal rule, 2; as sultanism, 94, 96
New PNI, 43
Ngadino, 142
ngebleng, 111
Nietzsche, Friedrich, 67
Notokariyo, 110

Operations Command to Restore Security and Order, 100
"Our Democracy" (Hatta), 50

Padmodipuro, R. Rio, 108
Pagliaro, Tony, 79n28
Pakpahan, Muchtar, 165; charging of under antisubversion law, 169
pamong pradja. *See* regional administrative corps
Pamungkas, Sri Bintang, 156, 167, 171, 206; charging of under antisubversion law, 172
Pancasila, 7, 8–9, 43, 47
Pangestu, Prajogo, 111
Panitia Persiapan Kemerdekaan Indonesia (PPKI). *See* Committee for the Preparation of Indonesian Independence
Panjang, 110
Papua: absence of regional parties in, 264; climate of fear in, 246; and

terrorist labeling of Free Papua Movement, 247; and murder of Theys Eluay, 246; PDIP vote drops in, 262; special autonomy legislation for, 245–46

Parliament: dissolving of in 1960, 29; and elections of 1999, 202–7; and establishment of Special Inquiry, 227, 228; fresh elections for, 192; and issue of memorandum of censure, 228; and laws governing, 203, 204; and maligning of parliamentary government, 100, 130; and passing of second memorandum, 231; relations of with cabinet under 1950 constitution, 13; and use of power of interpellation, 223, 225–26. *See also* People's Representative Council

Partai Amanat Nasional (PAN). *See* National Mandate Party

Partai Bulan Bintang (PBB). *See* Crescent and Star Party

Partai Demokrasi Indonesia (PDI). *See* Indonesian Democracy Party

Partai Demokrasi Indonesia Perjuangan (PDIP). *See* Indonesian Democracy Party of Struggle

Partai Indonesia (Partindo). *See* Indonesian Party

Partai Keadilan. *See* Justice Party

Partai Keadilan Sejahtera. *See* Justice and Prosperity Party

Partai Kebangkitan Bangsa (PKB).*See* National Awakening Party

Partai Komunis Indonesia (PKI). *See* Indonesian Communist Party

Partai Muslimin Indonesia (Parmusi). *See* Indonesian Moslems' Party

Partai Nasional Indonesia (PNI). *See* Indonesian National Party

Partai Nasional Indonesia Massa Marhaen. *See* Indonesian National Party of the Marhaen Masses

Partai Persatuan Pembangunan (PPP). *See* Unity Development Party

Partai Uni Demokrasi Indonesia (PUDI). *See* Indonesian Democratic Union Party

patrimonialism. *See* New Order; Soeharto

Pemerintah Revolusioner Republik Indonesia (PRRI). *See* Revolutionary Government of the Republic of Indonesia

Pendidikan Nasional Indonesia (PNI Baru). *See* New PNI

People's Consultative Assembly, 6, 10, 129–30, 132, 133, 134, 173, 205, 207, 208, 215; and annual sessions, 218, 226; and election of Abdurrahman Wahid, 214–18; and election of Soeharto and Habibie, 184; as exerciser of sovereignty, 8; and laws governing, 203, 204; power of to dismiss president, 228–29; and power "without limit," 230; special session of in 1998, 192, 203–4

People's Democratic Party, 166; and members charged under antisubversion law, 169

People's Representative Council, 6, 10, 129–30, 133; laws governing, 203, 204; strength of National Awakening Party in, 218. *See also* Parliament

personal rule: defined, 2; as charismatic leadership, 28, 97; as patrimonial leadership, 28–29, 93–99; and personality of leader, 2

personality: concept of, 3; versus culturalist view, 31–32; versus "intellectualist fallacy," 32; of personal ruler, 31; and sultanism, 95–96

Pertamina, 95, 151

pesantren. See Islam

Petisi 50. *See* Petition of Fifty

Petition of Fifty, 118

Phillips, Adam, 113, 117
Piagam Perdjuangan Semesta. *See*
  Charter of Total Struggle
POP magazine, 108–9
Pope, Allen, 105
populist attitudes, 14, 170; and fear of
  the people, 100–101; of Megawati,
  136, 196, 214, 241, 244; of Sukarno,
  44, 101; power state, 8, 173
Prananda, Mohammad, 147
Pratama, Mohammad Rizki, 147
Prawiranegara, Sjafruddin, 17
Prawirosudarmadi, 109
Prawirowihardjo, Ibu, 107, 108, 110,
  114, 115
Prawirowiyono, R. L., 108
presidency: and constitution, 4; as
  defined in 1949 Constitution, 12; as
  defined in the 1950 Constitution,
  13–14; and democracy, 1; and
  parliament, 229; as a patrimonial
  court, 25; personal nature of, 4. *See
  also* presidential democracy
presidential democracy: and direct
  elections, 255–56; majoritarian
  tendency of, 255–57, 258n12;
  personal quality of, 256–57; and
  rigidity of presidential constitutions,
  257; two-term limit of, 257
Pringgodigdo, A. K., 10, 12
Probosutejo, 108–9, 204–5

Rahman, Sheikh Mujibur. *See* Mujibur
  Rahman, Sheikh
Rahman, Tunku Abdul. *See* Abdul
  Rahman, Tunku.
Rais, Amien: attitude of to female
  president, 201; 204, 206, 207; and
  calling off of protest march, 188; and
  establishment of National Mandate
  Party, 193; and formation of Central
  Axis, 208–9, 215; as leader of
  Muhammadiyah, 172; and opposition
  to Soeharto, 182–89; and proposal to
  revise article 8, 223; and rejection of
  scapegoating of Sino-Indonesians,
  184; and seeking dismissal of
  Abdurrahman Wahid, 229, 230;
  speech of at Trisakti University, 186
Raleigh, Walter, 251
Ramadhan K. H., 112, 119
Rasyid, Ryaas: Team of Seven of, 202–3
regional administrative corps, 15
regional autonomy, 15, 29, 129, 135
regional conflict, 16–17
Religious Scholars' Council of
  Indonesia, 206, 207
Republic of the United States of
  Indonesia, 12
Res Publica University, 186
Revolutionary Government of the
  Republic of Indonesia: proclaimed in
  Padang, 17
Ricklefs, Merle, 264
ritual meal, 168, 177n39
*Road to Exile: The Indonesian
  Nationalist Movement, 1927–1934*
  (Ingleson), 36
Roeder, O. G., 103, 107, 110
Roem, Mohamad, 37–40; arrest of, 46
Roesmanhadi, 194
Roth, Guenther, 28, 96
Royal Netherlands Indies Army, 108, 116
Rudini, 183
Rukmana, Siti Hadijanti, 111–13, 115,
  162, 172; and blaming Sino-
  Indonesians, 184; rule of law, 30,
  169, 210, 211, 247–48; as
  smokescreen for Soeharto, 173. *See
  also* separation of powers
Rusdihardjo, 228
RUSI. *See* Republic of the United States
  of Indonesia
Ryacudu, Ryamizard, 246

Sadikin, Ali, 113
Saefuddin, A. M.: and calling for
  Moslem male president, 201, 225

Saidi, Ridwan, 167
Saleh, Chairul, 64–65
Sangidoe, Moedrick Setiawan: and Mega-Bintang phenomenon, 174; as related to Megawati by marriage, 179n75
Santoso, Maria Ulfah, 8
santri. See Islam, devout Moslems
Sara, I Gusti Ngurah, 197
Sarekat Islam, 62
Sastroamidjojo, Ali, 15
Sastroharyono, 110
Sastrosatomo, Subadio: arrest of, 46
Schwarz, Adam, 100, 118, 119
second-level region, 29; *selamatan. See* ritual meal
Sembiring, Radja Kami, 158, 197
separation of powers, 30, 133, 134, 247–48; and Montesquieu, 169, 210, 211; and Sukarno's rejection of *trias politika*, 169, 210, 211
Shastri, Lal Bahadur, 139
Shihab, Alwi, 216
Siahaan, Mangara M., 173, 176n21, 197
Sihaloho, Aberson Marle: and support of Megawati for president, 163–64, 166, 173
Simanjuntak, Marsillam, 226
Sinivasan, Marimutu: as owner of Texmaco conglomerate, 225
Sino-Indonesians: and anti-Chinese rioting, 186, 187; as cronies of Soeharto, 98; as "pariah entrepreneurs," 99
Siradj, Said Aqiel, 201
Siregar, Panangian, 193
Siremben, Ni Njoman Rai, 62
Situmorang, Sitor, 38
Sjahrir, Sutan, 10, 13, 14, 15; arrest of, 46; and attack on 1945 Constitution, 11; as Prime Minister, 12
Sjarifuddin, Amir, 10, 11
Smiling General, The (Roeder), 107–8, 110, 111, 118
Soedarman, Soesilo, 167

Soedharmono, 183
Soeharto, 1, 53, 76; autobiography of, 111–13; as president, 93; biographies of, 107–8, 110–11; comparison of with Sukarno, 111–12; composure of, 96, 113–19; and dynastic quality to rule, 95; fall of, 185–89; use of fear of, 99–101, 164; and General Attack, 117–19; influence of personality of, 95; and joining Royal Netherlands Indies Army, 108; and organizing of his personality around thinking, 119; as patrimonial leader, 29, 93–99; patronage machine of, 97–98; as personal ruler, 2, 3, 4; and the POP affair, 108–9; pride of, 167; role in massacre of, 53; and running for president in 1998, 161–63; and succession, 252
Soeharto and his Generals (Jenkins), 118
Soeharto, Dr, 50, 51
Soekarmini, 62
Soekarno, Guntur, 141, 142, 146, 148, 153
Soekarno, Rachmawati, 141, 142, 143, 146, 147, 156, 204; call of for dialogue in Aceh, 245; and defense of Abdurrahman Wahid, 231–32, 233–34; perpetuation of father's teachings of, 153, 231; and seeking revocation of decree 33/1967, 233
Soekarnoputra, Guruh, 140–41, 142, 152, 155, 156, 173, 209
Soekarnoputri, Sukmawati, 141, 142, 146, 156; and Marhaen People's Movement, 153
Soekowati, Edwin H., 205
Soemanto, Agung Imam, 242
Soerjadi, 152, 153, 155, 156, 168, 173, 174, 194, 209
Sophiaan, Manai, 156
Sophiaan, Sophan, 155, 156, 173, 176n21

Sosrodihardjo, Raden Sukemi: Theosophy of, 62; as chief teacher, 62
Staatspartij. *See* State Party
State Party, 10
Stokvis, J. E., 41
Subandrio, Dr., 45, 46; as first deputy prime minister, 28; as foreign minister, 26
Subianto, Prabowo, 96, 186, 187
Sudiro, Tarto, 197
Sudrajat, Edi, 162
Sugandhi, Mien, 187
Sugianto, Colonel Aloysius, 120n24
Sukamiskin prison, 40–41
Sukardi, Laksamana, 165, 176n21, 197; dismissal from cabinet of, 224–25
Sukarno, 1, 10, 11, 12, 14, 15; assassinations attempts on, 17, 45–46; attitude of to youth, 64–69; autistic world of omnipotent fantasy of, 119; autobiography of, 104–7; callousness of, 47–50; as charismatic leader, 29; and claim that Indonesia entering socialist stage, 87; comparison with Mao Zedong, 33, 66; dismissal from office of, 93; and favoring burial of political parties, 15; fear of death of, 32, 61, 63; feeling of desolation of, 32; funerary complex of in Blitar, 151; health of, 50–53; hopes of for Megawati, 141–46; hubris of, 2, 33–34; illness and death of, 54–55, 146–47; and integralism, 16; kidnapping of by youth, 64; *Konsepsi* of, 16; letters of to attorney-general, 36–40; Marxism of, 62–63, 81–89; as modern man, 61–63; mutual help cabinet of, 16, 65; and NASAKOM idea, 25, 71–76; as personal ruler, 2, 3, 4, 29–30, 31; and the "politics of being central," 32, 42–44; and "politics of rejuvenation," 32, 64–77; as president for life, 30, 51–52, 93; and proclamation of state of war and siege, 16; protection of Communist Party of, 25–26; quest for immortality of, 76–77; radical collectivism of, 7; reaction of to massacre of Communists, 53; and recalling his own youth, 69–76; and removal from power by General Soeharto, 33, 53; and separation, 32; and succession, 251; suffering of from the quiet, 40–42; and support of Yamin's fatherland concept, 8–9; suspicion of, 44–47; and undermining separation of powers, 30; vanity of, 202; view of history of, 33; and withdrawal from United Nations, 31
Sukarno: An Autobiography As Told to Cindy Adams, 104
Sukarnoputri, Megawati, 1, 96; attitude of to fear, 164, 178n70; as party leader, 155–58; as vice-president, 129; as beneficiary of New Order, 241; as beneficiary of new system, 135; and challenge of Soeharto for presidency, 163–64; and charisma, 165; childhood of, 141–146; concern of for her father's legacy, 3, 136; as daughter of founding father, 140; death of husband of, 147–48; victory speech of, 209; and elections of 1997, 171–75; and fall of Sukarno, 146–47; installation as president of, 130; legal challenge to Government of, 168–70; and marriage to Taufik Kiemas, 151; as mute symbol, 163; and opposition to Soeharto's nomination for presidency in 1998, 180–85; party leadership of threatened, 161–63; and people of Jakarta, 244; pilgrimage to Mecca of, 224; political thinking of, 166, 169–70, 195, 196, 197, 210–14, 244–45; as postparental woman, 163, 175n14; and presidential election of

1999, 214–18; pride of, 143, 202, 247, 248; and promise to Acehnese, 213; reaction to attack on party headquarters of, 168; and rejection of scapegoating of Sino-Indonesians, 184; as reluctant constitutionalist, 135–36; removal of from PDI leadership, 164–66; response of to father becoming president for life, 181; speech of at Trisakti University, 186–87; and spurning political suitors, 207–8, 214; standing for parliament of, 151–55; statement of on KKN, 240. *See also* KKN
Sukiman, 8
Sukirah, 110, 111, 114
Sukiyem, 110, 114, 115
Sulardi, 107
Sultan of Brunei (Hassanal Bolkiah Mu'zzaddin Waddaulah), 227, 228
sultanism. *See* New Order; personality; Soeharto
Sumitro, 109
Sumowiyatmo, 110
Suparlan, 197
Supeni, Mrs, 183, 204
Supomo: as principal author of 1945 Constitution, 7, 8; theory of integralism of, 7
supreme court and, 30, 134, 138n37; impartiality of queried, 170; and viewing declaration of state of emergency as unconstitutional, 235
Surindro Supjarso, 147
Suryoguritno, Sutardjo, 197
Sutarto, Endriartono, 133
Sutiyoso: attitude of Megawati toward, 243; election as governor of, 244; as governor of Jakarta, 241; as Jakarta military commander, 167; and responsibility for "Grey Saturday," 241–42
Sutjipto, 107, 110

Sutjipto, Ir: and defense of Sutiyoso, 242–43; and election of 2004, 262; as secretary general of PDIP, 224
Sutomo, 63
Sutoyo, N. K., 167
Sutrisno, Try, 135, 182
Suwondo, Mailana, 197
Syafei, Theo, 162, 171, 197

Takwin, Bagus, 56
Tambunan, R. O., 170, 193; criticism of Megawati of, 242
Tanjung, Akbar, 215, 235
Tanjung, Feisal, 161, 162, 164, 167, 168, 172, 173; as minister in Habibie cabinet, 193
Tanjung Priok Affair, 184, 190n25
Taslam, Haryanto, 170, 185, 197, 242
Tempo, 38, 148, 216
Terauchi, Marshal, 9; and meeting with Sukarno and Hatta in Vietnam, 20n21
Thant, U, 27
Tiwir, 107, 111
Tjikini Affair. *See* Cikini Affair
Tjitro, Mbok, 143
Tjokroaminoto, Umar Sayed, 62
To Achieve an Independent Indonesia (Sukarno), 82
Trisakti University, 186–87
Tsombe (Tshombe), Moise, 86, 89

Unitary State, 195, 211 244
Unity Development Party, 94, 154, 156, 171, 174, 175, 192, 201, 203, 208, 235, 263
unity of nationalist, religious and communist forces, 71–76
Universal Declaration of Human Rights, 13, 132

Wahid, Abdurrahman, 1, 4, 129, 182, 201, 204, 207; and acceptance of nomination of Central Axis, 209,

216; and antagonism of major parties, 225; and declaration of presidential ambition, 205–6; and declaration of state of emergency, 235; dismissal of from office by People's Consultative Assembly, 130, 234–35; and dismissal of Hamzah Haz, 223; election as president of, 214–18; and founding National Awakening Party, 192; and presidential election of 1999, 214–18; relationship with Soeharto of, 172–73, 175; and struggles with parliament, 227–31; and succession, 252–53; stroke of, 183; and suggestion to lift ban on Communism, 224; and Sukarno family, 157, 163, 168; and support of Soeharto, 187–88; as tolerant of separatist movements in Aceh and Irian, 226
Wahid, Hasyim, 197
Wahid, Hidayat Nur, 230
Walicki, Andrzej, 82
Walters, Patrick, 161, 165
Wayed, Sheikh Hasina. *See* Hasina, Sheikh
Weber, Max, 28
Widjojanto, Bambang, 166
Winnicott, D. W., 36, 113
Wirajuda, Hasan, 247
Wiranto, 182, 195
Wolpert, Stanley, 140
Wonogiri, 108
Wu, Jieping, 51
Wuryantoro, 107, 108, 110, 111, 114

Yamin, Muhammad: his fatherland concept, 8
Yani, General Achmad: as chief of staff of army, 31
Young Indonesia, 72
Yudhoyono, Susilo Bambang: as chief of staff at time of "Grey Saturday," 233; and claiming Free Aceh Movement terrorist, 247; dismissal from cabinet of, 232; party of gains substantial support, 263

Zia ul-Haq, Mohammad, 140

About the Author

Angus McIntyre acquired an area studies orientation in the Department of Indonesian and Malayan Studies at the University of Sydney while studying for his BA. He then undertook political research in Indonesia in 1966–1967. In the MA program in Southeast Asia Studies at Yale University, he attempted to reconcile his area studies background and fieldwork experience with the theories he was encountering in his political science classes, but without success. In his second year of study, under the influence of the professor of Southeast Asian history, Harry J. Benda, he settled for a political history approach to Indonesian politics. At the same time that he turned away from these theories, a post-doctoral fellow from Melbourne, Graham Little, introduced him to the political psychology stream within the same department of political science. He found this body of work more meaningful and consistent with Benda's emphasis on "the irreducible importance of the individual actor in history." He sought to acquire expertise in this area while studying for his PhD at the University of Melbourne under the supervision of Alan Davies, the author of *Private Politics*, and the same Graham Little, and, subsequently, as a special student at the Institute of Psychoanalysis in Chicago and as an auditor in David Gutmann's clinical course on the psychology of later life at Northwestern University Medical School. His next task, as he saw it, was to bring this newly acquired knowledge of political psychology into conjunction with his already formed political history approach to modern Indonesia. This was a difficult and time-consuming task that obliged him to think hard about human motivation in its individual, cultural, and universal aspects. This book is a product of the attempt to integrate these two strands.